GANDHI: IN THE MIRROR OF FOREIGN SCHOLARS

GANDHI

In The Mirror of Foreign Scholars

Editor
J.S. Mathur

Foreword
B.R. Nanda

NATIONAL GANDHI MUSEUM
RAJGHAT, NEW DELHI - 110002

In Association with:

GYAN

GYAN PUBLISHING HOUSE
NEW DELHI - 110002

Gandhi: In the Mirror of Foreign Scholars

ISBN: 81-212-0961-7

Price: Rs. 720

Published by
NATIONAL GANDHI MUSEUM
Rajghat, New Delhi - 110002
Telefax: 91-011-23311793, 23310168, 23328310
Email: gandhimk@bol.net.in; mkgandhingm@rediffmail.com
Website: www.gandhimuseum.org

In association with:
GYAN PUBLISHING HOUSE
5, Ansari Road, Daryaganj
New Delhi - 110002
Telefax: 91-011-23285914, 23261060, 23282060
Email: gyanbook@vsnl.com. **Website:** www.gyanbooks.com

Dedicated to

MY PARENTS

&

MY SON

Contents

Foreword

This is an excellent collection of essays on the various aspects of Gandhiji's life and thought mostly by foreign scholars, published in his 'Journal of Gandhian Studies' and 'Gandhi Prasang' put together by Prof. J.S. Mathur, who during the last thirty years has devoted himself to the propagation of Gandhian thought in his home town of Allahabad.

It is significant that most of these essays were written after Gandhiji's death during the latter half of the twentieth century by foreign writers. They would have been unthinkable in Gandhi's life-time. The reason is obvious. After Gandhiji had clashed head-on with the British Empire in 1919-20, he did not endear himself to countries which had empires of their own such as France, Belgium, Holland, Portugal or countries like Germany, Japan and Italy who wanted to build their empires. Only a few exceptional individuals in Europe and America, such as Romain Rolland in France, Albert Einstein in United States and C.F. Andrews in Britain were quick to recognize Gandhi's stature. An English Quaker John Hoyland noted in 1931, when Gandhiji was visiting England for the Round Table Conference, that satyagraha 'was looked upon in the West as ridiculous and undignified; it was regarded with cold disfavor especially by the educated class, because it was too unconventional, in word too Christian for us'. After Gandhiji's death some of the barriers to understanding him disappeared. Colonialism was dead or dying, racialism was under siege in its last bastion in South Africa. The life and thought of Gandhi could thus be viewed without the imperialist and racialist blinkers. His ideas and methods began to be invoked in Asia, Africa, America, and Europe. In South Africa, the African National Congress [ANC] carried on non-violent agitation and passive resistance for nearly forty years; it was, however, unable to sustain their struggle on non-violent principles in the face of ruthless oppression by the apartheid regime.

After the massacre of Sharpeville, and until the release of Nelson Mandela, the major liberation movement in South Africa turned into bloody guerilla warfare. This armed struggle would have been much more prolonged and difficult than it was, had not the students, industrial workers, religious leaders, youth, and women's organizations in South Africa joined in offering non- violent resistance to the racialist regime on specific issues such as rent, consumer embargoes, and bus boycotts. The liberators of the blacks in South Africa were thus not only guerilla fighters, but hundreds of thousands of men, women, and children - shop assistants, and workers living in shanty towns - who consciously or unconsciously adopted methods, which Gandhiji would have approved. In the United States the Mahatma's teachings and example inspired Martin Luther King Jr., a Baptist minister, who was able, in the words of an American writer, to 'meld the image of Gandhi and the image of the Negro preacher'. He advocated the non-violent method as a practical alternative, not only to armed conflicts within a country but between countries. 'The choice', he warned in his Stride Towards Freedom (1958), 'is no longer between violence and non-violence; it is either non-violence or non-existence.'

There were some remarkable examples of the application of Gandhi's methods in the last decades of the twentieth century such as in Czechoslovakia, Poland, Phillipines, Baltic States and other countries, which highlighted the potential power of the oppressed. However, it must be admitted that Gandhi's principles and techniques are still appreciated by only a small enlightened minority in the world. Gandhi himself had no illusions about the ready acceptance of his ideas. He did not claim finality for his views, which he regarded, within a broad ethical framework, as aids for bettering the lives of his fellow men; they could be altered if they did not work. Gandhi expounded his philosophy of life in hundreds of articles and letters, but did not build it into a 'system'. However, his deepest concerns have been increasingly becoming the concerns of thinking men and women stirring across the globe for a peaceful and humane world. As I have already mentioned that most of the articles in this collection are by foreign scholars or publicists. In India, for reasons which are difficult to fathom, the nationalist movement has ceased to interest our academic community and the media. We duly remember the Mahatma on his birth and death anniversaries; we go through the ritual of honoring him, and then go back to more 'practical' concerns.

I am reminded of a remark which Ivan Illich made when he visited India in 1978; 'it would be a tragedy if India had to re-import Gandhi from the West'.

New Delhi
14 August 2006

B. R. Nanda
Chairman
National Gandhi Museum

Preface

This book, *GANDHI – IN THE MIRROR OF FOREIGN SCHOLARS*, is a collection of 49 articles that were received from scholars from different countries (whose present addresses are not with us) during the course of last three decades.

Gandhiji wrote in the *Harijan* on 16 Jan 1937 – "...Out of my ashes a thousand Gandhis will arise". This has inspired us to take the message of Gandhiji to the present generation.

We at Gandhi Bhawan and later at Basant Bihari Jai Rani Foundation for Peace Studies, Allahabad, have been organizing several activities for the last four decades, such as (i) Painting competition on Gandhiji amongst children, (ii) Essay competition on Gandhiji's concepts, (iii) Debates, (iv) Setting up a Research and Reference Library, (v) Organizing seminars, and (vi) Publication of a Journal, to arouse the interest of the present generation.

We organized 16 seminars on different aspects of Gandhiji's thought and received papers from eminent scholars of our country and abroad.

These articles were serialized in various issues of the 'Journal of Gandhian Studies' and later in the journal 'Gandhi Prasang'. We now present them in a book form.

The world today is groping in darkness. A feeling of hopelessness and helplessness prevails. Winston Churchill had observed: "Dark ages may return, the Stone Age may return on the gleaming wings of science." (Quoted in the *Tribune*, p. 16). Russell had remarked: "We are perhaps living in the last age of man, and if so it is to science that he will owe his extinction." ('Impact of Science on Society', p. 27) Several quotations can be given. Gandhiji called this civilization Satanic. Among many problems we can mention are alienation of the individual, technology beyond human control, centralization and emergence of all powerful state, exploitative socio-economic system and materialism and consumerism.

Gandhiji initiated a number of revolutions to challenge these evils and laid foundation of a peaceful world order – revolution against consumerism and unbridled materialism, against technology beyond human control, for human motivation, for decentralization in all spheres, for rehabilitation of the individual, for full and gainful employment, for nonviolent and peaceful methods of change, for ecological balance and for maintenance of cultural identity of nations.

Gandhiji propounded nonviolent action/ Satyagraha and his theory of Trusteeship to attain his ideas of a new world order.

Gandhiji's thought and techniques of social change have been analysed by scholars whose articles are being published in the present volume. They have analysed the relevance of Gandhiji for the contemporary society – both national and international. These articles lay emphasis on the continued relevance of Gandhiji's principles and methodology for a peaceful world order. In the Introduction we have given a brief summary of the articles of these scholars.

Prof. Toynbee, the eminent historian had charged us in the following words: "You have incurred a rather formidable obligation both to Gandhi and history."

Nobel Laureate Pearl S. Buck remarks: "India, dare to be worthy of your Gandhi."

We are trying in our humble way to fulfill our obligation towards Gandhiji and are trying to take him to the present generation.

We are thankful to all who blessed our efforts to take the message of Mahatma Gandhi to the present ailing world.

I express my thanks to Dr. J. S. L. Srivastava who assisted me in this effort. I also express my thanks to Sri K. N. Sinha and Sri Pashupati Nath for their assistance and Sri G. R. Maini who prepared the manuscript.

This collection is a non-commercial venture with the sole objective of spreading the message of Mahatma Gandhi.

I sincerely thank Dr. Y. P. Anand, ex-Director, National Gandhi Museum, who initially approved the publication of this compilation.

Further, I am grateful to Dr. Varsha Das, present Director, who has taken great pains in getting the book published in the present form.

Dr. B. R. Nanda has written "Foreword" to this collection. He has very kindly given me the benefit of his august personality. This is a debt which can never be adequately acknowledged.

I dedicate this collection to my parents, late Sri & Smt. Basant Bihari Lal and my late son. My father initiated me to Gandhiji's thought. He was a member of the Mainpuri Revolutionary group. Later he came under the influence of Mahatma Gandhi and took a vow to wear self-spun clothes and serve the society as a teacher-doctor. He was both. My son was my right hand in my academic pursuits.

Allahabad
16 March, 2007

J. S. Mathur

Introduction

Dr. Rodrigo Carazo in his article 'Gandhi—A Man who Changed the Course of History' observes that "Gandhi gave a clear definition of India's identity through his spirituality and simplicity. But at the same time he was also a universal figure; though, the symbols he used to communicate with his people were local, the principles he inspired have permanent application for every nation of the planet." He continues, "Truly, Gandhi is the man that changed the course of history by leading his country to an indisputable victory, with the indestructible weapon of non-violence. Likewise, Gandhi has changed the course of history by showing that the poor nations can utilize non-violence as well as showing the rich nations and their leaders that it is never too late to implement justice."

Prof. Jan Tinbergen, Nobel Laureate economist from Netherlands, contributed six articles analyzing Gandhiji's thought from different angles. In his article 'Peace through Integration' he advocates that nation states in view of production of weapons of mass destruction and aggression should voluntarily think that polarisation be better replaced by tolerance, a view closer to the great Indian thinker and activist Mahatma Gandhi. In his article 'A New Life Style and Gandhian Thought' he points out to numerous problems that technological developments have given birth. One of these is scarcities of inputs that were considered free gifts of nature to which Club of Rome referred. Problems of pollution and ecology have gained importance. The problem of poverty in Third World countries, decreasing importance of western countries coupled with problems created by abundance, has led to degeneration due to more egotism and abundant leisure. Aware of the unacceptable poverty in some parts of the world, of new scarcities and of the past situation created by stubborn ideologies whether capitalist or communist, this movement for a new life-style tends towards a more modest level of prosperity, less inequality and more tolerance. New life style needs "an ethical, intellectual and cultural base". In his article 'A New World Employment Plan', Prof. Tinbergen lays emphasis on polices that create employment and satisfaction of basic needs with priority for the socially and economically weaker groups and policies based not on primarily private profit considerations but on the principles of social justice. In his article 'The New International Order and Gandhian Thought' Prof. Tinbergen observes, "To put in bluntly, Gandhi's ideas are by no means outmoded, as some believe, and, on the contrary might well be applied more often in to-day's world". In another article, 'Equality as an Aim of Policy', the author deals "with the instruments of socio-economic policy that can be applied, in economies at different stages of development, in order to reduce inequality." Describing Gandhiji's relevance Prof. Tinbergen remarks in his last article in this collection, titled 'Gandhi's Relevance' that, "Gandhian thought was not of a passive nature; it did constitute a revolution in thinking".

Prof. Gunnar Myrdal, Nobel Laureate from Sweden, contributed two articles, 'Poverty, Inequality and Gandhi' and, 'Challenge of Stagnation in Developing Countries'. Discussing the problems of poverty Prof. Myrdal refers to Gandhiji's emphasis on radical change in the social and economic order and decentralization, revolution and changes in the direction of education. Developments in post-independent India have belied Gandhiji's expectations. Prof. Myrdal observes, "It is unthinkable that today he would remain silent and idle. He would again take to roads and village lanes and begin anew his crusade". Gandhiji's approach of all-embracing planning (integrated planning) is needed which suggests a lower level of consumption of luxury goods in the upper strata, "austerity in consumption and living patterns of the rich".

In his article 'The Impact of Mahatma Gandhi on Martin Luther King' Prof. Stanley Wolpert discusses the influence of Mahatma Gandhi on Martin Luther King whom he describes as "American Gandhi".

Prof. Ulla Holmberg laying emphasis on 'Universal Brotherhood' discusses the impact of exchange of students between countries. His observation, "How should we make the people in the industrial countries understand and accept that brotherhood also includes lowering their own standard of living in order to give the poorest sisters and brothers a chance?" deserves full consideration.

Mr. Haflin Samdin in his article 'Gandhiji and Contemporary Ideologies Regarding Freedom, Peace and Equality' has analyzed his contribution to various problems that face the attainment of this ideal. He remarks "Gandhi has brought a clearer, truer, richer, and completer meaning to each one of the great principle so frequently handled about in political discourses and in the comity of nations; namely PEACE FREEDOM AND EQUALITY".

Prof. Unto Tahtinen in his article 'Gandhi on Natural Law' remarks that three experiments – racial discrimination in South Africa, colonial status of India and legal injustice involved in Hindu customs shaped his approach and "Gandhi came to realize that certain positive laws, even the whole system of law, as well as traditional social and religious institutions can be in conflict with an ethical law. The ethical law, however, is higher in authority and in the case of conflict, takes precedence.

Mr. Francis Ofosu Quartey from Ghana discusses Gandhiji's techniques of removal of economic inequality and after a brief review of Gandhiji's views remarks that Satyagraha can be used for non political objectives and that a "non-violent society had to be so organized as to reduce in-equalities and tensions within it and to remove the temptation for an assault from without." Such a society should be based on decentralized economy.

Mr. Amre M. Moussa, former Ambassador of Egypt, observes that people in Egypt hold Gandhiji in high esteem and affection because of his struggle against colour prejudice, war, race domination, untouchability and communal disharmony. Mahatma Gandhi will remain alive in the conscience of people all over the world.

Ms. Gudrun Loewner in his article 'Sarvodaya – A Way to a Better Life in Peace and Harmony – The Sri Lankan Experience' demonstrates the influence of Indian experience on Sri Lankan Sarvodaya movement which has spread in that country. The difference between Sarvodaya movement in India and Sri Lanka is distinguished, as "Gandhi's dream was the realization of independent village republics in India, Ariyaratne's dream is not going so far." In India after Gandhiji's death, time for big actions has passed away and small ventures by individuals are taking place. Sri Lanka represents a centralized system. The progress of the movement has been discussed. One weakness of the movement is its dependence on foreign donations.

Mr. Takaaki Pio Yasuoka in his article 'International Peace: Japan's Experience' describes efforts of Japan to evolve a policy for peace which will also mean fight against environmental pollution. This article also refers to Japan's involvement in U.S.A war efforts. However he refers to the close relationship between disarmament and development.

Mr. J. P. Pathirana in his article 'Gandhiji and the Concept of Power' describes Gandhiji as a 'champion of human dignity' who clearly analyzed the evils inherent in the materialistic modern culture and observes in his article: "No other current ideology, neither democratic Capitalism, nor democratic Socialism, nor dictatorial Communism, places before mankind the bright and noble idea of moral and spiritual development—."

Bishop Dr. Karoly Toth points out commonness of objectives of Gandhiji with Christian Peace Conference which was founded in 1958 much after Gandhiji's death. The Conference affirms with Gandhiji the unity of humankind. Gandhiji's views on peace, total disarmament and socio-economic structure that will make oppression and exploitation impossible, find echo in Christian Peace Conference and so also Gandhiji's views on the unity of word and deed in his concept of Satyagraha.

Peter Kempadoo lays emphasis on Sarvodaya as Gandhiji's alternative development strategy for today's world which starts with the conviction that salvation (well being) of oneself is inextricably bound up with the well being of all. Sarvodaya "is the application of the principle of Non-Violence in the transformation of societies: from their present forms which are mostly exploitative and imbalanced—."

In his article 'Gandhiji and Conflictlogy' Prof. Johan Galtung quotes Gandhiji to drive home his point while comparing him to Jesus Christ. Prof. Galtung observes that Gandhiji did not recognize difference between the mundane and transcendental. Various aspects of a conflict, its nature, its dynamics and its resolution, and these are many in Gandhiji's struggle, have to be studied. There can be several approaches and here is the role of social scientists and they should provide a language within which Gandhiji's views can be expressed.

Mr. Terence W. Miller won gold medal in the International Essay Competition on 'The Modern Search For Peace: The Gandhian Way'. Tracing the history of conflict in Ireland he observes that oppression of a minority is the one of the factors. Violence has vitiated the minds of children. He advocates the use of Gandhian methods and use of non violence, which should become a way of life. Ahimsa means a spirit of tolerance, truth and love. Gandhiji's strategy was that the immediate cause of Satyagraha should be selected within the larger cause. The next step should be to love the people – and that people should feel part of the organization and this can happen only when they contribute towards its continuance.

Detlef Kantowsky in his article 'Sarvodaya and State Power: Theory and Practice in South Asia' traces the history of Sarvodaya movement in India and Sri Lanka. Summarizing the movement in India, he remarks it as having moved from cooperation to confrontation. In India the Sarvodaya movement got divided, lacked organization, had little to show by way of its achievement. Sarvodaya has not yet given teeth to the rural poor. Sarvodaya in Sri Lanka has been summarized as from toleration to cooperation which is basically different from the Indian Sarvodaya movement. To quote Prof. Kantowsky "Whilst Sarvodaya in India envisages a stateless and highly decentralized political order..., Sarvodayaites in Sri Lanka hope that the rulers will always be righteous.... Whilst Sarvodaya in Sri Lanka legitimizes a revival of traditional functions of government, Sarvodaya in India is anarchic."

Prof. H. M. Delange in his essay on 'Work and the Meaning of Work' considers it "an improvishment were we increasingly to let work to be done by automation and bigger apparatuses, which produce goods only to be used by us. ... present styles of production drain energy resources, and for this reason too it would be wise to reflect on changes in our very production and consumption patterns." He suggests that "the problem is to search for a real new technology, a technology that accepts the idea that human work is a source of richness and welfare. Controlling technological innovation could be one of the most important issues in this field".

Mr. R. Scott Kennedy in his article 'Love is Real And Active' dwells upon the vital issues of nonviolence as a force of social change and as a means of seeking truth. Gandhi and the New Testament suggest that to be effective and active, truth has to be lived in deeds. Even truths expressed most eloquently and profoundly cannot match simpler but lived truth. The testing of truth can be performed only by strict adherence to Ahimsa or love-action based upon refusal to do harm and readiness to undergo self- suffering. This kind of Satyagraha has universal appeal and application.

In his article 'Civil Disobedience in a Democracy' Prof. Gene Sharp remarks that organized civil disobedience would provide an orderly and peaceful substitute to political violence which may otherwise be so dangerous to democratic polity. Democracy to be a living and dynamic system of governance has to be constantly and constructively responsive to the challenges of the time. One such challenge is the tendency of growing organized civil disobedience on the part of the pressure groups from within trying to give vent to their feelings of dissatisfaction and dissent. The proposal to permit civil disobedience in constitutionally representative political system may imply some modifications in the policies and legal provisions. But this would certainly strengthen and enrich the system by providing answer to the problem of how to express extreme dissent.

Prof. Seshagiri Rao in his article 'Gandhi, M.L. King and the Civil Right Movement' remarks that Martin Luther King Jr. the great crusader against apartheid and renowned leader of the civil rights movement in America was a Christian and had his schooling in Christian philosophy and theology. King was thus aware of Jesus's conviction in love as a force in the fight against injustice. King's conviction in it was however greatly fostered when he studied Gandhi's Satyagraha. Gandhi and King both believed that nonviolent resistance is not the coward's way out – it is a dynamic and spiritually active force, it seeks to conciliate. It is directed not against the sinner but against the sin. Nonviolence elevated to the scale of love –selfless and sacrificing love –is at the center of this struggle. Both Gandhi and King have faith in achieving rights through right means. Prof. Seshagiri Rao, the celebrated author of this article, has many useful suggestions to make the movement more effective for American Negros.

Major General Indrajit Rikhey in his article 'Non-violence, Truth and International Peacemaking' remarks that the job of international peace making is onerous and demands ideas, attitudes, outlooks and training of a kind that is not usually found in the bureaucrats brought up to serve concerns within national boundaries. An internationalist has to view things in global perspective and rise above the considerations of narrow nationalistic interests. Mahatma Gandhi had this perspective and there are many reflections of insight in his writings on this. In his 'Nonviolence in Peace and War' Gandhi's attitude towards opponents and his philosophy of means and ends have paved the way for international civil service as a profession. In view of the ever-increasing lethal weapons of mass destruction, evolution of some form of nonviolent and non-military defense strategy is required today more than ever before. Unfortunately the social psychology of conflict continues to remain belligerent. And hence the chance for nonviolent national defense system is rather bleak. But that should not deter us from trying to educate public opinion both at the national and international level and forge our resources together to attempt nonviolent and truthful solutions to international discords. Establishment of a Peace Academy on the pattern of National Defense Academies may go some way in this direction, feels the author.

Mr. Herold F. Bing in his article 'Revolution & Non-violence: A Pacifist View' observes that the rich-poor divide in our socio–economic order might have been born of unequal initial abilities, but it feeds on exploitation, proceeds on competition and persists on use of force. Drastic reforms based on equity, cooperation, justice and peace are the need of the hour if we are to survive and prosper as a civil society. For, changes and reforms wrought about by violent revolutions have only engendered reaction, violence and unpeace. Revolution should mean reconstruction and transformation of the existing structure towards a just, equitable, democratic and peaceful social order and the revolutions leading this change must shun violence, feels the author.

'Gandhian Concept of Non-violence' has been authored by Mr. William Stuart Nelson. Nonviolence is not just the renunciation of violence. It is not a single value of a single quality of life; it is a spirit, a way of life, a religion and the law of one's very being. It begins with a life which includes not only one's acts and behavior but one's speech and thought as well and embodies the qualities of compassion, selflessness, forbearance and fearlessness. It dictates a way of struggle against the civil forces in society and it decries violence and its accompaniment, malice, in all their shades and ramifications. These are the ends to which Gandhi dedicated his life in thought and action. Little wonder then that Albert Einstein could say that a thousand years from today men will scarcely believe that such a one as this had ever lived.

Article 'Violence – Non-violence at Koyoto and Beyond' was contributed by Mr. Homer A. Jack. He remarks that although the World Conference on Religion and Peace in 1970 at Koyoto was not sponsored by Gandhians, Gandhi and Gandhism occupied the center of debate and discussions there. Besides deliberating at length on nonviolence, considerable time was devoted to discussion on Disarmament, Development and Human Rights. The conference had overall support to nonviolent approach to resolution of conflicts yet it left "too many loopholes" for violence albeit "for a good cause". It is rather an uneasy stance on the subject. In view of the frequent failures of nonviolence it is urgently needed to demonstrate that nonviolence works and can both topple unjust structures and replace them with more just ones. Experiments with nonviolent truths and techniques in

Vietnam, India, Italy, and U.K and U.S.A etc. merit reference for those who are committed to the cause.

Mr. Paul Ekins in his article 'Creating a New School of Economic Thought: A New Initiative in the Field of Economics' heralds the advent of a new school of economic thought in offing, which he claims, is very much in tune with the social and environmental realities of the time. This new economic thought or the Living Economy as its protagonists call it, seeks to develop an economics of fundamental needs and their satisfaction. It gives great stress on human well-being rather than on total GNP and integrates economic concerns with those of society, ecology and ethics. In the Living Economics non-economic factors will also receive their due importance and there will be a proper balancing of market economy and local and central planning. In matters of size and scale, apart from input-output and cost-benefit considerations operational and human considerations will also come into focus. Steps are already afoot to accelerate publications on the subject and encourage interaction and exchange of views among the new fashion economist.

Mr. A.T. Ariyaratne in his article discusses the 'Role of *Shramadana* in Rural Development'. As a means of social reconstruction and positive change the voluntary sharing of one's time, thought and energy, known as *Shramadana,* was introduced in Sri Lankan Society recently, but the concept and its practice is embedded in the country's culture and tradition from ancient past. To consider it just a substitute for monetary and budgetary allocations is to miss the essentials of missionary zeal and nonviolent pacific content of the operation. It is free from bureaucratic complexities and does not result in distortions like inequality, exploitation and other form of oppressions. It promotes initiative and leadership in the society and strengthens economic democracy at the grass-root. However, suppressed entrepreneurship, extreme dependence on centralized bureaucracy, elitist approach and vested interests born of colonial rule for a prolonged period of time are informidable impediments in the success of the movement which need be fought through legislation and active and positive participation of political leaders.

Mr. Horace Alexander, close associate of Mahatma Gandhi, in his article 'Non-violence and The Rule of Law' remarks that Gandhi was not an anarchist in the sense that he has had no respect for rule of law. The fact is that he was himself a student of law and a legal practitioner of great repute and as such held the rule of law in high esteem. He was opposed only to such laws as were unjust and against the common interest of the society at large. His violations of law were specially significant just because he was a believer in the rule of law. Overtly in the name of maintaining law and order many a government is reigning a rule of terror and tyranny. The conception of a nonviolent war-free world can materialize only through an adherence on the part of the nation states to the rule of law. Nations must learn to compromise a part to their individual selfish interests and chauvinistic sentiments to join and run global institutions like the U.N. The author, in the last, makes a passionate appeal for enforcing the rules of the game both within the nation and internationally too.

The article 'Gandhi's Religious Quest in South Africa' was contributed by Prof. K. L. Seshagiri Rao, who observes that the basic tenets of Gandhian religion are truth, nonviolence, love, simplicity, dignity of labour, selfless service, equality and fearlessness. His religion admits of no rituals, dogmas and bigotry. Gandhiji's stint in South Africa was like a workshop of his religious formulations. Not only did he study major religions of the world there, he also came in contact with the writings of John Ruskin and Tolstoy which together exercised very profound influence on evolution and strengthening of Gandhi's ideals. Two Ashrams –Phoenix and Tolstoy Farm in particular and the African society in general served as laboratories for experiments and confirmation of his religious hypothesis.

Mr. Stephen Murphy in his article 'The Last Hours of Mahatma Gandhi' gives a detailed account of Gandhi's activities on 30th January 1948, the day he attained martyrdom. Early that morning Gandhi had said to Manu, "If someone fires bullet at me and I die without a groan and with God's name on my lips, then you should tell the world that here was a real Mahatma..." Did Gandhi have premonition about his mortal end and his journey to immortality? For answer read this absorbing tale by Stephen Murphy.

In his article 'Gandhi for Mere Mortals' Mr. Murphy remarks that deifying Gandhi, that we consciously or unconsciously often attempt, would do no service to the promotion of Gandhian ideals. Becoming Gandhi may not be possible, but becoming Gandhian is. One may not be able to do and achieve everything that Gandhi did, but one may become Gandhian. Even one step in the desired direction is better than no step at all. Signs of a true Gandhian "seeker" are belief in God, devotion to service of God's creation, devotion to truthfulness, practice of nonviolence, nonviolent resistance to injustice, devotion to simplicity, service and sacrifice and non-exploitation of lower species.

In his article 'Implications of the Limits To Growth Debate – Small Is Beautiful' E.F. Schumacher, a very celebrated and widely read author, declares that debates on desirability of limits to growth are meaningless unless we go beyond quantity considerations and enter into the realm of quality judgments. Our propensity to lay undue stress on 'quantity of goods' and 'quantum of profits' has relegated man to the background and in the process greed has taken precedence over needs. Accordingly, there came to be built a scientific and industrial civilization of monstrous dimensions resulting in mass production of luxuries, environmental degradation, mass unemployment, growing rich-poor divide, violence and other associated complexities. In short, the new technology and its consequences are incompatible with human nature and the resource endowment of the world. The author feels that the way out is to return to Gandhian gospels, to elemental simplicities of life, to sublimation of human desires and wants. And that in turn would ensure beauty and peace in life.

In his article 'Non-violence in the 21st Century: Challenges and Choices', Arun Gandhi states that "Non-violence, therefore, can be described as an honest and diligent pursuit of truth." In the article he further explains the four essential principles of Gandhiji's philosophy to be "Truth, Ahimsa, Trusteeship and Constructive Action."

Prof. George Paxton in his article 'Gandhi and War' gives an account of how Gandhi's ideas about nonviolence evolved into an abiding article of faith over time and how his initial ambivalence with regard to war culminated into making him a confirmed pacifist. Violence cannot be destroyed by counter violence. Mankind has to get out of violence only through nonviolence and love. Counter hatred only increases the surface as well as the depth of hatred. Gandhi however considered cowardice worse than war and should there be a choice between the two, preference must go to the latter.

In his review of the book 'We do not Want Violence; The Buber-Gandhi Controversy: A Contribution to Practical Philosophy' edited by Christan Bartolf, Piet Dijkstra compares the ideologies of Mahatma Gandhi and Martin Buber. The reviewer further suggests its translation into English from German.

Prof. Amalendu Guha in his article 'Gandhian Concept Of Equitable Equality' remarks that this is a "new concept in peace studies, which consists of (a) harmony of the heterogeneities, (b) uniformity of diversities, (c) equality with justice and (d) equity of equalities. The goal or end-result of the above is 'homonoia' or union of hearts at the behavioural level in society. Gandhi... used justice or equity as value determinant and homonoia as the union of hearts in the human and social behavioural process. Gandhi used nonviolence as the best and most effective means of changing human mind, effecting revolution in human consciousness and uniting the human and social beings under the common platform of human progress and human feeling type of bondage."

In his article 'Non-violent Philosophy and Culture of Peace: Gandhi's Contribution' Prof. Guha observes, "Human Peace is a culture which is the outcome of the feelings of humanity and humanism." He discusses the role of nonviolence, training in nonviolence and peace, and in his concluding remarks observes that "Gandhi's concept and philosophy of peace is considered to be secularist and humanist." He quotes Gandhiji: "I must love my enemy, I must apply the same rules to the wrong-doer who is my enemy or stranger to me, as I would do to my wrong doing father or son."

In his article 'Concept of the Philosophy of Peace' Prof. Guha points out that Peace has to be a positive peace. He discusses the impact of concepts and ideologies of several historical personalities in the evolution of this concept – Chinese Schools of Thought, European Schools of Thought and other schools of thought. He observes, "From confrontation to cooperation, hegemony to harmony, chauvinism to equitable equality, alienation to transparency, are the very basic missions and visions of peace philosophy."

In his essay on 'From Gautama Buddha and Gandhi to Ikeda: Missions and Visions of Peace and Truth' Prof. Guha's analysis is that "All these three great preachers for peace–Gautama Buddha, Gandhi and Ikeda opt for horizontal dialogues and approaches for removing wrongdoings, misunderstandings and crisis formation, as well as for reconciliation and self-realization. Nonviolence develops a culture of peace which (i) develops human instinct of propensity to forgive, (ii) removes the instincts of taking revenge, (iii) develops the rationality of tolerance and (iv) overcomes as well as prevents the evil spirit of direct violence." Earlier the author remarks that "nonviolence is neither a submissive and passive acceptance of violence pressed by the aggressor on nonviolent people, nor a coward and subjugated act of the helpless in the society." Mr. Daisaku Ikeda, the Japanese thinker has been quoted: "Gandhi's struggle in the name of nonviolence was a battle to make the people strong and wise... Gandhi was a rare leader who chose to live in the midst of the masses, sharing their sorrow and happiness and working to dispel the fear of authority bred by long years of colonial life."

Mr. Michelle Myres in his article 'Why Gandhi's Principles of Non-violence are Relevant Today' makes a fervent appeal to encourage peace studies and academies. The fact that the people belonging to various races and religions can live together in harmony and conflicts can be resolved without war and violence should be demonstrated in practice as Gandhiji actually did. Violence breeds more violence, similarly peace would breed more peace. Hence shun violence and practice peace, counsels the author.

Mrs. Nageen Sai Zinovieff in her article 'Gandhi's Philosophy and Sufi Doctrine' observes that Gandhiji has repeatedly asserted that he has not propounded any new philosophy or cult. He has only said what is already there in different religious scriptures. Many of his ideas are common with Sufism as they are with other religions too. His basic teaching that 'God is Truth' is similar to that of the Sufis who call God 'Haqq' meaning truth. Sufis are also known to have faith in dynamic nonviolence and love like Gandhi. Humility, Catholicity, austerity, simplicity, selfless service – all are basic to Gandhian as well as Sufi ideals.

Mrs. Nageen Sai Zinovieff in her article 'Gandhi and Imperfect Religion' remarks that Gandhi was a highly religious man. But he was not a blind follower of either Bible, Quran, Gita, or Avestas as he did not consider them to be revelations of God directly. They contain blasphemies, idiosyncrusies and hyperboles. Gandhi exercised his judgment about every scripture including Gita as he could not let a scriptural text supersede his reason. Gandhi believed in the oneness of God. He advocates a religion of service to humanity as the ultimate aim of coming closer to God, for he believed that man was created to know his Maker who is love, light and truth.

Mr. Paras Ramoutar from Trinidad in his article 'Need to Revisit Gandhi's Message' remarks that to a world tormented by violence, unpeace, threat of nuclear holocast, exploitation, inequality and terrorism etc., Gandhi and his ideals are the only hope. Abiding faith in God, truth, love, nonviolence, Satyagraha and their practice in actual dealings in life can rid the world of its present predicament and foster a culture of peace and universal brotherhood.

J. S. Mathur

Allahabad
16 March 2007

1

Gandhi – A Man who Changed the Course of History

Dr. Rodrigo Carazo*

Mahatma Gandhi is, from our perspective, the clear symbol of what he practised and preached: the local and the universal.

To the India of his time, Gandhi had a local meaning. For the rest of the world, he has a universal spiritual meaning.

For India, as a local figure, he was able to communicate to his own people the concepts of freedom, independence, techniques to improve development, self-sufficiency under conditions of extreme poverty, protection of the distinctive social values of his people, and the need to breach the enormous gap between the wealthy nations and his country.

Gandhi showed an undeniable capacity to strengthen his ideas with actions. This enlightened his country about fundamental truths, which were necessary to enhance, against the external pressure represented by British colonialism. Thus, salt, the spinning wheel, and the rejection of foreign cloths, symbolized autonomy and the use of spare time to obtain non-dependence and the identity of his nation.

Emancipation was achieved through non-violence, a concept practised by Gandhi, conceived as the only viable means to liberate a numerous and disarmed nation which was confronting one of the mightiest military powers of history. The spinning wheel represented the ability and will of a nation painfully affected by unemployment. The image of Gandhi at the spinning wheel personified, not only an effort against dependence on foreign nations, but also the proof that labour is basically a service which is neccessary not only for the worker but also for the community.

---

* President of the University of Peace, United Nations Organization, Santa Rica CA.

Published in *Gandhi Prasang*, Vol. 1 No. 2; January 1999.

Productive is not an essential factor, nor of direct immediate value, when the maximum effort is directed towards political independence, perceived as something fundamental before aspiring to achieve the social development of a populous nation living in abject poverty. Those who look for economic principles in Gandhi's action, will only find themselves in a never ending labyrinth and in an apparent web of contradictions. This is because Gandhi locally pertained to India, he was India itself: a distant and unknown factor for those who ignore the reality and identity of his people.

To depend on what is local and to abandon illusory benefits of what is foreign was fundamental to Gandhi's India. He was able to prove this with unique intelligence using the image and the word: Gandhi sought to illustrate with his spinning wheel and his march to the salt, the possibility of rural self-reliance as opposed to the subduing urban dominance, and the economic independence of a poor nation in the face of colossal dominance by financial centres. These, as well as local control over a nation's own natural resources, were fundamental goals.

Gandhi gave a clear definition of India's identity through his spirituality and simplicity. But at the same time he was also a universal figure; though, the symbols he used to communicate with his people were local, the principles he inspired have permanent application for every nation of the planet.

His ideas light the path that poor nations must travel if they really desire to overcome the gap that separates them from the industrialised world, a gap that originates from the exploitation caused by the prevailing relationship between countries.

As long as development is measured exclusively by the prevailing statistical system of the rich nations; as long as progress continues to be expected only from abroad; as long as natural resources are given away to be exploited by foreigners; as long as self-sufficiency is not strengthened, there is no possibility of overcoming obstacles which impede the self-improvement and the true development of the poor nations.

Thus, Gandhi's principles, which cannot be applied to all nations in the way he illustrated them for India, remain standing to be applied by the leaders of our nations, adapting them to each particular case. Those principles became universal guidelines to the governments of the third world countries, in as much as their leaders truly aspire to orient their actions, as

Gandhi proposed, on behalf of the impoverished majorities, those overwhelming and miserable majorities. With the certainty that the great differences between rich and poor countries can only he diminished when the needs of the poor are taken into consideration.

Gandhi was able to demonstrate the power of the majority, and India became independent and free as the result of a singularly peaceful revolution. However, we should not forget that the movement led by Gandhi was in fact a revolution which, as all revolutions, occur when government forget their primary responsibilities.

Gandhi was able to demonstrate the power of the rich nations: there can be no peace if you cannot walk the path of truth. Truth itself is justice and, we must emphasize this fact, there can be no peace without justice.

The wealth of the planet has to be utilised to cultivate happiness for the people — for all people of all nations. The rich countries cannot live in peace if they do not practice justice. The inexorable march of millions of human beings from the poor countries to the rich countries in search of food and shelter is dramatic evidence of this. An endless army of unarmed people invades rich nations, in spite of immigration laws and in spite of police security. It is an action of "non-violence" as opposed to the violence that has prevailed for centuries because of injustice millions upon millions of human beings are following the path through which, their country's wealth previously passed — and there is only one way to end this avalanche — through on integral development of the planet, so that all human beings may live contentedly in the land that saw them come to life. Peace through unity in diversity.

Gandhi's ideas were not perceived by the wealthy nations until their own technological achievements produced weapons from the effects of which no one can be saved. If there is an atomic conflict, there will be neither winners nor losers: the risk of extinction is shared by all of humanity. The generalisation of fear has driven the rich nations towards a desperate search for a superior force, superior to the weapons its technology has created. Many have already found it: non-violence.

But, what is non-violence? How is it practised? What is the inspiration behind it? People who are unaware of the origin of non-violence seem to be surprised to find behind this concept a small, simple, poor and thin figure's symbol of the country that is often regarded as backward by rich nations; a figure that sharply contrasts with all that contemporary power represents.

Gandhi is the symbol of non-violence and at the same time his image is beginning to reveal, for many, something the media has never reported; a sense of authenticity, justice, identity and self-reliance, of the true independence of nations, and of non-violence, understood not only as opposed to weapons that kill by explosion, but above all those other weapons represented by abuse, exploitation and ignorance.

Today, more than ever, the world is being nurtured by Gandhi's thoughts. The Third World sees him as an inspiration, and the First World is finding that history is written not only by itself; but that; the matrix of the destiny of nations seems to have been moving since the end of the Second World War, towards those continents, unknown and enigmatic, which held eighty percent of the earth's inhabitants. At the end of the Twentieth Century, these people, until recently spectators are swiftly becoming the protagonists, aspiring to achieve justice and to share in the wealth of creation.

Mankind today lives the reality of decolonisation, internecine wars, rebellions and inconformity. Hunger impels the people of the world towards any to overcome injustice.

Truly, Gandhi is the man that changed the course of history by leading his country to an indisputable victory, with the indestructible weapon of non-violence. Likewise, Gandhi has changed the course of history by showing that the poor nations can utilize non-violence as well as showing the rich nations and their leaders that it is never too late to implement justice.

Like a resurrection of the prophets of all times, like a remembrance of the teachings of Jesus Christ, from behind a spinning wheel, there appears to our contemporary civilization that figure, rising from the dust of India and the misery of the people: the image of Mahatma Gandhi changing the course of history.

All revolutions occur when man who have in their hand the destiny of the people forget their essential responsibilities... Mahatma Gandhi's local endeavour is expanding over time, to become a universal philosophy for humankind.

2

Peace through Integration

Jan Tinbergen*

1. War an increasingly risky means of conflict settlement

In history, mankind has gone through an innumerable number of wars; so many and so often that one is inclined to think that wars are part of human nature. As so many aspects of life, the activity of fighting has gone through a process of technological change and developed from a labour-intensive activity to an increasingly capital-intensive "industry". In a sense part of the process now occurs in factories where guns of all sorts, aircraft and, more recently, rockets are being produced.

Parallel with this change in technology other changes took place. Increasingly the victims of war became non-combatants, including women and children. Increasingly also the fighters were not only volunteers, but also conscripts, forced to take part in the process. Then, the use of more powerful weapons, some of them very cruel (chemical weapons), implied still worse suffering of all victims. This aspect of the war activity has now reached its absolute upper limit as a consequence of the discovery of nuclear sources of energy. At present a nuclear war means the high probability of making the earth uninhabitable and also means the end of most forms of life, certainly of human life. This constitutes a risk of so far unknown intensity, far surpassing the experience of the Japanese cities of Hiroshima and Nagasaki.

2. Alternative ways of conflict settlement do not always work

The cruelty of wars already before 1900 led to conferences on how to maintain peace and the city where I live and was born, The Hague, testifies of these endeavours by its Peace Palace, a building to which contributions in kind were made by a number of countries represented in

---

* Noble Laureate in Economics, Netherland.

Published in *Journal of Gandhian Studies*, Vol. 14; Jan/Apr 1987.

the Peace Conferences of 1899 and 1907. The Peace Palace was finished a few years before the First World War broke out in 1914. At present it is the seat of the International Court of Justice, part of the United Nations family of institutions.

The main alternative to war is to settle a conflict between nations by submitting it to the Court. Unfortunately nations may refuse to recognize the Court's competence to decide and possibly refuse to behave according to the Court's sentence. This bad behaviour was shown recently by the United States of America when a conflict with Nicaragua was at stake.

A somewhat different alternative is the submission of a conflict to the United Nations Security Council. This procedure does not work when one of the permanent members of that Council vetoes a decision made by its other members. Moreover, one of the nations in conflict may not behave as decided by the Security Council. The Council is not able to impose the implementation, since a United Nations police force does not exist.

Still another alternative is to seek mediation by an institution or a government which both parties trust and whose pronouncement will be accepted by both sides.

None of these alternatives is fully satisfactory, because the parties cannot be forced to act according to the settlement.

3. World Government: its meaning and feasibility

War would be ruled out as a means to settle conflicts between countries, just as the government of a well-organized country can deal with conflicts between provinces or, in a federal state, between states. There is much doubt and scepticism about the desirability of establishing a world government, but this is caused by misunderstandings about what a world government stands for. It is not, as some seem to think, a government that would take over all the tasks now in the hands of national governments. Rather it is a supplement to existing governments, which would remain the decision makers in the large majority of the tasks they have today. Only a small portion of their sovereignty would have to be transferred to the higher levels of a world government, or, alternatively, a continental or regional government. This transfer is necessary—for an optimal way of "managing the earth"—only for solving problems where the welfare of more countries than our own country is affected. These common problems are not so numerous, but they are very important. Examples known already for a long period are those of international trade, the international monetary system and international financing of development projects. This is why we do have United Nations specialized agencies dealing with these problems. For the examples just mentioned the agencies are UNCTAD and GATT, the IMF and the World Bank Group. Some newer institutions are those dealing with the environment, UN Environmental Programme (with its secretariat in Nairobi, Kenya) and with the oceans, the new Law of the Sea, not yet ratified by a sufficient number of member states. For the problem of maintaining peace it is the UN Security Council. The shortcoming of most of these institutions is their lack of power to implement their decisions and the creation of World Government in fact means that such power be given to these institutions.

It will take a long time before this transfer of sovereignty from national governments to the supra-national agencies mentioned will be implemented. In national government circles and among most national politicians there is a high "propensity to maintain national sovereignty". This high propensity partly rests on the *misunderstanding* that sovereignty is in the interest of nations. This is not correct for the elements of sovereignty just discussed. The solution of trade problems by maintaining full sovereignty will, for instance, be sought in protection by industrialized countries against a number of products of less developed countries. In UNCTAD and GATT conferences forces against protectionism are strong enough to counteract protection. Similarly, a better environmental policy will be obtained if we give the power to implement its decisions to UNEP. But again, it will take time to persuade a sufficient number of politicians that this is the better policy.

4. An approach from the base: integration

During centuries a change in government structure has been going on known as *integration*. A few centuries ago the number of independent countries in Europe and America—to start with these continents—was much larger than it is now. Germany consisted of an innumerable number of princedoms, and even a small country as the Netherlands consisted of several independent parts which coincide more or less with today's provinces. Also

Italy consisted of several independent kingdoms. A few centuries earlier even France was not a unit. In North America also a fairly large number of independent states existed. These smaller units fought many wars with each other.

Frontiers have been changed often; and history showed complicated patterns. Yet the general trend has been *towards greater units*. To be sure there have been opposite movements; for instance the dissolution of the "double monarchy" of Austria-Hungary into several sovereign parts, including the Slav nations of Czechoslovakia and Yugoslavia. Still the number of units in Europe as a whole has been reduced by integration; and with integration the number of wars has diminished. No wars have been fought anymore among German princedoms or Dutch provinces. Belgium, which did free itself from the 1813 — created Netherlands, did not fight any war with the (Northern) Netherlands after 1839, when it obtained its freedom. And at present the European Community is slowly integrating a number of non-communist nations. Starting with six, it now counts twelve members and the likelihood of a Franco-German war is felt to be weak.

In North America a similar process of integration brought us the United States of America. To be sure it did not happen completely smoothly. In the early 1860's there was the Civil War, between the Southern and the Northern states. Only after the confederation had been changed into a real federation American integration had become strong enough to completely avoid the possibility of war among American states.

The process of integration took place also in Asia, where two of the largest unified countries now exist : India and Indonesia. Here, ironically, the process was furthered by colonialism, which alongside its strongly negative aspects also brought some positive elements. Here, too, as in Europe and America, some process in the opposite direction took place, as, for instance separatist tendencies in the Punjab, but we can hope that the forces of unity will be stronger.

Even in Africa colonialism did bring some integration, but clearly Africa still has a longer way to go.

In Latin America some large countries resulted from integrative movements, but more remains to be done. The European Common Market is the most advanced result.

5. The necessary change in attitude

Since integration seems to be one of the most successful ways to a peaceful world the question may be posed whether this is also applicable to the relationship between the two superpowers, the Soviet Union and the United States. Alongside the classical reasons of war, those of nationalism or patriotism, these two countries also see their difference in socio-economic system as a cause for conflict. This conflict is less a question of a desire to occupy part of the other's territory than a desire to change the socio-economic system of one or more of the countries belonging to the sphere of influence of the other superpower. Both sides hate the other's order. If the policy of integration has to be extended also to this "last integration" a change in attitude will be necessary. The existence of different social orders should be regarded with more tolerance. There are some reasons for more tolerance. To begin with it is ironical that pure capitalism and pure communism don't exist. The US does have a social security system, although a rather weak one: in 1982, 21 per cent of gross national product was spent on public social welfare, whereas the Netherlands spent 36 per cent (cf. Haveman, 1985). The US does have the private plots of land. Between the extremes, a number of countries do exist with varying "degrees of socialism" (cf. Adler Karlsson, 1967). Income distribution also varies between the two extremes (cf. Wiles, 1978). So there is an almost continuous distribution of social orders, except the extremes, in contrast to the propagandistic polarized black-white picture. *Polarization had better be replaced by tolerance.* This brings us to a view closer to the great Indian thinker and activist Mahatma Gandhi. It was his spirit, which made possible the liberation of the largest colony, British India, without the use of violence.

3

A New Life Style and Gandhian Thought

Jan Tinbergen*

1. Introductory

For a long time Western public opinion did not show much interest in Gandhian thought. Many intellectuals considered it irrelevant to the problems occupying Western science, philosophy or art. In some quarters there was and is sympathy for the way India became an independent nation but the pattern of its liberation from colonial rule was considered in a way, correctly — exceptional. In addition, it was not quite clear to what extent the process of Indian liberation was due to the attitude of the Indian population and to what extent to the attitude of the British rulers; or, finally to the happy coincidence of their running parallel.

Unfortunately practically all other processes of liberation from colonial rule showed the pattern considered more or less normal in Western history and societies; as a violent struggle with much blood-shed. American liberation from British rule, Indonesian liberation from Dutch rule, Algerian liberation from French rule may be quoted as examples.

In the meantime important changes in the general situation of the planet earth have materialized. They will be dealt within the three following sections of this essay. Problems hardly heard of or discussed before World War II are now the ones that require the larger part of Western scientific and political thinking.

Moreover, the inner dynamics of Western technological, social and cultural development—amazing by its rhythm—has placed the national societies in front of numerous problems not expected by most politicians and cultural leaders of the nineteen forties. Features have come to the fore, which evoked grave doubts concerning the generally optimistic expectations prevailing around the early years of the twentieth century. Section 5 will deal with these features.

---

* Prof. Emeritus, Erasmus University, Netherlands

Published in *Journal of Gandhian Studies*, Vol. 9, October 1982.

An increased need to look ahead is now being felt; the certainties of the past are no longer there. All types of doubt have arisen around the national and social conditions, which in future period will codetermine the feasible standards of life. We propose to elaborate on them in the four subsequent section already characterized in the preceding paragraphs—in order to derive conclusions on a necessary change in life style now discussed in Western societies. In a final section (Section 7) some of the similarities of the new life styles needed with Gandhian ideas will be briefly dealt with.

2. The 'New Scarcities'

For decades, if not centuries, economic thinking of the West has been based on the assumptions that a number of resources nature supplied us with were "free commodities", that is goods and environmental elements available in unlimited quantities. This applies to air, water and minerals, the latter to be subdivided into ores and fuels. Almost everywhere air, in pure form, was around us, although in some industrial cities it was less pure if not even polluted. Of course deserts existed, but alongside them enough non-arid regions contained the fresh water wells needed for human and animal life. No price had to be paid, in most centres of productive activity, for air (that is, oxygen or nitrogen) or fresh water. Ores and fuels did carry a price, but that mainly reflected the efforts needed to dig them out of the earth crust or otherwise to move them to the location where they were used or processed.

At first, hardly observed, gradually changes in this situation come about. The area where smog was threatening people's expanded. The wastes of industries, especially chemical industries, step by step polluted brooks and rivers and finally lakes. Animal and plant life is some areas came under menace. Ores had to be hauled from farther-away deposits.

"New scarcities" were recognised as non-negligible elements of our economies (Hueting, 1974, 1980). The environmental problem was born and some biologists started giving attention to it. Action groups joined them; in some countries new political parties were based on the new challenge. In the Federal Republic of Germany the party of the "Greens" began to play a role.

In 1973 the Organisation of Petroleum Exporting Countries (OPEC) had started to understand that the base of their prosperity had a character fundamentally different from agricultural or manufacturing activities constituting the economic base of other countries.The unprecedented increase in oil consumption made it clear that OPEC member countries undermined their own future existence if they stuck to the very low price of their main source of income. Their situation was closest to what not so long before the Club of Rome had understood as an essential element of the "human predicament"; there are limits to a number of things considered endless before (Meadows et al. 1972).

The new scarcities can no longer be eliminated from our state of mind. They have profoundly changed the prospects of mankind, especially thanks to the Club of Rome and its infatigable chairman Dr. Aurelio Peccie. An impressive series of profound studies have been induced by his creative attacks on the problematique of mankind, put on the agenda of hundreds of meetings of all sizes and kinds. This also applies to the problem cluster now to be identified.

3. Third-World Problems

Started earlier, namely briefly after World War II, a cluster of problems had come into focus under the sub-heading of this section. Let us indicate it, alternatively, as the problem of world poverty. Immediately after the decolonisation process had started some believed that independence would raise well-being : they had considered "colonial exploitation" as the main cause of poverty — although Latin America could have shown that things were not that simple.

Around 1960 it was realized that a particular effort was needed in order to bring more prosperity. Still the size of the problem was underestimated by all experts. It was believed that additional investible funds of about one per cent of the income of the industrial countries per annum would be needed for a few decades only in order to help the Third World to get in a process of self-sustained development.

Now, twenty years later, we have experienced that it will take much more effort and time than we thought around 1960. To some extent this is due to the unexpected increase in population. If the annual rate of increase existing around 1940 had continued the figures of the investments needed might have remained about one-half of what is needed now for the same increase in consumption per capita. But other processes are involved, changes in attitudes and learning processes in several directions that require time. Not two, but five decades at least may be needed to attain a desirable level of welfare for the world's population; and a series of new efforts, of various types.

This aim is of the utmost importance; first of all from an ethical point of view. The poverty existing at present is unacceptable since the resources needed are available to give a life of dignity of this planet's population; but their distribution is highly inequitable.

The aim of such a more human distribution of welfare is also in the long-term interest of the prosperous part of world population. The main reason why the prosperous countries are so inactive in these matters is their short sightedness. Their citizens and their governments—with a few laudable exceptions—do not understand that if they maintain their present inertia in the next few decades an invasion of desperate migrant workers into their countries is to be expected. The beginning of this flow of migrants can be observed already in the Southern part of the United States of America and in the better-to-do (Northern) European countries.

4. Decreasing Importance of Western Countries:

Western countries have been accustomed to be the rulers of the world. Although they know by now that they are no longer, they still think they are the most important part of the world. If that importance is measured with the aid of their incomes in dollars it may still be true. This yardstick will not remain the most appropriate, however. The yardstick at the other end of the scale of alternative way of measurement is the number of human beings. It will be the yardstick of the future. And that yardstick tells us that the significance of the West is rapidly declining. In 1978 Western countries accounted for one-sixth of world population only. Part of the white population now lives under communist rule. Moreover, there is a continuing shift of what economically might be called the leading country. In the seventeenth century it was Holland. Holland's role was soon taken over by Britain, where the industrial revolution started. After World War I the U.S.A. has taken over. At present leadership is shifting towards a non-Western country: Japan. Among the many indicators of economic leadership let us take a very relevant one, the export surplus of technology sales. For the first time Japan showed such a surplus in 1980. Japan's industrial products are flooding European and American markets. American productivity is declining. New industrial revolutions, around electronics, data processing, information, and a trade towards complete automatization have started, and some of these new technologies are especially advanced in Japan, a non-Western country.

5. Problems Created by Abundance and Stubborn Ideology

Simultaneously, however, a number of spiritual developments seem to threaten industrial societies—including Japan and the communist countries— from within. What was once believed to be pure improvement, linked with growing happiness, the increased supply of material goods, is showing dark sides. Increased incomes are spent, in a number of cases, on too much of alcoholic beverages, or on drugs; or on innocent, but irrelevant luxury goods, the demand for which is stimulated by over-advertising. More prosperity is accompanied by more egotism. Less work creates more leisure and part of the prosperous peoples does not know how to use that leisure. Some groups, when looking for amusement, try to find it in vandalism, in violence directed at persons selected at random, often persons unable to defend themselves. The exact causes are not always clear, and less still the remedies. It appears to be difficult to motivate part of the population of the prosperous countries to make a more human use of the unprecedented possibilities. Fortunately, other parts of the same population do find a better use, although often still somewhat too self-centred. A small part only finds the road to really helping those who need help and so enrich human happens as understood by the finest personalities of human history. And as a matter of course there are numerous other forms of contributing to human culture, as understood by outstanding artists, intellectuals or wise personalities.

Without losing sight of these private developments it has to be started, unfortunately, that negative features, to be summarised as degeneration, are gaining on the positive ones. One particular form, often not even discussed as a case of degeneration, is the impossible position into which we have manoeuvred ourselves by armament. A complex mixture of social ideology, stubbornness, nationalism and greed for power is keeping humanity in its grip with a good deal of probability that it will extinct life on earth. The only solution, of a World Government with a Peace Force in which all armaments would be pooled, with a view to reduce and monopolize arms technology is still a far cry.

6. The need for a New Life Style

This close to hopeless situation of human society has given rise to a positive attitude adhered to by a non-negligible part of younger and not-so-young people in various parts of the world, which is often called the desire for a new life style. Aware of the unacceptable poverty in some parts of the world, of the new scarcities and of the part situation created by stubborn ideologies— whether "capitalist" or "communist"—this movement for a new life style tends towards a more modest level of prosperity, less inequality and more tolerance.

This movement is not a highly organized and clearly out-spoken political current. It is a combination of relatively small and rather diverse groups, often in the stage of protest against the existing power centres, and themselves not very powerful. Some of the groups emphasize environmental issues, others protest against nuclear power stations, or still others, against military service, often combinations of these aims are propagated, and differing methods of agitation recommended. An important aspect is that they often adhere to the economics of "enough" instead of looking for maxima of whatever components of life. It is not clear yet whether a strong organization—such as shown by some churches and non-church movements like nationalism or communism—is what is really needed. Strong organizations are almost incompatible with tolerance and pluralism and the latter two aspects are indispensable ingredients to escape from the fate threatening us.

The time has come to reformulate the concept of the sense of human life so as to integrate pure emotional and clear intellectual forces with wise experience into a guide to our destiny. This is what the new life style we are searching for needs as an ethical, intellectual and cultural base. Important contributions to it may be made by some religions, or other philosophies of life, but also by scientific thinking.

7. New Relevance of Gandhian Thought

It will be clear that the new state of mind in the Western world outlined very briefly in this essay gives new importance to Gandhi's ideas. Many of the features touched upon in the last section show similarities with Gandhian thought. This author is only vaguely aware of what India's great spiritual leader in his rich teachings had to say. Enough however, I venture to say, in order to state that for the Institute of Gandhian Thought and Peace Studies as a large new field of work now waits for being explored. In essence this new task consists of showing how Gandhian thought may assist not only Indian society, but also Western with its new and serious problems, and possibly to identify the main attitudes needed to solve them. It is this author's hope that this modest essay may contain a train of thought of some help to develop the additional tasks for the Institute.

References:

R. Hueting (1980), *New Society and Economic Growth, More Welfare Through Less Production?* Amsterdum, North Holland (English translation from Dutch, published in 1974.)

Donella H. and Dennis Fr. Meadows, *et al.* (1972) *The Limits Growth,* New York, NY Universe Books.

4

A New World Employment Plan

Jan Tinbergen, J.M.den Uyl, J.P. Pronk, W. Kok*

1. Introduction

The aim of this proposal is to launch a large scale international operation to stimulate the economies of and to raise employment in both the industrialised and the developing countries. As a first step thereto we plea for an operational study to formulate a new world employment plan. We do so because in our view a main gap in international economic policy formulating is employment.

The longer the international economic crisis lasts the less acceptable it becomes. In a world where so many of the most pressing needs are not satisfied no justification can be given to productive agents remaining idle, disregarding even the natural feelings of dissatisfaction of those unemployed and wanting to take part in the production process. Clearly a bold approach is needed for the world at large. The international character of any attack on unemployment is due not only to the fact that unemployment now prevails everywhere but also to the strongly increased interdependence of national economies. Increased international interdependence calls for an international effort to stimulate the world economy. At the same time this implies the futility of isolated national policies—an aspect of which public opinion seems insufficiently aware. What is needed is a simultaneous and co-ordinated policy.

Interdependence between the economies of the North and the South, leading to mutual interests between the countries concerned, is being understood much clearer nowadays than in the years before the international economic crisis.

The concept has been analysed within OECD, for instance in the framework of its Interfuture project.[1] It is a leading policy principle of the

* Netherland

Published in *Journal of Gandhian Studies*, Vol. 9, October 1981.

so-called Brandt-report.[2] It plays a major role in the North South dialogue, which this year results in the formulation of a Strategy, for the Third Development Decade and in launching a New Global Round of Negotiations. In these reports and consultations the whole of international economic relations between industrialised and developing countries is being dealt with.

In our proposal, as described below, we intend to elaborate a major part of it. It does not tackle all elements of the present international economic crisis. However, it tackles the main elements of this crisis. In our view an attack on unemployment in the world is an essential precondition for the solution of other structural international economic problems.

Our central thesis is that any large-scale operation to raise employment should be inspired by an attempt to approach an optimal international division of labour for the world at large. Stimulating government policies should be applied to the sectors in which each geographical unit has a comparative advantage viewed in a dynamic way.

Our proposal pertains to a combination of two policies: positive anticipatory structural re-adjustment of industries in industrialised countries and large scale international income transfers to developing countries, as recomme-nded by the Brandt-report.

In the following paragraphs we shall elaborate these policies in their mutual relation. In paragraph 2 we present some basic analytical remarks. In paragraph 3 an outline of a new world employment policy is being sketched.

A description of the framework of a plan underlying such a policy is given in paragraph 4. Finally we shall also make some procedural suggestions.

2. Some analytical remarks

In our view employment is the most appropriate vehicle of a new international policy to stimulate the economies of developing and industrialised countries, since labour constitutes the main factor of production. To direct such a policy to maximization of employment instead of economic growth—or even to a high increase of welfare in general—has the following advantages:

- it implies a direct attack on the major problem in the present inter national economic crisis: economic stagnation (and stagflation) can only be overcome by a parallel increase in production, productivity and purchasing power, hence by an increase in employment.
- there is a direct mutual relation between poverty and unemployment. The poorest of all are the jobless. In most developing countries to be unemployed means that basic human needs cannot be fulfilled. Economic growth only results in a general increase in welfare that is more equally distributed if it coincides with an increase in employment.
- in many societies to be unemployed means to be isolated from social process. Integration of people in their society can best be furthered through employment. Full employment is a major answer to increasing tendencies towards alienation in the economics both of developing and industrialised countries.
- environmental reasons and the prevalence of scarcity set limits to physical growth. Selective economic growth and a general increase in welfare therefore can best be attained by attaching priority to employment over material production in general.

Efforts to stimulate the world economy should be based upon the principle of an optimum international division of labour. A lasting structural economic recovery and a general increase in welfare can only be implemented through a maximization of world employment. Such a maximization of world employment can only be taught in the framework of an optimum distribution of employment throughout the world.

To call for a better international division of labour asks for an attempt to identify the sectors in which countries or regions have comparative advantages.

Thereby we must not forget the existence of a substantial volume of activities whose products cannot be traded internationally and hence have to be pursued everywhere. International trade in buildings being next to impossible constructions is one of these activities.

Most of the other non-tradable are services which by their nature either have to be near or on the spot of their consumption—retail trade, personal services, the overwhelming part of schooling, and a very large part of government activities. Crude estimates result in about half of total employment or total income to derive from the se activities. Activities whose products can be traded internationally include practically all material production—agriculture, mining, manufacturing—and a non-negligible variety of services, such as international trade and transportation and important parts of finance, insurance and consulting. It is with regard to the activities producing tradables that the international division of labour has to be optimised. However, producing tradable does require some non-tradable inputs.

We define the concept of the optimal international division of labour—in accordance with the Hecksche-Ohlin principle—as desirability of a maximum use of each geographical area's available production factors or resources, natural resources, labour and capital.

Each of these main types shows very considerable diversity and for analytical purpose a further subdivision is vital. Thereby a sub-division in two steps seems to make sense. Natural resources may be subdivided into exhaustible and non-exhaustible, labour into skilled and unskilled (where the dividing line can be chosen very freely) and capital into physical and human capital. All skills, of whatever level, can be translated into quantities of human capital. A final subdivision should be made into concrete natural resources (such as land of different fertility, ores of different metals), specified occupational or educational labour groups and different types of physical capital (building, different types of equipment, with perhaps different vintages).

It is appropriate to point out that the maximum use of exhaustible natural resources should be defined also in terms of some sort of optimum distribution over time. The problem faced at present by oil-producing countries illustrates this.

Now what are the comparative advantages of developing as distinct from developed countries or continents? It is commonplace to state that the characteristics of developing areas are their abundance of unskilled labour, an abundance of some natural resources and a lack of physical capital. (An exception to the last characteristics are some OPEC countries). Most developing countries have a potential of solar energy, which we hope will become a source of welfare to them within some decades. Developed countries show comparative advantages in quantities of capital, both physical and human, they command. Hence it is commonplace too that the economic perspective of these countries depends a good deal on knowledge-intensive activities. Almost all the services which have developed so quickly in western countries these last decades are knowledge-intensive.

On the basis of such commonplace knowledge national and international economic policies advocated and implemented in practice can be described as policies who favour or hamper an optimum international division of labour. However, much more research is necessary to identify the sectors in which countries or regions have a comparative advantage.

Some economists have attempted to specify comparative advantages by estimating "revealed" comparative advantages from observed trade figures. This is a somewhat tricky undertaking as long as we live in a world with many protectionist policies: the latter tend to obscure a number of comparative advantages rather than revealing them.

Recently some studies have been published in which research has been carried out on the optimum international division of labour (B. Herman[3]) and on comparative advantages (P.K.N. Tharakan a.o.[4]). It is highly relevant that governments and international organisations stimulate this research.

3. An outline of a new world employment policy

As indicated in the introduction of this paper a new world employment policy should consist of a combination of two policies: positive anticipatory structural re-adjustment of industries in industrialised countries and large scale international income transfer to developing countries.

3.1 Structural re-adjustment

Many governments of industrialised countries are under the pressure to protect industries, which are unable to compete on the world market. Understandable though they may be in order to prevent higher unemployment levels in the short run, these policies do not contribute to a long run world employment policy. Essentially protection is a negative policy especially if it is based on one-side decisions and if it is not used only temporarily and selectively as part of a restructuring policy. Western countries need a positive restructuring into the direction of activities where they have comparative advantages, meaning that they more intensively use their abundant resources: knowledge.

Which direction should such a positive anticipatory re-adjustment policy take? The answer to this question should be given against the background of three important trends. One trend—emphasized by Jean Fourastie already in 1949[5]—is the ongoing shrinkage in terms of relative employment and value added—of material production and the corresponding growth of the employment in the service sector. So in the European OECD countries the percentage of the labour force employed in agriculture decreased from 24 per cent in 1963 to 16 per cent in 1976, and in industry from 39 per cent to 37 per cent. In that period the percentage of the labour force employed in the service sector increased from 38 per cent to 47 per cent.

The figures refer to the formal economy, for obvious reasons the "under-ground activities" are not recorded in our statistics (vet); and only a relatively small part of household activities. It is our hope that through analysis like that of Gershuyny[6] we shall soon have more complete information; our impression is that Fourastie's discovery will apply also if we have the more complete information.

The second trend that cannot be overlooked is the element of great uncertainty introduced into our analysis by the rapid technological development in the field of the microprocessors. The progress of penetration of these new possibilities may well be slower than most people think, but they will result in both the greater access to information and Knowledge and in widening research possibilities. The difference with previous technological breakthroughs seems to be that this time the capital intensity of the new activities is lower, not higher than that of existing technologies. The similarity with previous breakthroughs may be that a growing demand for the new products will create offsetting employment. Much research is necessary in this field, especially to create and direct a demand for new products and services on the basis of needs which are considered to be important from the social point of view (e.g. improvements in the quality of work circumstances). This also asks for steering mechanisms with regard to the development of existing technologies.

The third trend is an increase in women's participation in labour force and a growing emphasis on a more just distribution of employment.

This applies not only to the distribution of employment between men and women, but also to that between employed and unemployed labour. There is growing tendency towards a shortening of the labour time per employed labourers, whether per day, per week or during his or her whole lifetime. This third trend is related to the other two: if it is politically necessary due to generally accepted views with regard to justice, it is made possible by productivity increase and desirable for welfare increases. This leads us to the following conclusions: given the necessity of a better international division of labour (as conceived in para 2, and in the light of some present trends described above it can be argued that Western industrialised countries, choosing for structural anticipatory readjustment policies should turn to knowledge-intensive and up to a point capital-intensive activities. The means used by some governments to encourage employment in general should be directed at branches with a future, that is, which will become competitive after an initial period of losses.

3.2 Research, investment and employment

Structural re-adjustment towards knowledge-intensive industries means that a high priority should be given to two sectors of the economy which are very much related to each other; namely:

1) research.
2) production of goods and services with a high research component in their development.

Today we are faced with a number of questions, the answers to which we do not know; these answers are of vital importance to the world's future. It is now absolutely clear that we know less than we urgently need to know and less than once we thought we knew.

So some key questions for planning the future are:

- what effect will the increased consumption of fossil fuels exert on the climates of various parts of the world?

- what are the comparative risks connected with alternative ways of producing energy—from fossil fuel through all types of nuclear reactors to solar radiation used in alternative ways?
- which uses of solar energy can be expanded at what rate?
- which part of the world surface must be left in its wildlife state in order to be available as a "gene reserve" for agriculture?
- what additional possibilities do exist to recycle wastes of one industry to be used by other industries?
- what have been the experiences of previous forms of automation, especially with regard to the expansion of demand for the process products and with regard to employment?
- what effects on labour satisfaction have been observed from changes in work organization, in particular from decentralization of such organization?
- can possible "social contracts" be proposed to link wages and salaries with the general price level and the oil price level?
- contracts, hence between Western trade unions, Western employer organisation and OPEC?

It seems clear that answering these questions requires a very large volume of intensified research activities.

Employment can also be created in sectors producing goods and services which require much research in their development. So industrialised countries can specialize, within the manufacturing sector, in the production of anti-pollution equipment, in new recycling activities—some of which formerly were too expensive now break even because of higher energy prices—and in the production of equipment for developing countries.

More orders for equipment will be received if (a) more industrial products of developing countries are given access to the markets of developed countries and (b) more financial transfers to developing countries are made, as proposed by the Brandt report.

Such a restructuring however, for two reasons also implies new activities in the sectors producing non-tradable. The first reason is that these sectors to a certain extent are complementary to the sectors producing tradable. The second reason is that there are still many unmet needs in industrialised countries, especially with regard to education, health and housing. So another part of employment programme may consist of innovation of dwellings, energy saving schemes such as energy saving insulation of buildings, recycling of utilised resources, antipollution schemes and of re-schooling programmes.

The question may rise how in an optimal international division of labour the available manpower can be used as fully as possible by the main economic sectors. Research done by Tinbergen indicates that the research and education sector may absorb several percents of total employment.[7]

For an analysis of the mechanism at work it is appropriate to make a distinction between three economic sectors: the primary sector (I), the research (II), and all that remains (III), which consists of the traditional secondary sectors (manufacturing, etc.) plus all service sectors except research. The labour force was distinguished into three categories: up to eight years of schooling (A), from nine to fifteen years (B) and sixteen years or more (C). On the basis of extrapolations of the changes during the last decades in the composition of the labour force employed in the three economic sectors in two countries (The United States and the Netherlands), its composition in 1990 was calculated. Combined with the then labour input coefficients per sector (also calculated of the basis of extrapolations of the changes in the composition of the labour force per economic sector) the total requirements of the three types of labour were estimated.

A comparison with existing estimates of available manpower in 1990 led to a considerable oversupply of A, a small over-supply of C and an under-supply of B. From this it may be concluded that it is likely that doubling the relative extent of research and education not only will occur but also uses the available labour force rather will (in 1990 research employment -C in III- would imply somewhat more that 2 percent of total employment in the Netherlands, as against somewhat less that 4 percent in the United States).

It is important to stress that such an anticipatory structural readjustment policy towards knowledge and capital intensive industries and towards social services cannot be implemented with the help of market forces alone. Planning is necessary. Such planning should help re-directing:

- investment capital
- research activities
- labour allocation, on the basis of, for instance, re-training programmes.

It is equally important to stress that such an anticipatory structural re-adjustment policy requires much more than restructuring specific weak industries. The aim is to create more employment in competitive industries and to distribute this more equally, both between and within nations.

Investment decisions should be based on social considerations with regard to the direction of production and the distribution of employment. This may require,

- national selective growth policies, which are based on social priority needs and which do not use too many scarce resources and energy,
- intergovernmental control of the long term investment policies of transnational companies,
- participation of the production factor labour in decision-making processes at the level of industries and of individual firms,
- longer term employment plans (next to longer term investment plans) for sectors and possible individual enterprises, to be agreed upon by the organisations of employers and employees and by the
- investing surplus profits made by stronger industries or firms also to create employment in other sectors,
- satisfaction of basic needs with priority for the socially and economically weakest groups and countries,
- international, industrial and investment policies, not primarily based on private profits considerations, but on the principle of social justice.

3.3. International income transfers

The second element of a new world employment policy consists of an increase in international income transfers to developing countries in order to increase employment in these countries. The resulting increase in welfare and purchasing power in these countries will lead to higher imports from the industrialised countries. This then will be an important economic stimulus to higher employment in the industrialized countries too.

This has been stressed recently by politicians and development policy makers like Barbara Ward[8], Judith Hart[9] and others. It has also been advocated in the report of the Brandt Commission. The question may rise whether there is a contradiction between recommendations for a slower economic growth and a plea for a big push to increase employment. This is not necessarily the case. A big push is meant to raise the level of production and employment for once only; slow growth recommendations refer to longer-term trends. Moreover, a contradiction between the two does not come about automatically: it is dependent on the nature of growth policies. We explicitly advocate employment based growth policies, oriented towards a balanced use of the world's scarce resources and energy because unbalanced growth may destroy future employment opportunities. A selective growth policy for the world as a whole means optimalisation of production in order to maximize employment. In order to be effective such a policy should be differentiated regionally. It should also be based upon an analysis of unmet priority needs, especially within the poorest countries. World demand should be steered (for instance by price policies and income transfers) in order to bring it in accordance with these needs and with the availability of scarce resources.

As indicated above the increased international income transfers to developing countries ought to result in an increase in the employment. Therefore, they should be invested in two sectors mainly: big infrastructural programmes (for instance a railway network in Africa, communication development schemes, road construction, flood regulation schemes, irrigation and desalination programmes, mineral resources exploration, development of alternative energy sources) which are too costly to be financed by individual countries' integrated rural development schemes and the furthering of small scale industries in developing countries.

It will be clear that necessary complementary policies in the field of international trade should be implemented. The industrial restructuring in the developed countries, increases the possibilities of developing countries to get access to markets for their industrial products. This will not only lead to import substitution but also to increased import. International trade measures, based on (indicative) long term planning of the world's industrial development thereby seem to be necessary. Temporary governmental support for weak and infant industries, both in richer and in poorer countries, may be acceptable if this support enables intergovernmental planning of the sectors concerns.

3.4. The financing of the program

How could the program, consisting of income transfers to the poorer countries and industrial restructuring in the richer countries be financed. In the reports and consultations referred to above various suggestions have been made. As some possibilities with regard to income transfers we would like to refer to : additional lending from the World Bank, whose lending capacity could be increased by doubling its borrowing-to-capital ratio(as advocated by the Brandt Commission).

- introducing a link between the allocation of Special drawing Rights and the financing of development activities. (We agree with the authors of the Brandt report that new SDR's should be created to the extent called for by the need for non-inflationary increases in world liquidity). Such a link could be established partly by allocating new SDR's through the World Bank or a new World Development Fund.
- part of the increase in Special Drawing Rights which are made available to the richer countries.
- introducing the use of automatically mobilised revenues (this also has been advocated by the Brandt Commission). Possible sources of finance for restructuring programmes are:
- savings on benefits to unemployed labourers by rendering employment subsidies lower than these benefits. An elaborate study of subsidizing employment has been made by the Swedish economist Gosta Rehn[10]. We come back to it below.
- increase in taxation on energy consumption and on toxical products.
- reductions of public financing of higher education by charging a larger part of its costs to the beneficiaries of it (by offering loans to them instead of making available higher education at a very small part of its real cost, repayment of these loans should depend on the incomes obtained after education).

- reduction of public expenditures by appropriate decentralization in the execution of some public tasks which may contribute to reducing their costs.
- increasing private financial allocations to research activities to be undertaken by private firms when subventioned.

(for an individual country) export of research products c.q. services.

A key question involved in such an operation is, of course, whether it can be financed without a reappearance of inflation. Recent experience seems to raise serious doubts whether this is possible. It comes to us, however, that some forces operating against inflation have not been given their full possibilities. Important anti-inflationary consequences can be expected from the elimination of protection (as has recently been shown by J. Waelbroeck.[11])

The introduction of more shifts in some industries (may be part-time shifts for those who prefer part-time jobs) so as to raise the average equipment utilization time to 45 hours a week would reduce costs and hence prices too. Next, we want to point to the use that can be made of employment premiums in order to reduce marginal costs of production. Important research done at the London School of Economics by Layard and Nickel[12] has shown that a clear pressure on the price level can be attained by such employment premiums. In addition we want to propose that an active price control has to be added in order to get prices down. Here the Swiss experience with a small but efficient Office of Price Administration in the period 1972-1987 lends support to this proposal. It seems to us that taken together these neglected possibilities might well constitute an arsenal of considerable anti-inflationary potential.

In our view both the need to raise the necessary financial resources, and the stipulations that thereby inflation should be avoided as such as possible, call for an incomes policy for all incomes: wages, salaries, fees of the free professions and profits.

4. New World Employment Plan

On the basis of the analysis presented above we propose that a New World Employment Plan be formulated.

This New World Employment Plan should be

- based on an adequate in-depth-analysis of present international and national social-economic developments.
- quantified, both in terms of its targets and of its instruments.
- related to a concrete specified time-period.
- both a macro plan and a plan with regard to the most important individual sectors.
- an aggregate of national plans or plans for regional groups of countries.
- related both to international and to national targets and instruments (with regard to policies of both industrialized and developing countries).
- directed already from the outset of the plan formulation, towards its implementation.

The plan thus should consist of elements both with regard to (anticipatory) industrial restructuring in industrial countries and to employment creation in infrastructural, industrial and agricultural sectors in developing countries.

The quantitative targets of the world employment plan should in first instance refer to increases in employment in specified sectors and regions. Additional targets with regard to changes in relative shares of specific regions in the industrial sectors distinguished may be necessary. Finally also targets with regard to the international distribution of income should be specified.

In the plan quantitative figures with regard to the following instruments will have to be estimated,

- investments in all relevant sectors by region.
- consumption of energy per country
- sources of finance, including international income transfers
- removal of trade barriers
- shares of national incomes to be spent on research
- shares of the labour force, by educational category and by region, to be retrained

Finally some institutional measures will have to be specified, at both national and international levels.

5. Some Procedural Remarks

A New World Employment Plan should not only be an exercise in economic analysis and forecasting, but very much also a political effort. We call upon governments, international organisations, organisations of employers and labour unions to commit themselves towards this. Recently many studies have been carried out on the basis of prognostic analysis. They often lead to qualitative recommendations only. A further step, consisting of a quantitative plan is needed now. And from the outset there should be no doubt that such a plan, when formulated, would be discussed amongst governments, in order to reach agreement on policies to be implemented.

In the introduction to this proposal we stressed the urgency of this plan. It may be asked why we need such a new proposal now. The answer is that we need a new initiative because at present the existing international organisations, producing quantitative projections and qualitative proposals, have not come along with quantitative plans. The possible contribution of the various economic geographical regions to the growth and employment in the world has as yet been quantified inadequately.

The turn from the decade of the seventies into the eighties provided us with a good opportunity for such an initiative. We see a deadlock in the North-South dialogue. We witness a failing economic recovery in countries whose economies could function as a flywheel for the world's economic development. We are also aware of the fact that the necessary international negotiations on the solutions of some major problems like energy and food hardly have started.

At the same time we know that in the forthcoming year important decisions have to be made with regard to the implementation of the Strategy for a Third Development Decade and with regard to the New Round of Global Negotiations. The work on a new world employment plan might be an important catalyst in the process.

We feel that, after consultations leading to political commitment in principle, the plan formulation would take about two years. Political negotiation on its implementation might take another half a year. This means that its implementation could start mid 1983.

This proposal is made to all whom it may concern. We want to be a bit more specific, however. Because the aim of a new world employment plan is to increase employment and welfare in both industrial and developing countries from the outset both groups of countries should be involved. We feel that it is highly important that a plan secretariat and a steering committee should consist of people from the South as well as from the North. For this reason we have addressed this proposal in the first place to the Secretary General of the United Nations.

We would like to add that we would welcome participation also from the Soviet Union and other Eastern European countries. Their participation in the solution of the world's economic problems is highly necessary. And these countries also have unemployment problems.

We would also hope for the People's Republic of China to participate. The future domestic and international economic policy of this big country has many important employment dimensions.

Finally we hope that Western European countries, both belonging to the European community, and others, would take a lead in the implementation of this initiative. Western Europe has a specific role to play, both in North-South and in East-West relations. It can do so by means of creative forward thinking "to master to future" and by catalysing international co-operation, in the interest of welfare and employment of all world's population, be it present or future generations.

We have sent this proposal to various international agencies like the Secretary-General of the United Nations, the Secretary-General of UNCTAD, the Director-General of ILO, the President of the World Bank, the Secretary-General of the Commonwealth, and others.

At this moment we specifically ask the institutions of the European Commission the Council of European Ministers and the European Parliament, to take a first decision to finance the study which should lead to a plan.

This paper essentially contains a proposal to make a plan. We also ventured some ideas on possible elements of the plan. These may be criticised. National and international employment policies may have to be different from what we sketched above. But we very much hope that the initiative itself will be taken over. It is high time to act.

References:

1. *"Facing the Future, mastering the probable and managing the unpredictable"* (Interfutures), OECD, Paris, 1979.
2. *"North-South: a programme for survival"*, The Report of the Independent Commission on International Development Issues under the Chairmanship of Willy Brandt, Pan Books, London and Sydney, 1980.
3. B. Herman, *"The Optimum International Division of Labour"*, Geneva, 1980.
4. P.K.M. Tharakan with L.G. Soete and J.A. Bussaert, in *European Economic Review*, Vol. II, pp. 221-239.
5. Jean Fourastie, *"Le grand espoir dus xxe siecle"* Presses Universitaires de France, Paris, 1949.
6. Jay I. Gershuny, 1949, *"The Informal Economy in the Development Process,* Science Policy Research Unit, University of Brighton.
7. J. Tinbergen, *"Which sectors should be stimulated by a Recovery Policy"*, Lloyds Bank Review, July 1980, pp. 30-40.
8. Barbara Ward, 1979, in *"S. Ramphal, One World to Share Selected speeches of the Commonwealth Secretary-General"*.
9. Judith Hart, 1979, *"Conflicts real and imagined"* Development (Society for international Development), 1979/4 pp. 31-33.
10. Gosta Rehn, *"Employment Premiums in Economic Policy"* (forthcoming).
11. B. Verreydt and J. Waelbroeck, *"Protection, Employment and Welfare in a Stagfalting Economy : Policy Issues for the EEC"*, Centre for Development Studies, St. Ignatius University, Antwerp, Symposium on December 11, 1979.
12. P.R.G. Layard and S.J. Nickel, *"The Case for Subsidising Extra Jobs"*, The Economic Journal,Vol. 90 (1980), pp. 51-73.

5

The New International Order and Gandhian Thought

Jan Tinbergen

In its sixth and seventh special session and in its ordinary session in 1974 the United Nations General Assembly has adopted as guidelines for international order three documents, known as the Declaration on the New International Order, the Plan of Action on the Establishment of that order and the Charter of Economic Rights and Duties of States.

On October 19, 1976, a group of independent experts published and offered to the Club of Rome a report "Reshaping the International Order" (RIO for brevity's sake)[1], formulated at the initiative of the Club of Rome's governing board and financed by the Netherlands government. This report expressed itself in favour of the overwhelming majority of the elements proposed in the official U.N. documents just mentioned, but not of all details. The report made an attempt to provide a scientific basis to the proposed new order, as well as a number of some seventy five concrete recommendations on steps to be taken in order to attain the New Inter-national Order.

It is the objective of the present article to show that several aspects of the ideas on the desirable new order show intimate relationships with some of the fundamental thoughts of Mahatma Gandhi. This constitutes, on the one hand, a tribute to the Great Master, and on the other hand a proof that closer study and elaboration of Gandhian thought can be of eminent relevance for the attainment of a better world. To put in bluntly, Gandhi's ideas are by no means outmoded, as some believe, and, on the contrary might well be applied more often in to-day's world.

The RIO report based its formulation of the aims the planetary order should seek to attain as a "life of dignity for all world citizens". The very

Published in *Journal of Gandhian Studies*, Vol.5; October 1977.

idea of establishing a new international order has sprung from the desire, in fact the necessity, to avoid violent clashes between nations, social groups and political parties. Among the principal elements of a life of human dignity the authors see less inequity among individuals, within as well as between nations.

A specific and very clear link between the recommended world-order and Gandhian ideas can be described under the headings of international division of labour and choice of appropriate technology. We will discuss in more detail these two subjects.

As one of the most immediate attacks on mass poverty the report sees— as did several international conferences, in particular the June 1976 International Labour Conference in Geneva—the creation of more employment. This should be an element of the highest priority in the development plan of any developing country. It immediately raises the question, however, of which activities should be chosen in order to create a maximum of employment with the aid of the modest amount of investible funds available to most developing countries. Here a distinction should be made between activities subject to international competition and those not entering inter-national trade. Examples of the former are apparel, the larger part of other textile industries, leather and leather processing, wood working and a few others. Examples of the latter are construction in the broadest sense and a number of so-called services, from domestic services to scientific research.

Although a combination of the activities just summed up would definitely make the highest conceivable contribution to more employment, some restrictions exist which may make this choice partially impossible. To begin with, the category of industries subject to international competition can only be expanded strongly if (a) it is competitive and (b) their products must be admitted on the markets of developed countries. The first restriction means that often not the extreme forms labour-intensity can be chosen. It is a question of calculations which is the optimal combination of labour and capital. Restriction (b) points into the direction of trade negotiations with developed countries and we all know that collective pressure only will be helpful to change the minds of policy makers from industrialized countries. One argument which in the long run may have some effect on their attitude is that it is the long-run interest of rich countries also to establish a division of labour not impeded by protective measures on their side. Their consumers will profit immediately from the lower prices at which developing countries are able to supply the commodities mentioned. Their producers may initially suffer—some categories will become un- employed—but with the correct policies of adaptation they too will gain in the end.

A few additional caveats are in place. Experience has taught us that the most labour-intensive methods of building, for instance, a dam may not be feasible if a very large dam is to be constructed. Too large a crowd may then be necessary and this may make the project almost unmanageable. For small objects, however, irrigation works and land levelling are excellent examples of labour-intensive activities able to provide employment to large numbers of people.

Some economists have doubted whether the choice of labour-intensive industries constitutes the quickest way towards further development. They advocate heavy industries as the starting point, because these make higher profits and thus supply more investible funds for future development. I think this is only correct if profits are the only source of investment financing. An effective government may, however, see fit to finance investment out of taxes. In such a situation what should be maximized is not profits, but the tax base and this is something closer to national income as a whole. And national income will be higher, the larger the part of production factors is used. An impressive example of a country which started its development by exporting textiles is Japan, which is now competitive in many other fields and no longer in textiles.

This brings us to the point that not only as much labour should be used as possible—the most abundant resources of most developing countries—but also the country's natural endowments should be used. Processing of the nation's own raw materials is one of the future priorities to be taken into account in formulating a development plan.

As announced, our subject of the international division of labour is intimately linked with the subject of the choice of technology. In fact we already selected activities on the basis of their technology. There is the further aspect that within a given industry there sometimes exist alternative technologies. Here priority—within limits—should again be given to technologies using the country's most abundant resource—labour and natural resources. The latter can be chosen, for instance, in building, where often a wide range of choice exists. Local materials should be preferred.

The link with basic Gandhian ideas is Gandhi's preference for technologies known by the people and for mobilizing people for the purpose of a common goal, and relying on their own inventiveness to improve their conditions, in a spirit of cooperation. Often such an approach is easier to attain in relatively small communities. A highly interesting example discussed and explored in India in recent years is the project to produce, at the village level, a combination of biogas, protein and fertilizer, as discussed in the Centre for Development Studies in Trivandrum, Kerala, India.[2]

In some respects Gandhian ideas may ultimately also become more relevant for the world at large. The long-standing tendency to bigger production units, still relevant to several sectors and nations may be some day weakened because it may be destructive. One example is the risks for mammoth tankers transporting oil to polluting, in case of accidents, the water to an extent hitherto unknown. The ever increasing size of aircrafts or of vans begins to stress too much the responsibility of the pilots or the drivers. The dehumanization of labour in very large organizations and the emergence of the demands for a better quality of life—in this case working life—may lead to pressure from trade unions for smaller units where participation makes sense. Experiments of enterprises in highly developed countries such as Sweden with different organization schemes are of interest here.

All this may be subsumed under the heading of the search for a new harmony between the various components of human life and as such is very close to Gandhian thought. It does not mean that we should stick to traditional behaviour, but it does mean that a rejection *a priori* of simple ways of life and work is not in the true interest of mankind.

What has been said so far constitutes only a few aspects of the new international order and their relation to Gandhian thought. Many more examples will be found by those studying the RIO report. The conditions formulated for international co-operation to function better than in the past two decades are throughout the report that for an equitable result to be obtained from negotiations the parties behind the table should be less unequal with regard to their power. The report sums up in what ways less inequality among parties can be attained. To some of the forms of collective self-reliance already applied it adds a few new proposals for co-operation between groups whose interests are parallel but which have so far been unaware of this parallelism. One example is parallelism in interests of western consumers and developing producers of industrial goods not permitted at the moment to enter the markets of rich countries. Another example is the common interest western farmers and consumers in developing countries have to accelerate the building up of reserve food stocks around the world, as recommended by the Rome Food Conference in 1974. In one way or another it is the element of human solidarity which permeates the export's proposals; a solidarity in serious need of being observed much more intensely than has been the case so far.

References:

1. Jan Tinbergen, *Co-ordinator, reshaping the International Order, A Report to the Club of Rome*, New York, E.P. Dutton and Co., Inc, 201 Park Avenue South, New York N.Y. 10003, 1976.

2. C.R. Prasad, K. Krishna and A.K.N. Reddy, "Bio gas Plants : Projects, Problems and Tasks", *Economic and Political Weekly* IX (1947), Special number, August, pp. 1347-1364.

6

Equality as an Aim of Policy

Jan Tinbergen*

1. Revival of Equality as an Aim of Policy

In recent years we observe a revival of the equality or equity ideal. Various democratic socialist political parties make attempts to express more explicitly through what policies they can hope to attain at least less inequility.[1] It is not a new concept; in fact socialist movements from the beginning of their existence have seen social justice as one of their aims; and they had taken over this goal from a long series of predecessors. What was lacking, however, was a precise *definition* of the aim, and a modern scientific analysis of policies which could help attain the aim. In this essay an attempt will be made to contribute to a more operational definition than the ones so far advanced from various angles. Its operational potential will be illustrated by some simple examples using figures for the Netherlands. This essay will not deal, however, with the problem of the influence of less inequality on the development process, but rather with the instruments of socio-economic policy that can be applied, in economies at different stages of development, in order to reduce inequality.

2. Interpretation of Equality

In the course of history various attempts have been made to define equality. As a preamble to the approach to be recommended here it seems useful to give a brief survey of the most notable attempts.

One interpretation which has to be abandoned rightaway is the primitive idea that *all human being are equal* in all relevant aspects. Some aspects of human beings are irrelevant indeed for the formulation of socio-economic policies and their being different need not concern us. Thus, the colour of eyes, hair or skin, the exact length and weight and numerous other characteristics are irrelevant. But aspects such as intelligence, the capability to take decisions,

---

* Nobel Laureate Economist, Netherland.

Published in *Journal of Gandhian Studies*, Vol.2; April 1975.

health and several others do play a role in socio economic life and there is no denying that in these relevant aspects various individuals are different indeed. This can be stated by measurement and any scientific approach has to accept the results of (repeatable) measurement.

Hence unrestricted equality of human beings can be dismissed as *non-existent*. There are, however, various forms of restricted equality which have been formulated, although some of them in a vague way, which cannot be dismissed at once.

"Equality before God" is *religious* version of equality, felt by many as a consolation for the underprivileged in our temporary human existence and by others as a warning to the privileged who are all too often inclined to use their privileged position on earth to the detriment of the underprivileged. The impact of this religious version on society has remained very limited.

Non-religious idealists, and religious idealists when dealing with worldly affairs, have at times mentioned *income* equality as a goal of socio-economic policies or orders. Such policies or orders are called egalitarian. As we will show later, it is questionable whether under present circumstances systems can be devised which introduce equal incomes and yet develop in an equilibrated way. Equal incomes for all with the present techniques of socio-economic policies will soon produce scarcity of applicants for difficult or responsible occupations and abundance of the supply of those wanting to take the more comfortable jobs. Attempts in the Soviet Union and Israel have shown this. This had to be abandoned.

More down to earth we find a *legal* equality concept, often presented as "equality in court." This covers a relatively small portion of members of society, namely those guilty of acts and has no implication for the normal activities in most societies which are the legal ones.

A *political* version of equality consists of equal voting rights in the election for bodies representing the population at large in a large number of decisions needed to run society. In most developed western countries such equal voting rights are now in existence, with the notable exception of some Swiss cantons and the question of the most appropriate lower age limit. It is rational that there be such a limit, since a minimum of knowledge about and understanding of the operation of present-day societies is required to participate in meaningful decision making. The sort of decisions at stake are not the current decisions of the production and consumption processes, but the more important decisions about the general framework within which these processes operate. This aspect of equality is important, therefore, but there remain other elements, especially the types of decisions entrusted to the general representative bodies, to which the equal voting rights apply. If the intervention in the processes of production and consumption is limited, the significance of these voting rights is also limited. In the liberalist era general voting rights brought political democracy, but hardly any socio-economic democracy, as a consequence of the principle of laissez-faire.

As a correction on the admittedly impossible concepts of complete equality and income equality the idea of creating "*equal opportunities*" has been forwarded. While in stratified societies such as the Indian society, with its different "castes" an element of equal opportunities has already been brought by the official elimination of castes, in present-day developed societies equal opportunities of that type are self-evident. What remains to be done can mainly be interpreted as access to all types of education? In practice the maximum of equal education opportunities means that every youngster receives, without cost, the education she or he is able to absorb. "Without cost", does not only mean that no fees have to be paid, but also that the student's cost of living is taken care of by the community. Even so differences in natural endowment and in socio-economic status of the parents will leave differences in the quantity of schooling, or of training on the job, the person in question will be able actually to absorb.

The various interpretations of equality discussed are indicative of the belief that, one way or another, human beings have something that entitles them to an as yet undefined type of equality. The proponents of the types of equality already discussed have not yet succeeded, however, to present society with a concept that opens up operational policies to attain the equality that we are looking for. For the moment let us speak here of some sort of "*fundamental equality*" to which a more precise meaning has to be given.

3. Another Interpretation: Equal Welfare

In recent years a new attempt has been to interpret the concept of equality as a possible aim of socio-economic policies[2,3]. As all the other attempts discussed in it suffer from some limitations to its applicability, but these limitations seem to be fewer than before. To a certain extent they can be overcome, as we will try to show. Put briefly, the aim of equality should be to reach a situation of *equal satisfaction* to every citizen. Here the word satisfaction is meant to be identical to what is called nowadays welfare or what has been called utility or ophelimity by economists. Another, word, to be used with much caution, might be happiness. But in any case there must be the restriction that we think of the concept as far as connected with the social position of the individuals considered. Elements of an intimately personal or spiritual character will have to be neglected, at least to begin with. It is also doubtful whether the concept can be applied to extreme cases such as heavily handicapped individuals.

The operational significance of the new interpretation depends entirely on the *measurability* of welfare. I see no reason to reject this assumption; it is not the first time that such an assumption is being made and examples from economics (for instance, job evaluation) and physics (for instance, the measurement of temperature or "degree of heat") show its scientific productivity. There seem to be, this author believes, a number of possibilities to measure utility by giving a concrete content to the concept of fundamental equality of men. For this to work it is useful to distinguish between *three different elements* in the mathematical formulation of the utility or welfare function. A first class of elements will be called *variables*; these may refer to phenomena beyond the control of the individual, such as income attached to a given job, or to phenomena the individual is able and free to chose, for instance the job itself, the number of working hours and the speed or intensity of work.

A second class of elements consists of *parameters*. These are figures indicating the individual's quality; they may be innate, or they may have been obtained by some learning process. I am not going to deal with the types of learning processes ethologists are distinguishing[5]: but I want to mention two classes of processes well known in present day society and measured already, although in a crude way: learning in schools and learning from experience.

The third class of elements in a welfare function are its *coefficients*. They indicate the intensity by which variables and parameters influence satisfaction. It is here that we can give concrete content to the concept of fundamental equality between human beings, by assuming that the coefficients *are the same for all individuals*. This need not even be seen as an assumption, but can be postulated, if we recognise the possibility to introduce as many parameters as anybody wants to. If some economist or sociologist feels that some coefficients must be different for different people, we can shift this coefficient to the class of parameters. In principle this means that we accept any suggestion about people being different, provided that the difference be proved by measurement. This is perfectly sound methodology, which has brought the enormous advances in the physical sciences first and in psychology and related disciplines somewhat later.

4. Measurement of Welfare

The equality of the coefficients occurring in the welfare function is the key to the measurement of welfare. To begin with, we can consider a group of people with the same parameters, but with different variables. The members of this group can choose the variables under their control so as to maximize their utility. In the equilibrium situation attained in that way the values of the variables, chosen and imposed ones, do still differ among the individuals of the group. Thus, some will have chosen a more "difficult" job than others, carrying with it a higher income. This enables us to find the trade-off between job difficulty and income. Elsewhere I gave an example of such measurement[6] and for the remainder of this essay it may be helpful further to pursue that admittedly over simplified example. Its features were that we introduced the two variables already mentioned: income (after tax) $\underline{X}$ and job (characterized only by the length of the schooling period $\underline{S}$ required). Moreover only one parameter $\underline{V}$ was introduced, meant to characterize the individual's capability, namely the actual length of the schooling period completed. For a clear presentation we may interpret the choice of the welfare function $\underline{W}$ as the logarithm of one more complicated entity "spendable income corrected for the inconveniences of the job held."

$$\underline{W} = l_n \{X - C_o S - \tfrac{1}{2} C_2 (S - V)^2\} \qquad (1)$$

where the variables are $\underline{X}$ and $\underline{S}$, the parameter is $\underline{V}$ and the coefficients are $\underline{C}_o$ and $\underline{C}_2$. For the Netherlands around 1962 we were able to obtain estimates for $\underline{C}_o$ and $\underline{C}_2$.

These values of $\underline{C}_o$ and $\underline{C}_2$ indicate how much income compensation is needed for a unit change in $\underline{S}$ (years of schooling) and in $\tfrac{1}{2}(\underline{S} - \underline{V})^2$, a measure of the "tension" caused by working in a job requiring more or less schooling than the individual completed.

As already observed, so far we considered groups of individuals with the same values of their parameter $\underline{W}$. We must now ask the question whether we can also estimate the influence of a change in parameter on welfare. In terms of our simple example the question would be, what compensation in spendable income is required for having a different value of $\underline{V}$? Here we cannot compare individuals with different $\underline{V}$ and different $\underline{X}$, since by definition an individual cannot choose another $\underline{V}$. Here, it might seem, we are before the same dilemma which induces the majority of economists to say that interpersonal comparison of utilities is impossible: nobody having the experience of "how it feels to be more intelligent than one is".

Again, however, this answer need not be the final answer. We will make an attempt to list the *conditions* under which it remains possible to measure the influence of a change in $\underline{V}$ or in other parameters.

i) A first possibility is to postulate that the only way in which $\underline{V}$ influences $\underline{W}$ is through the *tension* $\underline{S}$-$\underline{V}$, where the disutility, expressed in terms of spendable income units, of working beyond or below one's capabilities is equal to $\frac{1}{2} C_2 \ (\underline{S}-\underline{V})^2$. The square indicates the assumption that it is equally disagreeable to work beyond as to work below one's capabilities. In somewhat more general mathematical terms this possibility is that $\underline{V}$ influences $\underline{W}$ through an a-*priori* combination of $\underline{S}$ and $\underline{V}$.

ii) A second possibility is that the influence exerted by the tension is no-purely symmetrical, but is represented by an expression in $(\underline{S}-\underline{V}-\underline{C}_1)^2$, meaning that some amount of difference between $\underline{S}$ and $\underline{V}$— whether positive or negative— is preferred, other things (income in our example) remaining equal. The estimation of $\underline{C}_1$ must still be based on a comparison among individuals with the same $\underline{V}$, in order to avoid measuring the effect of the scarcity of $\underline{V}$ on income, as set out in the publication quoted.

iii) A third possibility is to assume that whatever satisfaction is derived from another value of $\underline{V}$ is experienced only through the satisfaction of an equal change in $\underline{S}$, the job variable; this cab be read from the value of $\underline{C}_0$ in formula (1).

iv) A fourth possibility estimating the impact of a change in parameter is that results of other sciences show this impact. An example in practical application already is the compensation given for a larger family by family allowances, or benefits from sickness insurance in case of illness; provided, however, that such allowances or benefits are based on medical advice and not restricted by financial implications.

v) A fifth possibility could be derived from such rare cases where by medical or similar treatment the same individual is undergoing a change in parameter and can compare the situation before and after the treatment. The opposite experience may be obtained by some accident, depriving an individual of part of its former capabilities.

vi) Finally, we may postulate that people with higher scores for some capability will feel happier than people with lower scores. Under these circumstances the omission of any term $\underline{C}_1\,\underline{V}\,(\underline{C}_1 > O)$ in the {} of formula (1) means an underestimation of utility for those with higher $\underline{V}$ compared to those with lower $\underline{V}$ and in some cases yield results "on the safe side", as again discussed in the previous publication already quoted.

5. Means to Reduce Inequality and Their Effectiveness

The very primitive attempt to measure welfare described in our previous publication must be seen as an illustration of a method which can be refined by the inclusion of several other variables and parameters. Variables characterizing job can be taken from job evaluation, whereas parameters characterising individuals can be taken from career planning files. While a huge programme or research is still due, it should be observed, nevertheless, that according to various authors the parameter "years of schooling" used in our publication is able to explain a considerable portion or the variance in incomes and may therefore give a fairly reliable first approximation to reality. According to our first approximation the income distribution, needed in order to equalize welfare among the twenty-one groups of the Dutch population, would have to show only *half of the inequality* actually prevailing in 1962.

Among the *instruments* of socio-economic policy likely to be most effective to help attain equality, *education* policies and tax policies stand out. Education policies can make a contribution by increasing the number of qualified persons, which implies diminishing the number of less or non-qualified. The former, through their increased numbers, will depress the incomes of their category, whereas the latter will reduce the supply in the corresponding market compartments and enable their incomes to rise. A major question, of course, what the quantitative impact will be and a second question, what the limits of the numbers who can be educated are. In a series of attempts to answer[4] the first question, I obtained widely diverging results. While this means that further research is needed, several of the most favourable results indicated that a doubling of the number of university-trained people as a percentage of total labour force might well reduce income inequality by one-half. These results were obtained from figures of a few developed countries. It has not yet been possible to obtain the statistical material needed for developing countries. The figures only dealt with education in schools and did not contain indications of what could be expected from changes in the quality of education.

One answer to the second question, namely what the limits are to the numbers able to absorb education of various levels, has been given by De Wolff[6] who calculated the "talent reserves" remained unused in 1963. For both the second and the third level of education he obtained figures of the same order as the numbers of students at both levels at that time. Interesting enough in the meantime these numbers have about doubled.

Then, however, a third question arises. Why have income inequalities not fallen to half of what they were in 1962? Two answers seem to apply. First of all the theory requires that the total labour force should show percentage of third-level educated double the one prevailing in 1962. It will take several decades before the present student numbers apply to the total labour force.

The other answer is that the theory assumes that technological change will not affect the relative demand for people with various levels of education. About this subject little systematic evidence is available, but it is likely that the relative demand for qualified personnel will rise. The subject deserves further research, the more so since the possibility may be considered so to influence technological change that no such shifts were to occur.

Tax policies, together with social services, have already been used to a considerable extent in the most advanced countries. This redistribution mechanism produces a considerable reduction in inequality, illustrated by large differences in the distribution of primary incomes (that is, incomes before tax) and that of spendable incomes (after complete redistribution). Thus, the ratio between incomes of the upper 20 per cent and the lower 20 per cent of Denmark is 8.2 for incomes before tax and 2 to 3 for incomes after complete redistribution. It is generally believed that with the present type of taxes not much more can be done in advanced countries. For developing countries there is much more scope for improving tax and general administrative discipline; and accordingly redistribution could be intensified considerably. At present tax collection in most developing countries, including some semi-developed countries, is subject to much corruption and its elimination would open the way to a much larger redistribution.

New perspectives for all countries are opened up by an analysis of the question – which taxes should be applied in an optimal socio-economic system.

Welfare economics teaches us that in the optimum taxes must be *lump-sum* taxes. This phrase stands for taxes not influencing marginal changes in production and consumption. Indirect as well as income taxes do not satisfy this condition. Only wealth taxes approximately do, but they affect a small part only of the possible tax base. Essentially a tax on all production capacity is the general type of lump-sum tax. Production capacity should include human capital as well as physical capital. It will depend on the future development of testing individuals' productive capacity, whether such a general lump-sum tax remains a dream or may once become reality. An effective test battery largely of a psychological character would open up the possibility to combine equality with a strengthening of incentives. Incentives would be strengthened to the extent the income tax could be replaced by the capacity tax. Equality could be approached by a sufficiently steep scale of that tax.

If these are the potentialities of a capacity tax, there can be no doubt that equal welfare for the great majority of the population is within reach. It will depend to a considerable extent on the test battery designers.

Rerefences

1. Jamlikhet (Equality) by SAP-LO's arbetsgrupp (Working Group of Socialist Party and Trade Union National Organization of Sweden), Boras, Sjuharadsbygdens Tryckeri AB, 1969 (Swedesh).

2. Kolm, S.C., Une suite a Justice et Equite: le fondamentalisme, CEPREMAP, Paris 1972 (French).

3. Tinbergen, J., An Interdisciplinary Approach to the Measurement of Utility or Welfare, Fifth Geary Lecture, The Economic and Social Research Institute, Dublin, 1972.

4. Tinbergen, J., "The Impact of Education on Income Distribution", The Review of Income and Wealth 18 (1972), p.255, including reference (9) given there.

5. Tinbergen, N., private correspondence with the author.

6. De Wolff, P., "Magelijkheden tot het vaststellen van begaafdheids-reserves", Weekblad van het Genootschap van Leraren aan Nederlandse Gymnasia en Lycea en de RLV, LVII (1963), p.327 (Dutch "possibilities to Estimate Capability Reserves").

7

Gandhi's Relevance

Jan Tinbergen*

In the course of the 1970, a series of studies have been published which have sown the urgent need for a reconsideration of a number of economic heses. The studies I am referring to have been sponsored by the Club of Rome, a Club of independent scientists and businessmen, concerned about the world's future. Certainly they were not the only ones and not the first to be alarmed by what ecologists and some independent economists had already discovered before the Club of Rome came along with their series of reports, but the Club of Rome has had a much larger audience in the political and business world. I am thinking of the impact of the Meadows couple and their collaborators executed with "The Limits to Growth", of Messrs Mesarovic and Pestel's follow up; of the reports formulated by Linnemann, deHoogh and Keyzer on the food situation to be expected around the year 2010 or so, and of the work done by the Barilche Foundation in Argentina.

The reconsideration needed is the consequence of the awareness of the "new scarcities", for instance in the field of food and of energy, but it is also the consequence of the failing attempts by the Pearson Commission and other to arrive at a better cooperation of rich and poor countries to give a push to the latter's development. One of the key questions here is what Western Tech-nology can do in this process; intimately linked with the question of what the proper role of transnational enterprises in the process of development should be.

Whereas they are believers in the large-scale operations, men like E.F. Schumacher told us; 'Small is beautiful.'

Social change remains as necessary as ever in present world of under-developed economics. The ratio between incomes of the "Highest" and the

---

* Based on forewords of Nobel Laureate Prof. J. Tinbergen to Economic Thought of Mahatma Gandhi & Non-violence & Social Change.

Published in *Gandhi Prasang*, Vol. 1; October 1998.

"Lowest" tenth of people measured according to their consumption possibilities has increased notwithstanding the efforts made to develop. Many schools of thought see no other way out of this terrible contrast than one of violence. Yet violence itself is making for much misery. Mahatma Gandhi was always for non-violent social change. India got its political independence without violence. Gandhian thought was not of a passive nature; it did constitute a revolution in thinking. So it seems clear that his thought deserves being spread again.

With this state of affairs the work of Mahatma Gandhi has in a few years come back to our minds. Almost suddenly we now become aware of the possibility that in many respects he may have had messages also for the world of to-day. In the new light of what we were almost unaware of ten to fifteen years ago we shall receive inspiration from what India's great spiritual leader already several decades ago was teaching.

8

Poverty, Inequality and Gandhi

Prof. Gunnar Myrdal*

I. The Liberal Legacy

Mohandas Gandhi's moral personality was a gem, faceted with immense richness. He will appear differently when viewed by different observers, depending upon where they stand and the background against which they perceive him.

The present author was for many years involved in a study of South Asia's and, in particular, India's problems of underdevelopment, development, and planning for development. My value premises in this study were the rationalistic modernization ideals as they had emanated in the early European era of Enlightenment and been preserved and developed in liberal thought everywhere. Together with Jawaharlal Nehru, Gandhi walks through my book as a spiritual leader upholding these ideals in a quite consistent way.

Viewed in this setting, Gandhi stands out as a radical and over-optimistic liberal of the post-Victorian English variety, though moulded by the Indian tradition and translating those ideals into folksy language. I realize that this characterization does not exhaust what can be said about Gandhi's world outlooks, but I do believe that it catches a significant and important trait and belongs to a fuller view of the "father of the Indian 'nation."

2. Civil Disobedience

Gandhi's political tactic of civil disobedience and non-cooperation with the colonial power structure was, of course, to him based on a philosophy in line with his moral imperative of non-violence. His absolutist concept of this

---

* Noble Laureate in Economics - Sweden.

The present article has been taken from the author's book 'Against the Stream– Critical Essays on Economics.- 'Gandhi as a Radical Liberal'.

Published in *Journal of Gandhian Studies*, Vol. 2; July 1975.

imperative was not endorsed by the rationalistic intellectuals in the Congress movement. That is evident from criticisms by Nehru and other contemporaries.

But to them, too, the application of the principle of non-violence seemed a rational means for a very large and very poor people to use in attaining national independence with a minimum of sacrifice from, the British¾with their specific ideals and inhibitions. Unlike so many of Gandhi's other political views, it did not even prove over-optimistic.

3. A Radical Leveler.

Gandhi spoke up *for* the "dumb semi-starved millions scattered over the length and the breadth of the land in its 700,000 villages" and he perceived their situation to be the result of systematic "exploitation". He saw clearly what later would become so forgotten in India, as in the whole Western economic literature, viz., that greater equality was not an aim in competition with economic progress but instead, a necessary condition for it.

Until Gandhi's crusade, social and, in particular, economic equalization has not been discussed much, either in India or anywhere else in South Asia. Gandhi's egalitarianism became one of the links between him and the rationalistic intellectuals of Nehru's type who, unlike Gandhi, were relatively unconcerned with religion. Together they persuaded Congress to accept a radical variant of modern liberal ideology. Confirmed at the Karachi session in 1931, it demanded that "in order to end the exploitation of the masses, political freedom must include real economic freedom for the starting millions."

In line with the golden-age myth, which Gandhi no more than any other Indian leader¾not even Nehru¾could entirely forsake, he held that "purer" and functional caste system could once upon a time have been a beneficial social organization. But the present caste system was to him a horror and had to be suppressed. He also stood for the liberation of women from their shackles. He cried out against child marriage and the religious and social compulsion hindering remarriage of widows. On all these questions, Gandhi was the opposite of a traditionalist.

In regard to the distribution of income and wealth, Gandhi's views were radical. Often he spoke as if he demanded complete economic equality, but his thinking became blurred with his concept of trusteeship. The rich could keep their wealth if they acted in the interests of the under-privileged. This notion was a practical compromise, mainly motivated by his rejection of violence and his realization that the rich would not willingly give up their possessions (see below, however). It was so flexible that it could serve as a justification for gross inequality. But Gandhi also demanded a moral revolution, a change of heart among the rich. Nehru, who doubted the likelihood of such a conversion, criticized Gandhi for inconsistency in regard to economic equalization.

4. Gandhi's Over-optimism

Gandhi remained optimistic on this score and often gave expression to his conviction of a radical improvement of the economic conditions of the poor, once India had become independent. He was equally optimistic about the rapid disappearance of caste and other social inequalities.

This optimism was founded on two judgments, which can now be seen to have been mistaken, but which were largely shared by Nehru and the rationalistic intellectuals in the Congress movement. One was that the British colonial rule over India had so suppressed the forces for economic progress that once the shackles of imperialism were removed, rapid economic progress would ensue and increase the elbow room for rich and poor. The other judgment concerned the political democracy that would come with independence and its expected revolutionary effects on Indian society.

To Gandhi, a radical change in the social and economic order was, indeed, the meaning and essential purpose of overthrowing foreign rule. Without it, independence and democracy would be an empty achievement. But Gandhi took for granted that once the power was transferred to the masses of the Indian people, these masses would assert themselves and carry out the economic and social revolution.

The rich and mighty would have to give up their privileges and do it willingly and peacefully. In his words: "Economic equality is the master key to non-violent independence....non-violent system of government is clearly an impossibility so long as the wide gulf between the rich and the hungry millions persists. The contrast between the palaces of New Delhi and the miserable hovels of the poor, laboring class cannot last one day in a free India in which the poor will enjoy the same power as the richest in the land. A violent and bloody revolution is a certainty one day unless there is a voluntary abdication of riches, and the power that riches give, and sharing them for the common good."

That independent India should be a democracy based on adult franchise, Gandhi held as above dispute, and so did Congress as a body.

The economic and social revolution to him then became simply an inference of the extreme degree of social and economic inequality existing there as a start.

5. Grass-Root Democracy.

Not as a qualification but as an amplification of the democratic principle, Gandhi was adamant, in demanding that a maximum of the political power should be dispersed and reserved for local and functional communities, and on this point also he won adherence .in the movement he led.

He feared centralization of power, even if founded on a majority vote, and wanted the villagers to be the makers of their own destiny, with only general rules laid down from above. This view had, with Gandhi, a moral basis in his concept of the dignity of individuals and his vision of their having an opportunity to organize their life together in a way that was conducive to peaceful cooperation, progress, and happiness.

Gandhi clearly perceived that development is basically a human problem concerning attitudes and institutions. It must imply that people everywhere begin to act more purposefully to improve their living conditions and then also to change their community in such a way as to make these strivings more possible and effective. The efforts in India to institute "democratic planning" or "decentralization" through various forms of cooperatives and agencies for local self-government have been an outgrowth of this Gandhian ideal that democracy is built "from below".

We can now see that when these policies have not, as yet, been very successful, a main explanation is that the social and economic revolution that Gandhi, like Nehru and the whole radical wing of Congress, so, confidently had expected to follow independence and general suffrage, did not materialize. The attempts made to cultivate a grass-roots democracy in the event came to bypass the equality issue and so were emasculated. Effective cooperation assumes greater equality, among many other things. This critique of mine, would, I am sure, have found favour with Gandhi.

6. The Blending with 'Traditionalism'

In practically all fields, Gandhi was thus an enlightened radical liberal. He demanded also a revolutionary change in the direction of education and not simply the sluicing of more children and youths through an unreformed school system inherited from colonial time and serving the interests of the metropolitan power and that Indian upper class which had flourished under its protection. In this, he was in line with the most modern contemporary philosophers of education, particularly prominent in the two countries where thinking in this field was already ahead of the rest of the world, namely, the United States and later the Soviet Union.

He stood, by words and personal example, against that serious obstacle to development, which persists in the contempt for manual work. Much of the educational reform he propagated had a major aim of elevating to its proper level the dignity of labor, all labor. He saw clearly its relation to the issue of social and economic equality, and he never tired of stressing this fact.

As Gandhi stood so undeniably on the side of the poor and down-trodden, he dared also to be more outspoken than any other Indian leader after him¾ with the occasional exception of Nehru¾in upbraiding his people for laziness and for not keeping themselves and their surroundings clean.

Blended with all these highly rationalistic opinions of Gandhi, which make him an outspoken radical liberal, he held at the same time more traditionalistic views that, seemingly at least, are contradictory. His hostility to modern industrial technology and to machines and, more generally, his pro-rural and anti-city bias were sometimes expressed in terms, which are hardly compatible with enlightened liberalism. But the recognition in recent years of the very predominant importance of agriculture in economic development and also of the primary necessity to put to work under-utilized labour resources in the cause of development has, to an extent, proved these ideas of his to be less irrational than they seemed *to* be at time when development was narrowly defined as industrialization and when it was believed that industrialization would rapidly create new employment that would make possible the "skimming off" of the "labour surplus" in agriculture.

Even at the culmination of that era¾approximately in the years when the Second Five-Year Plan was being prepared¾the planners found it rational to make a compromise with Gandhian ideas, viz., to reserve a large area of production of consumer goods for traditional labour-intensive technology.

In regard to central state planning generally, where Indian Policy has seemed to deviate most conspicuously from Gandhi's teaching, there may now be forewarnings of an evolution of thinking that comes closer to Gandhi's own. The plans produced in predominantly financial terms have turned out to be fictitious and misleading. Consequently, India is beginning to recognize the necessity of perceiving development as a process encompassing the entire social system. This was Gandhi's view, though he never elaborated it in clear terms. In this view, he was far ahead of the approach to planning that has been applied in India as well as other underdeveloped countries. It is only in the last few years that economists more generally have understood the need for a 'unified approach.'

To Gandhi, politics should be rooted in morals. In this respect, he only emphasized truly liberal principles, from which too many writers, particularly among the economists, have in the post-war era tried to run away. More questionable—from a liberal point of view—is Gandhi's insistence on basing morals on religion. But by his religious syncretism, stressing the affinities between all religions, he gave preponderant weight to the "higher" ideals which all religions, have in common and which are generally humanitarian and rationalistic, while playing down the importance of rites and taboos which are diversive and arational, if not irrational.

His reverence for sexual abstinence, however, and his consequent hostility to contraception are definitely anti-rationalistic elements in his moral philosophy. If adhered to; they would have become the more blatantly illiberal when the population explosion gathered momentum, but that occurred only after his death. Similarly, his support for cow worship—and sometimes idol worship—stands out as contradictory to his enlightened liberalism.

7. If Gandhi Came Back

Everyone who has studied Gandhi's teaching in depth must have pondered over what his intellectual, moral and political reactions would be if he returned to his India after more than twenty years of independence. Certainly, he would have to confess to himself that the unbounded optimism that inspired him and his contemporaries in the Congress movement during the struggle for independence had been mistaken,

The social and economic revolution he had looked forward to following independence has been, first, postponed and, later, shelved altogether—except for some continued rhetorical exuberances in public speaking. Instead of the economic equalization he had seen coming, inequality gaps have been widening; the concentration of financial power has increased.

Against the clear condemnation in the Constitution and special legislation, which had been adopted under the influence of the legacy from Gandhi, caste as a social institution has shown obstinate persistence and may even have gained in importance in some fields. The rise in the freedom and status of women, which he advocated, has, for the most part, remained a rather empty prescription—except in the top social strata.

The land and tenancy reforms have been little more than a sham, and there has been no fundamental reform of education, which still serves to preserve the gulf between those who work with their hands and those who, having acquired the badge of education, are not willing to do so. The efforts to lift up rural life—agricultural extension, credit and other cooperatives, community development, *panchayat raj*, and so on—have, contrary to proclaimed objectives, mainly favoured the better off.

And so the masses of people in the villages, where now, as in Gandhi's time, more than 80 per cent of the people live, have mostly remained in relative stagnation. The landless and poorer half of the villagers—Gandhi's dumb semi-starved millions—may be worse off in some respects than they were a quarter of a century ago and are certainly not decidedly better of.

Undoubtedly, the still unhampered population explosion has contributed in a mighty way to the severity of what, measured by Gandhi's predictions and honest expectancy, he would now see as large-scale failures. It is open to speculation whether Gandhi, when facing the population explosion and the cattle explosion, would have modified his views on contraception and cow slaughter. As rational liberalism was a major element in Gandhi's thinking, this does not seem entirely excluded. In any case, he would probably not have laid a main emphasis on these issues, but looked on them as peripheral to the general failure in the field of politics.

The development of Indian politics since the attainment of independence, which he himself barely survived, Gandhi would in all certainty have censured severely. He would have seen it to be affected with a progressively worsening moral illness, spreading out in the entire polity and society like a cancerous growth, to which the increase of corruption and the swelling volume of "black money" bore testimony.

He would have seen another sign of the downward trend of political life in the increasing prevalence of violence—on the one side, riots, usually without a major and rational political purpose, and police brutality on the other. Violence, as is often pointed out, has reached a higher level than it did during the struggle against the British, which Gandhi on the whole succeeded in keeping disciplined —though the British should be given part of the credit for it.

He would probably have judged the ailment of Indian politics as an *ex post* justification of his recommendation, at the time when India set sail as an independent state, that Congress should stay out of politics, not remaining a political party, but becoming a voluntary organization for social improvement. When Nehru and the majority of the Congress leaders chose to act differently, this was motivated by their correct view that a functioning democracy needed political parties and that there was already in existence the Congress with an effective machine which could become a national party. Its domination un-doubtedly, made possible the first ten years of relatively successful government in the country. But it was also during those ten years that the postponement of the social and economic revolution that would have been necessary if the exalted hopes of Gandhi, Nehru and many others were to have materialized.

If Gandhi could return to India after almost a quarter of a century, he would thus have to confess that he, together with most leaders of the Congress movement, had been grossly over-optimistic. It is equally certain, however, that he would stick to what were his fundamental valuations, rooted as they were in his moral convictions and in his religion. It is unthinkable that today he would remain silent and idle. He would again take to the roads and village lanes and begin anew his crusade, seeking to change the social and economic conception of the articulate upper middle classes of his nation, but at the same time trying to stir up the masses from their torpor. And he would have followers from many diverse backgrounds, now as then kept together as a unified force by his faith, resourcefulness and humor.

Often, when labouring with India's staggering development problems, I have felt inclined to believe that what that great country needs today, more than foreign aid and day-to-day adjustments of policies to meet the recurring emergencies, is spiritual leaders approaching Gandhi's greatness, his love, and fearlessness. Together with all the patriots who would undoubtedly come to surround such leaders, they might electrify the nation to undertake, late but perhaps not too late, the revolutionary changes in social, economic and political institutions, attitudes, and practices which are now so desperately needed.

9

Challenge of Stagnation in Developing Countries

Prof. Gunnar Myrdal*

In the country, which at this Assembly is our host country, India, Mohandas Gandhi was adamant in stressing the human factor in economic development. To him development meant that people everywhere in the country, and not least in the village where most of the people live, were brought to being to act more rationally and effectively and that they then changed their society to make this more possible. Gandhi was certainly a planner, and a rationalistic planner, but his planning was all-embracing and laid main stress on sanitation and health; the raising of nutritional levels by more intensive agriculture; a redirection and not only an expansion of education so that it becomes "basic" and not merely literary and "academic" and a redistribution of wealth and land to create greater equality.

Gandhi's Ideas

It is only in the latest years that we have more generally come back to Gandhi's ideas, when even some economists have been moved to press for an "integrated planning", which is the modern term for what Gandhi was all the time teaching. My Indian friends will not be offended when I say, that if Indian planning has not been more successful than it has actually been, the main explanation is that they have not kept so close as they should to the fundamental of the teaching of the Father of the Nation.

---

* Noble Laureate in Economics – Sweden.

Published in *Journal of Gandhian Studies*, Vol. 1; July 1974.

Prof. Gunnar Myrdal, Chairman of the Stockholm International Peace Research Institute, was invited by the One Asia Assembly early in February 1973 to present a paper on "The Human Dimensions of Economic Growth; Challenge of Stagnation in Underdeveloped Countries". The paper which evoked considerable interest among the delegates to the Assembly for its Gandhian perspective is being reproduced here.

The main responsibility for this failure should squarely be laid on my own profession, the economists, and in this respect there is no difference between the Western economists, the Asian economists and, indeed, also the economists from the Communist countries. All were too narrow-minded in their approach, too "materialistic" in a sense. When research on planning for development in underdeveloped countries began on a massive scale after the hurricane of liberation from colonial bondage, the economists all thought in terms of physical investment, mainly in industry, and of financial and dismal appropriations.

It should be noted, that this approach was definitely narrower, than the view applied by most of the great economists from Adam Smith to Alfred Marshall. They had their attention on people's attitude and the institutions in variety and reckoned with the possibility and need to change them through education and other devices. They were, in fact, institutional economists long before than the term was invented. And so were, of course, Marx and his nearest followers.

Just about the time of the Second World War when economists¾who earlier during the colonial time devoted very little research efforts to what then were called the 'backward regions', in great numbers moved to work on the problems of underdeveloped countries. Studies in some highly developed countries were supposed to have shown a very close relation between physical investment and economic growth. The so-called capital output ratio was by some economists actually hailed as similar to the constants in natural sciences, which permitted the natural scientists to make new contributions to knowledge at their writing desks by applying simple mathematical exercises on the basis of known facts.

As we all know, the approach to economic planning for development in underdeveloped countries was for a long time, and is partly today, dominated by the concept, capital/output ratio. It implied always the narrow attention in economic planning merely to physical investment and to the financial and physical appropriations as I have already noted. It thus meant a non-consideration on a large scale of the "human dimensions of economic growth".

Investment in Man

Closer studies again carried out in highly developed countries proved, however, that in reality physical investment could only account for a minor part of economic growth. Even in those developed countries with their supervisor statistics, we have not succeeded in planning down what these other factors are and how they collaborate in determining growth.

In the late fifties this "rest post of ignorance", as it must properly be characterized, was named "investment in man", which was then usually declared to be simply "education". It was often presented as a new thought, indeed a discovery that education had anything to do with economic development. The only basis for this pretension was, however, the fact that economists generally after the war had forgotten the importance of education, which had so prominently figured in the thinking of pre-war economists from Adam Smith to Alfred Marshall.

Worse still was, however, that "new school" immediately adopted their thoughts to the capital/output concept by treating education as simply an input together with physical investment. Quite aside from the fact that the output, that is the development effect, of education, cannot be calculated in the same simple way as of a new factory, this whole way of thinking focussed attention merely on the quantity of education input, while as we know its quality that is its direction and contact and what I might call its spirit, is what is paramount importance.

Much education in underdeveloped countries, following the pattern of colonial time and fashioned to serve the interests of the metropolitan power and the upper and middle classes that were privileged under its region is frankly anti developmental, particularly by bringing the educated to shun to soil their hands.

In India Jawaharlal Nehru had asked for a total revolution of the educational system, and in the other South Asian countries similar demands were often raised by their political and social leaders. Though all governments earlier expressed their primary goal to stamp out illiteracy within a very short time, what has actually happened, is that university education has increased most rapidly and high school education next, while primary education has lagged in spite of the fact that university schooling is some seven times more expensive than secondary schooling, and secondary schooling in turn, some three-four times more expensive than primary schooling. All schooling on all levels is still mainly of the general literacy, academic type, while vocational and professional schooling has been increasing only marginally. The channels of schooling have been widened where the pressures were felt to be strongest. These pressures were mainly exerted by the upper and middle classes, who have the power on the local, state and national levels.

Adult Education

Still more serious is the neglect of adult education. I know that in all South Asian countries there are devoted citizens, who have often formed associations for adult education and that some public funds have gone into aiding them in their work. But it has been too little and nowhere have the efforts reached far.

This is regrettable as adult education is particularly important in under-developed countries. It is needed until the population at large is all literate. And it is needed in order to make primary schooling effective. All our students have proved that even those children who successfully pass primary school will easily pass back into illiteracy when they live in an illiterate society. And what here in Asia is called stagnation¾the dropouts and the repeaters¾is more common in all illiterate surroundings.

In this issue we have something to learn from the Communist countries. Regularly, when a country goes Communist, a tremendous effort is made to teach literacy to all and particularly in adult education. This is not communist but simply common sense and good planning.

I must emphasise again, that the need is not merely quantitative expansion but much more fundamentally a change of what is taught, and how and to whom.

The millions of so-called "educated unemployed" are simply to a large extent mis-educated. The dream of many reformers in this region is, and has been, that they should be sent to the villages to teach people to read, write and reckon, instead of dwelling without purpose in the big cities trying to press Governments to let them swell administration on the lower level, where they are mostly under-utilised and, consequently, useless for society.

I cannot go deeper into the educational problem today but want at last to stress that the possibility to carry out a general reform policy, of the type that I consider essential for a steady and rapid development assumes, besides an enlightened elite, "pressure from below". This pressure should be for rational reforms. This assumes that the common people know their interests and understand how to organise for attaining them,

The uprisings guided by religious fanaticism or other particularistic impulses are not only useless for attaining better conditions for the common people but actually damaging to such rational strivings. The only way of counteracting such organizational impulses is education.

My regrettably brief remarks on the educational problem are only meant to exemplify the great number of reforms in the interest of greater equality which I see as necessary for a steady and rapid development in the under-developed countries here in South Asia. My main point is that they are not antagonistic in economic growth but rather a condition for growth, more specifically for raising the productivity of labour.

In this respect, economic theory has been biased severely much more than the classical authors a hundred years ago. Economists have generally always believed that social reforms carry their cowls, and that they are apt to slow down economic growth.

In my own country, Sweden, where the labour party has been in power for forty years, we have had an accelerating social reform activity, which cannot be ended because there are still and always will be inequalities and new ones are created by the development itself. During this time most economists, supporting the conservative parties have, at every time and at every substantial single reform, warned of economic catastrophy.

Sweden and U.S.

But, meanwhile, what has actually happened is that the country has experienced an economic growth that in my opinion has now placed Sweden even above the United States if the economic levels were not reckoned in the flimsy figures for gross national product but proper account were taken of the many things which imply an exaggeration of these figures for the United States.

I am mentioning this convergence between economic growth and egalitarian reforms, because it has a lesson for South Asia. If such a convergence can exist in a very rich country, it must be even more important in poor countries, egalitarian reforms are even much more needed to raise the productivity of labour, and there they can raise them very substantially.

In rich countries, the economists are allowed to use models of growth where consumption and the levels of living are not included explicitly but only stand as goals for economic growth. But when such models have been used in underdeveloped countries, the analysis goes seriously wrong.

In rich countries food intake, health and educational facilities, housing and sanitation are so much improved already and have reached such high levels, that a further change in these conditions does not have more than, at the most a marginal, influence on willingness and ability to work and efficiency in working. Incomes even in the lower brackets are high compared with incomes in under-developed countries, and they are regularly supplemented by social security payments when incomes drop out or fall off.

But in underdeveloped countries consumption of all sorts is much more important for productivity. The problem is complicated as an increase of some consumption is more important for productivity than of other consumption. This implies that not only must consumption be included as a factor of growth in the analytical model but that even the direction of consumption must be part of the planning for development. Quite ordinarily this will imply preference for public consumption, directed towards education, health, housing and sanitation, nutrition, etc.

Another implication, a common assumption of economists that increased savings even among the poor are usually pressed forward by inflation and the ordinarily very regressive indirect taxation is good for development. It might, indeed, make some more physical investments possible, but will at the same time press down living levels and so cause levels and so cause a smaller labour input and, particularly, lower labour efficiency, that is, for both reasons, lower productivity of the natural economy.

My view is thus that egalitarian reforms are not a burden on the economy, but that if well planned and honestly carried out, they not only pay for themselves but, are the means to lift that economy. They, in fact, belong to the most profitable national investment a Government in an underdeveloped country can undertake.

No Losses

It is true that sometimes they involve, an investment with a fairly long gestation period before they mature in return in form of higher productivity. This implies that for a time they involve sacrifices by those who are privileged and who will have to cut down on less necessary consumption. But even for those who are better off, I believe that this does not in the long run imply losses, at least insofar as they share in the common interest of economic progress, national integration and consolidation, and political stability.

I am thinking of reforms of land ownership and tenancy, aimed at creating such a "relation between man and land" that man is given the possibility to invest everything he can lay his hands on, in the first instance his own labour, to improve the land and raise the yields.

Assessment and collection of taxes need to be vastly improved in all countries of the region and corruption be stamped out.

In "soft states" alleged practices spread through the whole society, particularly persons who have political, social and economic power really use these devices for their own enrichment.

Taking effective measures against corruption and favouritisms is therefore, in the interest of social justice. But even more it is needed to improve human relations and to raise productivity of the economy.

About the crucial role of fundamental reforms of education I have already talked. Population policy of spreading birth control among the masses is an immensely difficult task for a Government, which has decided to carry out such a policy. Only if family planning were allowed to develop in conjunction with all the radical reforms in the interest of social justice and higher productivity, I have hinted at, could it be really effective.

Pressure from Below

What is needed is a comprehensive radical reform movement, which even if inspired from above, develops into a people's movement. There must be "pressure from below" to sustain it and that can only be engendered and given a constructive course when society has first been given by honestly carried out and effective beginnings of the reforms.

Another problem related to the topic is the human dimensions of economic growth. Warnings are expressional values. These warnings are often given the slant that the peoples in Asia should be suspicious against the modernisation ideals imported from the western countries and the Communist countries. The main modernization ideals, actually covering them all is however, simply rationalism. Let me continue by stressing that mostly there is nothing irrational *per se* what is traditional.

Rational planning, particularly if and when it has become successful will increase the possibilities of preserving and increasing the highly valuable traditions of appreciation of and pride in a country's history, its treasures of art and culture.

Housing Traditions

Traditional ways of constructing houses have often through centuries of experience, become functionally more adjusted to the climate than the type of houses we build for ourselves in the temperate zones. As they are rational, planning should certainly be based on this experience. The same is often true of the habits of dressing. There is not necessarily anything rational in adopting the dressing habits of the developed countries.

Even more definitely the languages should, of course, be preserved and improved. It is a practical question; to what extent dialects should be unified. In order to be able to use all knowledge available in the world, ability to master at least one foreign language may be needed, to begin with at least by some.

A country in Asia is in this respect not differently placed than Sweden. Though we Swedes are only eight millions, we are not willing to give up our inherited language. We, too, need knowledge of foreign languages for essentially the same reason as you, as we are rich we can afford to have every child taught in English in primary school. But among ourselves we will certainly continue to speak our mother tongue.

A script is a somewhat different matter. To have, as in India, different scripts and not only languages put an additional mental distance between states. It also sometimes makes the use of typewriters difficult or much expensive. A majority of Indian leaders on the highest level have long been in favour of going over to the Roman alphabets, as some other countries in Asia have done, which does not imply giving up the languages.

Vegetarianism in some groups is certainly not irrational in countries that are scarce on grains to feed cattle for slaughter. Abstinence from alcoholic drinks is not irrational for those who can discipline themselves enough to follow such a prescription. The Indian ban on cow-slaughter and similar taboos in other Asian countries, however, are compatible with rational husbandry. If such a tradition shall be preserved, it carries its costs.

On the whole, there is nothing in the traditions I have exemplified that brings them in conflict with rational planning. Traditional behaviour is either, as often or even mostly, rational or, when not, carries a cost which should then be counted against the attachment felt for a particular tradition.

When rational planning of policies to improve the living conditions of the people was not included in the inherited traditions, that is, however, a tradition, and the only tradition, that must be broken. And different from all the other traditions I have exemplified, it cannot be looked upon as valuable in any sense.

It implies the acceptance of a continuation of long bygone periods of stagnation mostly under foreign colonial rules. Particularly under the pressure of the very rapid and still, on the whole, accelerating population increase, holding to that particular tradition would mean inviting disaster.

It has happened even to me that I have met people who have told me that poverty itself is a tradition, and an Asia value. When this view is held by persons who themselves live in affluence, I must consider such a view as more than nonsensical, indeed as cynical.

Poverty

The poverty of the masses in Asia must be conquered. And this must be the supreme aim of planning in all Asian countries. Insofar as they succeed in their planning efforts and give it this rational direction, they will widen and not restrict the opportunities to invest in preserving their own cultures. In that sense, I see no conflict between rational planning and what is sometimes called the Asian values.

A planning aimed at liquidating mass poverty will however, imply that a much higher priority will have to be awarded for making labour scarce in under-utilisation of the labour force, which is the basic cause of extreme poverty, and to redirecting production towards producing goods and services for the poor masses

In the Indian approach to the Fifth Plan, 1974-1979, which I have just read, this is the theme stressed right in the beginning. To what extent this Fifth Plan and following Plans will succeed in adjusting the whole economy, production at all stages and consumption, to these goals, is still to be seen. But it is an advance in that the desired direction of change has been formulated more clearly than ever before.

Such fundamental changes will among other things, have to imply a much lower level of consumption of luxury goods in the upper strata. I do not say this with the simple meaning that it is needed in order to increase incomes and consumption in the lower strata. I do not believe it is realistic to think in the static terms of a total national income that is then distributed in one way or the other. The general statement so often repeated, that there must be economic growth in order to make egalitarian reforms possible, can be misleading. As I have pointed out throughout this lecture, the egalitarian reforms should themselves be productive and thus in a sense self-financing and, more than that, highly profitable from the national point of view, even if the gestation period be considerable.

But particularly with a small industrial base to start with, a need will be present from the beginning to redirect industrial growth from, as now to such a large extent, being directed upon ultimately producing consumption goods for the upper classes. It is for this purpose, to redirect production, that luxury consumption for the upper strata must be restricted. In a country like India this must imply a rather radical change in the functioning of the whole licensing system.

Industry

This type of austerity in the consumption and living patterns of the rich was what Mohandas Gandhi was demanding from them. Many in Asia would perhaps say that simple living is a tradition or even an Asian value. In the West we would call it a legacy of Puritanism.

In both types of countries we are now very much in need of cutting down a lot of unnecessary consumption. In the West, which is so much richer, restriction of less necessary consumption is needed in the higher income brackets, in order to stop inflation and also to raise the "quality of life". Our environment is threatened by our influence. In Asia austerity in the upper classes is called for primarily in order not to raise difficulties for the redirection of production towards what the masses of people need in order to liquidate poverty. Such a redirection of demand and production is an important element in building a more egalitarian society and at the same time a more productive economy.

10

The Impact of Mahatma Gandhi on Martin Luther King

Prof. Stanley Wolpert*

"Non-violence is not a symbol of weakness or cowardice", Martin Luther King told us when he came to speak at UCLA a quarter century ago, "non-violence transforms weakness into strength. We must never be bitter. We must meet hatred with Love, and physical force with soul force. I have heard the inner voice of God speaking to me from the dark night of my soul, telling me to 'Stand up! Stand up for righteousness! Stand up for the Truth! God is Truth, and Truth is Love!' Yea, though we walk in the valley of the shadows we must fear no evil! Every man has a right—beyond that, a *responsibility* to resist unjust laws, for there is a higher law that guides us, and that Truth shall one day make us Free!"

Martin's rich deeply resonant voice that echoed from the hills of Westwood that morning was a Black Baptists Preacher's baritone, but the words were Mahatma Gandhi's, as I well knew. For Martin Luther King was a "student" of Gandhi's, a true disciple of the Mahatma's. King followed Gandhi in spirit and through actions that transformed fallow words into deeds of greatness and self-sacrifice in the cause of Justice, Truth and Love. Martin had visited India in 1959, three years after the historic Montgomery bus boycott he lead that has helped to change America from a land of racial segregation and apartheid into one of the greater equality of opportunity for all and of justice before the Law for Blacks, Whites and people of every creed and colour from every corner of the globe.

King was, indeed, the "American Gandhi", a *Mahatma* in the truest meaning of that most meritorious accolade, a "Great Soul" filled with Love for every human being on earth, for every child of God's infinite creativity, no matter how misguided. "Our planet teeters on the brink of atomic annihilation,"

---

* Professor of History, University of California, Los Angeles, USA.
Published in *Journal of Gandhian Studies*, Vol. 15; October 1987.

warned Martin. "Dangerous passions of pride, hatred, and selfishness are enthroned in our lives; truth lies prostrate on the rugged hills of nameless calvarias; and men do reverence before the false gods of nationalism and materialism. The saving of our world from pending doom will come, not through the complacent adjustment of the conforming majority, but through the creative maladjustment of a noncon-forming minority .... Why should we love our enemies? Because returning hate for hate only multiples hatred, adding deeper darkness to a night already devoid of stars. Darkness cannot drive out the dark. Only light can do that, only the sunshine of Love in the floodlight of Truth!"

Martin read Mahatma Gandhi's *Autobiography* and his story of the struggle he led in South Africa (*Satyagraha in South Africa*). "As I delved deeper into the philosophy of Gandhi, my skepticism concerning the power of love gradually diminished", he wrote in his *Strength To Love*, "and I came to see for the first time that the Christian doctrine of love, operating through the Gandhian method of non-violence, is one of the most potent weapons available to an oppressed people in their struggle for freedom. At that time, however, I acquired only an intellectual understanding .... When I went to Montgomery, Alabama, as a pastor in 1954, I had not the slightest idea that I would later become involved in a crisis in which non-violent resistance would be applicable. After .... the bus boycott began.....the people called on me to serve as their spokes-man. In accepting this responsibility, my mind, consciously or unconsciously, was driven back to the Sermon on the Mount and the Gandhian method of nonviolent resistance. This principle became the guiding light of our movement..... and Gandhi furnished the method."

I walked with Martin to lunch at our University's Religious Conference building, and we sat together. He was much shorter than I had realised, barely taller than the Mahatma himself, whose ashes I had witnessed being immersed in the waters of Back Bay when first I arrived in India that fateful February of 1948. "How well you have mastered Gandhi's message and his method", I ventured to say. King accepted my compliment graciously, smiling and nodding. He would soon electrify the world that August from Washington, D.C., when he so fervently announced, "I have a Dream!" Tens of million of Americans watched him on television and heard his ringing battle cry of Freedom on radio tuned to their highest volume.

"We refuse to believe that the bank of justice is bankrupt", shouted Martin before that sea of faces in the shadow of Washington's marble monument. "Now is the time....Now.....This sweltering summer of the Negro's legitimate discontent will not pass until there is an invigorating autumn of freedom and equality.....I have a dream......Let freedom ring! From every hill and molehill....from every mountainside let freedom ring!.....Free at last, free at last; thank God Almighty, we're free at last!"

Speaking after lunch at UCLA, Martin recalled the vernacular words of an old Southern Baptist post-Civil War prayer, which he recited for us the melliflous tones: "Lawd, we ain't where we oughtta be, and we ain't where we gonna be! No, Lawd, we ain't where we wanna be, but thanks to You, Lawd, we ain't where we waz!" It was, he told us, much the same with his valiant struggle, the Satyagraha he had launched in the South, the Boycott Movement, the Freedom Struggle. It was a long march from Montgomery to Birmingham, to Washington, but Martin never wearied or broke his stride. Just the way Mahatma Gandhi led the Salt March to Dandi, and the way Vinobaji led his countless *Pada Yatras*, Martin Luther King marched with Love in his heart towards the golden dawn of Freedom. And like Mahatma Gandhi, Mahatma Martin Luther King was murdered by a madman's bullets, but his Soul marches on.

11

Universal Brotherhood

Ulla Holmberg*

As a background to what I am going to quote the Declaration of the Rights of the Child:

"The Child shall be brought up in a spirit of tolerance, of friendship among peoples, of peace and universal brotherhood, conscious that his talents should be devoted to the service of his fellow men."

I think we could say that the same should be true in the case of everyone, not only as a rule of the education of the children. All of us need to learn tolerance and to feel the tolerance and friendship of our fellowmen. All of us should devote our talent to the service of others.

It would be very interesting to ask a hundred people in Finland what the words "universal brotherhood" might mean to them. I think many—may be most of the people interviewed would answer that it means giving to different funds like UNICEF, the Red Cross, the Christian mission and so on. Unfortunately, very few people in my country have had the possibility to take part in any kind of action for the developing countries involving other activities than giving money. And what is still worse—people are quite often suspecting that the money they are asked to give will not be used for food or other good and necessary things, but for arms.

May be Finland is something of an underdeveloped country in the aspect of international cooperation on a popular level. I must admit that I know very little about what our government does and how much money it gives to the developing countries—I only know that the aid is much smaller than it should be. But I happen to know that the idea of having a "sister community" in a country far away from Finland is quite unknown and new. There are only about ten communities which have established such friendship

* Finland

Originally published in *Journal of Gandhian Studies*, Vol. 15; October 1987.

bonds with communities in Asia, Africa or South America. As a comparison I can mention that in Belgium there are only five communities which *do not* have such sister communities in a developing country.

Of course, there are examples in Finland of school children sending home-made toys to refugee children in Africa, young people travelling to remote countries in order to take part in work camps etc. There are also people giving lots of money, time and devotion to the restoration of an old ship with which they will begin to import food and other things directly from African and Central American countries. But, as I said, the main part of the people never have had the chance to meet a person from a distant country and speak with him or even send some personal greetings to someone living far away from their own country.

There are many reasons why we in Finland are such "slow learners" in the matter of internationalism. One reason is that our own country is a bit remote from the main part of Europe and this means that our trips to other countries are more expensive than they are from e.g. Germany or Austria. We also have very few immigrants in Finland and extremely few refugees, so we are not used to foreigners.

In Finland there are two official languages, Finnish and Swedish, and this means the school children study English as their third language (and in some instances even as the fourth language). Those who go to school today learn English in elementary school, but among grown-ups there are many who have never learned English. The language problems are of course even greater if you try to establish contacts with a place where people do not know English, but understand e.g. French. The community where I live, Narpes on the west-coast of Finland, has had some contacts with Nyakizu in Rwanda, but one of the difficulties is that in Narpes there are very few people who have even the slightest knowledge of French and in Nyakizu very, very few people speak and write English.

Sending post parcels from Finland to, for instance, Asia or Africa is extremely expensive. I think it is the same everywhere. There are lots of things we could send to a "sister community" in a developing country, but we cannot afford the postage. For example: I think it would be possible to gather some old sewing-machines in Narpes and send them to women in Nyakizu. But the cost of sending them would be at least 60 or 70 US dollars each of the machines, may be even more (and the parcel would arrive several month after we have sent it).

These problems of postal costs etc. are things we cannot do much about, but there are also problems and questions I think we could discuss and maybe find a solution for. I would be very glad to hear what you think about my question, both you who are from the so-called developing countries and you who may be active in some kind of program for aid to poor countries.

First, what should we say when people ask how we know that their money will be used in the right way? Should we always trust the local (or government) authorities or should we send people from our country (or our organization) to control how the money is used? Is it wrong to send clothes from Finland to Africa or Asia¾would it be wiser to send money and promote domestic production?

Is it true that a twin program between a school or community in Finland and an equivalent in Africa or Asia would cause a lot of enviousness among those people who do not have their children in that school or who do not live in that community which gets some kind of parcels, letters and so on from Finland? (I have heard this from a bishop in Finland who has been a missionary himself in Africa).

If a community in Finland is in contact with a community in a very poor country, should the contact consist of principally economical assistance, or is it also reasonable to send letters, photos, etc. and expect the other part to answer the letters? What if the lack of paper and writing material is immense in the other country, or the postage are too high? Should we try to feel satisfied with only the pleasure of sending letters and parcels? I must say that for most people it is much easier to feel the joy of inter-national brotherhood if they are in a personal contact with some concrete people in another country.

An example, again from my own community and the efforts to establish contacts with Nyakizu, Rwanda: In order to overcome the language difficulties we asked the kids in our school to draw pictures or make collages, which would describe Narpes and Finland. (As I said, if they had written letters they should have had to do it in French and very few of the pupils have studied French). Our pupils get everything they need for this work; paper, pencils, crayons, scissors, glue and a great amount of beautiful brochures of Finland from the nearby travel bureau to cut pictures from. Some of the kids have written letters in English. They ask for pen pals and they tell the receivers of their drawings and letters to write back and tell about Rwanda or at least to send some drawings or photos. I hope we will be able to find out how to make this possible, but when I write this I only know that in Rwanda children in the grades 1-4 do not have paper and pencil at all and there is a great lack of everything needed in school.

Another question that I would like to hear your opinion on is whether it is reasonable to try to arrange some kind of student exchange between "sister communities" in an industrial country and a developing country. I imagine that the travelling expenses would not be too high compared to the benefit of sending one or two teenage students from Narpes to Rwanda or India for one month. I also think that people in Narpes would like to have a student from Rwanda or India as their guest for some weeks and we could probably arrange some kind of fundraising in order to pay the costs of the trip to Finland and back again. But the problem is that I have heard about people from developing countries who have had the opportunity of visiting Finland or Scandinavia¾and the result has been a real shock. They did not expect us to live in such abundance and maybe they could not morally accept our style of life.¾ My question is then: can it be dangerous to ask young people (17-20 years of age) to visit our community and our school for a short time? And what about sending our students to visit developing countries?

My own opinion is that the risks anyhow must be small compared to the benefits. What people will see in a foreign country is the truth. We are living on a too high level, we are wasting our resources¾maybe it would be very whole-some for us to compare ourselves with people living in another way.

In Finland, like in other western countries, most of the people still believe that the "natural development" will improve the situation little by little in the poor countries. And the result will be that the people of these countries in the future will live at least as well as we are living now. I must admit that I also thought in that way earlier. It was not before during this decade we began to understand that this idea is very unrealistic. And as I said, most of the people do not understand it yet. The new insight that we have to lower our own standard of living in order to make a reasonable improvement in the standard of the poorest countries possible is very hard for us to accept.

I think that many of the thoughts I have brought to you are not new and maybe you had expected me to analyse the situation more abstractly and deeply. I am asking for your opinions more than I am giving answers. I hope to learn a lot from this seminar about how we should teach universal brotherhood in our schools and in our communities. My contribution will therefore, be these questions and problems, which I hope we could discuss.

Finally I want to say that one of the greatest thing with being a peace activist is that there will always be new challenges, new problems to solve. I have taken part in the peace work for about ten years. The questions I am asking you to discuss are only a small part of those I have thought of this year, the International Peace Year. I am sure there will be new questions and new challenges for every year during the rest of my life—and this will be one of the reasons for me not to try to struggle alone, but to stay in contact with other peace activists all over the world.

Is it necessary to know exactly how the money is used, if you are raising funds in one country in order to help people in another country?

Should we always think of promoting domestic production in a country, no matter how poor it is, or can it be reasonable to send clothes, school materials etc. instead of money?

Can a twin program e.g. between a school in a western country and a school in a developing country cause enviousness in other schools?

How should a twin program be arranged in order to promote universal brotherhood and not to cause a lot of economical and practical problems for the more disadvantaged part?

Is it reasonable to send young people from one part of the world to another for a short time as "exchange students" or are the benefits smaller than the risks?

How should we make the people in the industrial countries understand and accept that brotherhood also includes lowering the own standard of living in order to give the poorest sisters and brothers a chance? Is it always a negative thing to lower one's standard or can we learn to find pleasure in cheaper things?

12

Gandhiji and Contemporary Ideologies Regarding Freedom, Peace and Equality

Haflin Samdin*

"Liberty is the principle of our public life" declared Pericles some two thousand years ago. It was love of truth and a concern for good government that made him to think so.

It was the love of Truth and the love of freedom that impelled men to go into the wilderness, and seek the great values of life. It was the love of TRUTH that impelled Siddhartha to forsake his young wife and infant and regal joys and pleasures and go in quest of the inner peace and of the human welfare: the '*Andha Hridaya*' the concealed core of one's being and becoming process. It was the love of Truth that drove Abraham and even Moses and many others to roam the desert wilderness and hear the truth. And some 2500 years after Buddha, another man in the person of Mohandas Karamchand Gandhi came in the desert milieu of Kathiawar, Gujarat and perhaps heard the very same strain born on the brine spray laden air. It was the Truth that he was in quest of. It was the grand theme that he experimented on. A century or so before, the very same "Satyam" the thirst for liberty, equality and fraternity, found its way into the heart of Abraham Lincoln. He made the noble and sublime declaration of Independence: not the mere theoretical and political idea; but he laid considerable stress on the basic principle that all men are born free: and all men Black or White or Yellow shall be free; that the several members of the human family, shall be equal, for they are all brothers.

Gandhi saw the Truth: and he felt it: the thought coursed through his veins and suffused his whole being. And it was this basic principle that had

* Coordinator, Sarvodaya District Centre, Batticola, Sri Lanka 11.

Paper contributed at the '*International Seminar on Contemporary Ideologies regarding Freedom, Peace and Equality*' held in October 1986 under the auspices of Gandhi Bhawan, University of Allahabad, Allahabad.

found a permanent slot in the Time Record of his being. It was this: That man in order that he might see the Truth has first and foremost '*to be free'*. For ensnared and encumbered, how can he think? The very essence of man, creative is *FREEDOM.* It is the essence of all development, of all growth, of all forms of creativity. If that be so, how comes it that man having been born free is found everywhere in chains? The first and foremost principle that Gandhi discovered and later formulated is this: *Man shall be Unconditioned and Free.* Liberty shall prevail in all human groups: be it the State, be it the township, be it the village: be it the educational institution, or be it the home. According to Gandhi: Freedom shall not come only to a few. It shall be the possession of all: of every individual that goes to make up any social or political group country or nation.

Are you a man? Then you shall be free: you are meant by Nature to be 'Free'. This is the sublime Truth, whose genuineness, no one *dare* question and whose perfection in all universal relationships, no race, no religion, no doctrine, no dogma, not even a Stage shall doubt.

Gandhi was par excellence a great scientist. His theme was 'the Science of Life' and he had experimented with TRUTH (Satyam) and attempted to trace all the relationships that he could trace between man and nature.

Gandhi had experimented in the art of living a meaningful and purposeful life. He had thought out these principles, which his western counterparts had thought out in a slightly different way. His western education and his Asiatic culture have enabled him to see the great relationships. There resides not any humbug in it: no hypocrisy in his ways; no meaningless utterances and no empty and misleading designs in his style of thinking.

In his endeavour to get at the Truth, Gandhi had reposed his faith on "the one noble truth" namely ACTION, the right thought and right action. The Vedic rishis have given him this simple and universal principle.

The basic thinking in the 'Gita' is this: Action-*detached action.* The western way of thinking had got at one end of this thought: and the eastern way of thinking at the other end. The means adopted had been slightly altered, and the ends appear to be at variance. The 'West' believed in action: mere mechanical action; bleach bone action; action minus the 'moral' or value appendage. The western States and Governments, have it would appear, not gone sufficiently deep, into this question of evolving life's designs and issues: namely, the 'ends and means of Existence'. The Asiatics, in the sandy wastes of Arabia, Palestine, Gobi, in India and China and Persia, had given sufficient thought to it and seen and conceived, in a detached condition of mind. *The End: and means of attaining the ends.* The Asiatic thinkers appear and stand out here and there, like a few Himalayan heights having lost sight of the sprawling plains and the immensity of the desert vastnesses. The West, has on the other hand, focussed its attention on the evolution and the maintenance of their 'State systems' and social organisations, to wit: Democracies, capitalistic States, Fascist and Communist and other totalitarian patterns of state organisations. Some of them were more concerned with the welfare of the individuals, and most of them more bothered about building up cast iron, thoroughly disciplined authoritarian and totalitarian states where dictatorship was the principal mode.

And so in the West the ideologies of Individualism, Socialism and Communism and Fascism have had to confront each other, wage constant cold wars; wars of prestige and power. Now the question poses: Do you want bees? Or do you want Gods? Do you want service authority, order, discipline, and clock work regularity in all that you do and perform, and cent percent efficiency? Or do you want Freedom and Equality and a sort of perfection in a free society? The former aims at the begetting of an authoritarian order of social events: the latter aims at the perfections of the democratic system where the begetting of the greatest happiness for the greatest number is aimed at: Give me security and peace and harmony and I am prepared to forego a portion of my birthright, namely, an Individual Freedom. What is aimed at in the safeguarding of individual freedom is the attainment of this ideal: We ought to be able to do for the others *What we expect them to do to us*. That is to say, we have to mutually safeguard our Liberty. And unless and until people are free, and learn to protect the tips of their noses from the blows dealt by the others, on a mutual understanding of our rights and duties and of the other's rights and duties, they cannot even dream of attaining peace and harmony, equality and liberty. The simple democratic view is that the government and the society should interfere as little as possible with the individual. Another point of view is: Everyone should respect the right of others, to do what they like, and should therefore, live on the principles of doing 'Unto others as he would have them do unto them'.

In other words an ideal State should be one where there should be as little interference as possible by government and society with individual freedom. It is in brief the principle of: 'Your Freedom ends where my nose begins'. In a Democratic State, "Individual Liberty has to be curtailed in the interest of other individuals and of the whole society."

None of the freedoms according to western political thinking namely, Freedom of Speech, Freedom of Press, Freedom of the Stage, were obtainable in an imperialist controlled state such as India under the suzerainty of the British Raj. This is the view of M.K. Gandhi. Orderliness in society is a dire necessity for maintaining a just and lawful administration. This is a recognizable fact. But the question was: how can there be law and order, let alone orderliness, in a slavishly cringing and crawling society, gavelling in the dust and borrowing into the mud and sinking into the mire, exploited to the marrow of its bones by a supremely capitalistic and imperialistic power?

M.K. Gandhi fully agreed with the poet Rabindranath Tagore, in what he *proclaimed as the true life's objective of man,* 'Man in the inner depth of his being will have to realize human unity........Our first duty, at dawn is to remember Him who is one, Who is indistinguishable through class or colour and Who by His varied forces provides as is necessary, for the needs of each class and of all. Let us pray to Him, who gives wisdom to unite us all in understanding.' People will have to learn to maintain a free spirit; and we shouldn't surrender our reason into anybody's keeping. Here is at last the real essence of Freedom.

That M.K. Gandhi cared a lot for the maintenance of individual Freedom—has been given sufficient recognition by the Imperialistic British Raj in India, indicated by this statement appearing in the state sponsored newspaper—INDIA (1919).

'Gandhi's readiness to take up the cudgels on behalf of any individual or class whom he regards as being oppressed has endeared him to the mass of his countrymen.'

Here is 'LIBERTY' in its essence which M.K. Gandhi has nursed and cherished as the basic principle of a Nation, and from this he swerved not even an iota throughout his life's career, namely, *the winning of freedom for the least of the Indian people.*

M.K. Gandhi's 'Tolstoy Farm,' and his 'Phoenix Settlement'—both he established to South Africa—were tangible social experiments that confirmed his intrinsic and unshakeable faith is Freedom, Self-help, Self-respect, Equality, Fraternity and a peaceful way of life that he had formulated for the Indian nation. Any nation, be it small, be it mighty, should have as its foundation the rock base of a solid culture: Neither anarchy nor chaos nor disorder. His book 'Nature Cure' is an outspoken document of his philosophy of life. It had much in common with the sort of life that Henry Thoreau led in his Walden Ashram. Live and let live: and live in harmony with Nature, for '*You are a child of the Universe no less than the trees and the stars are'*. Exploit her not, for you, who haven't the skill and the capacity to build has no right to break and demolish and make a painful and gaping dent in Nature's sides.

Now let us come to what a great political thinker of the West has to say on democracy. These are the works of Leonard Woelf. 'Do you believe in Democracy'? Then if you do so, you must believe in equality. For all democrat, in some sense for another believe in equality, and this belief has caused immense political changes in recent years, as immense as the changes caused by the democratic ideas about happiness'.

Gandhi in no way deviated from this way of thinking. He conceived a '*Rajya*' which was no other than a 'Kingdom of Peace' and contentment, where the right relations and correct understanding shall prevail, where intellectual freedom and individual freedom shall reign supreme, where equality of opportunities for all and sundry shall be given due respect. The 'parayah' was for him an important and as useful and dignified a member of his Rajya as the Brahmin and the Kshatriya. The state had to serve 'Unto the last' that is to say one and all.

Gandhi was a great student of the society of man. He strongly believed in the notion: 'As long as I live, so long do I learn'. And I create this world after my hearts desire. And life according to him, has to be lived in true earnest; it has to be learnt and experienced. It has to be chopped and chipped and chiselled, moulded and shaped, cut into from and assigned the much-desired, much-longed for shape. Throughout one's life one is busy learning, planning, designing and creating. In short it is a process of doing learning and creating. Life is like a chunk of clay in the hands of a potter. You can deal blow upon blow on it, with your shaping mallet and fashion it, mould it and shape it after your own sweet will: *Your intrinsic heart's desire.* You are a creator, in no way second to that "MIGHTY PLAN" that had been designed long ago in the deepest depth of the void and of time.

Gandhi had reposed infinite faith on this idea: That life has to be lived, and lived meaningful; life is an individual concern. It has had to have it multi-stringed relationships with the entirety of its circumbient circumstances; immediate and distant, its cordial relations, with all that one meets with in one's life. There is sweetness and suavity, a genuine bond and cordiality and a harmony that have to be forged in this miraculous sojourn on the face of the earth, the journey of life.

M.K. Gandhi has had his dream of human life, and he dreamt it in all true sincerity and his greatest wish was that the entire human race should live its life meaningfully, significantly and purposefully, having lived his life in perfect harmony with the rest of humanity and with the totality of Nature. Gandhi may be said to have designed his pattern of society in tone, each with its native ambience.

Here is a Criticism: Wasn't he trying to achieve the impossible? Achieving the Utopia of a '*Ram Rajya'*? His politics, it would appear, was not on this world, but of one that rested on the descriptions given by Valmiki in his *Ramayana.* His '*Ram Rajya*' belonged to the puranic age of some three thousand years ago. Is this criticism reasonable?

Well, all this is very, very radical and unfair criticism. Gandhi knew that India suffered from a fatal malady. The malady of poverty, the malady of ignorance, the malady of a chaotic understanding of events, and these maladies needed a radial cure. Hence, he made up his mind to perform very Gargantuan task. Hercules in its efforts and proportions. He studied the question of Indian Nationhood and had come to the conclusion that man all over the world was in chains, despite the fact he was born free. Man was ensnared in every way, economically, socially and politically. He was in chains. He had to be willy-nilly liberated. First and foremost he needed *mental liberation*; then should come *moral liberation*; then *economic liberation.* He saw that man in India hadn't the bare animal needs—food, clothing and shelter. A starving man cannot think. In any empty stomach how can one beget clear understanding.?

Superstition in its worst form had crippled the people's beliefs and faiths. Caste, racism, creedal and linguistic differences had befouled the country's understanding. He had thus to work out a system that might help to free the people politically, economically, morally and socially. Man in India had to be divested of all his age-old prejudices: his religious and linguistic entanglements. In order to effectively rig out a 'Rajya' where the people shall live in peace, contentment and harmony: where they can beget social equality of status, equality of opportunities, and enjoy freedom from fear, from hunger, from ignorance, all which have come upon the land like a vast gloom. He realized that the fundamental need was '*Swaraj*'. Freedom of the heart, *Freedom of the head, Freedom from want.*

Gandhi knew fully well that the remedy rested on the country's freeing itself from the stranglehold of a crippling imperialistic power, that cared not, that felt not for the well-being of all and sundry.

Contemporary political thinking aimed at the attainment of this sublime goal in any land: western or eastern. And M.K. Gandhi had this clearly defined end in view when he initiated the 'Freedom Movement in India' *It was the human Freedom that he had in mind.* But it was too difficult a task for a single man to perform. He was good; he was strong; his morality was sound; his heart was pure, but the effort to attain all these qualities had overstrained him.

And when he met with his end at the hands of his assassin, what that great critic of human conduct, Mr. George Bernard Shaw had said, still rings true in our ears. '*It is far too dangerous to be too good*'. Gandhi was too good a man for facing the problems of India and for finding solutions for every one of them. But the human kind can still be proud of one thing. That one its kind had ventured to seek out and find a solution for every one of its problems at one single sweep of vision. Gandhi has brought a clearer, truer, richer and completer meaning to each one of the great principles so frequently handled about in political discourses and in the comity of nations; namely PEACE, FREEDOM AND EQUALITY. His was a slow but sure process where the ends are clearer and means purer, and as such, the great ideologies can become solid realities, and can be achieved by employing only one factor and one power, and that is SOUL FORCE: ATMIC POWER and no other.

13

Gandhi on Natural Law

Unto Tahtinen*

1. The meaning of 'Truth'

It is not always so easy to say what Gandhi precisely meant by 'Truth' with a capital T. He understood 'Truth' to be several different things on different occasions. At the very beginning, it is essential to rid ourselves of the idea that Gandhi thought of Truth as being the same as isolated facts. He distinguishes synthetic Truth from detailed knowledge. Gandhi did not appear to attribute any special significance to empirical knowledge in the overall search for Truth. Sense perceptions, he said, are often wrong and deluding, however, real they may seem to us. External evidence is insufficient; one must have changed behaviour and character. (*Truth is God*, p.6).

Sometimes Gandhi speaks of 'Truth' as truthfulness or the attempt to achieve Truth. In this case the term refers to a moral norm or virtue. One ought to strive after truth, one should struggle, endeavour, try hard, make efforts to attain truth. Ought-ness, rather than is-ness related to doing is the essence of a moral norm. The emphasis is on the endeavour, on the striving itself.

As a moral norm truthfulness resembles honesty. One may be expected to be honest or truthful towards other human beings. In this case it is a social moral norm of verbal communication, it may also be applied to action. Yet one may be honest towards oneself, too. Being truthful to oneself is, again a self-regarding moral norm. Honesty to oneself is, I think, for Gandhi more essential and primary than social honesty. One ought to be

---

* Finland.

Paper contributed at the *'International Seminar on Contemporary Ideologies regarding Freedom, Peace and Equality'* held in October 1986 under the auspices of Gandhi Bhawan, University of Allahabad, Allahabad.

straight forward in one's own essence, thereafter and consequently towards others and the society at large.

Generally in non-Gandhian writing—'truth' is understood as an epistomo-logical concept. However, for Gandhi, corresponding with facts, and also coherence with other beliefs has mainly an instrumental value. He even seems to have disregarded logical consistency and replaced it with consistency of thought (in general) and life, theory and action. (*My Religion*, p.112)

If any conventional Western theory of truth can be applied to Gandhi's thinking, it is the pragmatic theory. A belief or hypothesis is true if it works satisfactorily or is successful when applied to action. Yet Gandhi differs from the Western pragmatists in this view of what is determined to be successful or satisfactory. Therefore, values are essential. Thus, what is true is shown by value-consequences reaped by the application of the hypotheses.

So Truth, as Gandhi thought of it seems to be derived to this epistemological sense, to a largely normative character. In one sense of the word 'Truth', is moral norm, in another sense it implies a value-consequence. Gandhi often said that Truth is the end not just an end or any end: any desired object, but the end. 'Truth' finally implies metaphysics, value-metaphysics.

2. Gandhi's life—'experiments' revealing Truth

Truth as truthfulness also points to a certain content: that which should be discussed or the aim, which ought to be achieved. Now it is this sense of Truth as an end that I wish to expand on, and I may elaborate somewhat on Gandhi's life.

Gandhian philosophy took shape in a different way than academic philosophy in general. Usually a scholar studies the writings of other scholars, ponders over the problems and often teaches at some University. Yet Gandhi's view of life did not come into existence in such a conventional way.

Gandhian philosophy was born out of an abstraction of his own and his co-workers' lives and actions. The philosophy is the nucleus of his life-story and may be recognizable after-words. Gandhi applied certain ideas or ideals to action so far as they applied to his conscience. Through application the ideas developed and were gradually transformed.

Three 'experiments of life', I think, were especially substantial for Gandhi. They were all essentially concerned with his own life and the people round him. One, the first, was racial discrimination in South Africa. He had moved there in 1893 as a young lawyer. He was continuously degraded and molested, as was the whole Indian community.

These bitter experiences gave rise to an idea that the positive law can be at least, in part, morally unjustified, that the law in many obvious cases is not morally binding.

Another basic experience was the colonial status of India. Britain controlled Indian foreign trade, bought raw materials from India and sold her back industrial goods. This ruined the handicraft industry and made India poor. Gandhi clearly understood that colonial exploitation was morally wrong, as was the legal system backing it.

The third basic experience of legal injustice involved Hindu social custom. The lot of the outcasts was miserable. Gandhi felt that it was his moral duty to help the Harijans to live a humanly acceptable type of life. Gandhi found that a social system can also be unjustified from a moral point of view. Social custom based on ancient authority and on highly regarded religious institutions was in this respect faulty.

Thus Gandhi came to realize that certain positive laws, even the whole system of law, as well as traditional social and religious institutions can be in conflict with an ethical law. The ethical law, however, is higher in authority and in the case of conflict, takes precedence.

Starting with his own personal life-experience, his individual hardships, then gradually widening to the Indian community in South Africa, thereafter to India, Gandhi came to realize that there is a higher normative law above positive law. For a person originally a lawyer, this proved to be drastic mental development. He grew to be a greater man for this moving onward in pursuit of a higher law.

3. Ancient Indian and modern Western sources

Gandhi must have come across the Western theories of Natural Law while studying Law in London. Anyway, the ancient Indian traditions also contain ideas resembling the Western ones. In the Vedas *Rita* is mentioned.

It means first and foremost a cosmic rule. As such stars orbit and cows eat grass according to their inborn nature. *Rita* means the wholeness of the laws of nature and the harmony implied in the wholeness of existence. But it also represents a standard for human beings, an ethical law which men should observes in their actions. Thus *Rita* is also a metaphysical ethical law above all social institutions. It is unseen and a non-positive moral law of higher authority than the human law.

In this respect, as in many others, Gandhi was influenced by ancient Indian ideals, especially normative ideals, which he had imbibed in childhood. He became conscious of these latent through their Western equivalents. The experience of injustice offered a moral provocation and catapulted these dormant ideals into his full consciousness.

4. Truth as Natural Law

The most primary normative ideal for Gandhi was Truth. It was inderivable and was not a means to anything else. In the final analysis it is the eternal principle, the absolute Truth, God. (*Collected Works XXXIX,* p. 4) This Truth has an intrinsic value. To seek Truth is the *summum bonum* of life (*CW XXXIX,* p. 263). This seems to mean that seeking the final Truth has the highest moral value. In the above senses Truth is a formal concept, which cannot be analytically defined. However, it may also attain material content and its meaning then becomes manifold. For instance, the independence of India and the removal of untouchability are part of Truth. (Bose: *Selections*, p. 43, *CW LIII*; p. 427).

To use Western terminology, many meanings of Truth, and central meanings are absorbed into the concept of Natural Law. Gandhi himself did not want to use the 'Natural Law' nor (ethical) 'Justice', he rather preferred to speak of 'Truth'. He insisted on his specific vocabulary, although other vocabularies would also have been possible.

In the West, Natural Law means a higher and more authoritative principle as opposed to the positive law of a state. Natural Law has been supposed to be universally valid irrespective of time and place. It consists of principles of practical reasoning in ordering human life and community according to certain ethical ideals. It has arisen in opposition to positive law yet in origin and nature distinct from it. References to Natural Law have been used as the guiding light in changing positive laws.

Natural Laws have in the West been sometimes considered as an eternal law derived from the existence of God or being ultimately subjected to a divine law.

Gandhi also equates Truth with God. In this sense Truth is purely formal by nature. In a letter Gandhi explains that a perfect definition of God is impossible, so too, is one of Truth. The truth, he adds, which can be defined, ceased to be his God. (*CW LXV*, p.398) The final Truth can never be reached; it can only be approached in approximation. (*Selections*, p. 45).

Gandhi shuns the thought of describing the final end in detail. He rather says, "one step is enough for me". Anyway, he believes that it is possible to approach, even to attain, the absolute Truth if we faithfully and steadily practice a relative truth, as we ever know it. (*CW LIV*, p.372).

Thus Natural Law or Truth has, according to Gandhi, two meanings. The most primary meaning is purely formal. The other is a material having a relative validity.

5. How to know the truth?

There are two main problems involves in the realisation of Natural Law. One is the question of how we ever know it, whether can we have objective knowledge about it. Another question is, how we are capable of realizing it in practice.

The most central problem is that of knowledge. Is our assumed knowledge about Natural Law subjective or relative or is it possible to have objective knowledge and on what conditions?

Gandhi asked, "What is Truth", and answered that it is what the inner voice tells us. He further asked how it was possible that different people consider different and mutually conflicting things as truth. He tells us that human mind is not at the same level of development. What seems to be truth for one may seem an untruth to another. Therefore an experimental knowledge to truth has certain preconditions. Ardent moral practice is preparatory to this knowledge. Truthfulness, non-violence, limitation of wants, self-control, non-possession and humbleness are virtues, which train the mind. (*Selections*, p. 5-6).

Thus Gandhi basically understood Truth in a formal way, as that which the inner voice tells us or as an end to which all human endeavours is a means. Truth is consequently something of border-value. The goal, he says, always recedes from our way. (*Selections*, p.19).

According to Gandhi we have a right to err and so long as we do not see our mistakes, we must act in accord with the ethical norm which we understand to be true. (*CW XXXVII*, p.21). Thus Gandhi accepts a putative truth justifying action. Truth as we grasp it has relative validity, even then we have an ethical obligation to act according to it and subject it to a pragmatic test. Conditions of the justifications of action are a phenomenological analysis of one's mind and moral purity of motivation.

Gandhi says that by having undergone a deep internal search, he has analysed every psychological situation. (*CW XXXIX*, p.4). Praying and fasting can make mental effort more intense and represent ascetic self-purification. (*CW LII*, p.376).

Gandhi's method of seeking truth should be described as ascetic-phenomenological. The emphasis on moral purification shows the influence of the ascetic Indian schools of thought, Upanishads, Yoga, Jain and Buddhist.

Yet Gandhi did not respect ancient traditions as such. He respected them only so far as they responded to his own moral consciousness. He resorted to intuition, which in the final instance is always something personal. He believed a phenomenological analysis of one's consciousness to be the criterion for truth and justice. In this respect Gandhi could depart from ancient authority, even the authority of the Holy Writings such as the *Vedas*.

Actually, anyone who clings to Natural Law as a primary principle is to be considered a radical. Natural Law is by definition, as concept, already separate from the existing society and its legal, political, social, economic and religious institutions. One who resorts to Natural Law as the final authority will always demand for improvements and changes in society. Many of the changes may be possible within the legal and political framework, others may not.

6. Natural duties versus natural rights

Thus Gandhi essentially meant Natural Law by Truth, but was reluctant to use the vocabulary of Natural Law. Sometimes he, however, mentioned a natural right. (*Selections*, p. 255). Obviously he preferred to speak of 'Truth' instead of justice or law even the ethical sense of the term. He was also reluctant to speak of rights.

Possibly Gandhi felt that the vocabulary of Natural Law or natural rights could, in the mind of some listener or reader, be wrongly identified with legal rights or privileges, which aim at expression personal benefit. Gandhi definitely wanted to avoid this interpretation.

The term 'right' did not much appeal to him either. He saw the performance of duty as the source of rights. (*Selections*, p.284). Without duties there are no real rights. If everybody demanded rights and nobody performed the duties, it would lead to complete chaos. If, on the other hand, instead of holdings on to his rights everyone performed his duty, it would immediately lead to order in human society. (Datta. P. 88).

The relationship between duties and rights can be described by saying that if duties are correctly performed, they are sure to bring good results. (*The India of My Dreams*, p. 101). Duties are thus the source of rights. Apparent rights not based on one's performed duty, are seizure of power. The seizure of power or priviledge is not morally justified (*Hindu Dharma,* p. 223). Seizure of power is, besides being unjustified, also evil, because it leads to violence when secured. It increases social, political and economic structural violence. Violence becomes necessary when one tries to insure his own rights without performing his duties (*Non-violence* II, pp. 269-70).

Thus Gandhi did not sign the Proclamation of Rights. Instead, his moral philosophy stands for a proclamation of human duties. In this respect he follows rather the ancient Indian way of moral thinking, where the whole stress is on *dharma* and not on natural rights as in the West.

7. Natural Law and non-violence

Gandhi considered 'non-violence' the means of realizing Natural Law. Real justice cannot be secured by evil means, the means must be morally pure. Here also, I think, lies a difference between the Natural Law theorists of the West and Gandhi. The Western thinkers did not realize the importance of the ethically correct means of realizing the end.

14

Gandhi Techniques for the Removal of Economic Inequality

Francis Ofosu Quartey*

Gandhi's techniques for the removal of economic inequality may be classified under the following:

a) The revival of village industries.

b) Pursuance of the policy of self-reliance.

c) The building of socialism.

d) Elimination of Capitalism.

The most fundamental problem of life in an organised society is the conflict either potential or actual between the "haves" and "have-nots", the self-evident is the elimination of this distinction.

Many renowned leaders have in one way or another renounced economic inequality and advocated equitable distribution of wealth. Among many such leaders were Mahatma Gandhi of India and Dr. Kwame Nkrumah of Ghana Those who are alive and continue to advocate equitable distribution of wealth are Presidents Ahmed Sekou Toure of Guinea, Julius Nyerere of Tanzania, Kenneth Kaunda of Zambia, Mrs. Indira Gandhi, Prime Minister of India and many others too numerous to mention.

Many developing countries in Asia and Africa are struggling to develop their countries with their limited resources towards socialism in order to eliminate economic inequality. They are building roads, bridges, dams, highways and mansions. More children are going to schools. The population doctor ratio is improving. New Industries are going up, accompanied by slight increase in agricultural production. Even so often, we parade the accoutrements of political sovereignty, Coats of arms, National Anthems, National Flags never ending rounds of economic

---

* General Secretary, Mahatma Gandhi Brotherhood League, Nibiani, Ghana.
Originally published in *Journal of Gandhian Studies*, Vol. 2; April 1975.

conferences and meetings of Commissions, Development Boards and Agencies.

No nation can develop where wealth is concentrated in the hands of its few citizens to the detriment of many. Hence many countries in Asia and Africa on attainment of independence struggle to build socialism as the only system that can correct these abuses.

The progress of mankind consists in eliminating everything that causes dependence and makes for the subjection of man by man, class by class and sex by sex.

The concentration of wealth in the hands of few people in any given society amounts to capitalism at home, which in itself is domestic colonialism. It does not allow for any development whereby the Gross National Product will be equitably distributed.

If the GNP is produced by many, people in general will share in the material benefits of economic growth, whereas if it is limited to a few, the gap between the rich and poor will continue to widen.

In Africa today the Gross National Product (GNP) is still below 300 US dollars per capita. Social services are growing rather slowly. The masses still live in squalor and at or below subsistence level. Africa's external debt stood at 7,95,20,00,000 US dollars by June 30, 1968, having more than doubled in under eight years. It is still growing. Africa's balance of payments in 1965 was adverse to the tune of 1,652 million US dollars. This trend continues.

Yet notwithstanding the difficult economic problems of development besetting many developing countries in Africa and Asia and the need to facilitate equitable distribution of wealth, a few citizens possess more than they require for the upkeep and maintenance of their families much to the detriment of their next door neighbour.

Mahatma Gandhi foresaw the danger in the concentration of wealth in the hands of a few people as antithetical to economic development hence he opted for socialism. Gandhi claimed that he was a socialist long before many Indian socialists had avowed the creed. "But my socialism" he wrote; "was natural to me, and not adopted from any book. It came out of my unshakeable belief in non-violence. No man could be actively non-violent and not rise against social injustice wherever it accrued". A deduction can therefore be made from the foregoing that Satyagraha can be used for objectives, which are not purely or on the surface political. These may be superficially social, religious and economic. Gandhi points out that "widespread social and economic injustice is a sure index of the undemocratic nature of the state" and felt that the capitalist must regard himself as a trustee.

Socialism was in the Mahatma's opinion the best system that can solve India's problems. What then is Socialism? In the definition of Socialism many books say different things. There is the Western concept of Socialism, and there is the Eastern concept of Socialism. But for the purposes of this paper I shall attempt to define Socialism as an order of society in which exploitation of man has been abolished for ever; a society in which there is no unemployment; a society in which economic crisis does not exist; a society in which every body strives on his or her own work; where man works according to his ability and receives payment or wages according to his work; a society where the standard of living of every individual will be continuously praised; a society in which there is no race or caste discrimination; a society in which tribalism does not exist; a society in which the spirit of brotherhood constitutes the predominant social and cultural factor; a society in which national patriotism prevails and is accepted by all the people.

In capitalist developed countries where the means of production, distribution and exchange are concentrated in the hands of a few people to the detriment of a great majority of the people suicide attempts are rife. In England and Wales out of 40,000 reported suicides attempts yearly 5,000 succeed. In the United States 225,000 yearly suicide attempts were reported of which 25,000 succeed, the world's figure is attempted suicides 3,300,000 yearly 365,000 of which succeed.

Capitalism has proved too complicated a system for developing countries and therefore should be eliminated. What then is Capitalism? It is an economic system under which the ownership of production, distribution and exchange are concentrated in the hands of a few who form a financial oligarchy. The gap between the "haves" and "have-nots" widens because the majority of the people become propertyless and are thus compelled to sell their labour power cheaply in order to earn a living.

Under this system the private owners who are directed only by profit motives form an upper class and enjoy their wealth at the expense of the workers. This is exploitation of man by man.

To prevent competition the capitalists, who in several cases raise no figure to work, unite into large monopolistic concerns, pool their capital resources together and undertake large scale production to control the market.

Equality is the cherished dream of toiling mankind. It has always served as the banner of struggle of the oppressed against the oppressors. To eliminate inequality it is necessary first of all to abolish private property – that basis of exploitation of man by man.

Unlike capitalists and socialists, Gandhi considered property as the debate about ownership of property, which had little relevance for millions of people who were no more than at a subsistence level, if not below it. Addressing the women of India he said: "Let them remember that millions of men have no property to transmit to posterity. Let us learn from them that it is better for the few to have no ancestral property at all. The real property that a parent can transmit to all equally is his or her character and educational facilities".

If even Gandhi tolerated the institution of property, it was not because he loved it or considered it essential for the progress of humanity, but because he wished to abolish it with the non-violent technique. Gandhi would have vested ownership of property neither in the individual nor in the state but in God. Those who had the possession of property were to consider themselves as trustees, but they were not to be its primary, let alone exclusive beneficiaries. No one was to keep more to himself than he needed; everyone was to work according to his capacity and to receive according to his real need. In fact, it was a radical theory, which called for voluntary sacrifices from the "haves" in the interest of "have-nots".

Besides being a natural born socialist Mahatma Gandhi was very much concerned with the purchasing power of the village dwellers. He was of the opinion that fostering village industries could create employment and pump purchasing power into the villages; it could also shake the villagers out of their lethargy. Gandhi wrote "The 400 adults of Segaon can easily put ten thousand rupees annually into their pockets if only they would work as I ask them. But they wont....." He felt that by increasing the purchasing power of the villages and reviving old industries the growing gap in economic standards and social amenities between the village and the town can be bridged. Gandhi started to plead for a new deal for the village communities as far as 1915 when he entered public life. His concern centred around chronic unemployment and under-employment among the peasants whose appalling squalor never ceased to weigh heavily upon the Mahatma's mind. Exploitation of the village in the interest of the town was what he described as "a species of violence" and advocated that the growing gap in economic standard and social amenities between the village and the town had to be bridged. Rural industrialisation, accompanied by the necessary infra- structural and public health development has a significant impact on the rural populations both in terms of the population drift and in increased employment opportunities.

Another area where he expressed concern was the use of automatic or machinery for production "relating them to his fundamental doctrine of non-violence".

His criticism was based on the fact that it tended to concentrate the production of wealth in a few hands. But after a period of 40 years he was able to elaborate his ideas. He said that in a country where the hands were too many and the work too little, machinery could only add to unemployment and poverty. In 1921 he wrote "I would favour the use of the most elaborate machinery if thereby India's pauperism and resulting idleness could be avoided". As stated previously Satyagraha can be used for objectives, which are not purely or on the surface political. That is to say that a non-violent society had to be so organised as to reduce the in-equalities and tensions within it and to remove the temptation for an assault from without. Such a society needless to say be based on a decentralised economy where the Gross National Product would be shared and enjoyed by many people. In this connection Gandhi wrote, "You cannot build non-violence on a factory civilization, but it can be done on self contained villages. Even if Hitler was so minded he could not devastate seven hundred thousand non-violent villages. He would become non-violent in the process. Rural economy as I have conceived it eschews exploitation altogether and exploitation is the essence of violence. You have, therefore, to be rural minded before you can be non-violent".

As stated in paragraph two supra Gandhi was not alone in his quest for socialism as the best system for removing economic inequality. The late

Dr. Kwame Nkrumah of Ghana and Africa shared the same views with him. At the second conference of Non-aligned States held in Cairo, October 7, 1974, Osagyefo Dr. Kwame Nkrumah said:

"We who claim to be non-aligned must have the right to choose the political and economic philosophy which we consider most suitable for our rapid development and advancement. For example, the fact that Ghana accepts socialism as a means of our political and economic development does not and should not place us in opposition to any other country or people. Socialism does not belong to the Soviet Union or to China or for that matter to any other country; it is an international idea. Similarly, Capitalism does not belong to Britain, Western Germany or the United States of America. It is an economic doctrine and political philosophy which some of us consider unsuitable to our present circumstances. But this rejection of capitalist exploitation does not mean that we are politically opposed to the countries who have embraced capitalism. We are Socialists. We are also non-aligned. We are opposed to political and economic exploitation and domination, injustice and inequality against racism and racialism, we stand for progress, peace and justice".

Traditional African society was humanist and egalitarian. There was no concentration of wealth in the hands of a few to the detriment of the others. There was equality because nobody possessed the tools for production. Life was based on communitarism. No sectional interest was regarded as supreme; nor did legislative and executive power aid the interests of any particular group. The welfare of the people was supreme.

But colonialism came and changed all this. As a result, our continent has suffered a lot under the colonial era. Some of the legacies bequeathed to us were poverty, disease, squalor, distorted economy based on the exploitation of man by man and a pattern of education aimed at Europeanizing the African for white collar jobs bringing in its trail "colonial mentality".

The Government of Ghana under the late Dr. Kwame Nkrumah embarked on an extensive socialist programme in which every member of the community was given every encouragement and opportunity for progress and development irrespective of his creed or original conditions of birth.

In fact it is under socialism as the only way of life which will enable Africans developing their capabilities and rediscover themselves and live by the tenets of traditional African society which are:

1) That all men are equal.
2) That each man is an end in himself and not just a means to an end.
3) That the group is responsible for the individual.
4) That the free development of each is the condition for the free development of the group.

And yet socialism in Africa today tends to lose its objective content in favour of a destructing terminology and in favour of a general confusion. Discussion centres more on the various conceivable types of socialism than upon the need for socialist development.

The socialism of a liberated territory is subject to a number of principles if independence is not to be alienated from the people, when socialism is true to its purpose, it seeks a connection with the egalitarian and humanist past of the people before their social evolution was ravaged by colonialism, it seeks from the results of colonialism those elements (like new methods of industrial production and economic organization) which can be adapted to serve the interest of the people; it seeks to contain and prevent the spread of those anomalies; and domineering interests created by the capitalist habit of colonialism; it reclaims the psychology of the people, erasing the "colonial mentality" from it; and it resolutely defends the independence and security of the people. In short, socialism recognizes dialectic, the possibility of creation from forces which are opposed to one another; it recognizes the creativity of struggle, and, indeed, the necessity of the operation of forces to any change. It also embraces materialism and translates this into social terms of equality.

But the cynics among us will sneer at us for pursuing the improbable. They will always point to the power of the gun now in the political saddle in many African countries. It is true that military power has been employed to put back the hands of the clock in Africa. But look closer: Military power has also come to the assistance of national independence:- Boumedienne, Gaddafi, Gowon, Aeheampong! How are we sure, that military power will not one day come to the aid of socialism in Africa?

In any case, those who fear the might of the army should listen to the words of Victor Hugo:- "No army can withstand the strength of an idea whose time has come".

15

The Gandhian Phenomenon

Amre M. Moussa*

Mahatma Gandhi was a phenomenon, which cannot be repeated. The will-power of this man was such as to mobilize a whole nation in a manner unprecedented in recent history, for a cause which was clear to his mind and which he made clear to the minds and hearts of many millions of people.

His method was simple but most effective in its non-violent resistance towards the British occupation and domination of the Indian sub-continent. This method suited very well the circumstances obtaining at the time when no other conceivable method could have achieved the same results within such a short span of time.

What he did borders on the impossible since he had no other than his mere will-power which transpired to his fellow citizens from all castes, religions, languages and sects. The masses saw in him an idol and a symbol of staunch resilience, unwavering belief in what he was doing and uncompromising freedom fighter. They followed him whole-heartedly and gave him unqualified trust.

The result was thus a matter of time which he gave and which he took into consideration during the arduous task of negotiating with the representatives of the occupant forces and long prison sentences and detention without trial which did not break his morale or make him accept anything else than complete freedom for his nation.

But the Gandhian example remains a torch for the people deprived of their rights to self-determination, freedom and economic livelihood, etc. Everyone can find in Gandhi something to learn and to benefit, also nation as well as leaders. Therefore, it is doubtful whether this method could be suited to this day and age for example, for the Namibian freedom fighters against the occupation of racist South African regime. Times change

---

* Ambassador, Egypt.

Published in *Journal of Gandhian Studies*, Vol. 14; July 1987.

and circumstances change also and every epoch is governed by different rules of action and perception.

Mahatma Gandhi, however, did not confine himself to struggle for freedom of the nation, but also struggled against colour prejudice, war, race-domination, untouchability and communal disharmony. That is why Mahatma Gandhi will remain alive in the conscience of people all over the world, whatever their race, colour, religion, creed and tongue.

We in Egypt hold Mahatma Gandhi in very high esteem and affection. We cannot specially forget the close friendship between him and our national leaders the late Saad Zagloul Pasha who led the Egyptian struggle against the British occupation of Egypt in the same period.

Sarvodaya – A Way to a Better Life in Peace and Harmony: The Sri Lankan Experience

Ms. Gudrun Loewner*

There is nothing new, I can tell you about Sarvodaya in India. Sarvodaya and Gandhi are one, since Gandhi gave his translation of Ruskin's "Unto This Last" the significant title of Sarvodaya. For a period of one year I stayed with the Sarvodaya Movement in Sri Lanka in order to study their "religious path to peace and building a just world".[1]

In 1958, Mr. Ariyaratne, a teacher from a prominent Buddhist High School in Colombo, started together with his pupils and some colleges a shramadana camp in a backward village; this means that the mostly middle class youth donated voluntarily their labour force for some days in order to uplift the living conditions of the villagers and to help to awaken the own capacities of the village population by setting a good example. Although the beginnings of the Movement were very moderate, Mr. Ariyaratne was described as the '*Little Gandhi of Sri Lanka*', when he got the Ramon Magsaysay Award for Community Leadership in 1969.[2] The reward was somehow a starting point for the Movement to gain international recognition and interest and very soon donor agencies gave financial support and partnership.

The growth of the Movement is not yet stopped and today Sarvodaya is the largest non-governmental organization in Sri Lanka, which is also represented in Tamil areas. The Movement is active in 6037 villages. Those villages can be divided in four stages. To the Shramadana stage (introductory

---

* Department of Comparative Religion, University of Heidelberg, West Germany.

Paper contributed at the '*International Seminar on Contemporary Ideologies regarding Freedom, Peace and Equality*' held in October 1986 under the auspices of Gandhi Bhawan, University of Allahabad, Allahabad.

stage) with shramadana camps (which means gift of labour) belong 1937 villages, to the Group Formation Stage, where Sarvodaya groups are functioning such as Children's Group, Mothers' Group etc. belong 1646 villages and to the active stage, where the village groups are functioning with a fairly high spirit with the guidance of their own trained workers belong 2335 villages. The Self-financing Stage was reached by 119 villages and no village has yet achieved the Surplus Stage, where it could help other villages. This means that nearly one-third of the villages in Sri Lanka have more or less contact with Sarvodaya. About one thousand paid Sarvodaya workers are spreading the message all over the country and they are helped by 5000 preschool-teachers and thousands of volunteers.[3]

These few figures should only give you a recent picture of the Sarvodaya Movement in Sri Lanka. I think that you all know about the general work of it and if you want some detailed information, I think that the best book is still from Prof. Dr. Detlef Kantowsky: *Sarvodaya-The Other Development*,[4] which was translated into Hindi and published by the Gandhi Peace Foundation recently. I don't recommend the book, because it is written by a German, but because it is the only comprehensive book written by an outsider on all aspects of Sarvodaya.

Kantowsky was also one of the first who stressed the relationship between the Indian and Sri Lankan Sarvodaya Movement, and he was followed by the Dutch Wismeijer with his book "Diversity in Harmony", which represents a study of the Sarvodaya leader similar to "The Gentle Anarchists—A Study of the leaders of Sarvodaya Movement for Non-violent Revolution in India" by Geoffrey Ostergaard and Melville Currell.

I dare to say that Sarvodaya in Sri Lanka would have never come into existence without the great example of India. The decay of India doesn't mean that Sarvodaya in Sri Lanka must also decline, but a lot of people are of this opinion and therefore Ariyaratne, "the little Gandhi" said in an interview: "If I would start again I would rather try to avoid the name Sarvodaya. Not that it does not give the exact meaning of what we are doing, but we are thereby identified with Sarvodaya in India and measured by a yardstick that is not our own."[5]

In this talk I will try to answer three questions and the first is dealing with relationship Sri Lanka-India: What are the main differences between Sarvodaya in India and Sri Lanka ?

The second question: What is the contribution of the mainly Buddhist Sarvodaya Movement towards peace and harmony in the Sinhala/Tamil conflict?

The third question: What are the future perspectives of Sarvodaya in Sri Lanka?

Coming back to the first question about the difference between Sarvodaya in India and Sri Lanka, I want to divide between aims and practical action. It is obvious that both are going hand in hand, but it is possible to achieve the same aims with different means, and I think that this is here the case. For a person, who isn't an expert, he will put both Sarvodaya Movements in the same drawer as alternative (whatever that is), indigenous, independent, concentrated mainly on the poor and outcast; struggling for freedom, human rights, peace, harmony, mainly village orientated, charismatic leaders, fulfilment of basic needs, no wish of an affluent society; spirituality, philosophy and religion play an important part; the western model of development with growth and industrialism is not the only solution etc. And this person is right, because all these aims and descriptions are relevant for India and Sri Lanka. The differences start, when you look in detail. Gandhi's dream was the realization of independent village republics in India, Ariyaratne's dream is not going so far. His stress is also on villages and their population, but he can imagine those villages being inter-dependent and all being ruled by a righteous government—as it was in the glorious past, when there was a unity between the Buddhist king, monks, tanks for water and the villages. Gandhi is more radical, because he doesn't want state to exist, whereas Ariyaratne is taking the ancient welfare state as a model, as it might have been similar in the time of King Asoka.

What concerns the practical aims, Sarvodaya in Sri Lanka has developed a list of Ten Basic Human Needs: clean and beautiful environment, clean water, sufficient clothing, enough food, health care, housing, communication, alternative energy, basic education, culture in all forms. Although I didn't find such a catalogue formulated by Gandhi I think he wouldn't disagree. The fight against westernisation in dress, habits, thinking and behaviour, the struggle against gambling, drinking, smoking, sex films, they all aim at a *moral upliftment of the individual*. In discussions with Sarvodaya workers in Sri Lanka, I found that the *moral upliftment* is a very important point for them, then comes the philosophy, which is deeply influenced by Buddhism and only thirdly comes the fulfilment of the ten basic needs. The idea is that people should be satisfied with the fulfilment of their basic needs and grow spiritually, so that they can accept their situation as *voluntary simplicity*. Sarvodaya doesn't talk of voluntary poverty, but as the middle path in Buddhism they are going a middle way. The implementation of this programme has to face many difficulties, because once the basic requirements are met, wants are going further and it needs a lot of philosophical understanding to be satisfied with the achieved status-quo in material things, specially when the non-Sarvodaya members of the society are living a life according to the Singapore development growth model. The idea of "small is beautiful" is relevant to Sri Lanka and India, and means that production units should be mainly small and in the village surroundings to cater to a specific village community. The ideal is to make the villages nearly self-sufficient units. Special emphasis is given to a lifestyle, which resembles to me a bit to the lifestyle I experienced in the Wardha ashram, where no harsh words are spoken, the elders are respected by the community, all members are treated equally irrespective of caste, class or creed and physical labour is necessary for everyone.

To have aims is one thing, to implement them can be very different. What concerns India I would see two stages. Stage one is the past with Gandhi being alive, with Satyagraha for political independence from Britain, the struggle for the upliftment of the Harijans, the emphasis on Swadeshi and Vinoba Bhave with the Bhoodan Movement. Stage two is operating in the last years up to now. The time of the big actions has passed away. Now individuals; who are Gandhians have started all over India, specially in the North to implement Gandhi's ideals in practice. Mostly these are rather small ventures, which include ashrams as centres of spiritual life and base for village development. There is no central structure combining these efforts, only the spiritual attachment to Gandhi and his philosophy. Subba Rao is implementing the philosophy in the Chambal Valley with robbers, Prembai is working with tribals, who have less than the means to survive. In Wardha appropriate technology, vocational training for the youth and the fight against leprosy are going together with the ashram life.

Compared to the mostly micro cosmos activities of India, Sri Lanka represents a centralized system, with a paragovernmental structure, head- quarters in Moratuwa, 27 district centres and 220 divisional centres and about 1000 workers paid by the headquarters. Because the main emphasis is on personality change, the main emphasis is on the children's programme and youth education. In an earlier stage you could have even talked of Sarvodaya as a Youth Movement, specially after 1971 riots, when lots of young people joined Ari as a new alternative.

The most widespread activities are preschools, educating nearly 100,000 children and trying to feed them with nutrious food, vaccinate them and educate their mothers on nutrition and health care and drawing the mothers' attention towards the Sarvodaya Movement. The second are children groups and youth groups and mostly from these groups are drawn the young people who are trained for being preschool teachers in their own villages, learn various vocational skills in the centres and some of them are also trained in community leadership and eventually become new leaders in the Sarvodaya Movement itself. The village leaders initiate programmes for the welfare of the villagers like the digging of roads and wells, the starting of small income generating projects, the building of preschools and the paying of the preschoolsevika etc.

Besides such work, which can be done in any village there are couple of very special programmes taking place; the Community Leadership Bhikku Training Institute, which tries to educate bhikkus in the modern role of development in the Sarvodaya Way, the Meditation Training Institute, the Agriculture Training Institute etc. Special Welfare Projects for the visually handicapped, the disabled, the deaf, those suffering from Malaria and those suffering from Epilepsy are also on the programme.

I want to finish my picture by enlisting those activities, where according to my mind, there is the greatest potential for the establishment of some kind of a Sarvodaya alternative society within the present conditions.

The Saving Scheme, which is mostly utilized for educating children in the habit of saving could potentially grow into an alternative banking system. Upto now about 100,000 accounts have altogether a deposit of about 200,000 American Dollars, that is not much, but a starting point.

Another try in this direction is the establishment of small community shops, legal aid services, indigenous medical services, home-gardening and libraries.

It is obvious that Sarvodaya in Sri Lanka is trying to cover all aspects of life and to establish an alternative system for the fulfilment of basic requirements within the existing system under the idea of Swadeshi, although Khadi doesn't play any role and the perspectives of Sarvodaya are worldwide. From the cradle to the grave, specially the weaker sections of the society should be educated and profit from the new way of life, which wants to bring about change only by non-violent means—a main reason, why Marxists don't like the movement, because according to them only a revolution can at once bring a total change, whereas someone who tries to work within the existing structures is only helping those who profit from the status-quo.

Let me now try to answer my second question: What is the contribution of the mainly Buddhist Sarvodaya Movement towards peace and harmony in the Sinhala/Tamil conflict?

You are all informed about the conflict, but let me give you a few figures. The population of Sri Lanka amounts to 15 million people, with a large Buddhist majority belonging to the Sinhalese race, 11 million are Sinhalese and the rest 4 million are Tamils and Ceylon Moors. The Ceylon Moors are Moslems and amount to 1 million, that means that in Sri Lanka there live about 3 million Tamils, who came only during the British time as teapluckers. Upto now there is no great unity between the Ceylon Tamils and the Indian Tamils who are mostly low caste, uneducated and restricted to the plantation sector. The Sri Lankan Government fears a coming together of these groups and an infiltration of the plantation sector with militant Jaffna Tamils. A starting point was Talawakelle and Hatton, where a lot of shops were burnt in February 1986, which I witnessed myself. 12.6% of the population are Ceylon Tamils and 5.56% Indian Tamils. The violent terrorists are nearly 100% coming out of the Ceylon Tamil group, which came once from India, and they have deep connections with Tamil Nadu. Since July 1983 about 200,000 refugees have left Sri Lanka, mostly Tamils to live in India or Europe or Canada etc. Within Sri Lanka, 150,000 people belonging to all races are living in refugee camps, mostly in the north and east, 15% of all schools in Sri Lanka are closed. Nobody knows how many people have exactly lost their lives and their property during 1975 till 1985, but several thousand people on both sides are the victims, and mostly the victims are innocent people, neither army nor terrorists.[6] This is only the recent history, but a look into the past shows that the two communities have never lived together in peace and harmony for very long. Elam is not only a new demand, it has been reality for centuries in Jaffna. Peace was there only for some time between the two wars. To be sarcastic it is possible to say that only during colonial rule there were no open riots between the two communities.

Sarvodaya and Ariyaratne knew about the problems from the very beginning of the starting of their movement, but their first aim was to make

Sarvodaya attractive for the Sinhala/Buddhist majority, who were neglected during British rule. In fact, Sarvodaya in Sri Lanka only started to be successful, when it was linked deeply with Buddhism in alms terminology and got the support of Buddhist Bhikkus for their work. Prof. Dr. Hewage initiated together with Ari this dipping of Indian Sarvodaya in Buddhism and in the glorious past, which was similar to a myth, and which should be revived, to become partly the model of the future. Here lies the uniqueness of the Movement, because it was the first Movement, which started this type of activism under the Buddhist flag. The rapid growth of the Movement brought about the question: What does Sarvodoaya do for the minorities, specially the Tamils?

I think that three steps can be seen. The *first step* was the integration of the northern and eastern provinces into the Sarvodaya system. Already in the beginning of the 1970s a few Tamils joined the Movement and started the work in Jaffna. The work started quite successfully and at the peak up to 1000 villages, which were Tamil or had parts of a Tamil population were with Sarvodaya. The district-coordinator of Killinochchi, Mr. Pillai, is himself a Gandhian of the typical Indian style, who had started an Ashram years ago, wears khadi and can only speak Tamil. That too makes him an outsider in the Movement, but at the same time he is the symbol of continuity. Due to the political situation I was not able to visit Jaffna personally, but what I had heard indicated, that most of the current Sarvodaya work had to stop there. Nearly no village is registered at Shramadana Societies from the Tamil part. The whole of Sarvodaya was deeply moved, when the army shot dead the pregnant wife and the parents of the Vavuniya Tamil district coordinator, a very devoted young man. Normal activities had to be replaced by *relief work*. Sarvodaya is very active in distributing food, providing shelter, giving medical help etc., specially in the refugee camps around Anuradhapura, Batticola etc. They help everyone. The *second step* was to work in the plantation sector together with UNICEF and to initiate there a cretche-establishing programme together with a training-programme for cretche attendants. In Norton Bridge a special centre was established for this purpose and it is headed by Ms. Leela Jayasekere, an old woman, who according to my mind together with Mrs. Ariyaratne is the leading force within Sarvodaya, that concern women. Sarvodaya as a whole has a huge number of serving women as pre-school teachers, but fingers of my hand are more than enough to count those women, who have responsible leading tasks. Nearly 1000 cretches were newly established or restored in the plantation sector. When the financial initial aid of UNICEF is over, the costs will be met by the Plantation Cooperations, which are owned by the State, because they used the mothers as pluckers. Within the plantation sector, there are several areas with a mixed Tamil-Sinhala population, who are working and living together. Here Sarvodaya sees a starting point for integration, for example the trainers of the preschool teachers are about half Santhalese and half Tamil. There 20 women are a very good example, how human beings, who are different can live together in peace and cooperative harmony. I have made a special study of these unmarried women, who divided into groups move from plantation to plantation in order to give an on-the job-training to the preschool-teachers in their existing situation.

The *third step* are special actions undertaken by Sarvodaya in order to bring about an understanding between the two communities. Mr. Chandrasena is the Co-ordinator of the Shanti Sena Amity Project, which regularly holds camps with young people of both communities. These camps are taking place till today now mainly in the plantation sector, because the political situation makes travelling insecure. The programme consists mainly of three parts: (1) Social interaction and integration, activities such as games, shramadana camps, camp fires, singing of songs in different languages, entertainment etc., (2) Gaining theoretical knowledge through lecture sessions and discussions, (3) In-life-experience, that means that a Tamil is living in Sinhala family and a Simhala living in a Tamil family. I have the impression that the in-life-experience is the most important, but also the most difficult to achieve, because housing conditions poverty and fearful parents do not allow easily this great event. Nonetheless about 400 young people have had this experience for about three months in the past. Talking to some of the participants I found, that they had come closer, they had learnt a few words of each others language, they saw that their religious customs are similar and that their hopes, dreams are very much the same; they want to leave poverty behind.

Such an exchange programme seems to me very useful, but it looks as if it is already too late or already too early for each programmes. They are only a drop of water on a hot stone.

The Sarvodaya Movement is a strong force, also politically, although it doesn't want to interfere in politics. Rumours are going around that Ariyaratne should run for presidentship, because the country needs a figure with an integrative force, who is not bound by party politics. From all sides, including from the moderate Tamil side, which doesn't want an independent state, people are approaching Ari to do something—what should and what can he and his Movement do?

I think the most noticeable event is the starting of a peace march on 6th December, 1983 at Kataragama, an auspicious place, holy for Hindu, Buddhist and Moslems. The idea was to walk from Kataragama hundred of miles to Jaffna and people joining the march. This march should have shown the unity of the country, but it was stopped by the government, although it had first allowed the march. When the religious ceremonies were over at Kataragama and already 5000 people assembled, the government asked Ari to stop the march, because his life and the lives of his followers were in danger. They threatened Ari by thugs who were hidden in the woods through which the white dressed unarmed pilgrims would have had to go. Ari stopped the march.

This didn't stop Ari's activities altogether, but from that time his relationship to the government was no longer as good as it was before. In March this year the Sarvodaya Movement organized another peace march to the Adam's Peak, a mountain which is holy for believers of Buddhism, Hinduism, Islam and even Christianity. Although Sarvodaya was the leading force to organize this march, their name appeared nowhere in the headlines of the newspapers—it was organized under the leadership of the government—otherwise it would not take place.

In the village lots of small peace marches are going on, poojas for peace are conducted, lectures and exhibitions on peace take place, language courses are established to bring about at least an understanding language-wise, mixed groups are fighting together against drugs, liquor and gambling, plants are planted and distributed as symbols of peace, creation of friendly ties between the two groups is tried between schoolchildren, youth and trainees, peace and literature on peace is created etc. —but there is still no peace. It is true that all these methods are not very effective, but what else can Sarvodaya and Ari do? I want to close my description of the peace activities by telling you a true event. A young Buddhist Bhikku was invited in 1985 to Madras to a Youth Meeting organized by the Christian Type of Ashram Taize. Naturally, in Madras the majority of the participants were Christians and also Tamils. The Sinhalese, Buddhist Bhikku attracted a fair amount of attention and were attacked a lot as being responsible for the civil war in Sri Lanka. The Bhikku said: "Kill me, if this can solve your problems." His statement was followed by complete silence.

I want to finish with answering my third question: What are the future perspectives of Sarvodaya in Sri Lanka?

There is no answer to the question about Sarvodaya, without an answer to the question: What is the future of Sri Lanka? Although there is no solution visible at the moment, I think that in the time to come some more violence will take place and a situation similar to Ireland will establish or a division like Zypre, whatever will happen politically, I think that if Ariyaratne is asked to join politics he should give it a try—it would be a unique chance to try to put Sarvodaya philosophy in everyday politics. That the closest friends of Gandhi and he him-self were not in favour of politics should not be an example for Ariyaratne as he has found an independent Movement and he might be able to implement a bit of it for all Sri Lankans.

Although Ariyaratne is surely belonging in the category of a charismatic leader, I don't think that his Movement must cease to exist with his death. His Movement is according to my opinion no longer a Movement alone, but it is a *moving institution*. In his close circle there are several persons who could replace him. The biggest threat to the existence of Sarvodaya is the lack of money. About 90% of the income is coming from foreign donor agencies, who are more and more reluctant to pay, because Sarvodaya should become self-sufficient. Can it ever become self-sufficient?

I think it can't. All efforts in this direction with income generating projécts are giving employment, but are nearly never able to gain a surplus, which could finance the Movement, which needs roughly 500000 American Dollars, just to finance the basic structure. The reason is that in no country of the world welfare and education activities are earning money, they only cost money. If you look back in the past of Europe and America, you can see very clearly, that mostly the churches took the initial steps to provide schooling etc, but then the state took over on a large scale. Sarvodaya in Sri Lanka is supplementing state activities, but the state will never be able to finance all the activities of the Movement nor does it want to do it.

Otherwise the State has learnt from Sarvodaya and now conducts shramadana camps etc. on its own, not so efficiently as Sarvodaya. But none-theless. It looks to me as if the Sri Lankan State is looking towards the Singapore development Model and in the days to come, they might not like to have a strong opponent to this type of development.

Even if the structure of the Movement will fail, that doesn't say that the message is wrong—it will only show that loving kindness, compassion, sympathy and equanimity must be practiced more by the individuals in order to walk towards a Sarvodaya society. Buddhism was put into existence in India, but nearly vanished in its country of origin. Possibly the torch with the flame of Sarvodaya was also given to Sri Lanka and might possibly flourish there.

I want to close with a word of Gandhi, which Dr. Aryaratne also likes to quote:

"Satisfaction lies in the effort, not in the attainment. Full effort is full victory."[7]

References:

1. Ariyaratne, A.T., *Religious Path to Peace and Building a Just World*, Lecture 1984.
2. Dasgupta, Sugata, *Sarvodaya in Sri Lanka*, Salt Lake City, Calcutta 1982, p. 10.
3. Statistics are taken from *Sarvodaya*, 19th Annual Service Report Moratuwa, p. 711.
4. Kantowsky Detlef, *Sarvodaya The Other Development*, Vikas Publishing House, Delhi, 1980.
5. Ariyaratne, quoted from Kantowsky, *Sarvodaya The Other Development*, p. 77.
6. Statistics are quoted from: *Statistical Pocket Books of the Democratic Socialist Republic of Sri Lanka, 1984 and Sub-Asian-Info* No. 4/1986.
7. Ariyaratne: *New Approaches to Development, Building a Just World*, 1984, p. 19.

17

International Peace: Japan's Experience

Takaaki Pio Yasuoka*

Hony Director, Professor J.S. Mathur, distinguished scholars and Ladies and Gentlemen:

It is a great honor to participate in the International Seminar on Gandhi And Contemporary Ideologies Regarding Freedom and Equality on the occasion of celebration of Silver Jubilee of the Institute of Gandhian Thought and Peace Studies at University of Allahabad. Congratulations on your happy anniversary!

On the occasion of the International Peace Year this year, Japan marks her 30th year since the entry of the United Nations. It is therefore, a good opportunity today to reflect upon what Japan has done to achieve international cooperation toward peace and what Japan can do to foster international peace through non-violent means.

Post-war Japanese "Peace" Constitution

Our defeat in the last World War II is certainly blessing in disguise. A new path of Japan's militarism was prescribed clearly in the 1947 Constitution which set its peaceful and democratic state-building as well as nation-building as the prime goal of political development in wartorn Japanese society.

The most unique feature of the constitution is the Article 9, the provision completely renouncing war as an instrument of national policy. Here I quote:

"Aspiring sincerely to an international peace based on justice and order, the Japanese people forever renounce war as a sovereign right of the nation and the threat or use of force as means settling international disputes.

---

* Institute for the Study of Social Justice, Sophia University, Tokyo, Japan.
Published in *Journal of Gandhian Studies*, Vol. 14; January/April 1987.

In order to accomplish the aim of the preceding paragraph, land, sea, and air force, as well as other war potential, will never be maintained. The right of belligerency of the state will not be recognized."

This provision fully reflected the principles and objectives of the Potsdam Declaration of 1947. De-militarization, de-centralization and democracy, as what we call 3 D Policies of the Allied Powers (SCAP—supreme commander for allied powers), were implemented as definite step toward democratisation of Japan.

The sentiment and aspiration seeking for a new path of peace by the Japanese people who had been betrayed and experienced the horrors of war which include the early deaths of many young lives and victims of nuclear disasters through the action of government are clearly stipulated in the preamble of the Constitution. Here I quote :

"We, the Japanese people, desire peace for all time and deeply conscious of the high ideals controlling human relationship, and we have determined to preserve our security and existence, trusting in the justice and faith of the peace-loving peoples of the world. We desire to occupy an honoured place in an international society striving for the preservation of peace, and the banishment of tyranny and slavery, oppression and of intolerance for all time from the earth.... We, the Japanese people, pledge our national honor to accomplish high ideals and purposes with all our resources".

After the surrender of Japan, "democratisation" thus became the supreme symbol toward which, at least superficially, everyone channelled his efforts. Until the end of the Occupation of Japan by the Allied Power in 1952, critical attitudes toward Japanese traditional value were phenomenally observed. It is interesting to note that one prominent American scholar, Dr. Reischauer commented the inclusion of the above mentioned Article 9 of the new Constitution struck a responsive note in the hearts of the war-weary Japanese and contributed strongly pacifistic sentiments that have swept Japan ever since the war.

In the early part of the post-war period, a certain reality was reflected in the three propositions.

1) The anti-militarism of the Japanese people could effectively prevent militarization. The Japanese peace movement during the 1950s was most active crying in the wilderness to try to disseminate the message of

Hiroshima and Nagasaki where the reality of a nuclear age with instantaneous death of 200,000 citizens, which I deal later.

2) Out of devastated national economy, the economic rationalism for rehabilitation of the Japanese business would favour limited military expenditure. Take for example in the special war procurement in Korean War.

3) U.S. dominance over the Japanese military would make militarization less dangerous.

Cold War System in Asia and Japan

The emergence of the Cold War at the close of World War II in Europe sooner or later moved into the scene of Asia. The postwar state of confrontation and tension between the United States (US) and the Soviet (USSR) had meant to Japan a re-examination of US led Allied Powers occupation policy and forging Japan's alignment with the United States.

Let me just briefly refer to the content of the Cold War. For the US, the Cold War was a strategy of using threat to check, contain and roll back Soviet advances as the part of the outcome of World War II by assuming leadership of the capitalist world from Great Britain and France and to maintain American superiority over the USSR. The power diplomacy of the US meant Cold War for the USSR and "hot war" for the socialist countries in Asia, especially China, Vietnam and Korea. Asia was less important to Soviet security than even Europe. Thus Asia was never a primary battleground of the Cold War. The USSR had no major priority in East Asia. And the US never had any intention of going to war with the USSR. It was a policy of threats, rather than the use of force.

War began in Korea in June 1950. When the Korean War broke out, Japan was ordered to build new army to support indirectly the US forces to repair weapons and vehicles. Various Japanese industries seized the opportunity to start military production. The US and Japan concluded a treaty and established the US-Japan Security System, and the United States obtained the right to continue to stationing troops in Japan.

The then Chief of the Allied Powers, General D. MacArthur announced that Japan had to become the bulwark against communist aggression and in July 1950, on American initiative, the conservative-led Japanese government established the armed forces of 75,000. The conservative government was aware that this establishment of new military was incompatible with the war-renouncing clause of the 1947 Peace Constitution. The government therefore used willingly the label such as "the Police Reserve Force", or "*Military without military power*". It grew into the size of 200,000 men with tanks, artillery, destroyers, and over a thousand planes by the end of 1960s.

That is how Japan was drawn into a military alliance with the US as an integral link in the Cold War system.

The role of intellectual community—its impact on Overall Peace movement in 1950-60

Under these circumstances, however, we should not forget the fact that the Peace Issues Discussion Group which consisted of about 50 individuals including intellectuals and scientists ranging from Liberals to Marxists issued the joint statement on the problems of peace which undoubtedly *provided a theoretical and intellectual foundation* to the "overall peace" movement around 1950. Let me just briefly introduce to you its content on peace.

Chapter I. *Our Basic Thought on the Peace Issue*

1) *War as a Self-Defeating Means.* Here it says that there is no doubt that war has now become the *greatest evil* on earth. No other evil is as great as the evil of war. For all men of the world, the maintenance and consolidation of peace has become the primary objective without which *no other* value can be realized.

2) *Paradoxical Truth of the Nuclear Age.* Here it says that in the light of the tragic experience of our own country, it is only too clear what was the outcome of having sanctified war at the expense of peace for the sake of what was deemed to be the Divine cause.

....The spirit of our new Constitution, whereby we renounced our right to belligerency not only as a means of national policy but also as a means to any ends, might be viewed by some as a most impractical idealism. But this is the very attitude that is most firmly founded on the awareness of the reality of the modern war. I cut it short now due to space limitation.

Chapter II. *Conflict and Accommodation Between the "Two World"*

1. *Conflict between the "Two Worlds" re-examined.* Here it introduces conflict on three distinguishable levels, namely

a) the conflict between liberal democracy and communism as ideologies;

b) the conflict between the bloc of Western states with the United States and the United Kingdom as nucleus and the block of communist countries concerned around the Soviet Union;

c) the conflict between the United States and the Soviet Union as the super-powers of today. The statement warns that we must guard against confusing the three levels, for such a confusion can also lead to a dangerous way of thinking – the tendency to judge the problems of world politics and diplomacy not as a product of a composite of conditions but in terms of *a priori*.......

2. *Fallacy of the Inevitability of Armed Conflict.* Here it says that even though the external behaviour of the Soviet Union may appear from the outside extremely unpredictable, sober observers the world over are already in agree-ment that underlying behaviour are profound fear and suspicion concerning the formation of an anti-Soviet crusade by the capitalist countries...... In order to overcome such psychological obstacles on both sides of the "two worlds", we must open up free communications between the two as the first step.

3. *Conditions Promoting Coexistence.* Here the statement confirms that the "co-existence" of the two worlds is the basic requisite for peace... In order to effectively secure world peace, we must at the outset accept the existence of the "two worlds"¾in every sense. The most forceful representative and spokesman of Asian nations today asserting autonomy and independence is, Prime Minister Nehru of India. Concerning present Korean incident, he opposed all moves that might irritate Communist China and the Soviet Union, while making every effort to realize the representation of Communist China to the United Nations as a way to achieve a real settlement of the Korean incident and to restore the proper functions of the United Nations...... the fundamental principle of Nehru that disputes should always be settled by peaceful means reveals his penetrating insight into the nature of the modern war. At the same time, it is none other than

the expression of his boundless self-confidence regarding the historical position and mission of the Asian people. It appears that this move for inde-pendence exemplified by India will be, and must be, followed in the future, with certain variations, by other Asian peoples filled with youthful vigor.

4. *Again on Our Basic Thought*. Here it says that we are convinced that Japan must firmly maintain the policy of strictly avoiding interference or involve-ment in any international disputes... Under the existing conditions the policy of neutralism is the expression of the position of genuine self-reliance and independence for Japan...... To those who say that our position is fraught with difficulty, we can only admit it frankly and say, "Nevertherless".

This group sought "to determine the extent to which people's understanding could be gained in order to preserve pacifism" and aimed to develop "a national consensus" on pacifism. They embraced the following doctrine: "to think according to principles, to maintain a standpoint based on principles, and to act according to principles—in a word, to become a person of principles."

Anti-nuclear Weapons Mass Campaign

On 6 August 1947, in commemoration of the second anniversary of the atomic bombing, Hiroshima city issued its first "Peace Declaration". It expressed the fervent affirmation of peace that Hiroshima and Nagasaki, rising above their physical and spiritual wastelands of atomic "death and darkness", have continuously addressed to the whole world. Let me quote here in brief.

The citizens of Hiroshima will never be able to forget August 6, 1945. On that morning, exactly two years ago today, the first atomic bomb to be unleashed on a city in the history of mankind fell on Hiroshima........

Mankind must remember that August 6 was a day that brought a chance for world peace. This is the reason why we are now commemorating that day by solemnly inaugurating a festival of peace, despite the limitless sorrow in our minds.........

The horrible weapon brought about a "Revolution of Thought", which has convinced us of the necessity and the value of eternal peace........

Let us join to sweep away from this earth the horror of war, and to build a true peace.

Let us join in renouncing war eternally, and building a plan for world peace on this earth. (Source : *The Impact of the a=bomb,* 85, p. 195)

Such common voice of Hiroshima and Nagasaki appealing for peace and the abolition of nuclear weapons began to be heard and taken seriously only after the hydrogen bomb became a reality. Prior to that the Occupation's strict censorship had suppressed Japanese research on A-bomb damages and also stifled the free flow to the outside world of information on the realities of A-bomb damages and suffering. It was therefore the advent of the hydrogen bomb (United States, 1952; Soviet Union 1953) that finally impressed upon peoples throughout the world what nuclear arms really mean for the fate of the earth and for all its inhabitants.

On August 6, 1955, the first World Conference of Anti-Nuclear Weapons was held in Hiroshima and 50 thousand people gathered. The Japanese student groups such as the National Federation of All Students Government Association, established in 1948 sponsored the "All Japanese Students Rise Up Against Nuclear Wars" campaign in 1957 which involved more than 200 universities and over 350 thousand participants. Trade union such as the General Council of Trade Unions, the Japan Council against A & H Bombs and the Japan Congress against A & H Bombs were main organizers of World Conferences mentioned above.

Peace Movement of late 50s-70s

From the mid-sixties, the anti-Vietnam War campaign surged across the nation. People were opposed to the war itself and to the fact that the US bases in Japan were used for the war, but they were also afraid of the prospect that in the war escalation. Japan might become the main advance base for the war. A noteworthy development in this period was the establishment of the Japan 'Peace for Vietnam' Committee (Beheiren) which was a politically non-aligned citizen's league composed of 'ordinary' citizens, housewives, intellectuals, students and workers. By the end of 1965, the Beheiren mobilized more than 1.5 million people throughout Japan.

The anti-Vietnam war movement which flourished from the late sixties on to the seventies added a new character to Japanese peace movement. The peace movement hitherto had been built around the experience as victims of Hiroshima, Nagasaki and Bikini : a movement of refusal to ever be victims of war again. In the anti-Vietnam war movement Japan ceased to be viewed a mere victim and recognized that it was also an aggressor. Under the security arrangement between Japan and US, the Japanese government could not remain neutral concerning the Vietnam war. In return this indicated that Japan stood by the side of US and become another enemy of the Vietnamese people.

Furthermore people started to realize that the standard of living in Japan was not only something to be defended from the rage of war but that Japan's economic situation was supporting the whole structure which propelled the Vietnam invasion. This lead our peace activists to question the life-style of Japan. And furthermore this effort to see oneself through one's relationship with the people of the Third World was made simultaneously by people active in their community opposing development and environmental destruction.

The Rise of "Grass Roots Community Movements Today Opposing Environmental Pollution and Development"

It is rather important to refer at this point to the local movements opposing development and pollution. Because I note that the Japanese people *gradually* began to consider the meaning of culture and civilization being confronted with the post-war transformation of Japanese society. Sharp criticism of the rapid economic growth and industrial development (maldevelopment) came from localities such as from farmers and fisher-peoples living far from the metropolis.

Let me here consider the Minamata Disease (crippling disease due to environmental contamination known as the tragedy at Minamata in Kyushu island for example).

The damage from pollution was already obvious in the 1950s when Japan began reconstructing its industrial base. The people's movement in that period as I have just introduced to you, however, focused on political issues rather such as 'Ban the Atom and/or Hydrogen Bombs" or "Terminate the Japan-US Security Treaty". During the 1960's, however, local people began to rise against large-scale industrial development which resulted in environmental pollution. This movement spread gradually and, during the 1970s, people organized many *non-violent* direct action against such development.

In 1956, the Minamata Disease was discovered to be caused by organic mercury in the food chain. This poison, a by product of nitrogenous fertilizers, had been dumped with the wastewater into the sea by the manufacturer. The administration took the side of this polluting enterprise. People were reluctant to stand up and defend their rights. Since the latter part of the 1960s, people—mainly Minamata area residents—began organizing themselves in support of the ailing victims, demanding humane treatment. A ground swell of popular indignation grew against the polluting enterprise in the early part of the '70s. The first victory came in 1973 when the courts decided in favour of the patients' demands for compensation from the manufacturer. Citizens groups in support of the Minamata victims were composed of the *concerned individuals*. The aim of these organizations was simply to support the struggling Minamata patients. Groups in different areas acted independently of each other, yet together they formed a horizontal network, what I call *solidarity*. Grouping for solidarity is the case in point. "Symposia for Alternative Community Development" since then become a new style. This type of symposium may be regarded as a beginning of the people's school, or the people's seminar, where the people educate each other and learn from each other, what is called *conscientization process* Each individual local movement with the will to universalise its ideas and experience, should on its own initiative, call upon other local movements, visit them actually, and directly learn through dialogue and study. This is, what is called, *Exposure Program for Peace and Development.*

Japan's Contribution to effectively establish relationship between Disarmament and Development

I have dealt so far the post-war Japanese pacifism in brief how it evolved from the people's security perspectives. To this end, I would like to discuss Japan's contribution to effectively establish relationship between Disarmament and Development.

In 1978, at the General Assembly of the United Nations Special Session devoted to disarmament, the following position was explicitly endorsed.

"There is a close relationship between disarmament and development. Progress in the former would help greatly to the realization of the latter. Therefore, resources released as a result of the implementation of disarmament measures should be devoted to the economic and social development of all nations and contribute to the bridging of the economic gap between developed and developing countries." (*Source:* Study on the relationship between disarmament and development: Report of the Secretary General, Thirty-sixth Session, 5 October, 1981, p. 11).

And the main conclusion of this report is that an effective relationship between disarmament and development *can and must be established.* Let me here clarify the term 'development' used in the report. As we understand very well today, *development is another name of peace.* Development involves the opportunity and responsibility for full participation in the economic and social processes and a universal share in its benefits as a result of profound economic and social changes in society besides the need for sustained economic growth.

The report warns that the danger of war is currently growing, owing to the new dimensions assumed by armaments competition quantitative and qualitative, conventional and nuclear and to the use of threat of use of force by State in non-conformity with the principles of the United Nations Charter. The greatest danger to all mankind, and one that would put its very existence in jeopardy is the risk of any conflict leading to the use of nuclear weapons. *The need to prevent this risk is becoming all the more urgent.*

The report recommends that *Governments create the necessary pre-requisites, including preparations and, where appropriate, planning, to facilitate the conversion of resources freed by disarmament measures to civilian purposes, especially to meet urgent economic and social needs, in particular, in the developing countries.* The report also recommends among other things that Governments undertake to inform their own people of the social and economic consequences of the arms and the potential benefits of disarmament measures. And finally, the report calls for the important role to be played by non-governmental organizations to continuously showing a strong interest in awareness of public information and education activities to the social and economic consequences of the arms race and to the corresponding benefits of disarmament.

Considering the present political economic milieu of Japan, there exist many elements we should have a critical self-analysis of our own country when we desire genuinely how we function in the peaceful evolution towards a united world order in which this UN report clearly suggest.

The Japanese government officially announced *the three non-nuclear principles which state that nuclear weapons will not be produced, possessed or introduced into this country.* I personally believe strangely that as a legacy of the demilitarisation and democratisation policy taken by the Allied Powers right after the World War II as I mentioned at the beginning of this paper, the Peace Constitution of Japan in its preamble and Article 9 clearly define de-nuclearization of Japan in the present context of the world situation with the faithful implementation of the three non-nuclear principles. It has also factors that make the issue universal. That is to say, the legalization and internationa-lization of the three non-nuclear principles as a concrete approach to establishing a non-nuclear zone in Asia. Thus, Japan can contribute to the world.

I personally believe strongly that the Peace Constitution of Japan in its preamble and Article 9 clearly define a new path of *unarmed neutrality*. These two major principles are my commitment for the positive peace to be attained. There should be always a hope¾That is a spirit of challenge of peace.

In order that the university may fulfil successfully its educational function in the peaceful evolution towards a unified world, a program that the UN report suggest and recommended should be planned well that would convey to the students the very necessary knowledge and principles for the furtherance of international peace.

I will work for it, and why don't you join with us in this endeavour.

I thank you very much.

18

Gandhiji and the Concept of Power

J. P. Pathirana*

To think of Gandhiji, as essentially a freedom fighter however inspired is to do him less than justice. He was above all a champion of human dignity. He recognised political freedom as an essential, though by no means sufficient, condition for dignified existence. But he had no use for political freedom if it countenanced the exploitation of one social class by another. He once said "I am not anti-Government but I am anti-untruth, anti-humbug and anti-injustice." Words have power and thus Gandhiji without any fear and favour uttered in no uncertain terms; words with brevity and courage, however the authority be mighty or great. He spoke words with emotion and strength and in this same strain lived up to it and put into concrete action that power into reality¾that is the greatness of Mahatma.

Violence; he was convinced, was the root of all evil, so that opposing violence could not yield any good. His unique contribution lay in demonstrating how Satyagraha or "Soul-force pure and simple" as he puts it, could be used to defeat violence. For him non-violence was not a matter of mere expediency, it was both an article of faith and a way of life. As he repeatedly explained, non-violence was nothing but truth in action and power. And how valiantly he strove to make his own life the perfect embodiment of truth in action and this unfailing concept of power.

The Satyagraha Saga began in 1893 with Gandhiji's ejection at Maritzburg from a first class railway compartment, despite having a valid ticket. He forthwith set about organizing the Indians of South Africa so they could fight for their rights. By the time the humiliating Transvaal Asiatic Registration Act was passed in 1907, he had become the accepted leader of the Indian Community in South Africa. The non-violent struggle, he launched

---

* Managing Editor, 'DANA' Jayanthipura, Battaramulla, Sri Lanka.

Published in *Journal of Gandhian Studies*, Vol. 11; October 1983/January 1984.

against this Act lasted eight tortuous years and ended in his first major triumph, obliging General Smuts to concede that Gandhiji, was a great man, in whose shoes he himself was unworthy to stand.

Gandhiji though small in stature possessed an enormous power within in his heart and soul to fight any aggression with firm determination and resolve with his powerful armament of truth and non-violence.

In the words of Martin Luther King as explained in "Pilgrimage of non-violence", where he so rightly admitted "It was in this Gandhian emphasis on love and non-violence that I discovered the method for social reform that I had been seeking for so many months.......In accepting this responsibility, my mind was drifting to that Sermon on the Mount and the Gandhian method of non-violent resistance. This principle became the guiding spirit of our movement. Christ furnished the spirit and motivation and Mahatma furnished the method."

The perennial source of power were these two elements of Truth and Ahimsa (non-violence). Gandhiji was not a visionary nor a revivalist harking back to a past Golden Age. He had the advantage of knowing and coming into close contact with the modern civilizations. But, unlike others he refused to be dazzled and overawed by the fantastic progress made by science and technology during the last hundred years or so. With far-sightedness rare among political leaders, and even among religious teachers and thinkers, he clearly analysed the evils inherent in the materialistic modern culture as represented by the industrialised West, and boldly criticized it. Gandhiji's insight has not been unerring and his insistence on non-violence, which he always advocated as power absolute, has now become the only correct remedy for achieving world peace and progress of mankind. He deprecated the craze for the machinery and the incessant search for endless sophistication in gadgetry for the satisfaction of a number of artificially created wants. Simple living and high thinking are good not only for individuals, but also for Communities and Nations. Modern man has lost his way and does not know his destination as a species, which is endowed with not only with intellect but spiritual aspiration also. Material plenty and abundance of creature comfort rapidly provided by modern science and technology even for one and all, cannot be the sole aim of all human endeavour and existence. Gandhi's concept of non-violence and the awakening of man 'Paurushodaya' had been the perennial source of power, which is inherent in man within himself, if only a proper awakening is stimulated as advocated by the great Mahatma. And Gandhi and his ideology are unique in this particular respect. This has been Sarvodaya's credo as practical in Sri Lanka and propagated by its leader of the Sarvodaya Shramadana movement, Dr. A.T. Ariyaratne, popularly known as the 'little Gandhi' of Sri Lanka. The word Sarvodaya was coined by Mahatma Gandhi, it is a compound of two Sanskrit words, 'Sarva' which means all, and "Udaya" upliftment or welfare or prosperity. We are really deeply indebted to Gandhiji for this unique inspiration and his concept of power through "Sarvodaya" which has now spread into global proportions. With that unique Gandhian thought besides the total awakening of human personalities the "Paurushodaya" we have in turn awakened the human families "Kutumbodaya", to village communities "Gramodaya", to urban groups "Nagarodaya", to national communities "Deshodaya" and lastly to the word community "Vishvodaya". For no other current ideology, neither democratic Capitalism, nor democratic Socialism, nor dictatorial Communism, places before mankind the light and noble ideal of moral and spiritual development in preference to more material progress.

If individuals, whole communities and even Nations decide to observe as far as possible Truth and Non-violence in their relations with each other, most of the problems faced by modern societies whether in the developed or developing countries would just melt away. Untruth in trade, business, courts of law, settlement of marriages, educational institutions, politics, international diplomacy and way plays havoc in human relations and distorts values. Gandhiji was no doubt a Mahatma, a spiritually great soul but, he was different from other religious leaders. He did not subscribe to maintaining the social and economic hierarchical system; he believed in a just and more egalitarian one.

In very unambiguous words Gandhi once remarked "By the non-violent method, we seek not to destroy capitalism......If capital is power, so is work.... Either power can be used destructively or creatively."

Mahatma Gandhi, describing his life and findings as a voyage of experimening with Truth, began his theological analysis of contemporary reality with the words which always gave him strength and power. "There is no God than Truth". The only means for the realization of Truth is Ahimsa (love). Gandhiji set a criterion which is sublimely religio-philosophical, from which he analysed events both as they flow Truth and as they lead up to Truth. In humility as a seeker, Gandhiji did not make claims to having found the whole meaning of Truth, but ever kept his sights clear, never closing the doors to continuing exploration.

Gandhiji's method and approach of Truth and non-violence which were the two cardinal concepts of power which was within him should be adopted hook, line and sinker for the settlement of all disputes and let us adopt this Gandhiji thought for a sane socio-economic development and for a better and a peaceful tomorrow in this modern world.

On the one hand, Gandhi incarnates India's traditional idea of a Saint, but on the other he belongs to the most modern type of mass lealder; venerated, emulated and followed for the benefit and welfare of mankind.

This humble tribute to the Great Gandhiji, I can but only close with the words of Albert Einstein, "Generations to come, it may be, will scarcely believe that such a one as this ever in flesh and blood walked upon this earth."

19

Gandhian Insights — Religion and Peace

Bishop Dr. Karoly Toth*

I would venture humbly to examine the foci in the Gandhian thinking which bear on progressive Christian insights. Realizing the fact, that the stature of Gandhi's life and thought cannot be categorized in any religious or philosophical mould, one can yet dare to seriously consider the manner in which Gandhi adversely reacted to the Christian message which was presented to him in a Western colonial framework. However, Gandhi affirmed that, he revered the New Testament and was touched by the Sermon on the Mount "which went straight to my heart". Christians need to recognize that what was repellent to Gandhi in the Christianity as practised by them—their militancy, their record in the spheres of discrimination on the basis of race, colour and caste and their attitude to peace etc.—was quite understandable.

An important bifurcation exists in the stream, which flows from Christ, whose sacrifice on the Cross Mahatma Gandhi highly regarded. We would even describe these as being two opposing traditions. One of these traditions in Christianity we have already spelt out is basically detrimental to the Gospel. It is this tradition of distorted view of Christianity, which Gandhi confronted and rejected. The other tradition, which could be described as enlightened, seeks to work out in theological terms the Gospel as calling for the total development of individuals and nations, through liberation, mutual understanding, harmony and peace. It was unfortunate that the Mahatma in his lifetime did not have the opportunity to encounter the pacific understanding of the Gospel. It is here that I wish to offer tribute to Gandhiji for his mainstream discoveries in the spheres of religious experience as they filter through political, economic and social channels in a

* President, Christian Peace Conference, Hungary.

Published in *Journal of Gandhian Studies,* Vol. 10; October 1982/ January 1983.

given situation, bearing a posture similar to the searchings of International Christian Peace Conference.

Before we embark on this exploration, let me acquaint the readers with some background information regarding the Christian Peace Conference, which operates in over 80 countries today with peace thrusts in all continents. Born at the height of the Cold War in Europe in 1958, the Christian Peace Conference activates with unflagging zeal the demands of peace and justice, based on the principles of the Gospel, bearing on global issues of the arms race, and disarmament, poverty and its degrading concomitants, racism, racial discrimination and apartheid and strives for the elimination of evil that stunt human development, while projecting ingredients for the wholeness and well-being of humankind.

Mahatma Gandhi, describing his life and findings as a voyage of experimenting with Truth, began his theological analysis of contemporary reality with the words, "There is no God than Truth. The only means for the realization of Truth is Ahimsa (Love)", Gandhi set a criterion which is sublimely religio-philosophical, from which he analysed events both as they flow from Truth and as they lead up to Truth. In humility, as a seeker, Gandhi did not make claims to having found the whole meaning of Truth, but ever kept his sights clear, never closing the doors to continuing exploration. The search in the Christian Peace Conference is of a similar nature and it is in such an enterprise that we honour the memory of Gandhi. Where we differ is that we confess through an act of faith that Christ is "the Way, the Truth and the Life". But, Christians, however, cannot make any claims to be in possession of the whole Truth, for they are but pilgrims exploring and manifesting in their lives the Truth revealed in Christ.

This incessant search for Truth led Gandhi to two experiences. It brought home to him the fact that the march towards Truth must be on the road to self-purification. Conquest of anger, selfishness, hatred etc. is central. Gandhi's words cut to the deep: "A man who is swayed by passion may have good enough intentions, may be truthful in word, but he will never find the Truth. A successful search for Truth means complete deliverance from the dual throng such as of love and hate, happiness and misery",—as it is written in his autobiography. One realizes self-purification as a sine-quo-non in the search for Truth, and sees how closely it relate to Christian principles.

In the second of these experiences, we in the Christian Peace Conference find close kinship with Gandhi's thinking. "To see the universal and all-pervading Truth face to face, one must be able to love the meanest of creation as one-self. And, a man who aspires after that cannot afford to keep out of any field of life. That is why my devotion to Truth has drawn me into the field of politics; and I can say without the slightest hesitation, and yet in all humility, that those who say that religion has nothing to do with politics do not know what religion means." It is therefore, no wonder that Gandhi stood in the vanguard for swaraj, that he underwent much pain and agony both in his struggle against British imperialism and Hindu-Muslim communal conflict. Using the weapons of fasting, prayer and non-violence (ahimsa), he wrote in his weekly paper, "Harijan": "All the religions of the world describe God pre-eminently as the Friend of the friendless, the help of the helpless and the Protector of the weak. Who can be more friendless or helpless or weaker than the forty million or more Hindus of India, classified as untouchables?" "Harijan" means "children of God" which was Gandhi's name for the untouchables.

From the foregoing we can draw out three valid drives of the Christian Peace Conference, which are closely allied both to Mahatma Gandhi's thinking and our service for Peace in the CPC.

1) We affirm with Gandhi in the unity of humankind. This is not an outcome of a belief only, but the fact that beyond all artificial divisive factors is the basic human person, which is a commonality. Arising from the fundamental basic, we need to accept the unity of entire humankind, irrespective of religious, political, ideological, colour, racial, national, cultural and linguistic barriers. Without attempting to moralize, one has to confess that such an understanding leading to the realization of the unity of humankind has to be gained in an over-whelming and tremendous love for human beings as children of God Himself.

2) Our work in the Christian Peace Conference draws us to the increasing conviction, which was basic to Gandhi's thinking that religious experience of God as "Truth cannot end as an ethereal endeavour but be footed in religious faith in dynamic relation to political and social objectives. It is this factor galvanizes the Christian Peace Conference to making its stances clear. Such stands can be stated as follows:

— the preservation of peace and peaceful resolution of international disputes without recourse to violence;

— general and total disarmament, justice and cooperation among all peoples based on the principle of coexistence;

— social and economic structures that will make oppression and exploitation impossible, ensuring a life worthy of the human person. The CPC support new national economic orders and a new International Economic Order. The CPC is in solidarity with popular liberation movements struggling for national independence, against oppression, racial discrimination, hunger and illiteracy. It is redundant to repeat that all these stances are the direct outcome of religious commitment as is found in the basic Gandhian principles.

3. Gandhi advocated the unity of word and deed in his concept of "Satyagraha"— "Satya"—Truth and "Agraha" firmness which was Gandhi's designation for struggle. The weapons of satyagraha are Ahimsa (Love), self-restraint (brahmachari), silence, fasting, meditation, prayer and discipline. Gandhi confessed "it was the New Testament which really awakened me to the rightness and value of the real beauty of doing good against evil. When I read the New Testament, I was simply overjoyed, and found my own opinion confirmed where I least expected it." Gandhi never permitted divorcing the instruments of Satyagraha one from another, but created the whole as a single package of indissoluble unity motivating faith and action.

The Christian Peace Conference has through the years endeavoured to do away with the gulf that exists between words and deeds. It is tragic to witness leading world politicians make noble pronouncements, which are never translated to deeds. Such situations only bring tragedy and death to human survival. We need men and women whose words pass into deeds and whose actions come out of deep religious commitment. Such men and women are loved and feared. Such persons cannot be bought but they always shine incorrupt. They are dedicated sons and daughters in the struggle.

This humble tribute to Gandhiji I can but only close with the words of Einstein: "Generations to come, it may be, will scarcely believe that such a one as this ever in flesh and blood walked upon this earth."

"For me humanitarian service, or rather service of all is religion. And I draw no distinction between such religion and politics. Indeed, I cannot conceive a life full of service without its touching politics....... I believe that the time is fast coming when politician will cease to fear the religion of humanity and humanitarian will find entrance into political life indispensable for full service."

Collected Works of Mahatma Gandhi, Vol.25, pp. 52-53.

20

Sarvodaya: Gandhi's Alternative Development Strategy for Today's World

Peter Kempadoo*

Throughout history, there have always been men diligently searching for meaning of life; Who Am I? Whither I Go?

There are those whose searches have led them to leave their communities and withdraw to some form of seclusion: a mountain top, a forest clearing, a desert island—where they hope to concentrate exclusively and meditate on what they perceive as self-realisation. Lets call this Way One:

And let's say Way Two is for those thronging millions of humanity with a religious turn of mind, who instead of secluding themselves, remain in their communities among their fellow-men; committed to a search for meaning of life. Like those in Way One, they too are seeking salvation—their own personal salvation. Many on this track might also achieve their goal, proudly so; and, again like those in Way One, without having to bother themselves about their fellow men 'who sit outside the gate. Our Way Two-ers are those who remain physically in the rough-and-tumble of society—but isolate themselves morally and spiritually.

Then there are those who while pursuing their personal solution within society do not shut their eyes to the suffering of their fellow men. But in their way—Way Three—they claim their conscience when facing the reality (of human suffering, by resorting to the giving of alms: feed the beggar, run the soup-kitchen, entertain the orphan—plaster the sores of society but leave the status-quo well alone !

Way Four is for those who might or might not be concerned with personal salvation (of soul), but are very concerned about the inequalities

---

* Sarvodaya Development Education Organisation, Guyana, South America.
Published in *Journal of Gandhian Studies*, Vol. 10; October 1982/January 1983.

within our communities. The way out, many of these feel, is the Revolution: nothing short of smashing through the whole rotten structures that enmesh man. And since, they argue, to do anything to mitigate human suffering *now* might only shore-up the present state of things and thus help put off the coming of the day of the revolution, they turn away from service to the unfortunate ones, the 'downpressed'. Agitation is their way.

All these four Ways have been tossed about on Planet Earth for a good long time. And yet we realise only too well the mess in which man and society still dwell. We must be on the search for alternatives; a Way Five.

Sarvodaya as conceived by Mahatma Gandhi, seems to be one such Way Five: a purposive blend of the best intentions of the Ways One to Four; a way which searches for meaning of life, but starts with the conviction that the salvation (or well-being) of oneself is inextricably bound-up with the well-being of all; a way through which man can strive for his personal self attainment without isolating himself; do something within his community to meet the challenge of the *here-and-now* suffering but in such manner that would not impede the development of a social consciousness as to the need for society to transform itself into one in which there would be no need for alms-giving; a new society in which people can translate their 'religious truths' into public values, a society in which "shall rest perpetually a system that will provide a new race, where poverty and crime and helplessness cannot enter." Sarvodaya's Way Five even provides the Revolution: but in new terms, so beautifully put by Charles Reich in his book "The Greening of America": "There is a revolution coming. It will not be like revolution of the past. It will originate with the individual and with culture, and it will change the political structure only as its final act. It will not require violence to succeed and it cannot be successfully resisted by violence......Its ultimate creation will be a new and enduring wholeness and beauty—a renewed relationship of man to himself, to other men, so society, and to the land......At the heart of everything is what we shall call a change of consciousness. This means a 'new head'—a new way of living—a new man. This is what the new generation has been searching for and what it has started achieving."

GENESIS

The word Sarvodaya was coined by Mahatma Gandhi, it is a compound of two Sanskrit words: *Sarva* which means all, and *Udaya*—

upliftment or welfare or prosperity. Therefore Sarvodaya really means the upliftment or welfare or prosperity of ALL.

Gandhi first used the word Sarvodaya in a booklet he published in his own language (Gujarati) after he was inspired by an essay by the Englishmen, John Ruskin. This essay called "Unto This Last", was based on a parable from the Christian Bible, from the Gospel according to Matthew, Chapter 20, verses 1-16: concerning the owner of a planation and his hiring of labourers to work in his vineyard.

In his parable, Jesus made the Master of the Vineyard declare, "I will give unto this last, even unto thee." The emphasis of Ruskin's essay is certainly that the ideal Society is one in which there is concern for ALL: even "Unto this last", that is, the neediest and the humblest. (Wasn't the essence of this parable also a forerunner of the maxim: from each according to his ability, to each according to his needs?)

Mahatma Gandhi used the word Sarvodaya to describe the principles that he felt should guide us in our efforts to build ourselves, our communities and nations. He had arrived at these principles of Sarvodaya society on the basis of his studies, his observation and his experiments with Truth and Non-Violence. He felt very strongly that the soundest foundation on which societies should be built were the qualities of Truth, love and Compassion in both our personal and public lives. The theory of trusteeship, elimination of exploitation in every shape and form; a classless society which offers no privileges by birth or wealth or talent; mutual cooperation and not individual competition being the driving force of motivation and behaviour; and above all, securing the welfare of all without any distinction whatsoever by race, religion, political affiliation, or else; these may be said to be the highlights of the Sarvodaya Society envisioned by Gandhi.

Indeed our Caribbean author, Arnold Apple, summarises the same vision of society, when he writes— "We must be able to close the gate of unfairness, racialism, untruthfulness and selfishness. To say that we are equal in every respect is indeed a misguided thought, but we must find a system to give every man the initiative and right to perform in his fullest capacity.....a system to make us seek out and discover new attitude in which we could move to transform our selfish talents into usefulness, and eventually a progressive nation."

Its Application

Sarvodaya then is the application of the principle of Non-Violence in the transformation of societies: from their present forms which are mostly exploitative and imbalanced: towards a more balanced and equalitarian form in which could become enshrined the principle of 'Social Justice for ALL.'

"Economic equality is the master key to Non-violent independence", wrote the Mahatma. "Working for economic equality means abolishing the eternal conflict between capital and labour. It means the levelling down of the few rich in whose hands is concentrated the bulk of the nation's wealth on the one hand, and levelling up of the semi-starved naked millions on the other. A non-violent system of government is clearly an impossibility, so long as the wide gulf between the rich and the hungry millions persists."

A recent publication by the World Council of (Christian) Churches (by Dr. Francisco Cato, the Brasilian theologian and private financial consultant) stresses the same point thus: "As a general rule, therefore, we may say that economic disorder apparent amongst other things in the violation of the underlying ethical imperatives of social life, cannot be directly tackled with moral weapons alone. The justice demanded by morality must equip itself with instruments of a strictly economic nature of it is to transform the basic mechanisms of the system and ensure that economic activity is integrated into it in a way which respects the deep ethical imperative of which we are increasingly conscious today. These instruments are precisely the alternative proposal we are looking for; although initially inspired by the concern for justice and the right of peoples, they cannot be other than economic".

The most disadvantaged section of the community being the economically poor, it is obvious that no equalitarian society could evolve without the poor taking part in the evolving process; and for this sector to take part, focus must be put on raising their economic status to an acceptable level.

However, as it should be for all the other sectors of society, if an acceptable level of economic status is to be reached and maintained for the disadvantaged sector, it is desirable that it should be self-sustaining:

"Wherein thou appliest charity, and it be not self-sustaining, judgment is rendered against thee.

Wherein thou appliest charity and it be self-sustaining; judgment is rendered in the favor.

Thou shalt go to the foundation of things, and go systematically.

Thy efforts shall not be single-handed, but thou shall unite with others; and together, ye shall provide a remedy against poverty.

Thou mayst feed three drunkards' families, and flatter Thyself thou hast done charity worthily; but if thou has not done that which will make them no longer need of charity, thou hast done little.

Another man may not feed them, but he may reform them, and put them in the way to be self-sustaining. Such a man will have done a hundred-fold greater charity.

To open the way for employment and industry, this is the greatest of all charity. For, by these avenues, charity will not be needed, even for the aged, nor for orphans.

It is not sufficient that ye feed and cloth little ones; but ye shall teach them a trade and occupation, and given them learning, so that, when they are grown, they can sustain themselves.

But, even yet, your work is not the highest; but ye shall so provide them, that they will not only be self-supporting, but that they shall be willing and capable of rescuing others as they were rescued.

Let your charity be not for a year, nor for a hundred years; but, be ye the corner-stones, founding places on earth where shall rest perpetually a system that will provide a new race, where poverty and helplessness cannot enter."

OAHSPE's Book of Judgment

CREDO

If we are to be faithful to the fullest definition of non-violence, a system must be allowed to evolve genuinely through participation by people at all levels, without coercion in any shape of form¾whether such coercion is précised by governments or political, religious, economic, military or other entities with vested self-interest.

No blue prints—not in socio economic targeting, nor methodology—are necessary as advance preparation for such work in social transformation other than respect for 'grass-root' people's intelligence, experiences and contribution to their own development plans. This, the heart of the Sarvodaya philosophy (and genuine democracy), could be summed up in another way, poignantly set out in the words of an ancient poet :

Go in search of your people

Love them

Learn from them

Plan with them

Serve them

Begin with what they know

Build on what they have.

(This is very much contrary to the usual methods of political parties which design development plans, in accordance with some ideology, and then expect people to fit into them and carry them out¾whether those plans are acceptable or not; in some cases they might even be diametrically opposed to people's cultural sensitivities, economic priorities and so on).

If we think along these lines it naturally follows that the main characteri-stics of Sarvodaya work are discipline of thought and a wide sharing of authority. In the present state of things in the world in general it seems that the Sarvodaya way is the way out of our dilemma. If we are to hope to re-build our communities on the principles of brotherly love, community workers must be fully committed to the concept of service to people and respect forpeople's rights, without any thought of coercing them into pre-conceived moulds, however admirable and intellectually satisfying these moulds might be perceived.

The Sarvodaya ideal could also be expressed in this way:

"Turn inward to that which unifies all—not intellect but the spirit—and then to devise and put into operation new forms and modes of economic and social life that will truly and vigorously express that spirit".

Richard Gregg – "Voluntary Simplicity"

What greater gift to humanity could a Brother-man, Mahatma Gandhi, have bequeathed, than the SARVODAYA WAY!

21

Gandhi and Conflictology

Johan Galtung*

In this paper the approach that is chosen is the study of Gandhi as a theoretician, and above all a practitioner, a *Karmayogi*—a man of action, not merely meditation—in the field of conflict. It is an effort to analyze Gandhi's implicit and explicit Satyagraha as a contribution to the theory and practice of behaviour in-group struggle from a social science point of view. By this we mean, loosely, that we want to see what Gandhi wrote and what he did in the framework of a theory of conflict. The concern is not with the relationship between various parts of what Gandhi thought and practiced, but with writings, and action-reports, that seem to have a direct bearing on social conflict. Ideally, our basis should have been the projected eighty volumes of *Collected Works*, but much can be said, fortunately, on a less complete basis.

This should then be distinguished from a study of the subjective and objective role of Gandhi during his life-time, and particularly during that segment in space and time—South Africa and India, 1893-1948—where Gandhi enacted his principles into practice, reformulated them, and built on them as a result of his "experiments with truth", Gandhi's real, deepest intentions and motivations, as something hidden to the ordinary students of his writings and the records of his actions, but (perhaps) revealed to the biographer whose mind is sharpened through exceptional empathy or psychoanalytical insight lie outside our field of study. And the same applies to the concrete, historical study of the objective consequences of his actions.

There are two immediate objections to this effort to detach Gandhi's conflictology from its concrete relation to space and time. First, in the name of empiricism, would one not have to study very carefully the exact impact

---

* Institute Universitaire, d'Etudes du De'veloppement, Geneve.

Published in *Journal of Gandhian Studies*, Vol. 6; October 1978.

of his doctrine in that particular setting to ascertain its applicability in other contexts? The world will never re-experience exactly India's struggle for *swaraj*, but it may go through similar experiences in a general class of experiences, of which *swaraj* is one case.

This objection seems valid up to a certain point. Only a study of concrete reality, not to mention social practice itself, can give an indication of what the practice of satyagraha really leads to for instance in terms of counter strategies pursued by a non-satyagraha adversary. Empathy with the adversary and good institution about how he might act may be a poor substitute for records of what really happened. But the significance of such studies is limited by the general limitation of empiricism: it tells us, at its best, what happened in the past, not what might have happened or what could happen in the future. It gives us only empirical, not potential reality. For this reason the focus here is on transferable, generalizable aspects of *satyagraha* that can be detached from that particular segment in space and time. Failure or success in one time-space context does not guarantee the same in any other time-space context—there are too many relevant and changing conditions for any kind of exact replication to take place. It is the basic perspective, the general approach that is of interest, not whether it once worked or failed.

The second objection is that Gandhi only lived there and then and he developed his conflictology in relation to the challenge he had to countenance. Had he lived in a different time-span and at another place, his conflictology might have been different, hence we should respect the singular nature of Gandhi and his reaching and not try to stretch it outside those time and perimeters. More particularly, if he had not been murdered on 30th January 1948 but had lived through the following twenty years, in command of his full faculties might he not have been challenged further to develop his teachings so as to deal with a *national* government, not only with a foreign—imposed one—and might he not have done so from a position of opposition? Moreover, he would have had to face direct violent encounters with outsiders (China in 1962, Pakistan in 1965) as opposed to internal communal riots. And in addition to the structural violence from within, indigenous (caste) as well as imposed (colonialist), he might have reached to the neo-colonialist types of structural violence. In short: if Gandhi had continued in his double role as acting politician, and an unusually explicit intellectual reflecting on his own actions (a profuse writer: some ten million words), we would have been equipped with much more material. By that we do not mean "more guides to Gandhi thought", but an *even richer Gandhi thought*, because Gandhi's thought would have developed further through the need to reflect on a still richer variety of situations. And since the whole assumption underlying this particular exercise is that the particular person, that mind, was to conflict like a Newton, and Einstein to physics, a man who could see what was unseen to others, it may be said that the assassin's bullet in 1948 deprived the world of insights and experiences extremely hard to come by.

But one consequence of this way of reasoning is, in our mind, exactly the desirability of an effort to detach Gandhi from his context. He happened to live at those places at that time, be he observed and acted for mankind at all times. We will see Gandhi, as he seemed to see himself: as a scientist presented with specimens of extremely intractable empirical reality, trying to distill from these encounters general maxims of truth. If he had sampled reality, conflict reality that is, at some other region in time and space it is impossible for us to say how large the overlap with the doctrine he did develop would have been. Gandhi got a glimpse of *the human condition*, unusually rich and varied due to his longevity, the duration (over fifty years) and extremely high level of his involvement in active conflict participation, the large variety of conflict experience—but still it was only a glimpse. He tried to extend it, partly forced by questioners who extolled from his views on conflict at other places. But it was a biased sample, and he did not claim to pronounce the ultimate truth, in his sense of that word, even on what he himself had encountered. Just to take one example which touches on the comparison with Mao, with whom Gandhi has so much in common: what would have been Gandhi's conflictology if he were to work for the liberation of peasant masses against Chiang Kai-Shek's "extermination campaigns" and Japanese imperialism? We do not know. All we have is our biased sample of Gandhi's reflections in words and deeds, on his biased sample of encounters with the human condition.

Is it then worth while? A metaphor might be appropriate here. Gandhi is in a sense like a new telescope for an astronomer. The claims made for the telescope, not so much by the advertising agents, are immodest; it is said to peer more deeply into the depths of the universe and yield insights so far hidden from man. On close examination it is revealed that the telescope indeed gives new visions, but it has only been tested in some directions, and if the images are different, then that may also be because of systematic distortion, blurred reflections in the lense system, etc. In short there is a need for comparison of the new images with old images, e.g. to test whether the new telescope is capable of replicating what "we" already "know". To this the advertising agents might retort that this is no test: discrepancies in images should be interpreted to mean that the other telescope used so far is all biased. But that is unacceptable: there has to be *some* element of continuity in the accumulation of human insight So let us use the test on Gandhi.

We can get some idea of the validity of Gandhi as an instrument if we see how he reflected on conflicts remote in space from the field where he was an expert, India. As a first example, take the following quotes from Gandhi on Palestine:

"Palestine belongs to the Arabs in the same sense that England belongs to the English or France to the French. It is wrong and inhuman to impose the Jews on the Arabs. What is going on in Palestine today cannot be justified in any moral code of conduct. The mandates have no sanction but that of the last war. Surely it would be a crime against humanity to reduce the proud Arabs so that Palestine can be restored to the Jews partly or wholly as their national home." (*Harijan* 26.11.1938).

"And now a word to the Jews in Palestine. I have no doubt that they are going about it in the wrong way. The Palestine of the Biblical conception is not a geographical tract. It is in their hearts. But if they must look to the Palestine of geography as their national home; it is wrong to enter it under the shadow of the British gun. A religious act cannot be performed with the aid of the bayonet or the bomb. They can settle in Palestine only by the goodwill of the Arabs. They should seek to convert the Arab heart." (*Harijan* 26.11.1938).

What is interesting about these quotes is that Gandhi did not accept the concept that has prevailed in many circles until recently: that Palestine was a "state without nation", which could then appropriately be filled with a "nation without a state." On the other hand Gandhi does not rule out the possibility that the Jews could settle in Palestine, only that it would have to be "by the goodwill of the Arabs". But this idea he seems to have given up when he writes about the same question eight years later:

"But in my opinion, they have erred grievously in seeking to impose themselves on Palestine with the aid of America and Britain and now with the aid of naked terrorism. Their citizenship of the world should have and would have made them honoured guests of any country. Their thrift, their varied talent, their great industry should have made them welcome anywhere. It is a blot on the Christian world that they have been singled out, owing to a wrong reading of the New Testament, for prejudice against them. If an individual Jew does a wrong, the whole Jewish world is to be blamed for it. If an individual Jew like Einstein makes a great discovery or another composes unsurpassable music, the merit goes to the authors and not to the community to which they belong." (*Harijan,* 21.7.1946).

It is clear that Gandhi here sees the Jews as potentially "honoured guests of any country"; whereas Palestine belongs to the Arabs. In this reading of the situation Gandhi has probably been partly guided by his scepticism towards the British and his sense of identification with Palestine Arabs since they were somehow in a situation corresponding to the Indians in India. Moreover, he has probably been guided by his strong sense of geographical belongingness. He who has tilled the soil, to him does the soil belong.

Thus, it may be objected that Gandhi in his interpretation of what today usually called the "Middle East" projected from the Indian situation. This may also be true about the next quotation, that says something about Japan that still may have considered validity:

"I want to assimilate all your good points, but unfortunately no one comes here to give us the good things of Japan. You believe only in dumping your goods on us. How can I take a single yard of Japanese cloth, however fine and artistic it may be? It is as poison to us, for it means starvation for the poor people of India. You have left the West far behind in diplomacy, in skill, in cheap manufactures, in armed warfare, in exploitation. How then can there is friendship between you and us, so long as you see nothing wrong in exploitation?" (*Harijan,* 24.12.1938).

In this quotation Gandhi points our what to him is basic in the concept of "exploitation": destruction of local production patterns, by "dumping your goods on us." But it is interesting to see how Gandhi does not generalize from this to a general verdict concerning Japan. He sees this as one aspect of Japan, "but unfortunately no one comes here to give us the good things of Japan." In this there is an invitation of Japan to turn her face and show another aspect of herself, not a rejection of Japan in general.

There is prophetic doom in Gandhi's reflections on the atomic bomb:

"So far as I can see, the atomic bomb has deadened the finest feeling that has sustained mankind for ages. There used to be the so-called laws of war, which made it tolerable. Now we know the naked truth. War knows no law except that of might. The atom bomb brought an empty victory to the allied arms but it resulted for the time being in destroying the soul of Japan. What has happened to the soul of the destroying nation is yet too early to see." (*Harijan,* 7.7.1946).

It is not so difficult to imagine from the last sentence how Gandhi would have reacted to the Vietnam war. But in a sense he fails to combine the last two quotes into another important question: what happened to the soul of a destroyed nation, Japan? What has the message imprinted on Japan with the explosion of the atom bomb? It was probably "never again." But was the implication that the key to "never again" lies in copying the conqueror, or in rejecting the methods of the conqueror? In general, this is a point that seems to be missing in Gandhi's writings: the impact violence has on the vanquished, not in the sense of hurting and hitting them bodily, but as a message that may become firmly engraved on their minds. Two another examples with more direct bearing on non-violence:

"Well", said Gandhiji, bidding good-bye to them. "if it comes true, it may be through the Negroes that the unadulterated message of non-violence will be delivered to the world". (*Harijan,* 14.3.1936).

In this quotation Gandhi predicts Since there is no indication of time-span, the prediction cannot be said to be falsified. And twenty years later, at the time of Martin Luther King and Albert Luthuli, one would have said that Gandhi's foresight in this quotation was remarkable. Today there might be room for doubts. On the other hand, in the Black Power movement there are also so many elements that are similar to Gandhi's way of thinking and acting about society that the distance from Black Power to Gandhi's type of active non-violence may be shorter than the distance between non-violence on the one hand and some type of passive acceptance on the other.

What, then, about this quotation?

"The Indian community there was a mere handful in the midst of an overwhelming majority of Europeans and Negroes. The Europeans had arms. We had none. So we forced the weapon of Satyagraha. Today the Indian is respected by the White man in South Africa, not so the Zulu with all his fine physique." (*Harijan,* 1.12.1946).

It is difficult to tell. It may be that Gandhi here falls prey to an exaggeration of the significance of the events in which he himself 50 years earlier, had participated. And even if it may be true that the Indian is respected in South Africa, more than the Zulu, this may also be for the wrong reason: because of the way the Indian enters into the production pattern of the South African society. In similar societies, but not dominated by the White man, like in East Africa, the reverse seems to be true: the Indian is not so much respected, the African is, or at least increasingly so. But there may of course be something to Gandhi's claim that this was because the Indian did assert themselves through an act of basic courage that established their self-respect and hence also the respect of others.

Let us then return to the telescope metaphor again. This metaphor, when applied to Gandhi, leads to a certain element of elitism that it would be vain to try to deny. The idea is that Gandhi not only witnesses and participated in more than most, but also saw deeper and further than most. At this point this belief in Gandhi is axiomatic. Its justification would lie in the scope and the range of insights that can be gleaned from him, and the quotes given show strengths and limitations.

But here it is tempting to make a reference to the comparisons sometimes made with Jesus Christ. Gandhi's life was a sample of real life situations, as was that of Christ. But Gandhi's life has the advantage that the sample was more relevant for our time. It has the lagoons noted above, but it also has inclusion of colonial, class, caste and communal struggle. Although Gandhi's reality certainly was not Western reality, fewer links have to be interspersed, fewer hypotheses have to be introduced, fewer inter-pretations have to be made in order to make Gandhi relevant than for the case of Christ. Moreover, there is an obvious linguistic advantage: Gandhi writes in an exceptionally clear and rich English: what Christ said will always remain a conjecture.

But the basic difference would be the extent to which the two can be said to have developed a social doctrine. There are obvious similarities. Like Christ is reported to have done, Gandhi lived among the publicans of his time. But the purpose was different. They were both prophets of a Kingdom, of a "social order" if one may use that expression. But they differed basically as to the location of this Kingdom. For Christ the kingdom was not of this world which makes it much more difficult to interpret what he did and what he said as a social doctrine—at least if one accepts that Christ had no real intentions as a politician, introducing a new social order in this world. If Christ can really have been said to want to purge *society* not only the *temple* of the money-lenders, it might have been more interesting from the point of view of social doctrine. But the temple was to be purged because it was the symbol of the Kingdom of Heaven an embassy so to speak, not because it should serve as a nucleus, a model social order from which a new social order in this world should gradually, or quickly, spread. On the contrary, established Christianity has tended to be tolerant of social condition in this world, and focussed its social doctrine and practice on individual suffering: on helping the victim of direct structural and violence rather than removing the causes.

In general, the mundane Kingdom and the transcendental Kingdom are not continuous with each other, they are two separate components in an ideological space. But it seems clear that Gandhi had goals in both directions, that his "kingdom" had both components. He can only be understood in terms of order *and* also be instrumental to a self-realization that ultimately would be transcendental. To discuss which of these components was more fundamental to Gandhi is probably meaningless, but it is quite clear that a social doctrine for this world is involved—and this adds to his relevance.

This doubleness in Gandhi, his refusal to see the mundane vs. transcendental as a dichotomy combined with an effort (like for many branches of Christianity including the Jesuits) to transcend it, is basic to Gandhi's conflictology as to other sides of his doctrine. Thus, it leads to a doubleness in the criterion of "victory" in a conflict—to be developed later.

Let us then in conclusion say some words about the term "conflictology" which will be used quite often. It is used to refer to any systematic body of thought and set of statements about conflicts. By this, in turn, we mean roughly the following: A *statement* is a verbal formulation that excludes something. If it is a descriptive statement it excludes something as false; if it is a normative statement something is excluded as wrong (to do). (There are also other possibilities, but these two are particularly important). A set of statements about conflicts is *systematic* if relations between the statements are explored. Such relations are usually referred to as relations of interference, deducibility, etc., but we have relatively weak types of relationship in mind. What matters here is that the concept of conflictlogy is broad: it includes an *empirical conflictology* (today usually based on an interdisciplinary social science approach) out of which descriptive conflictology would be a part, as well as a *normative conflictology* with more or less explicit norms about conflict behaviour, and all kinds of mixtures of the two. Depending on what kinds of statements are included there will be different kinds of validation procedures. Thus, an empirical conflictology may be validated by confrontation with basic axioms and data, and a normative confictology by confrontation with basic norms and hypotheses. Gandhi is rich on both, particularly strong on the latter, but also full of description and empirical hypothesis.

It is customary, and shall stick to that tradition, to divide conflictology in three parts: statements on the *nature, or genesis* of conflict: on the of conflict: on the *dynamics* of conflict and on the *resolution* of conflict. Since Gandhi himself never formulated a conflictology, nor indeed gave any indication as to how he would react to efforts to divide his statements into three parts, we have to proceed with a certain care. Only if this customary tripartition permits us to see what other–wise would have been more hidden should it be made use of.

Gandhi himself would probably have had a rather dim view of this type of undertaking, in fact of writing in general. His reaction to no longer running *Young India*: "I did not shed a single tear" (*Harijan* 13.5.1939). And

"A friend suggests that I should write a treatise on the science of *ahimsa*.

To write such a treatise is beyond my powers. I am not built for academic writings. Action is my domain." (*Harijan*, 3.6.1946).

This is written in 1946. And it is precisely this period of Gandhi's writings that we are drawing most heavily upon, since they seem to us to give precisely what Gandhi denies they have: considerable theoretical substance. They are the writings of a Gandhi with a maximum of experience, some of them extremely bitter, perhaps lacking in some of the exuberance of younger years, but not the less valuable for he who wants to understand Gandhi's thinking for that reason. In short, we have found the old Gandhi particularly valuable.

But at the same time one understands and respects the feelings that Gandhi expresses himself in two famous quotes:

"Let Gandhism be destroyed if it stands for error. Truth and *ahimsa* will never be destroyed, but Gandhism is another name for sectarianism, it deserves to be destroyed. If I were to know, after my death, that what I stood for had degenerated into sectarianism, I should be deeply pained......... Let no one say that he is a follower of Gandhi. It is enough that I should be my own follower. I know what an inadequate follower I am myself. For I cannot live up to the convictions I stand for."

"I have said before in these pages that I claim no followers. It is enough for me be my own follower. It is by itself a sufficiently taxing performance." (*Young India*, 7.5.1931).

There are many elements in what Gandhi seems to be communicating in such quotes. Evidently, he is afraid that something called "Gandhism" should freeze into a dogma, a Gandhiology. It is not quite clear what Gandhi means by "sectarianism", but with his emphasis on *experiments* one aspect is probably that Gandhi is afraid of a doctrine that is completely insensitive to empirical experiences and changing empirical circumstances. That the doctrine in Gandhi's view has a nucleus that is unchangeable, independent of any experience, is probably correct—but that is not the same as sectarianism. But it may also be that there is no such sacred nucleus in "Gandhism" according to Gandhi's own view, since he can imagine that it can be destroyed "if it stands for error." The criterion of error is not clear from this context, but it seems to be the failure to capture universal truth and *ahimsa*. Gandhi's emphasis, again, is on the *search*, and a dynamic doctrine, everywhere modifiable.

There is also an element of Gandhi elitism in this when he says, "it is enough for me to be my own follower." One interpretation is that these are values and norms set by Gandhi for himse!f. Another interpretation is that they are also set for others to follow, but only as values and norms to be followed, not because a person should be followed because somebody "is a follower of Gandhi". Gandhi seems to indicate that a personal, direct relationship to Truth and Ahimsa is needed; not the relationship mediated through a doarismatic leader, Gandhi himself.

What is the role of social science in this particular conclusion? We see it as one, of many, ways of approaching Gandhi's truth. It may appeal to some more than to others; to many it will no doubt look more like social science than like Gandhi. But social science provides a language within which Gandhi's view of conflict may, to some extent, be expressed, for Gandhi pronounced himself explicitly and implicitly on many of the problems social scientists, and particularly political scientists, are wrestling with.

But basically what we hope to show is that a confrontation of Gandhi with conflictology is primarily a way of enriching and expanding conflictology; that the use of conflictology as a way of understanding Gandhi is a secondary purpose and also in a sense self-defeating. The parallel would be with some kind of instrument that improves by being used, not with an instrument that is given and fixed and deals with objects according to unchangeable rules.

22

The Modern Search For Peace: The Gandhian Way†

Terence W. Miller*

Gandhi's Way of non-violence must be the reaction to the unjustified acts heaped upon men by men in the future. For too long violence has been the response, and destruction of mankind the outcome in human history.

But in 1978, the possibility of a violent response, through the use of nuclear weapons, could mean the extinction of Homo sapiens as a species. As Gandhi eloquently stated: "For we are all tarred with the same brush, and are children of one and the same Creator, and as such the divine powers within us are infinite". Thus, another human being's death is our own death. Therefore, the subject "The Modern Search for Peace: The Gandhian Way" must not only be a topic of an essay contest but should be a subject raised in education, the media and in Government because it is a vital question for survival of mankind.

But, I am also very hopeful with the appearance of such an essay contest, because it is a start in a very important and basic area—education. Through discussion, research and exchanging ideas on non-violence more people will become aware of it as an effective alternative to violence producing the end result of peace based on justice which will be long lasting. Therefore, I hope my essay is as practical as it is idealistic, because both philosophies must be attained for non-violence to work.

The subject matter for this essay contest has vast possibilities, from the family and its conflicts to international conflicts. I firmly believe that

---

† This essay was adjudged the best essay in an International Inter-University Essay Competition organised by the Institute during 1977-78 and was awarded 'Mother Teresa Gold Medal'.

U.S.A.

* Published in *Journal of Gandhian Studies*, Vol. 5; April 1978.

non-violence could be effective in every one of these areas and must be used to build and reinforce non-violent action.

Due to my partial Irish background and personal interest, I have decided to write on the North Ireland situation and to apply Gandhi's methods to this civil war torn area, in the hope of suggesting an alternative to violence with justice which would provide a lasting compromise for both sides. From this description, this essay could be termed idealistic, but by the end I hope to show that it is practical and possible.

One of Gandhi's methods was to study the conflict situation. Many books have been written on the North Ireland situation, but I will try to outline the complicated and long history of this conflict.

It started with the breaking away of King Henry VIII from the Catholic Church, which led to the Protestantism of all of England. Ireland remained Catholic country, especially in the South, even though still under British rule, but in the North there developed a population of English Protestants. If a date could be picked for the start of the conflict, it would be 1690—a date still immortalized in the graffiti throughout the North. In that year King William of Orange, a Protestant supported by the Pope, lost in battle to King James II of England, a Catholic. The struggle of Irish independence from England is the history of Ireland until 1949 when it was granted. But, the North was developing into a highly industrialized, Protestant area. Therefore, when the break came in 1949, North Ireland asked to break away from the Republic and remain under partial jurisdiction of the English. This was granted, but only because it provided for the establishment of a free State in the South.

Thus, with this break away of the six counties of Ulster into North Ireland, we have the development of a nation based on religion with a ratio of 3 Protestants to every 1 Catholic. By sheer number and economic, social and political abuses, the Protestants remained in control and still do.

In 1969, with the development of a Catholic Civil Right Movement, violent strife once again returned to this Island. They began with peaceful marches, but these soon developed into violent outcries by the Catholic for their rights. One thing led to another and para military organizations developed for each side, intensifying the conflict. British troops were called in.

First seen as a peacekeeping force, they quickly became hated by both sides—specially the Catholics. Due to the violence the Government of North Ireland collapsed and Westminster began to rule the country.

Since that time North Ireland has been ripped open with hatred, strife and violence, although the accounts of violence have decreased since 1969, the situation remains the same with little or no alleviation in sight.

Reading about the circumstance of North Ireland is one thing and experiencing it another. I left for North Ireland in July of 1977 to work on a Playscheme in Lurgan, 30 miles outside of Belfast. The International Fellowship of Reconciliation sponsored the playscheme whose objective was to provide the children of both groups activities to avoid any conflict during the summer months. I talked to everyone I came in contact with—young, old, Protestant and Catholic, constantly probing, asking and trying to understand the conflict.

My conclusions at the end of my stay were mainly centered around the belief that the conflict is not a religious one any longer. It evolves around civil rights and an oppressment of a minority by a majority. It is filled with injustices that must be corrected. For too long this majority, through job, housing and political sanctions, has prevented the minority from living as human beings.

Another factor that weighs very heavily in the conflict is the daily reminder of history throughout North Ireland. From July 12 to late August there are marches, parades and demonstrations by both sides to commemorate different historical events. There are excellent photographic essays on the graffiti of North Ireland, but they do not do justice to the graffiti I saw. "The handwriting on the wall" informs any individual as to which area he is in, and who controls that area, and is filled with abusive sayings about the other side and historical reminders of one group's dominance over another. The constant searchings, the British Army's guerrilla warfare tactics, bombing, infringements on both groups' human rights by the conflict, all contribute to the physical atmosphere of the situation which must be accounted for.

The most disturbing component of this problem is the acceptance by the population of all these measures. Life, remarkably, goes on through all this terror. People have adapted to it. Thus they are living, and most importantly raising children, within a totally violent environment. The effect is devastating.

Working with children aged 3-17 this summer I can say that although everyone puts new hope for North Ireland with the children, the odds they are up against are tremendous. In a culture that force feeds its heritage to their children, how can the children overcome this to make a better world for themselves? The children I talked to speak of only one thing¾getting out of North Ireland one day. With all this discontent among the children, it is difficult to talk about them as the future.

But, there is another side. A 17-year-old boy exclaimed: "It's all so stupid and senseless." It is this segment of the society that is the hope of tomorrow for North Ireland. I would also like to mention the 13 Peace groups now in existence within North Ireland and the countless number of religious and community projects in existence, which is trying to alleviate the violence.

From my readings and personal experience, I believe that the Catholic population, due to the injustices, cried out violently and this prolonged the situation instead of shortening or changing it. Therefore, my following remarks are addressed to this minority, for I feel their application of the Gandhian way will strengthen them and bring justice so that their children may enjoy the peace that will follow.

The Gandhian way is not only in reference to the method of non-violence used by Gandhi in his struggles in South Africa and India, but it also refers to a philosophy of a way of life. As Gandhi continually states throughout his autobiography, the method of non-violence without the ideas of Brahmacharya and especially Ahimsa could not work. It is only with the acceptance of non-violence as a way of life, not only as a workable political method, that it will triumph in practice. As exemplified in Gandhi's and also Martin Luther King's struggles the leadership and the population trying to use the method must accept and believe in its viability.

There are many concepts that must be a part of the philosophy of Ahimsa, most important of these being tolerance, truth and love. Gandhi in his teaching places a great importance on each of these in order for the method of non-violence to work. I would like to quote what I feel are the most pertinent saying for non-violence to work in North Ireland in each of these three categories. This might appear to be a digression, but I feel that it provides a foundation for a later discussion on viability of non-violence in North Ireland.

On tolerance Gandhi said: "My experience has shown me that we win justice quickest by rendering justice to the other party." "We are all one family". And, finally, Gandhi's idea that all men are brothers. All these concepts are vital in the functioning of non-violence and all are lacking in North Ireland, but not by the majority of people who statistically want the conflict end, but by the extremists on both sides who terrorize the majority. There is no tolerance, no understanding, no compassion for their fellowman and this middle majority terrorized by the extremist can't display it for fear of economic and social sanctions.

If there is no tolerance it goes unsaid that there is no love in North Ireland. But the antithesis is displayed openly and flagrantly by everyone. The children especially display this hatred, not only for the opposing group or the British, but also I found children expressing hatred of people of their own religion if they didn't know them. Frequently I stopped and thought how could so much hatred be present in one place. It is by far the most depressing and saddening feature of the North Ireland situation. Gandhi saw the need of love of your enemy as a prime concept of Ahimsa. I firmly agree. One of Gandhi's quotes particularly comes to mind: "There only is life where there is love. Life without love is death. Love is the reverse of the coin of which the obverse is truth. It is my firm faith......... that we can conquer the whole world by truth and love."

Finally, the concept of truth builds upon the other features of tolerance and love. In a quote that must be learned by the world Gandhi states: "Truth is One: The Path to It are Many", and "Truth is like a vast tree which yields more and more fruit the more you nurture it". It is this truth that will especially profit the Catholic population if it is build on tolerance and love.

In a recent study released by a Government agency set up in 1976 to outlaw religious discrimination in employment, it was found that Roman Catholics are 15 per cent more likely to be unemployed than Protestants. Certainly, this truth could only rectify the injustice Catholics must deal with if it was used within a non-violent framework.

There is one other area that Gandhi speaks on that applies specifically to North Ireland—religion. Although I feel that this situation is no longer based on religion, it certainly played a major role in originating the conflict and the opposing forces still go under religious symbols and identification. It disturbed me immensely to see the prostitution of Christianity by both sides in North Ireland. It is unimaginable that so much hate, intolerance, injustice and violence could be generated from the philosophy of Christ who specifically abhorred these things and taught and exemplified the tolerance, love, forgiveness and truth as outlined in Gandhi's philosophy. It would be truly miraculous if acceptance of the following quote would not only be believed but practices: "Religions are different roads converging to the same point. What does it matter that we take different roads, so long as we reach the same goal ? In reality, there are as many religions as there are individuals". As one person I spoke to in North Ireland said: "There is too much religion in North Ireland and not enough belief."

The most ironic factor is that if both groups practiced their religion the base of Ahimsa would be firm and thus the method of non-violence could function and quite effectively due to both parties being in agreement on certain fundamental precepts. The most remarkable feature to the situation is that non-violence is operational within that society and is not contrary to certain Western principles. It could work!

It is at this point where the philosophy of Ahimsa could be adopted by the population through their religious beliefs that we must turn to the second phase of Gandhi's way of non-violence.

In a contest Gandhi ran in South Africa for a name for non-violent action the winner coined the word "satyagraha". The meaning being firmness in truth. Gandhi then outlined steps to be taken once the philosophy of Ahimsa is accepted in order to procure justice. It is quite extensive and each step must be taken and fully followed before going on to the next step. What is more fantastic about satyagraha is that it is viable, exemplified through Gandhi and King.

Gandhi in outlining step number one stated that in selection of a cause you must be selective within the larger cause. In other words, in North Ireland the larger cause would be justice for the Catholics economically, politically and socially. But to tackle all that would be self-defeating, therefore a selection must be made within the larger cause. For this example, although many things could be picked, we will choose the need of jobs among the Catholics. Then a step furthers the need of jobs among the Catholics among the Goodyear plant in Craigavon.

In selecting a cause that is approachable and practical, result will be seen which will strengthen the movement. As far as gathering knowledge and statistics dealing with the economic conditions, as already seen with the recent Government study, the figures are available and need only to be used to speak the Truth to the majority to show the injustice involved. Not only is there this recent study but also a report by the British on unemployment in each town in North Ireland. The figures show that the towns with the larger Catholic population have the larger unemployment and the opposite is seen with the Protestant figures. It is not areas of the country involved, but differences are seen in towns next to each other, and in Belfast it is seen from neighbourhood to neighbourhood. No economic wizard is necessary to interpret and inform the people of this injustice. For our smaller cause we could receive the figures for the Goodyear plant of the ratio of Catholic to Protestant workers and the corresponding population of the town of Craigavon.

To live like the people is a step that must be carried out to prevent prejudice within the minority group. Surely, dissent would rise should the leaders live somewhere else under different conditions and try to convince the majority of the economic injustice being heaped upon the minority. Also it provides first handed information on the living conditions of the people, which is the valuable information in any conflict situation. Finally, the people will respect and admire the leaders who are living with them and fighting 'the battle' every step of the way. Also, this daily struggle will provide self-discipline and valuable experience on the part of the leaders in future struggles.

A permanent organization with symbols, titles and a flag would especially be esteemed in North Ireland. This is due to the importance of physical symbols to the people for identification. In North Ireland flags, saying symbols, and membership in organizations reflect your position in struggle. Thus a non-violent identification would be important and people could relate to it. North Ireland places great emphasis in organization.

People will also feel a part of this organization when they contribute to its continuance. Money from the people will only intensify their loyalty to organization. In pàrticular one peace group has come under fire due to its procuring funds from everywhere except the people involved, leading to failures in its attempts to secure peace.

The true Christians among the people will easily see and be convinced in non-violence as a way of life. It is the people who profess the religion but not its philosophy who must be educated and disciplined in non-violence. Self-discipline in the face of violence is by far the most difficult rule of satyagraha. Yet it is the most powerful component of the method. As Gandhi did several times when this self-discipline broke down, the leaders must show through personal self-sacrifice their own belief in the method. This will reinforce the participants' belief in satyagraha.

For the next steps of the struggle it must be remembered that the original foundation of tolerance, love and truth must be reinforced and grow or else the method dies. Negotiations with the opposition should be encouraged as first step of direct action. If this has been exhausted with no results, the media could be introduced. The power of the media, especially the television, is an effective force within the modern world, which should be used to publicize the fact and the belief in non-violence as a way to rectify injustice.

The power of law courts, especially in democratic countries, should not be underestimated. Legal action could be sanctioned against the factory in accordance with certain laws. In North Ireland there has been created a Fair Employment Agency to safeguard against economic injustice, which could secure legally the rights of the Catholic workers to jobs.

If all else fails, there are methods available that require strict self-discipline of all involved and a dedication to non-violence. These are direct action responses civil disobedience, strike, boycott, non-cooperation, economically and socially, and, finally, politically, exemplified in an alternative Government.

These methods are extreme but do produce results. Especially effective again exemplified through Gandhi and King, are economic sanctions. There is a saying that money talks, and it is true. Besides, it doesn't involve the direct conflict the other measures suggest, thus preventing a display of a breakdown in self-discipline that would show the organization's weakness.

An important factor also is the realization that if satyagraha worked here in the Goodyear plant of Craigavon, it would give real impetus into the movement and establish its credibility.

In conclusion, North Ireland is filled with injustice by a majority against a minority. In 1969 the Catholic population, although it was contrary to many of their basic beliefs, cried out violently. The Protestants retaliated. Civil war tore open the country through para military organizations. In fact, two groups developed within the Catholic Irish Republican Army (IRA). Today, it is fact that there is more violence between the Provos and the Officials than there is between the Catholics and the Protestants.

From my personal experience and my readings, the time is ripe for non-violence to occur. In August of 1976 three children's deaths led to a mass march of women, both Catholic and Protestants, for peace. Unfortunately, as Married Corrigan personally admitted to me, they do not have an educational background in the study of peace or the Gandhian method and are desperately in need of it. The People's Peace Movement has also failed because of two breaks with the satyagraha method as outlined by Gandhi¾namely, to live like the people, and the importance of finance coming from the people themselves. I still have hope in this movement, but education is so important. The analogy has been made that you wouldn't use an intern to perform complicated brain surgery. So it is the same, therefore, with non-violence¾education is the key to success.

The world today is filled with specialists and the peace specialist familiar with the prime example of Gandhi's way will serve a vital function if Homo sapiens are to survive.

23

Sarvodaya and State Power Theory and Practice in South Asia[†]

Detlef Kantowsky*

South Asia's soft states are characterized by a limited capacity for goal attainment. Their dual economies, with a foreign-oriented capitalist sector, are unable to integrate the rising expectations that the educational subsystem and a socialist ideology of planning have created. Thus we have recently seen repressive policies to maintain the existing institutional patterns in all four South Asian States. This state of emergency has led to sharp reaction and political crises.

In India and Sri Lanka new governments have been voted into power that try not to repress public grievances and demands but to integrate them under populist slogans. If we accept a western paradigm of development, it is in this context that the role of the Sarvodaya movements in these countries has to be seen. In the Marxist version of this paradigm Sarvodaya can still be described in the way M.N. Roy assessed Gandhi as "the most acute and desperate manifestation of the forces of reaction". In the structural-functional version of the paradigm Sarvodaya is a strategic instrument for effective crisis management, i.e., it helps to absorb the unavoidable repercussions of capitalist modernization.

In this paper I shall avoid such disputes and focus instead on an immanent description of the recent development of Sarvodaya in India and Sri Lanka. I am convinced that none of our Western concepts, neither the Marxist nor the neo-liberal version can adequately explain Sarvodaya's

---

† This paper is based on material collected in India and Sri Lanka in October 1977 and in February/March 1978. Travel grants from the German Research Association (DFG) are gratefully acknowledged.

* University of Konstanz (West Germany)

Published in *Journal of Gandhian Studies*, Vol. 5; July 1978.

political philosophy. I am, however, not yet in a position to present here an alternative model of interpretation. Such a model would first of all have to correct our misconceptions about Hindu, and especially Buddhist, social ethics. Emanuel Sarkisyanz's (1965), Louis Dumont's (1970), R.F. Gombrich's (1971), and S.J. Tombiah's (1976) studies would be the platform on which to construct an Eastern model of the relation-ship between individual and society. Probably we could then prove that Gandhi's anarchic concept of Sarvodaya, Kisan Raj and Lok-Niti provides the most suitable framework for the self-realization of "homo hierarchicus" in India, whilst a "righteous ruler" and central power is necessary in Sri Lanka to provide an infrastructure for human beings whose supreme aim it should be to gain some insight into their own non-identity.

Sarvodaya in India—from cooperation to confrontation

The history of Sarvodaya in India is the history of two charismatic personalities. The following chronicle of events is, thus, written around their names.

1951. Confronted with rural unrest *Vinoba Bhave* discovers the concept of *"Bhoodan"* in a village of Andhra Pradesh. He later (1957) develops the Bhoodan concept into *"Gramdan"*. Contrary to the Gandhian technique of non-violent resistance to wrongdoers Vinoba favours "positive satyagraha", i.e. non-violent assistance in right thinking and action.

1954. *Jayaprakash Narayan* joins the Bhoodan movement and explains this decision to his socialist friends in a fascinating personnel document: *"From Socialism to Sarvodaya"*.

1965. With Government support the movement starts a *"whirl-wind campaign"* to bring Gramdan to all Indian Villages.

1969. By the end of the Gandhi Centenary Year the movement claims to have reached 140,000 villages, of which 60,000 are in Bihar; with nearly 90 per cent of its villages covered, *Bihar* is proclaimed the first *"Statedan"*.

1970. In response to the challenge by the *Naxalites*, Jayaprakash Narayan concentrates all his energy on a non-violent change in *Musahari Block* (Bihar). In the block's 120 villages he comes "Face to Face" with the realities of village politics and the *failure of the movement* (Narayan, 1970).

1971. At a Sarvodaya Conference in Bhopal in October 1971, some workers raise the question as to whether the time has not come for the movement to recognize the landless and small peasants in a massive *non-violent confrontation* with the large landowners and power holders in Indian rural society (Ostergaard 1976, p. 3).

1972. A Gramswaraj Workers' Conference *discusses the movement's relationship with the Government.* One group advocates "coordination" the other wants to remain independent of the Government. Sarvodaya Workers organize several satyagraha in Tamilnad and are sent to jail.

1973. In July, the Executive of the Sarva Seva Sangh passes a *Resolution on the National Situation* in which the Government is held responsible for "famine poverty, unemployment, miseducation, sky-rocketing prices,............ increased concentration of power, widespread corruption" (People's Action, New Delhi, Aug. 1973).

1973. In September, during the half yearly meeting of the Sangh, no consensus can be reached as to the further work of the movement. Together with Vinoba a minority pleads for a "spiritualization of politics" whilst the majority is with Jayaprakash for a "*politicisation of the Sangh*".

1973. The Youth Peace Corps of the movement participates in the *Youth Against Famine Campaign*, during which 750 summer camps are organized, including 73 in Gujarat and 51 in Bihar.

1973. In December Jayaprakash Narayan publishes "*An Appeal to Youth Power*" in which he asks Indian Youth to enter the national arena and play a decisive role in establishing the primacy of the people and securing their victory over the power of money, falsehood and brute force". (People's Action, New Delhi Dec. 1973).

1974. In March *J.P accepts the invitation from the students in Patna* to give guidance and direction to their movement. *Vinoba Bhave retreats* into one year of silent "action through inaction".

1975. On October 2, Gandhi's birthday, JP notes in his *Prison Diary:* "Vinobaji did something miraculous for some years. It appeared as though a new Gandhian process of social change and reconstruction had emerged. But *after his stormy Bhoodan* experiment *not even a mild breeze blows,* not to speak of the mighty storm of the Gramdan, Gram-Swarajya or any other constructive experiment. Later he withdrew into his inner self.................. One is reminded here of a statement by *Bapu* who, while defining democracy, *had said that* it did not only mean a government established by the people's vote; it also meant that the *people had the power to oust their rulers* when found unworthy to rule". (Narayan, 1977, p. 83).

1976. During the *emergency* the organization of the *movement is destroyed* and many Sarvodaya Workers are sent to jail.

1977. Though seriously ill, Jayaprakash Narayan becomes the charismatic leader of the united opposition parties. After a landslide victory in the Lok Sabha elections the Janta Party delegates meet on the campus of the Gandhi Peace Foundation, *where Jayaprakash nominates Morarji Desai* as candidate for the office of Prime Minister.

1977. Referring to a note in his *Prison Diary* that a "total change" has to be brought about either with the cooperation of the Government or in confrontation with it (Narayan, 1977 p. 49). I ask JP on October 9 when he will begin to *challenge the Janata Government* and remind its leaders of their election promises His reply: "Whatever position I may have, I may also find myself ineffective and withdraw. I can only *dissociate myself* from what I may find wrong".

1978. In February, *JP* issues a statement from Patna saying that he is *severing his connections* with all the institutions and organizations he has been associated with. "By releasing me from all formal responsibilities, they will not only help me but also the cause I hold dear, he said (Ceylon Daily News, 21.2.78).

I had interviews with N. Krishnaswamy, Director of the Voluntary Action Cell, and K.S. Radhakrishna, Secretary of the Gandhi Peace Foundation, in October 1977 and February 1978. Our talks on the future of Sarvodaya in India and in particular the position of the movement vis-à-vis new Government and its so-called Gandhian Approach. Furthermore I had the opportunity to discuss details with Indian delegates to an International Sarvodaya Conference held in Sri Lanka in April 1978. The following are statements made by these leading Sarvodaya Workers in India:

"When we came out of jail the apparatus of the movement was not only destroyed but the *workers* were *divided. Vinoba* had some 25 people, *and* the bulk of the workers were with *J.P.*"

"The decision to *support Janata* was not an easy one, but JP persuaded us that this was a *choice between freedom and democracy.* Yet within two months there was a great *disillusion.* Regarding the State elections we decided that there was no point in continuing our linkage with Janata. We have been friendly, but we did not participate as in March. *Our organization* will not be a *wing of the Janata Party* but be independent. Whenever, there is an occasion of injustice, we must be prepared to do civil disobedience."

"If the Gandhians have a chance at all, it is within these next three or four years. Yet you have to reckon with people who fought the Gandhian approach. So we have to develop a *programme that will strengthen our roots* within the next four years: formation of *people's committee; organization of the rural landless and poor* for a peaceful and non-violent struggle".

"The Gandhi Peace Foundation will work on a *complementary programme* and cover the *colleges* so as to build up Gandhi Peace Centres in each college. So we thereby cover the *urban* as well as the *rural sector* and have a network if there is a reversal to dictatorship within the next four years."

"J.P. has *no powerful organization behind* him. Sarvodaya has not yet reached the district level; we have only rebuilt our committees at the State level. Leaving out the Khadi people we have *not more than 200 Sarvodaya workers now.*"

"Most of *our* many Welfare *Institutions are sand*, we have to give them a new structure, then they might be shaped into a concrete building. Moreover, half of *our people are over 60*. So we have to start from scratch and create the symbols of a new movement. What *we have*, to begin with, is an *enormous fund of good will*. JP was in jail and we are greatly respected by the people".

"Sarvodaya has not yet given teeth to the *rural poor*. The land-owners bribed Vinoba. This enabled them to keep control, but no change of heart was achieved. You can't get money from the Tatas and fight them; our *structure must reflect our commitments*".

What does this chronicle of events show? What is the meaning of the statements summarized? Is the heyday of Sarvodaya and Satyagraha over or are we witnessing a new beginning, since its leaders have at least come to realize the "fool's paradise made by State practice, of the moralities of a Mahatma Gandhi, or of all the pieties of a Vinoba Bhave" (Selbourne, 334)?

I shall return to these questions after a short description of Sarvodaya's development in Sri Lanka.

Sarvodaya in Sri Lanka – from Toleration to Cooperation

The Sarvodaya Shramadana Movement of Sri Lanka traces its history back to the year 1958, when Ahangamane Tudor Ariyaratne, science teacher at Nalanda Vidyalaya, a leading Buddhist High School in Colombo, took his students and some other teachers and volunteers to a village 67 miles away from the capital to hold a Shramadana Camp. Though the following chronicle of events is also meant to give an idea of the basic principles of the movement, it lays particular emphasis on the relationships that developed with the Government over the years. For methodological reasons I shall quote from the movement's own documents, whenever possible.

1958. "The *first experiment* was carried out in a remote village called Kanatoluwa, by students and teachers of Nalanda Vidyalaya. It is fair to say that the *pioneers* of the movement *belonged to a higher* class—both economically and socially—than most other youth in the country. The *community* they *selected* for their experiment, on the other hand, was *one of the worst* communities in *Ceylon* at that time" (Ariyaratne, 1971, p. 12).

1958. From the very inception of the Movement in 1958, there was *ideological similarity* between the official point of view of the Hon. Mr. Bandarnayake's *Government and the Sarvodaya* Shramdana Movement (Sarvodaya Shramdana Movement, 1977, p. 7).

1958. "We in Ceylon were *inspired by* this Sarvodaya thought of Mahatma *Gandhi* and the Bhoodan-Gramdan action of Acharya *Vinoba Bhave*. We do not allow our national pride to stand in our way when we choose to accept, the best of any culture. While the word '*Sarvodaya*' with its literal meaning was adopted from India, the *interpretation* of its deep meaning as relevant to *our own* Sinhala Buddhist Culture and national population is completely our own. We have our *own indigenous character both in thought and action* as far as the Ceylon Movement is concerned" (Aryaratne, 1971, p.3).

1958. "The Hon. *Mrs. Bhandaranaike* (who later became our Prime Minister), seeing the project, made the following entry *in the Camp Log*

Book on 16 Dec., 1958: "It has given us great pleasure to see the *wonderful work* done by all those who have been responsible for the development of the village. The wonderful spirit of service and the enthusiasm displayed by the students of the Nalanda Vidyalaya is very praiseworthy. We hope all other schools will follow their *example* and come forward and help in the development of our backward villagers" Aryaratne 1971, p. 14).

1964. With foreign aid the Department of Land Development starts a scheme under the name "National Service Branch". After some time the scheme is changed to "National Shramadana Service". The Sarvodaya Movement comes to a *working arrangement with the Government* and undertakes some projects such as cyclone relief and rehabilitation *programmes on behalf of the Government.* For the Movement's own projects the Department loaned vehicles, tools and implements.

1958/66. The word "Shramadana" had a magical effect. In effect the *Shramadana* action *spread* faster than the Sarvodaya thought. Between 1958 and 1966 more than *three hundred thousand volunteers* were taken to hundreds of rural areas to participate in community development projects through Shramadana Camps. (Aryaratne 1971 p. 14).

1965. The Government of Sri Lanka declares the Movement an *approved charity* by gazette notification No. 14490 of 27th August.

1966. The *new director* of Government Shramadana Scheme points out that it was not correct to have supplied vehicles etc. to a voluntary organization. The *Movement* has either to *shrink back* to a volunteer social service or approach donor organization.

1967. In preparation for the celebration of the centenary of Mahatma Gandhi's Birth the Movement starts a "*Hundred Village Department Scheme*", for which the Freedom from Hunger Campaign gives some financial assistance.

1968. The movement claims to have *250,000 trained volunteers* working in 182 villages of the country.

1969. A.T. Ariyaratne, who is called "the little Gandhi of Sri Lanka", receives the *Ramon Magasaysay Award* for Community Leadership in Manila.

1969. *Jayaprakash Narayan* comes to Sri Lanka and stays with the Movement for two weeks.

1970. "Under the leadership of the Hon. Prime Minister, Mrs. Sirimavo R.D. Bhandarnaike, Sri Lanka society is undergoing the most revolutionary non-violent structural changes which no other democratic country in the world has yet seen. Rural Society is being structurally liberated and the *Sarvodaya* Shramadan Movement is *determined to supplement* this *effort of the Government* by injecting its spiritual, cultural and social organisational input" (SSM 1977, p.7).

1970. A substantial *donation* from the World Assembly of Youth allows an expansion of the educational programme for young community leaders.

1971. "In April 1971, there took place an unforgettable event in the island's history. That was the violent youth uprising better known as the '*insurgency* of 1971'. Violence was met with greater violence. What is significant here is that the *Sarvodaya workers*, being already engaged in non-violent social revolution, *did not get involved* in this unfortunate incident. Therefore, the stature of the Movement grew fast" (Sarvodaya Research Centre, 1977, p.15).

1972. The Movement is incorporated in Sri Lanka by an Act of Parliament (Act No. 16 of 1972).

1972. *Massive aid* from various Western development organizations *begins to flow* in.

1974. A Bhikkhu Training Centre is inaugurated in which sixty *monks* can be accommodated and *trained* in village development work during six month courses. The three main Nikayas of the island support the centre and ask young monks to participate.

1974. *Home Minister* Felix R.D. Bhandaranaike grows suspicious and *tries to control* the Movement's rural activities. The Prime Minister intervenes.

1976. The Movement sets itself the target of bringing about *one thousand villages* to a self-development stage.

1977. After the elections and the sweeping victory of UNP an "*Electorate Programme*" is drawn up to start development work in those 41 of the 163 *constituencies* in all whose delegates asked Sarvodaya for assistance.

1978. The movement has developed into a massive organization with a *permanent staff* of some two thousand semi-professionals. It maintains 62 *extension Service Centres*, situated mainly in the Buddhist South- Western and Central regions of the island.

1978. "Our *Government and the Sarvodaya movement have many things in common* and both endeavour to create a peaceful righteous and prosperous society in Sri Lanka based on the teaching embodied in Dhamma Chakka Sutta of the Buddha "*says President* J. R. Jayawardene after opening the Movement's New Building at Moratuwa. (Ceylon Daily News, 22.3.78).

1978. "The *Government* has decided to enlist the *support of the Sarvodaya* Movement to build the righteous society it envisages. The Sarvodaya movement will also be made use of by local authorities to serve the people", *said Mr. R. Permodasa, Prime Minister* after he inaugurated the first International Conference on Sarvodaya and Development (Ceylon Daily News, 3.4.1978).

1978. In a panel discussion with the participants at this conference the *Members of Parliament* invited vehemently *reject* suggestions *that Sarvodaya has been drawn into politics*. They make it clear that according to their point of view politics and the work of a non-political organization are two distinct things. Though they hope to make use of the Movement for development work in their electorate, they expect it at the same time to remain neutral.

Is this just another case of open exploitation of Buddhist religious elements and enthusiasm "in the interests of party politics" (Leach, p. 48. In how far is the Sarvodaya Movement in Sri Lanka a direct offspring of Buddhist modernism), a revolt against the techniques of Western planning skilfully floating on an international wave of requests for indigenous and more appropriate solutions to the modernization problems of post colonial societies? What interests motivate the present 384 members of the in-corporated Sangamaya, most of them from the urban upper middle class, to initiate "Buddhist" development in the rural areas? And what would the future of the movement be if outside assistance dried up? I hope to be able to answer these questions in my forthcoming study on the objectives and methods of the movement. Here I must confine myself to a few comparative remarks.

From Movement to Structure and Institution

The Sarvodaya Movements in India and Sri Lanka developed from voluntary groups that went to the villages, into an organization that relies for its social work activities on a staff of semi professionals. Even Sarvodaya was unable to invalidate a well-tested law of the social sciences, i.e., that the development of at least a semi-permanent organizational structure is essential for the realization of the goals of a movement. This "routinization of charisma" and the gradual bureaucratic corruption of its idealism, missionary zeal and spontaneous emotional commitments seems to be an unavoidable paradox in the life history of any social movement. The other paradox refers to a movement's gradual acceptance.

If a social movement is successful, it contributes to the formation of public opinion by providing conceptual alternatives for the discussion of social and political issues. If these alternative concepts are accepted and if some of the movement's followers become part of the political elite, then the point is reached where a movement, having changed or modified the social order, becomes part of it. Its life cycle has thereby come to an end; it has become an institution.

Sri Lanka's Sarvodaya is not an institution yet, though its Shramdana concept has become part of official development planning and quite a number of its early supporters are now members of the ruling party in Parliament. Compared with the situation in India, Sarvodaya in Sri Lanka had the advantage of non-cooperation with the Bandaranaike Government until 1977.

Yet Vinoba Bhave and his followers were given the official blessing and Government support from the very beginning. Sarvodaya Gram Sevaks worked together with the Block Development personnel, and the concept of Panchayati Raj was the official label under which Gandhian visions were institutionalised. By the mid-sixties Sarvodaya's challenge had been accommodated into Indian state doctrine and community development machinery. May be this was also gradually realised by Vinoba Bhave who retreated more and more, thereby successfully taking on the classic Hindu rule of the saintly hermit.

Thus I think that we have good reason to speak of a "JP Movement" and the "Bihar Movement" as new phenomena of political agitation and mass mobilization. Though JP tried to convince the students that only the

Sarvodaya approach would lead them to success it was not the old Sarvodaya that challenged the Government. JP's message of "total revolution" was basically a negation of the entire political superstructure that Vinoba's Sarvodaya had supported in one way or the other.

Today the New Janata Government is using exactly the same accommodation strategy that Jawaharlal Nehru used in the early fifties to institutionalise the Gandhian approach: A twelve-member "Rural Development Committee" was set up in February 1978, "to ensure the full and active participation of constructive workers and voluntary organizations in the rural development of the country." And Mr. Asoka Mehta, Chairman of the Committee for the Restructuring of the Panchayati Raj institutions assured the public, that these institutions are vital democratic institutions and that their roots must be strengthened to make democracy stable.

These surface phenomena, the Janata Party's "Statement on Economic Policy" and the Government's New Industrial Policy have led foreign commentators to speculate on a "Gandhian Revival" in the country. I think "The Times" had a more realistic interpretation to offer when it spoke of "More funds for Indian agriculture" in a headline on 16.11.1977. And Romesh Thapar was as well informed as usual when he commented on the "Arrival of the Farmer" in his 'Capital View' of 31.12.1977 (EPW, Vol. XII). Charan Singh may be a true Gandhian, as many say, but it remains more than doubtful whether he will be able to implement his "Gandhian Blueprint" (Singh, 1978) in the face of the powerful interests of rural entrepreneurs which developed during the green revolution period. It is not the spinning wheel but the tractor that symbolizes the new self-image of rural India's dominant minorities. The note on "Economic Policies and Priorities" that the *Sarva Seva Sangh* issued after the State elections in June 1977, is not an appropriate response to their demands.

Compared with the situation in India, Sarvodaya in Sri Lanka was spared the dubious benefits of close Government cooperation until 1977. However, as the last entries in our chronicle have shown, the new UNP Government is making open attempts to integrate the movement and to use its philosophy as an umbrella under which a variety of development policies can be sheltered. Yet I presume that we have to search for explanations which reach beyond the movement-institution dichotomy used here so far, and it is with this in mind that the following remarks are made.

Bilingualism and the Role of Sarvodaya in Sri Lanka

To be "culturally bilingual" is, under the present circumstance of a country like Sri Lanka, essential for politicians if they want to obtain local support as well as international cooperation. Starting from that assumption *Edmund Leach* distinguishes four alternative models of correct behaviour, two on a secular and two on a religious basis (Leach, p. 51):

Scale of Public Esteem

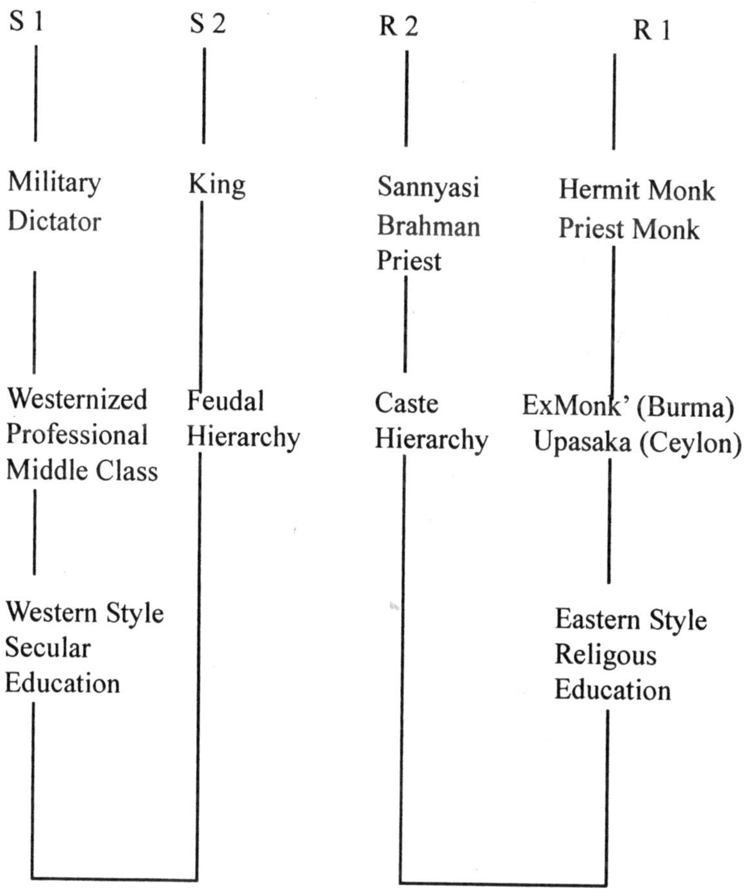

Secular Pole of Values——Religious Pole of Values

It is not difficult to relate recent events in Sri Lanka to this diagram. The "*secular project*" of a free Trade Zone north of Colombo is counterbalanced by the UNP Government's pledge to complete a meritorious irrigation project (Mahaweli) within six years. By changing the constitution and assuming the office of Sri Lanka's first President J. R. Jayawardene moved as close to the role of king as modern constitutional thinking allows for; and by stepping into muddy rice field for the ceremonial first ploughing at the beginning of the maha-season in October 1977 he performed the traditional duties connected with this role. The statement reported elsewhere in this paper makes it clear that President J. R. Jayawardene sees himself in the Sinhala-nationalist rule of a defender of righteousness. It is not only on these occasions but also on various minor ones that Sarvodaya in Sri Lanka clearly serves to bridge the gap between international modernism and traditional local sentiments. Sarvodaya's development strategy of self-reliance, based on a modern interpretation of Buddhist principles, carefully balances the secular and the religious poles of values and thereby allows for "overlapping" behaviour. Far from being astonishing, it was in fact to be expected that a party which ousted a regime claiming to be socialist should make such open advances to the movement.

I do not think it is necessary to illustrate here in great detail the value of Leach's diagram for the explanation of the behaviour of India's political leaders. Indira Gandhi, for instance, who had moved up on the S_1 scale of worldly power tried to link herself with Vinoba's charisma on the R_2 channel of religious merit. And the present Prime Minister misses no occasion to openly declare his prefe-rence for a vegetarian diet and traditional medicine.

But what about the Indian Sarvodaya movement? It obviously does not fit the model as in Sri Lanka. I maintain that this notion leads us to a basic difference between the movements in the two countries.

Welfare State vs. Village Republics

Sarvodaya's work in Sri Lanka and its cooperation with the Government is supported by a Buddhist theory of the welfare state that Hindu political theory lacks. Sarvodaya's ideologists in Sri Lanka can draw upon a "glorious past" of harmonious relationships between ruler and Sangha, between the tank and the temple. Gandhi, however, had to develop a model of the ancient autonomous Indian village republic, since the history of the feudal Indian Raj had no other modern concepts to offer. Whilst Sarvodaya in India envisages a stateless and highly decentralized political order which would consist of a network of self-governing agro-industrial communities, Sarvodayites in Sri Lanka hope that the rulers will always be righteous and provide the means for the pursuit of Nirvana. Whilst Sarvodaya in Sri Lanka legitimises a revival of the traditional functions of government, Sarvodaya in India is anarchic.

Seen in this context JP's life work and his intellectual development from Socialism via Sarvodaya to Total Revolution is quite consistent. In a Hindi Poem, which he composed while in solitary confinement during the emergency, he says (Times of India, 14.2.78):

"The ways of renunciation of service,
Of reconstruction, of strike, of "total revolution"
Were steps in search of revolution?
The world may call it a failure.
The steps are countless,
The destination is still far off,
I cannot stop midway
No matter how rugged the road,
I have no personal desires,
They were all returned to the Lord,
I am satisfied with my failures,
This failed life will be rewarded a thousandfold
If the road of young fellow revolutionaries
Paved with thorns
Is now easier to transverse."

It is indeed informative to contrast this poem with the last verse of the song that A.T. Ariyaratne composed to welcome Sri Lanka's Prime Minister and his wife at the inauguration ceremony of the International Sarvodaya Seminar in April this year:

"Your life is for the nation, your service is to humanity,
With blessings of the Triple Gem and the protection of the gods:
May you both be healthy, prosperous and victorious!"

24

Work and the Meaning of Work

H. M. DeLange*

Thinking and talking about labour and employment, about the efforts to humanize labour, and about the fight for better labour conditions mostly occur from the angle of economics and politics. From the point of view of social ethics one can at least add one dimension, because ethical thinking is aiming at responsible and just acts. The key work is righteousness, to be understood in our context as a "*relation word*". This is a permanent call to restore broken human relations. It is the old story that human relations are disturbed not only by individual sin and guilt but also by some particular economic and political developments. Significant of the biblical way of thinking is that justice is not a set of rules, but a way of living with both God and people. Biblical thinking brings us not to the question "what is justice", but to the question "who acts justly". It has a sharp reference to those who are oppressed and suffering. It is to these people that a new hope has to be given. Modern labour organisations (private and public—industries and others) show serious problems and many people (not only on the shop-floor) are suffering.

It strikes me that during the last years there is more reflexion on work and the meaning of work than during the decade before. The rather unexpected and persistent unemployment is a strong motive. In the Netherlands almost all the political parties hold the idea of full employment as one of the most important goals of economic policy. On the other hand, the goal of a "full" "dignified" (or worthy) employment is also being more and more important and already even been proposed by the government. This turn to more qualitative aspects can be seen as a consequence of the extension of education after World War II. A deeper awareness of human

---

* Netherlands.

Published in *Journal of Gandhian Studies*, Vol. 5; July 1978.

existence grows simultaneously with a higher level of vocational training. There is an increasing likelihood of growing frustration and alienation, especially where forms of work cannot take into account this cultural trend.

The demand for work

The total demand for work is decreasing and qualitative work is restricted. On the other hand the labour supply is growing especially when we look at the supply of women. From this point of view a technology which is a labour saving technology and a monotony-stimulating technology is related to an epoch in which we accepted these phenomena because the first priority was economic growth. Our background and starting point is: *man needs work and especially meaningful and creative work for his/her existence. Production and technology are made for man and not vice versa.*

With this conception in mind we have to reflect on possibilities for the renewal of work and the shaping of a less violent technology (Schumacher). We should never forget that the present manner of production is a very costly one indeed, especially when one looks to *total* costs. The assault of nature occurs in a way for which not only future generations, but already the present generation is hearing a heavy burden. The sustainability of the earth is at stake. The *spiritual* sustainability is threatened by psychological strain – suicide, drug addiction, heart disease.

People become ill, as we can see in the very serious increase in sick leave and the 12% of the labour population rejected as medically unfit. More and more people are consigned to the social security system that in itself puts a heavy burden on society (unemployment rate 5% by the end of 1977).

Next to these new problems we are still struggling with an old one: how to create more meaningful work in production?

What can be done ?

Must we accept that work is probably slipping away from human life? Are we moving towards a society in which leisure can contribute to the meaning of life? I am not so sure and I would still consider it an impoverishment were we increasingly to let work be done by automation and bigger apparatuses, which produce goods only to be used by us.

Moreover, one has to remember that present styles of production drain energy resources, and for this reason too it would be wise to reflect on changes in our very production and consumption patterns.

With the assumption that work is an intrinsic and irreplaceable part of human existence the idea of full employment and full dignified employment should be held on to as long as possible as one of the goals of economic policy. It is true that the pressure of work for society as a whole has fallen off in recent decades. However, this does not mean that we should abandon work in our lives. It means that in future, much more than in earlier times, we have the freedom to arrange the work as is good for the well being of mankind. Especially in the "structure of labour" people not only have an opportunity to earn money but also to gain some self-realisation and respect, and finally to have a relationship with others. Reviewing the last aspect, one can sometimes hear that from a Christian aspect "work is inseparable from service to our fellow-men. The understanding of work in this sense is inherent in the conception of man as existing not in individual isolation but in community and in his responsibility for his neighbour. Work has a Christian meaning only if the occupation is one in which society is truly served."[1] Oldham, whom we are quoting here continues on the same page: "It follows from the conception of work as ministry that the purpose of the economic order and of industry is to produce goods for the benefit of the consumer. If an economic system fails to meet the fundamental need of sustaining human life no other virtues which it may embody can compensate for its default in realizing its primary aim."

Outside the "labour structures", our modern society offers few opportunities to earn money, to realize some self-respect and to have relationships with others. Maybe it would be preferable to develop such other structures—may be we should extend the whole idea of work, like human efforts in unions, churches, sports committees, etc.

Another way of dealing with the problem is to search for a real new technology, a technology that accepts the idea that human work is a source of richness and welfare. Controlling technological innovation could be one of the most important issues in this field.

A third range of possibilities points in the direction of reduction of working hours, early retirement, and extension of compulsory education.

The Scientific Council for Government Policy in the Netherlands has just completed a study analysing the changing relationship between so-called economically active and non-active persons. The Council expresses the desirability of creating jobs in the non-commercial service sector, however not exclusively from an employment viewpoint. The basic premise is that unfulfilled needs exist in society, which can be filled by means of labour-intensive provisions.

The instrument traditionally applied by governments in the Northern Hemisphere to fight unemployment—stimulation of production—has lost its glamour and has its limits too. More production in our countries has less and less to do with needs. But this brings us to a different discussion and this is the problem of the economic order itself. It leads to the discussions on the economic of the just and sustainable society.[2]

References:

1. J.H. Oldham, *Work in Modern Society*, SCM Press, London, 1950, p. 50.

2. A small group of economists (all Christians) is now studying this problem, going through the ideas of Kenneth Boulding, *The Economics of the Coming Spaceship Earth*; Tibor Scitovsky *The Joyless Economy*; E.J. Mishan, *The Economic Growth Debate*; Herman E. Daly, *Steady-State Economics*.

25

Love is Real and Active

R. Scott Kennedy*

During the early 1970s there were several periods of turmoil involving youth, students and police in Isla Vista, replete with street-fighting, small-scale trashing, bonfires, barricades in the streets, and police occupation of the small town in which we live. During one such period, a friend happened upon a crowd gathered around a trash receptacle in a parking lot behind a large apartment building. The milling crowd surrounding the "dumpster" numbered nearly forty persons.

One young man shouted to the crowd, "Let's light it up and push it into the street." By this time nearly every street corner had one or more such firey barricades.

"No, don't light it", others from the crowd entreated. There was a standoff, with no sense of how to resolve the conflicting views.

Finally, another person, seemingly the most imaginative of the crowd, shouted out, "Let's have a vote."

This person climbed onto the dumpster and asked for ayes and nays. The nays had a majority of the crowd and he declared that by vote of the majority they would not set fire to the dumpster. For a brief moment the situation seem to have been fairly and definitively dealt with.

Another voice arose from the crowd, offering a challenging and striking rejection of the process of the group. "I'm going to light it anyway!"

Raising the ante, he approached the dumpster with matches in hand. His act cut through all that had gone before and the dumpster was seemingly his with which to do as he pleased.

---

* The Thomas Merton Unity Center, 892 Camino del Sur Isla Vista, CA. 93017 U.S.A.

Published in *Journal of Gandhian Studies*, Vol. 3; January 1976.

At that point a young woman emerged from the crowd and withought a word climbed up and into the dumpster. Sitting atop the pile of garbage, she looked at the match-wielding young man and spoke clearly and calmly. "OK, go ahead".

She had equalled his ante and called the bluff. There was no firing of that dumpster that night.

The above short tale touches at several points the vital issues of nonviolence as a force for social change and as a means for realizing the truth.

Gandhi created the word *Satyagraha* to describe a dynamic process whereby humankind might come to know more and more of the truth. As Joan Bondurant has written, "The technique to which Gandhi gave the name *Satyagraha* is at once a mode of action and a method of enquiry." (*Conquest of Violence*, p. v).

It was Gandhi's combination of two Sanskrit words and concepts which created the activist principle of non-violence, *Satyagraha* combines two Sanskrit nouns, *Satya* which means "truth" and *agraha* meaning "firm grasping", to hold on or to adhere. *Satyagraha* then means grasping or holding to the truth.

Satyagraha presupposes the synonimity of love and truth. Love and truth are one. Significantly, to carry this exploration one step further, the root of *satya* is *"sat"* which is Sanskrit for "being". Truth, and the discovery of truth, therefore, are rooted in *being*.

In I. John 3:18-19 we find written:

My children, our love is not to be just words or mere talk, but something real and active only by this can we be certain that we are children of the truth."(Jerusalem Bible).

In another translation we read:

Let us not love in word, neither with the tongue, but in deed and truth.

Thus, in the New Testament truth is also directly linked to being. Truth must be embodied, not in word or talk, but in deed. Deed, or being, is equated with truth.

For many of us Truth has become a principle which has been articulated and which is shared by a group of people as an abstraction or concept. The veracity of a truth is normally determined by its articulation, the clarity and applicability of its definition.

Gandhi, and the New Testament suggest another approach to testing the veracity of a truth. Truth is lived, it is to be found if it is something "real and active" or "in deed".

In the short story with which this meditation was commenced, we saw an escalation in deed, an escalation in truth-seeking. At one point on the scale, the risk is minimal, and the truth abstract: "Should one participate in firing the trash container?"

Perhaps it is fair to phrase the question in terms of a classical point of issue in discussions of non-violence: "Is the destruction of property as a provocative act a correct and efficacious choice of action ?"

A response to this question in word or "in tongue" by asserting an opinion is relatively cheap. The risk is minimal. If you oppose such an action, and your argument fails to persuade others, you may simply dissociate yourself by walking away. If you favour lighting up the dumpster, but the will of the crowd contradicts your own, you may seek out another situation, another dumpster and another crowd which might share your views.

The discussion took on a higher character with the suggestion of a vote-taking. In what might be viewed as a classical American response to such a dilemma as the discussion provided, people were asked to express their view by exercising the vote. This decision lends a certain clarity to the situation...... and permits a free expression of preference by all involved.

But, again, the risk-taking is minimal. The personal stake is small. The degree of personal commitment to the expression of one's view is fulfilled by the mere act of voting. The raising of a hand or shouting of aye or nay is an act in word or tongue. While advocating a position, and in that sense asserting a truth, there is no clear expectation that one feels any responsibility for acting on the same truth. The vote is the beginning and end of responsibility.

And, more importantly, the vote is found lacking in many cases as a means of resolving conflict. Bondurant refers to "a central weakness in liberal democratic thought: the failure to provide techniques of action for those critical occasions when the machinery of democratic government no longer functions to resolve large-scale, overt conflict."(p.x).

Therein lie the limitations of electoral politics.

By challenging the outcome of the straw vote, the young man threatening to light the dumpster raised the level of the exchange to one step higher. His act implied a clear risk of assuming responsibility for violating a process agreed to by those who both agreed and disagreed with him. His decision expressed a certain willingness to take personal responsibility for his act, in spite of the expressed will of the majority. His truth-asserting the appropriateness of a provocative act of arson-would not be found wanting for lack of personal responsibility or risk-taking on his part. At some level he sensed the validity of his truth, the appropriateness of his acting on said truth, and moved to act on it, to *embody* it.

In most situations such an assertion would suffice to carry the day, if for no other reason than such a level of commitment appears rare. As it evolved, his truth would not be so easily won.

For another person, with a variant understanding of truth and an equal commitment to it, matched his truth in deed as well as in word. By placing himself in the dumpster, the young placed herself in a position of personal jeopardy, and said in effect, "I'll meet your truth with my truth and raise the bet."

Truth is affirmed and enters the course of human events in an embodied form. The young woman cloaks herself in the truth in order to test it. To do any less is not to disprove the truth, but to indicate one's unwillingness to live it. As Gandhi said, "those who believe in the simple truths I have laid down can propagate them by living them."

Disembodied truth, no matter how articulately defined or defended, is no truth at all. A simple truth, embodied in the life of one person, shines far brighter than the greatest profundity expressed in the most eloquent terms, but which remains to be lived in deed and "in truth".

One is called to "*do* the truth". A disembodied truth is relegated to the realm of banal irrelevancy or reduced to pious platitude.

A truth unlived is no truth at all.

This story offers an example of Gandhi's method of truth seeking. It is indeed a parable of *satyagraha*. One sees that the level of discussion, discovery and truth is heightened, as one is willing to embody that truth which is affirmed. Words are cheap; voting is not much more useful as a mechanism of enquiry into truth.

The key for Gandhi was one's willingness to cloak one's self in the truth and to adhere to it unfailingly, perhaps at one's expense but never at the expense of the other person. This is likely to involve or even to invite a degree of self-suffering.

As Bondurant has observed, "To proceed towards the goal of Truth—truth in the absolute sense—the way must lead through the testing of relative truths as they appear to the individual performer. The testing of truth can be performed only by strict adherence to *ahimsa*—action based upon the refusal to do harm, or, more accurately, upon love." (p. 26).

Gandhi has written, "Non-violence in its dynamic condition means conscious suffering. It doesn't mean meek submission to the will of the evil-doer, but it means the pitting of one's whole soul against the will of the tyrant. Working under this law of our being, it is possible for a single individual to defy the whole might of an unjust empire." (p. 26 Boundurant) and "Suffering injury in one's own person is........of the essence of non-violence and is the chosen substitute for violence to others." (p. 27 Bondurant).

When advocates of countervailing truths are willing to accept personal responsibility for living the truth and accepting the consequences of affirming their truth, there is a greater clarity to the discussion and truth-seeking is served, Gandhi would relate the degree to which a truth might be made known to the degree to which self-suffering is accepted. The young man risked ostracism and going against the will of the majority to embody his truth. The young woman met his bet and raised the ante-risking her physical well-being in behalf of her truth.

The lesson is well stated: brothers and sisters, our love is not to be just words or mere talk, but something real and active. Only by this can we be certain that we are children of the truth.

26

Civil Disobedience in a Democracy

Gene Sharp*

"One may well ask, 'How can you advocate breaking some laws and obeying others?' The answer is found in the fact that there are two types of laws: There are *just* laws and there are *unjust* laws......One has not only a legal but moral responsibility to obey just laws. Conversely, one has a moral responsibility to disobey unjust laws......."

"One who breaks an unjust law must do it *openly, lovingly*........ and with a willingness to accept the penalty........and individual who breaks a law that conscience tells him is unjust, and willingly accepts the penalty by staying in jail to arouse the conscience of the community over its injustice, is in reality expressing the very highest respect for law."

—the late Dr. Martin Luther King Jr.
"Letters from Birmingham City Jail."

"I ask you to consider what would happen if other bodies adopted the same course (of organized civil disobedience). If that happened, it would be an end, would it not, to the rule of law? It would lead to the end of democracy, to anarchy and possibly dictatorship."

[The British Attorney-General, Feb. 1962, in his summing up at the trial of six members of the Committee of 100 for organizing civil disobedience against the British nuclear weapons programme.]

Is organised civil disobedience democratic? Is it justified in a liberal democracy in which citizens possess the right of free speech, assembly, a parliamentary system and periodic elections? Should dissident groups in such a system be permitted to organize to express their dissent in open disobedience and to encourage others to join them? Or does such behaviour strike hard against such a system itself? As the application of organized civil

---

* Lecturer, Department of Social Relations, Harverd University, U.S.A.
Published in *Journal of Gandhian Studies*, Vol. 1; July 1974.

disobedience in political conflicts is historically relatively new, so the constitutional questions it raises are new. They are, however, crucial and may influence not only future legal cases but the whole future development of democratic society.

In this chapter I shall attempt to analyse the issues of stake, and to demonstrate, not only that *individual* civil disobedience is justified in a constitutional representative democracy, but that *organized* civil disobedience may play an important role in the preservation and development of that system. This argument will not be based on the view of the late Dr. King as quoted above. From the perspective of what behaviour is appropriate in a constitutional representative democracy, there are severe dangers in saying that civil disobedience is right for "good" causes but wrong for "bad" causes. Opinions differ widely as to when a cause is good and bad. Most people who differ with each other extremely believe that their own cause is right, and that they are acting from noble motives From the perspective of the problems of civil disobedience in a constitutional representative democracy, political principles and standards must be developed which would apply equally to civil disobedience by anti-segregationist Negroes and by pro-segregationist whites, to religious men and atheists, to supporters of capitalism and committed socialists, to pacifists and to militarists, and to many other contending groups with opposed viewpoints.

The discussion in this chapter is limited only to possible role of civil disobedience, especially organized group civil disobedience, in a constitutional representative democracy, and does not apply to the multitude of other methods of non-violent action, such as economic boycotts and forms of non-violent intervention.

I. The Problem of Extreme Dissent

The ancient moral problem of the limits of individual obedience to the established government has not been eliminated by majority rule. As far as the *individual* is concerned, when it is demanded that he submits to what he believes to be a violation of his basic beliefs, it makes little difference to him whether the evil is one approved by a single man or by all of his fellow citizens. Nor has the system of constitutional representative government solved the problem of how extreme dissent should be expressed. One of the sobering aspects of politics is the number of occasions in history when the government's laws and policies have, in the perspective of later years been condemned as wrong. The simple extension of the franchise is no guarantee against similar errors in the present or future. Yet in the past such laws and policies have generally been passively or actively supported at the time by the majority of the citizens. In such cases it was the minority dissenters who opposed and, at the cost of persecution, often disobeyed those laws, who were thanked by later generations for their part in bringing about changes in those policies.

There have also been other dissenters who, seen from a later perspective, were not right, but who sincerely believed that they were and were therefore willing to take strong actions in support of that belief. Both these groups dissented on moral or political questions on which they rightly or wrongly, believed submission or compromise was not possible without a betrayal of their basic principles. They therefore, pose the same problem for all political societies including parliamentary democracies: how to express extreme dissent, and whether this can be done in a way which is effective but at the same time respects the opinions, persons and rights of their opponents and the majority. Representative governmental institutions and procedures however, imperfect, mark a distinct advance over the use of open political violence to achieve political ends. But if democracy is to continue, their usefulness must neither be under-valued nor their limitations ignored.

It is often forgotten that these institutions and procedure are able to function effectively only so long as the issues with which they must deal are those on which there exists a fundamental agreement within the society. The disagreements must be limited to secondary matters on which compromise—, which is essential to the present system,—is possible or on which the dissenting minority is willing and able to acquiesce.

However, there do exist moral and political issues involving conscience or fundamental questions concerning the nature or future of the society on which compromise or acquiescence are—rightly or wrongly—regarded as morally and politically unacceptable. Some of these are issues on which most of us would agree. For example, the election by majority vote of a party pledged to destroy liberty and democracy permanently could not bind the democrat to submit passively to the ensuing dictatorship. Racial segregation, untouchability or slavery do not become acceptable because of majority sanction. Majority support can never justify the extermination of a minority. Abolition of religious liberty by the majority cannot bind the democrat. There may be other issues on which agreement is not so widespread but on which the dissention minority neverthe-less believes that they can neither compromise nor submit to the majority. The possibility of error—seen by others—does not alter the intensity of the minority's convictions.

These "no compromise" issues arise even when constitutional representatives democracies operate as they ideally ought, with full civil liberties, full dissemination of information and genuine debate. Almost by definition the moral procedures of a political democracy are inadequate in these cases of fundamental conflicts.

Much popular discussion about civil disobedience and constitutional repre-sentative democracy proceeds on the assumption that all differences of opinion and conviction are of equal intensity and that compromise or acquiescence is always possible. This is a false and dangerous view, which may weaken the democracy in whose name the argument is offered.

In addition to these "no compromise", issues, the problem of how to express extreme dissent is important for another reason. Increasing concentration of social, political and economic power often reduces the degree of effective decision-making left to legislature, the degree to which minorities even on lesser issues may effectively influence others not sharing their views and the degree to which legislatures and governments may be really controlled even by the majority of the subjects. Where the normal institutional processes are thus imperfect, the need for examining how to express dissent is extended beyond the "no compromise" issues into ones of lesser importance on which the subjects feel they have no effective conventional means to express their grievances.

In a world in which liberty is widely threatened, and resort is frequently had to violence in political conflicts, democratic society will be strengthened by finding creative ways of expressing strong dissent.

It is no answer to a dissenter on fundamental issues (of the type cited above) to say that he has a right to maintain his personal opinion, to exercise freedom of speech and to work through established constitutional channels.

When the dissenter regards an issue as crucial, he cannot be expected to compromise or acquiesce passively during a transition period while he works for the cause in question. He feels he must express his disapproval by some form of action lest he be involved in moral or political complicity in the policy he opposes. Any such action to have a chance to influence opinions and policy necessarily leads to organization and the cooperation of others. To argue that while *individual* dissent is permissible, *organized* dissent by non-violent means is not, is to postulate the atomising of the population, isolating the individual in face of vast organized forces determining his fate, and rendering the dissent impotent and ignored. This is hardly a democratic theory.

A firmly established regime need not take serious note of a minority opposition, which is restricted to verbal dissent while continuing passive submission, which is restricted to verbal dissent while continuing passive submission and cooperation with the regime. If even a majority dissent only in words, while refraining from any action, which the regime would have to take seriously, there is nothing that *requires* the regime even to consider the advisability of a change.

The problem therefore, is to find a mode of dissent which is both capable of wielding power proportionate to 'the number of dissenters and which simultaneously does not violate the rights of others or seek to impose minority rule. This mode of dissent must, however, be one, which can be applied in *group action*. The dissenters face an organized opponent possessing vast resources; to deny their right to act together is to destroy any content in democracy.

II. Inadequate "Answers" to The Problem:

If the established institutional channels are inadequate to resolve these issues, these of course include the judicial system. It is unreasonable to assume that simply because a court of justice is involved the basic "no compromise" issues somehow disappear or become secondary ones where compromise or submission is possible. Judicial decisions may usefully settle a variety of social and political issues; but 'there will be certain issues on which judicial ruling will not be accepted by both parties as a final settlement.'

There are a limited number of possible ways of the type cited above of acting when "no compromise" issues arise (i.e., conflicts concerning morality, religion, justice, or the whole nature and direction of the society, or when people believe the conventional channels to be effectively blocked even on lesser issues. One common response to such crises has been political violence—rioting, assassinations, terrorism, violent revolution or civil war. These have occurred both in the presence and in the absence of a constitutional representative system of government. This is a response to a problem, which we must reject. Political violence in our time has taken such forms as to convince most serious democrats that it is destructive of moral principles, justice and democracy itself.

Another response to such conflicts of principles has been passive submission. But although the dissenter may thereby avoid the undesirable consequences of political violence, there are good reasons why passive submission must also be considered unacceptable. Firstly, the dissenter may be right. The Nuremberg and the Eichmann trials are particularly relevant here. The only legal basis upon which both those trials could be held was that the men charged and had a *legal* responsibility to *disobey* the orders of their political or military superiors. The Allied Governments accepted this legal position at Nuremberg.

When people have a deeply felt moral conviction it is dangerous to them personally and to society for them to suppress it and to do nothing about it. Their ability ever to act responsibly and true to their best convictions is reduced when they knowingly passively submit to what they believe to be a grave wrong The history of the consequences of increasing political passivity, authoritarianism and dictatorship ought to be a warning that passivity on deeply-felt issues may weaken democracy.

There has always been a third, less common, response to fundamental conflicts, namely, to attempt to withdraw from the "world" and to live as true as possible to one's convictions without attempting to influence the course of political events. This is, however, unsatisfactory for those who feel their convictions require them to exert a wider responsibility for influencing the course of society as a whole, and is, therefore, no answer to our problem.

If, therefore, there is not to be an acceptance of either passivity or political violence, there must be an alternative means of democratic peaceful action to express extreme dissent which while **being effective,** also recognizes the democratic rights of the majority.

III. Civil Disobedience

Civil disobedience—one of the methods of non-violent action—has been suggested and practiced as a substitute non-violent way of responding to these conflicts and of expressing extreme dissent—in place of both passivity and violence. Civil disobedience is a deliberate peaceful violation of particular laws, decrees, regulations, ordinances, military or police orders and the like. These are usually laws etc., which are regarded as inherently immoral, unjust or tyrannical. Sometimes, however, laws of a largely regulative or "neutral" character may be disobeyed as a symbol of opposition to wider policies of the Government. This may take place where it is difficult to find a point of direct contact between the individual and the wider governmental policy. Civil disobedience may be practiced by individuals, by small groups, and by masses of people. It may be reluctantly practiced by those who have no desire to disturb the status quo *per se*, but wish only to remain true to their convictions. Or it may be undertaken with the limited aim of changing a particular policy, law, etc. Or it may be used along with other methods of non-violent action in times of major social or political upheaval as a full substitute for violent revolution. Civil disobedience is not likely to be lightly undertaken in the absence of strong feelings, for it involves always the strong risk, and in certain situations, the virtual certainty of incurring at least the penalties provided for disobedience in the law.

IV. Problems of Civil Disobedience in a Democracy:

Where ordinary civil liberties exist, organized civil disobedience is not a substitute for verbal persuation and the use of the existing constitutional means of influencing and changing governments. It is, an alternative to political violence. This is basic for understanding its role in a democracy.

Organized large-scale civil disobedience inevitably presents certain problems to the government and the majority. They cannot ignore it because of the dissenters' challenge in openly disobeying a law, *with willingness to accept the legal penalties*, in order to bring wider public 'attention to their case and in order to withdraw their consent and support from the policy they oppose. Established governments will rarely feel they can tolerate open deliberate disobedience without their imposing the sanctions provided in the law for disobedience. This means that Governments, operating from their established premises must arrest the civil resisters and impose fines and sentences of imprisonment upón them. *This is to be expected and when this is done the civil resisters normally cannot complain.* They must instead regard the sentences as a means of furthering their cause and strengthening their movement. Where civil disobedience is widespread the government is compelled to provide the necessary enforcement personnel, administrative, machinery, and punishment facilities to cope with the large number of disobedient subjects.

The enforcement problems for governments facing large-scale organized civil disobedience are peculiar, partly because deliberate, open, peaceful disobedience is not usual, but mainly because the dissenters not only are not afraid of the penalties but virtually ask to be arrested. Governments have therefore, often reacted with some uncertainty. The example of people willing to undergo penalties and hardships for their conscientious dissent may lead increasing numbers of the public to think about the issues for the first time. This thus encourages policies to be chosen consciously, rather than accepted passively. It may even result in the minority becoming the majority. In that case, of course, the change of policy may be made by the usual constitutional methods. Where the Government does not bow to the changed views, or does not allow the usual constitutional means for changing governments to be used, then the new majority of dissenters to Government policy have peaceful means of civil disobedience and other forms of non-violent action by which they can act peacefully to alter the policy or the Government and restore majority rule.

But it may not happen that the dissenters are successful in convincing the majority. In that case the minority cannot force the majority to accept the change of policy. There is no such thing as a "non-violent *coup d'etal.*" Those who envisage that they could become some kind of incongruous "Gandhian Jacobins", and, while a clear minority, impose their will on the majority which believes in the existing policy are obviously ignorant of the nature of non-violent action and are harbouring ideas which are irresponsible and dangerous in the extreme.

If a policy is to be permanently secured by non-violent means it can only be done by building up conviction in its rightness among the population to the point where it has majority support and strength to carry through its policy and to defend it non-violently against minority attempts by violence to impose the old policy. It is possible that a minority could by purely obstructionist non-violent tactics bring about the fall of a Government in a democratic system. But to think that this would amount to a victory is pure ignorance. This would not necessarily nor even probably, bring about the desired new policy. *With the majority still supporting the old policy and alienated from considering the minority's case by their obstructionist, a new and more repressive regime supporting the old policy could come to power-either constitutionally or by coup d'etat.* Obstructionism thus could lead to the minority becoming a still smaller minority with reduced chances of achieving its objectives.

If, as is unlikely, a minority Government should come to power favouring the new policy against the wishes of the majority it could only maintain itself against the probably strong opposition on such a crucial issue by itself becoming repressive of the majority and depending for its existence in the last resort upon the very military means it allegedly opposed.

Understood in terms of the nature of civil disobedience, and of non-violent action in general, a minority cannot impose its will upon a majority which believes in its own policy. There is no substitute for quality and genuine strength in a non-violent movement, and there is no alternative to building up majority support for the view of the dissenters. If, therefore, non-violent action in general, and civil disobedience in particular, are to advance the minority dissenters' cause, it must conform to certain standards which not only make it effective in the long run but also simultaneously make it compatible with democracy.

V. Democratic qualities of civil disobedience:

Civil disobedience withdraws support and obedience from a policy or regime in proportion to the numbers of citizens who disapprove of it and are willing to pay the price for that withdrawal—usually imprisonment. Given the maintenance of the quality of the action, the seriousness of the challenge of the civil disobedience to the Government is thus roughly in proportion to the numbers among the citizens who feel strongly enough on the issue to take part in it.

Organized civil disobedience combines certain qualities, which have formerly been believed to be incompatible. It allows for direct, immediate militant action by those strongly dissenting from the established policy and who feel that they "must" act, against it at once. This quality was formerly believed to be possessed only by political violence. With civil disobedience, however, there is no injury or death inflicted by the dissenters, and no destruction of property. There is respect for the opponents and for the majority. The dissent is expressed in an orderly and peaceful manner—important qualities of democracy. It has even been argued that civil disobedience involve a profound respect for the law itself, the disobedient acting openly and being willing to accept the legal penalty for disobedience as the price in a democracy for expressing extreme dissent in direct action.

All these are qualities, which, it was formerly believed, were possessed only by adherence to the normal constitutional procedures of a representative democracy. *Civil disobedience, it is thus argued, combines the strength of both direct action and gradualism in political conflicts, while avoiding the undesirable moral and political consequences of both political violence and inaction in face of fundamental conflicts.*

VI. The choice : violent or non-violent action

The distinction between non-violent action in general and civil disobedience in particular on the one hand, and political violence, on the other cannot be overemphasized. The moral implications and immediate human consequences as well as the long-run social and political effects are radically different. Civil disobedience is an attempt to act peacefully and democratically in case of basic conflicts on which the minority finds itself unable to compromise on essentials or passively to acquiesce. It is resorted to only in cases of extreme dissent on which—in the absence of a non-violent alternative—the dissenters would very possibly have resorted to political violence, such as assassinations or bombings. *Civil disobedience is thus not a substitute for conventional constitutional means, but for political violence.*

It is, therefore, disturbing that the attempt is often made to equate civil disobedience and violence. In a legal sense admittedly, the breaking of the law is the breaking of the law, and preparations to break one law may be technically as illegal as preparations to break another law. However, the social and political consequences for a democracy of acts to express extreme dissent by minority political violence and by minority non-violent action including group civil disobedience, respectively, are vastly different. Such consequences differ so much that a legal distinction should be made between organization for violent disobedience and for civil disobedience. This difference is crucial in answering the question whether there should be prosecution for *organizing* as distinct from *committing*, civil disobedience. In considering the constitutional question of whether or not people should be prosecuted for *organizing* civil disobedience, the question of whether the dissent is violent or not is therefore a highly important one. The attempt to equate the two techniques, by ignoring their different consequences and implications can only be seen as based upon ignorance of these differences or a desire to crush the expression of dissent by civil disobedience at all costs.

One widespread erroneous view of organized civil disobedience is that it must cause social or political obstruction or disruption. In civil disobedience, however, it is not the actual successful committing of the intended specific act, which is the most important. It is the attempt to do so. For example, in India in 1930, when there were massive attempts to manufacture salt illegally, if the person was arrested before the making of the salt was completed, this did not defeat his object: the salt tax law had been violated by his attempt, and the State had demonstrated that in order to maintain its policies it was necessary to arrest thousands of peaceful subjects. This revealed the normally hidden violence of the system, trained the population in resistance and further alienated the people from the Government. Similarly, if anti-racial segregation demonstrators in the U.S. Deep South were arrested as they enter a segregated waiting room instead of after they have been in it for a while, their action has not been defeated but has achieved its essential purpose.

If the numbers of disobedient subjects grow so large, owing to decreasing support for the government's policy, or there is a "change of heart" in the opposition, so that the dissenters are ultimately permitted to continue the specific act without interference, so much the better from their stand point. But—and this point is important in considering the role of civil disobedience in a constitutional representative democracy—*it is attempt to commit the act which constitutes the civil disobedience and if all the demonstrators are arrested as soon as this attempt is made and outward formal "order" is thus quickly restored—thus satisfying the government—the act has still achieved its purpose in being an act of defiance and of withdrawal of consent which the government has been forced to recognize.*

VII. A democratic expression of extreme dissent

The answer to our original question, is organized civil disobedience democratic, thus gradually becomes clear. Basic to that answer is our view of democracy. It involves, of course, basic civil liberties and respect for both the minority and the majority. But democracy, as I see it, means essentially that the citizens have a genuine voice in determining the course of their own lives and of the policies of their government and country. With the present increasing centralization of all kinds of power, the active participant of the citizenry—basic to democracy—is more important than ever. Equally important, democracy means that social and political changes are to be made without resort to political violence. Representative institutions have served as a means towards this end. It was always clear, however, that these were not the sole means of making peaceful changes.

No one questions the democratic qualities of public protest meeting, distribution of leaflets, publication of political articles and books, a picket line or a strike, a petition to the government or a campaign to educate the public on a particular issue. All these actions may be aimed at influencing the majority, the legislature and the government. But they all clearly operate outside the formal structural arrangements of elections and the institutional framework of repre-sentative government. This does not make them less democratic. Similarly, organized civil disobedience is not intrinsically undemocratic because it too operates outside the electoral and legislative procedures.

Civil disobedience is often dismissed as coercive, but, as we have noted though it may cause difficulties to the government and the majority, *minority* civil disobedience cannot *force* a government to reverse its policies if it and the majority really believe in them and are determined to carry them out.

It is my contention that the view of the British Attorney General quoted at the beginning of this chapter, is simply not true. *Rather than destroying democracy, the introduction of the right to organize civil disobedience would strengthen it by meeting one of its major weaknesses¾the absence of a democratic means of expressing extreme dissent¾and reduce the more serious dangers to democracy posed by passivity and political violence.* Rather than being horrified at the prospect of other groups adopting civil disobedience one might be gratified that they had thereby rejected political violence with its anti social and anti-democratic effects.

Organized civil disobedience is somewhat comparable on the political level with strikes in the industrial field, except that in the former only a portion of the persons involved withdraw their cooperation with the system. Strikes are designed to take place when established procedures for dealing with disputes have failed to produce agreements. They, too, are substitute for violent action, such as murdering the employer or bombing the factory. Instead, the men non-violently withdraw their cooperation with the opponent. However, misused strikes have been at times, it is generally agreed that the right to strike is an essentially democratic right.

Even so, there are of course sanctions against strikes. While refusing to work the workers get no wages and this, though not a legal sanction, operates to discourage strikes except where the issue is deeply felt. Similarly in organized civil disobedience, sanctions exist which would in a much greater degree discourage people from practising it except in extreme cases. The numbers of groups, therefore, likely to adopt civil disobedience are not large, being limited to those who feel sufficiently deeply about the issue to be willing to accept imprisonment and other suffering for their refusal passively to submit. If the dissent is that deeply felt it is desirable that the group should have some strong, but peaceful, means of expressing its objections.

It is therefore, suggested that our present democratic system be improved by making provision for the expression of extreme dissent through recognition of the right to *organize* civil disobedience with no prosecutions being made for such organizing and promoting. The *committing* of civil disobedience would of course by definition continue to be illegal, and as long as arrests and prosecutions were made under the law chosen for disobedience they would be regarded as fair and reasonable within the framework of existing constitutional representative democracy. This would provide the society with a democratic outlet for extreme dissent and with a kind of barometer by which the extent and intensity of extreme dissent would be measured. *Organized civil disobedience thus would provide an orderly peaceful substitute for political violence with its anti-democratic qualities.*

On the other hand, the attempt itself to *prevent* the peaceful expression of radical dissent by organized civil disobedience poses grave threats to democracy. By interfering with such organization the government forces the society to restrict the normal civil liberties which a dissenting group may wish to use either to discuss their views or to publicize a demonstration by civil disobedience (as leafleting, public meetings, and the like).

If the approach advocated here were adopted, prosecutions for *committing* civil disobedience would be quite in order, but such restrictions on normal civil liberties for publicizing grievances or future civil disobedience would be unne-cessary. Lifting these restrictions could thus at certain stages of a movement considerably ease and simplify the task of the police. At times in the past when restrictions were placed on civil liberties, one result was an increase in the numbers committing civil disobedience, for people then saw a connection between that act and the preservation of freedom. At times, such restrictions have simply enlarged the scope of civil disobedience, by making it possible to commit by holding prohibited meetings, distributing prohibited literature, etc.

What if a government faced with a significant movement of extreme dissent persists in making organized orderly civil disobedience not only illegal but seriously attempts to make it impossible? Unless knowledge of the principles, theory and application of non-violent action is widely permeated throughout the movement and population, there is a strong likelihood of the movement organizing itself on an "underground", i.e., secret basis. This would have serious consequences for the movement as well as for the society. It would probably lead to a numerically smaller but more desperate movement, tending to use whatever means it could, very possibly including acts of political violence.

As Gandhi said when the British were so furious at his 1930 civil disobedience movement—would they prefer violence? That is in fact the alternative in such case of radical conflict, and unfortunately it is often the case that rulers *do* prefer their protesting subjects to revolt with violence, for they are more easily crushed and discredited when they do. This development would however, be disastrous both for the cause of the dissenting group, for the society, and destructive of democracy. The chances of it occurring will be greatly reduced if it is recognized that a democratic society requires some means of expressing extreme dissent and that this need can best be met by a legal recognition of the right to organize civil disobedience to do so. Whether this is accepted may depend upon whether the citizens and government are more interested in suppressing dissent or in maintaining and improving a democratic society.

VIII. Standards for civil disobediences in a democracy

When organized civil disobedience is to be practised in a constitutional representative democracy, there must then be certain standards of behaviour to which *both* sides must conform if fair play is to be observed and if the democratic qualities of that society are to be maintained and enriched. The failure of either side to conform to these may severely threaten the democratic qualities of that society. I tentatively suggest the following standards: For the non-violent actionists:

1) The action must be absolutely non-violent in all circumstances, in face of all provocation, retaliation and repressive measures. The actionists ought even to seek to avoid engendering permanent animosity and hostility and to maintain friendly relations with all involved (while recognizing that temporary hostility may despite all efforts sometimes be aroused by the mere existence of dissent).

2) The group responsible for laying the plans for the action must operate openly and above broad. All plans for action must be revealed publicly in advance of the action, including to the police and other relevant governmental agencies.

3) As long as prosecution is brought under the law or regulation chosen for disobedience, the actionists must be willing to accept the penalties provided in the law for disobedience, such as fines or imprisonment.

4) Except where brutality, attempts at humiliation or other unjust treatment have occurred, or in very special cases, the prisoner should cooperate with the police and prison authorities from the time of his arrest. Imprisonment is seen as the penalty the democrat must accept for practising civil disobedience as a means of furthering his convictions.

5) The non-violent actionists must behave in a disciplined, dignified manner jin all circumstances.

6) The demonstrators will not seek to be simply obstructionists nor to bring down a government supported by the majority.

For the government:

1) Where a law is not being violated, the non-violent action must be followed to proceed peacefully without interference. Basic civil liberties, including the right to picket, distribute leaflets, hold parades, public meetings, etc., must not be interfered with, even when these advertise civil disobedience.

2) The penalties imposed on the disobedient demonstrators must be limited to the maximum—*and this must be reasonable*—contained in the law chosen for disobedience and other laws which were not intended by their authors to deal with such behaviour must not be invoked.

3) Extra-legal measures, such as beatings, shootings, brutalities, etc., either before or after arrest must in no circumstances be permitted.

4) Disproportionate punishment of a few only of the demonstrators or organizers must be regarded as selective justice and hence unfair.

(5) The right to organize and practice collective civil disobedience, subject to the above standards, must be recognized as a peaceful democratic substitute for political violence.

(6) While conforming to the above standards, a government if justified in arresting and sentencing demonstrators practicing civil disobedience under the normal provisions of the law chosen for disobedience.

With both sides conforming to such standards as these, regardless of the rights and wrongs of the disagreements, the contest while admittedly causing inconveniences to the government and the majority will enrich the ability of the democracy to deal with extreme dissent in a democratic manner.

IX. Conclusion

The general proposal that the organizing of civil disobedience be permitted in a constitutional representative political system, admittedly involves a modification of some existing policies and perhaps even legal concepts. But, it is argued this would enrich and strengthen the democratic system by providing an answer to the problem of how to express extreme dissent—a problem which existing democratic theory and practice has never really faced.

The development of non-violent action including civil disobedience, in facing conflicts within the society may, in turn, help the country to resolve other problems. It could assist in providing a means—along with other forms of non-violent action—by which the majority itself could act to defend the society and constitutional government when liberty is threatened; for example, by *coup d'etat* for which there is also at present no constitutional answer. The use of civil disobedience and other forms of non-violent action within the society could thus help to prepare people as a whole for meeting such crises as this, and even invasion, by producing experience in the application of an alternative technique of struggle. The country as a whole would thus be more capable of effective action against internal or external threats to its liberty.

27

Gandhi, M. L. King and the Civil Right Movement

K.L. Seshagiri Rao*

In 1935, while talking to a group of Negro visitors in India, Gandhi observed, "perhaps it will be through the Negro that the unadulterated message of non-violence will be delivered to the whole world"[1], Martin Luther King, Jr. was a six-year old boy living in Atlanta, Georgia, at that time. Dr. King is perhaps, the one Black leader who came closest to fulfilling this prophecy of Gandhi by employing the technique of non-violent resistance in all his struggles.

Satyagraha has received much publicity in America over the past two decades because of its employment in the Civil Rights Movement of the American Negroes. For nearly fifteen years the American Black Community, until 1964, was led by Dr. Martin Luther King, Jr., who had been staging one type of struggle or the other. After listening to a lecture by Rev. Mordacai Johnson, a Baptist minister who had returned from India with a great enthusiasm for applying Gandhi's techniques to the Civil Rights Movement, Dr. King was intrigued, and studied several of Gandhi's books. Gandhi's *Satyagraha* exercised the mind of Dr. King, and the impression of his first encounter with Gandhism is given in his book, *Stride Toward Freedom*:

Gandhi was probably the first person in history to lift the love ethic of Jesus above mere interaction between individuals to a powerful and effective social force on a large scale. Love for Gandhi was a potential instrument for social and collective transformation. It was in this Gandhian emphasis on love and non-violence that I discovered the method for social reform that I had been seeking for so many months. The intellectual and

---

* Professor of Religious Studies in the University of Virginia, U.S.A.

Published in *Journal of Gandhian Studies*, Vol. 2; April 1975.

moral satisfaction that I had failed to gain from the utilitarianism of Bentham and Mill, the revolutionary methods of Marx and Lenin, the social contract theory of Hobbes, the "back to nature" optimism of Rousseau, and the Superman philosophy Nietzsche, I found in the non-violent resistance philosophy of Gandhi. I came to feel that this was the only morally and practically sound method open to oppressed people in their struggle for freedom".[2]

The Civil Rights Movement is concerned with racial equality for the Black people. The crisis began in the United States of America in 1955, and since its beginnings, it has been typified by sit-ins, freedom marches, demonstration picket lines, etc. The movement was aimed at, among other things, (i) bringing pressure for the passage of Civil Rights Act of 1965 (which it achieved); (ii) increasing Black Voter Registration; (iii) challenging the all-pervasive and over-riding fear that dominated the life of the Blacks in the U.S.

Martin Luther King, Jr., was brought up in the Christian faith. His father was pastor of the Ebenezer Baptist Church in Atlanta, Georgia, and was also an active champion of civil rights, being a militant member of the NAACP. So it was as a child that Martin Jr. began to see how Christianity could work in the world to combat social evils. When he was in high school, returning from an oratorical contest in which he had won second prize, he was forced to give up his seat on a bus to a white student. "I don't think I have ever been so deeply angry in my life"[3], he later recalled. This and similar encounters left a deep impression on him, convincing him of the evil of racial prejudice and hatred, and of the need for reform.

While in college, he began a search to find his own philosophy one which would have meaning to him. He studied philosophers and theologians; but the influence that moulded his life were his Christian beliefs and the ideas of Gandhi. King feared that he had too much faith in the kind of love Jesus spoke of as the answer to over-coming injustice. But he was heartened greatly by Gandhi's idea of *Satyagraha*. "As I delved deeper into the philosophy of Gandhi my scepticism concerning the power of love gradually diminished, and I came to see for the first time its potency in the area of social reform."[4]

King called *Satyagraha* love-force, and it became the heart of his doctrine of non-violent resistance. He felt that Gandhi showed that Jesus' ethics could work effectively on a large scale as well as between individuals. In his later years, non-violent resistance became more than just a philosophy; it became a way of life. Dr. King, like Gandhi, was strongly influenced by Jesus' teachings of 'social gospel'. They both experienced racial prejudice which left its indelible mark on them.

King adopted many of Gandhi's ideas concerning non-violent resistance. Non-violent resistance as practised by both men has several basic principles. It is not the coward's way out—it is dynamic and spiritually active. It does not seek to humiliate, but seeks to conciliate. It is directed not against those who commit evil, but against the evil they commit. Non-violent resistance is characterized by its willingness to accept suffering without retaliation; the center of the struggle is love—the kind of love that is unselfishly concerned for others, loving for their sakes alone, responding to their needs. Love is the great healing force. King told the Blacks that "Since the white man's personality is greatly distorted by segregation, and his soul is greatly scarred, he needs the love of the Negro."[5]

Both King and Gandhi agreed that ends do not justify the means. This belief underlies the philosophy of non-violent resistance. "Constructive ends can never give absolute moral justification to destructive means, because, in the final analysis the end is pre-existent in the means."[6] In this and many other respects, we see a similarity and close resemblance between the stands of King and Gandhi on non-violent resistance. Let us now look at the impact Dr. King had on his movement.

Dr. King began his career in 1955 when a Negro woman in Montgomery, Alabama, was arrested for refusing to give her seat on a bus to a white person. King, a young and enthusiastic minister in Montgomery, interested in civil rights, was asked to help organize a Negro boycott of the bus system of the city; he agreed. The Montgomery Negro leaders who met to plan the boycott formed the Montgomery Improvement Association, and elected King president. The movement was on its way. King was a leader—an excellent leader—and was available when a leader was needed. His success as a leader was, in large part, due to his ability to get the Blacks to work together; he was able to channel their hates, their fears, their prejudices, and their resentments into a constructive programme of non-violent resistance. And because he had studied non-violent resistance and was well acquainted with Gandhi's demonstration of it, he was able to make non-violent resistance effective on a large scale.

The best way to dramatize a cause is to personify it. King became the spokesman for the Black people, and they identified with him. He was the champion of their rights. To people all over the world, King became the symbol of freedom for the Blacks.

On February 1, 1960, another phase of the Civil Rights Movement began with the first sit-in at a Woolworth's Counter in Greensboro, North Carolina. This phase also embraced non-violent resistance as its official policy. The idea of the sit-in gave the movement a philosophy and a direction. It was intended to break down the segregationists' will while, at the same time, gaining public sympathies. All over the United States, sit-ins were employed. The sit-in was the catalyst for the organization of groups like S.N.G.C. and C.I.O.R.E. which soon branched out into national powers.

Protesters became the victims of police scorn and brutality in the South. In Birmingham, 3,000 non-violent demonstrators were jailed. The nation became electrified. The fear of a sit-in leading to adverse publicity and nuisance caused many restaurant owners to be happy to serve anyone. Consequently large numbers of restaurants even in the South were integrated.

Several marches were sponsored by the Black community; for example, one was organized from Memphis to Jackson, Mississippi and the other from Selma to Montgomery, Alabama. In these marches the Negroes were beaten, jeered at and tear-gassed. However, they did not resort to violence (actually violence came from other quarter). Dr. Martin Luther King repeatedly claimed: "I am not a consensus leader and I will not turn to violence." These acts of non-violent resistance greatly helped the Blacks to achieve the Civil Rights Act of 1965.

The method of violent protest riots by the Blacks later on, the increase in the popularity of the 'Black Power Movement', and the assassination of Dr. King would indicate that non-violent resistance has suffered an eclipse of late. This may be only partly true; to an extent it may have been brought about by differential news coverage and by the more vocal of the violent segment of the Black population.

Dr. King adapted *Satyagraha* for American needs and condition. Blacks, under the leadership of Dr. King endeavoured to win through Gandhi's method, and many are consciously aware of it. They drew inspiration from Gandhi; but they realize that there are some flaws in practice. The Indian culture with its tradition of *Ahimsa* (non-violence) and the American Black culture with its "western tradition of defense" account for many differences in the practice of non-violent resistance by Gandhi and by King.

The Blacks have practiced Gandhi's *Satyagraha* to achieve social equality in an ad hoc manner and by 'bits and snatches'. They have turned the other cheek and practiced discipline. They have learned to suffer in dignity. However, the weakest point seems to be the lack of sustained constructive activities among the people. If they engaged themselves in more constructive activities, their cause would benefit to a greater extent. If their goals along with their reason and their willingness to help themselves are communicated to the wider public, there would be much more progress and more rapid progress than at present. This has to be done if the Civil Rights Movement is to achieve greater success in the future. Properly utilized and with the proper motives, non-violent resistance has an important role to play in the American Civil Rights Movement, or in any other situation of injustice and oppression.

Refrences:

1. Lerone Bennet, Jr., What Manner of Men (Chicago, 1964), p. 4.
2. Martin Luther King, Jr., Stride Towards Freedom (New York, 1958), p. 97.
3. Robert Stranns Fenerlicht, Martin Luther King, Jr., (New York, 1958), p.21.
4. Martin Luther King, Jr., Stride Towards Freedom, (New York, 1958), p. 96.
5. ibid., p. 105.
6. ibid., p. 92.

28

Non-violence, Truth and International Peacemaking

Indrajit Rikhey (Major General)*

As a professional soldier, I was trained by the British and fought alongside them in the Middle-East and Italy. As an Indian, I was deeply influenced by Gandhi's non-violent struggle to free my country from the British rule. For a man schooled in the disciplined use of force, the doctrine of ahimsa can only be made appealing if it is interpreted as courageous if non-violent action. That is why I was ready to listen when Gandhi talked about non-violence.

"I would rather have India resort to arms in order to fend her honour than that she should, in a cowardly manner, become or remain a helpless witness to her own dishonour.

"But I believe that non-violence is infinitely superior to violence, forgiveness is more manly than punishment. Forgiveness, adorns a soldier." (From *Non-Violence in Peace and War*).

Nationalism and Truth

In spite of Gandhi's teaching and example, I am afraid that my understanding of this adornment—the quality of mercy in Lincoln's words—was rather narrow until I stepped out of my role as an officer in the Indian army to become an international civil servant. I suppose that those who recommended me for the post of Military Advisor to the UN Secretary-General must have thought I possessed some of the traits needed for this sensitive job. But ten years of United Nations experience have taught me

---

* Chairman, International Academy Committee, U.S.A

Originally published in *Journal of Gandhian Studies*, Vol. 1; October, 1973.

that whatever an individual's personal characteristics, national service is not the kind of preparation needed for international experience and peace-keeping.

The reasons are obvious enough: national governments train their military officers and diplomats in adversary attitudes and strategies. Whether practiced on the battle-field or in the conference room, the objective of adversary methods is to win the contest rather than to resolve the conflict. Every issue or situation is refracted through mental lenses ground to national specifications.

This "ingroup" bias has a subtly distorting effect on the way national representatives see the world and interstate relations. It is an inescapable aspect of individual identity : our personal values, attitudes, and interests are shaped by our "reference groups", as the sociologists call them. Conformity to the outlook of the groups with whom we identify ourselves gives us our social bearings and ballast. This is the essence of nationalism. It explains why an Indian Army officer thinks like an Indian Army officer rather than an American officer or Indian pacifist.

With the exception of gifted or great souls, our normal roles lock us into stereotyped way of perceiving conflict and reacting to it. Consider the problem of accurately explaining the causes underlying a particular conflict. There is an Arab and an Israeli truth about the Middle East crisis, just as there is an Indian and Pakistani truth about Kashmir. I am directly acquainted with both of these situations. I have added up the pros and cons of the case advanced by each side in its favour and come to my own conclusions, though I must concede that I am able to do this more impartially when I am looking at the Middle East than when I am looking at Kashmir. Political truth is subjective: it involves *preference* regarding the distribution of population, natural resources, and power. It is largely defined by territorially based social attachments, though it can be argued that an evolutionary process has fitfully but steadily widened the effective loyalties of men. Loyalty to India is more universal than loyalty to Simla.

In an international dispute, the peacemaker's function is not to expound to those involved an indivisible, immutable Truth, but to help them *create* a new truth about their relationship by finding firm ground for agreements that will benefit both parties and bring their vital interests into closer harmony. When this happens, Arabs and Israelis, Indians and Pakistanis, Americans and Russians, will be able to say. "The truth of the matter is that peace and cooperation are in our mutual best interest." I am not suggesting that this is easy, or that it is possible at every point in the development of conflict, but in the end it is the only alternative to mutually devastating violence or chronic and debilitating conflict.

Gandhi's Philosophy and Third-party Roles

The creation of new political and social truths, new sympathies and rela-tionships, is always the goal of great peacebuilders such as Gandhi. There are many reflections of this insight in his writings on *Satyagraha.* It can be found in his *Non-violence in Peace and War* "I did not consider Englishmen, nor do I now consider them, as particularly bad or worse than other human beings. I consider them to be as capable of high motives and action as any other body of men and equally capable of making mistakes." Or from *Young India:* "We must try patiently to convert our opponents. If we wish to evolve the spirit of democracy out of slavery, we must be scrupulously exact in our dealings with our opponents." "Means and ends are convertible in my philosophy of life."

It strikes me forcibly that Gandhi's attitudes towards opponents and his philosophy of means and ends have helped to open the way for inter-national civil service as a profession. The U.N. officer commits himself to an institutionalised third-party role, whether its incumbent is a military officer wearing the UN's blue beret, a diplomat acting temporarily as a mediator, or an FAO technical specialist, requires scrupulous impartiality in dealing with all parties. It also demands adherence to the principles of justice expressed in the UN Charter and Covenants on Human Rights. This calls for difficult and sometimes painful judgments.

Like Gandhi, the international civil servant and other practitioners of peace will protest their fallibility, but the intent and thrust of their roles are clear and distinguished them from those who represent national and other partial interests. Peacemaking, peacekeeping, and peacebuilding require a high degree of consistency in the conduct of those who seriously profess them.

The Limits of Non-Violence

While I recognize the contradiction, and the frequent futility, of using violence to achieve moral ends, I am unable to accept Gandhi's faith in non-violent non-cooperation as a means of national defense.

I have the same problem with this concept that Congress had with it in 1939. I grant that it represents the highest manifestation of bravery and humane patriotism, but it requires a capacity for collective self-imposed suffering which I fail to observe in any nation, including India. To me, the measure of its impossibility is implicit in Gandhi's 1940 "appeal to every Briton", "I want you to fight Nazism without arms, I would like you to lay down the arms you have as being useless for saving you or humanity ....(if necessary) you will allow yourselves – man, woman and child to be slaughtered, but you will refuse to owe allegiance to them."

That was too much to expect of Britons, or Indians, then. The arguments in favour of non-violent or non-military defence are far more relevant and compelling today. Strategic thermonuclear weapons threaten the extinction of states, probably whole population, even the human race. Yet this quantum leap in the technology of warfare has not brought about a revolution in the social psychology of conflict, in spite of the impact of World War II and the cumulative carnage of the "small wars of last twenty five years." Leader and their peoples alike have reacted to these psychic shocks with habitual responses, which made some sense before Hiroshima. Unfortunately the rate and magnitude of change are continually outrunning our ability to adapt to radically new conditions.

I regret to say that I see few, if any signs, that whole nations, or a large enough proportion of their populations, can be mobilized in support of non-violent national defence. To pin our hopes for the prevention of nuclear war on that prospect would be like planning a future based on the merger of the Kremlin and the Holy See.

A step at a time

So, I can be called a pessimist. But I am also an optimist. Like Mark Twain, I believe that habit is habit, but I also believe with him that it can be "coaxed downstairs to step at a time". I suppose I am hoping for grace, for enough time to change our habits. And since institutions are habitual patterns of action, to talk about changing habits is to talk about changing institutions. How is this to be accomplished? Not, I think, by sudden radical innovations, which totally transform present international patterns into somebody's ideal system. As I have made clear, I do not expect the world to be swept by a religious passion which would turn us all into *Satyagrahi*. Nor do I foresee the establishment of world government by consent, or, for that matter, by conquest. But I do see the possibility of breathing renewed life into the politics of international cooperation.

At this moment in history the world's problems are not basically constitutional; they are political. We do not need to revise the United Nations Charter. We need to change the foreign policies of governments by changing the attitudes of political leaders and their followers. There is a starting place for this effort, though it is no more than that: their mutual interest in national survival.

The twenty-fifth anniversary of the United Nations has been celebrated. We face the uncertainties of the next quarter century with an unsettling mixture of anxiety and desperate hope. The illusions about the UN experiment generated by early enthusiasm have evaporated. Where once they were only untested dreams about what wartime allies wanted the UN to be, there is now the truth of experience. It is the truth of this inter-nationally shared history which we must build on in the future, realistically but courageously, patiently but with the determination that every possibility of expanding functional cooperation between nations will be vigorously explored and supported.

The United Nations and the Specialized Agencies provide the structure for collective action by governments, but they are also the institutional embodiment of compromises between governments. That is both their strength and their weakness. The will to international action is generated in the political decision-making process within the member states of the UN. If we have not learned that, we have not learned anything in the last twenty-five years. Non-violent change in the international system depends on national attitudes, goals, and policies.

The implications of this fact seem clear: first, national leaders must educate themselves and their people to look at international issues from a much less parochial, more global point of view, and second, we must train popular leaders, diplomats, military officers, international civil servants, educators, journalists and others in the values, attitudes and practical skills needed for third-party and other peace-related roles.

There is a critical shortage of men and women who are prepared to plan and participate in UN peace observation or peacekeeping operations, or to serve as supporting staff on mediation missions, or to bring "transnational" discernment to the issues before them on the negotiating table. That is why I have devoted myself since leaving the UN to the establishment of an international peace academy.

The pilot projects run by the International Peace Academy Committee at the Austrian Diplomatic Academy in Vienna during the summer of 1970 demonstrated the eagerness of young practitioners and scholars for a new kind of training for peace-related responsibilities. Their more experienced colleagues agreed that the time has come to institutionalise this training in the form of a peace academy analogous to a military academy in its focus on practice informed by theory. More than 140 individuals from fifty countries took part, a majority of them supported by foreign ministries defence agencies, intergovernmental and nongovernmental organizations. The world's major regions and ideologies were represented, and the crosscurrents shook all of us into questioning some of our suppositions and dogmas.

I think it accurate to say that the spirit of truth-seeking illuminated the encounter of participants with one another. In both formal classes and work groups, and in informal contacts between participants and staff, the climate favoured the kind of communication that transcends partial and partisan versions of the truth.

Regardless of our different assumptions about the causes of violence and the best means to eliminate it—attributable to our various worldviews and political beliefs—we were able to agree that justice was the fundamental condition of peace. This sweeping generalization is, of course, easy to accept. It must be brought down to specific situations before its meanings can be translated into public policy. All of us recognized that we would part company on many issues. But whether we were from the southern or northern hemisphere, from East or West, the will to find a few common point of departure was reassuringly strong. When it came to the concrete procedures and skills of third-parties in peacemaking and peacekeeping, or the role of the outside catalyst in peaceful social change, there was a surprising measure of concurrence. It reminded me that "objectivity" in human affairs is the outcome of communication which leads to a common definition of the problem to be solved, and agreement about the steps which should be taken to solve it..

In spite of all the differences and divisions in the world, the spirit of non-violence and truth can find conditional significant embodiment in world institutions, which are labouring to draw together the breads of human aspirations into a life-preserving mantle with seams that will hold. My personal faith is that one of the most important investments we can make is in every transnational educational requirements of a future for which the past has failed to prepare us.

29

Revolution & Non-Violence: A Pacifist View

Herold F. Bing*

Today, as at the end of the eighteenth century, the word Revolution is being used everywhere either with enthusiasm or with fears. Opponents of the *status quo* proclaim the need for revolution to destroy the evil of the existing order, while the supporters of that system denounce the revolutionaries as the greatest enemies of peace, social order and humanity.

We live in a controversial age. Technological development has made possible the production of large quantities of necessities and even luxuries quite unimaginable to our forebears. Technically it is possible for every human being to enjoy the necessities and even some of the simple luxuries of life, but things are so unequally divided that we have rich nations and poor nations, and rich and poor within the same nation. The rich are apt to claim that their greater wealth is the result of hard work and/or superior intelligence, while the poor blame the inequality on an unjust social order which permits of exploitation and maintains a so-called judicial system to enforce the maldistribution of property. They declare (as indeed Rousseau declared two centuries ago) that the position of the rich rests solely upon force and that it is therefore changeable and ought to be changed.

Observing the contemporary gap between rich and poor (nations and individuals) one might imagine that time would reduce it. In fact, the gap is widening, even between the social classes in the developing countries. Contrary to the belief of some early nineteenth economists, there is no natural tendency towards equality.

Since revolutionaries believe that the present social order rests upon force, it is natural for them to think that only by force can it be changed.

---

* War Resisters International – England

Published in *Journal of Gandhian Studies*, Vol. 1; October 1973.

Certainly it is true that any social system can be changed by force, providing that its opponents are stronger than its supporters. But with what result ? Power passes to a new group of people. Resistance to the new order will almost certainly continue in an effort to restore the old. The new rulers will find themselves more and more driven to use force to maintain their position and carry out their plans. Thus the new order will even more closely resemble the old with the sole difference that power and profits will be in the hands of a different, but possibly not much larger group than before.

This problem is today closely bound up with that of war and peace. No longer do we regard war as an isolated phenomenon. It is an essential expression of a society based on competition and exploitation. To get rid of war, we must create a society based on co-operation and brotherhood. The great question is whether this revolutionary change is to be accomplished violently or non-violently.

If we recognize the rights of man, as set forth for example in the United Nations Charter, and more fully in the U.N. Declaration of Human Rights, we must strive to secure the right of every man to live free from hunger, war and disease; to live free from economic, social, racial or cultural exploitation. He must be enabled to express himself freely and to develop to his full potential a social capacity, which will allow him to live in community and to rise above egotism.

From a belief in freedom stems opposition to war and to systems which exploit and corrupt, such as colonialism, capitalism and totalitarian communism. Such a belief touches every aspect of human activity. It requires an educational system which liberates rather than cramps the human spirit: an economic organization which is democratic and gives power to the workers involved. It demands nothing less than a total non-violent revolution.

The Violent Structure

A violent revolution creates a violent structure in which, having killed one's enemies, it is all too easy to kill one's friends for holding "wrong positions". Having once taken up weapons, it is difficult to lay them down. If, as some suggest, the use of violence can have a liberating effect on the oppressed, it also has a brutalizing effect. If it be argued that a non-violent revolution is too slow, we need only refer to Vietnam, where a violent struggle has raged without pause for 24 years, more than one million people have been killed, and the revolution has not yet been won. The Russian revolution which began with the enthusiastic support of practically all progressive movements in the world, eventually produced a State which killed millions of its own citizens in purges and forced labour camps, oppressed the nations of Eastern Europe, and to this day is still imprisoning writers who seek to exercise the most elementary freedoms.

Man is not free when he is subjected to violence. Therefore, the struggle against violence must be seen in the context of a revolutionary effort to liberate humanity. Violence takes many forms. In addition to the direct violence of bombs and guns, there is the silent violence of disease, hunger and the dehumanization of men and women, caught up in exploitative systems.

While recognizing that we do not have answers to all the problems of revolution, we say that men should not organize violence against one another, whether in revolution or in civil or international war. To those who claim that a non-violent society will be possible only after the Revolution, we reply that unless we hold firmly to non-violence now, the day will never come when all of us learn to live without violence. The roots of the future are here and now, in our lives and actions.

A commitment to non-violence does not mean hostility to all contemporary revolutionary movements, but a rejection of their methods. Non-violence has its setbacks, it is no panacea. On the other hand violent revolution destroys the innocent as surely as does the violence of the oppressor.

Is there a pacifist answer to the problem of South Africa? Probably not, in present circumstances. But is there a non-pacific answer either? Every non-violent movement in South Africa seems so far to have failed. But so has every violent movement. There are moments in history when we find situations that cannot be immediately resolved by violence or non-violence. In Spain for example, there have been organized appeals for violent action against France for the past 20 years. Yet Franco still holds power. The murder of Martin Luther King is sometimes cited as evidence of the defeat of non-violence in the American civil rights struggle. But in fact it no more proves the failure of non-violence than the murder of Che Guevara proves the failure of violence in Bolivia.

Probably, the greatest contribution we can make to the liberation movements is not by involving ourselves in abstract arguments as to the methods they should use—arguments which are not likely to have much influence on them— but by working to bring an end to colonialism and imperialism by attacking its centres of power in the West. This means changing the Western economic system insofar as it is based on the exploitation of the less developed parts of the world, and this, we shall find, involves a complete revolution in our socio-economic pattern.

The basic reason for holding to non-violence, even when it seems to have failed, or when it cannot offer a ready answer to an immediate crisis, is because the non-violence revolution does not seek the liberation simply of a class or nation or race. It seeks the liberation of mankind. Experience shows that violence merely shifts the burden of suffering and injustice from one group to another; that it liberates one group and imprisons another; that it destroys one authoritarian structure but creates another.

A society without violence must begin with revolutionaries who will not use violence.

30

Gandhian Concept of Non-Violence

William Stuart Nelson*

In recent years the word non-violence has come into very wide usage but without a clear understanding of its meaning. Indeed, it has been given many meanings. For some years Gene Sharp, former researcher in the Institute for Research in Oslo, labored on the development of a typology of non-violence. He identified nine types describing them as non-resistance, active reconciliation, moral resistance, selective non-violence, passive resistance, peaceful resistance, non-violent direct action, *Satyagraha*, and non-violent revolution.[1]

A wide lay interpretation of the word, certainly in the Western world, is simply the absence of physical force in personal and group encounters. For many this non-elaborated version is a source of profound doubt concerning, and often in opposition to, the non-violent principle. This is unfortunate.

For Mahatma Gandhi non-violence is not a single virtue or a single quality of life; it is a congeries of qualities or virtues; it is a spirit, a way of life, a religion or, as he would say, the law of one's being. In Gandhi's moral structure, there are two basic pillars—truth and *ahimsa*, that is, nonviolence or, as he called it, love. Truth is the end; non-violence is the means. But the end and the means are bound irrevocably to each other, for a vision of truth is dependent upon the realization of non-violence. As truth is God, so also love is God. Love, surely, is not a single virtue; it, too, is a way of life. Gandhi considered his life one indivisible whole. "What", he asked, "was the larger 'symbiosis' that Buddha and Christ preached?" It was gentleness and love[2]; it was non-violence.

---

* U.S.A.

Published in *Journal of Gandhian Studies*, Vol.1; October 1973.

Let us now look at certain major qualities of life, which compose non-violence as Gandhi defined it. Non-violence relates not simply to the act but to what transpires in thought and speech as well. For Gandhi hate is the subtlest form of violence. He advised, further, that one had better not speak if he cannot do so in gentleness. He held that there is no truth in one who is unable to control his tongue.

Violence, moreover, does not simply include killing in the physical sense. Gandhi held a man may be killed by inches by one's deceiving him in a trade or otherwise. A devotee of non-violence cannot properly be non-violent in one of these ways and violent in the other. For Gandhi life is one. All of its modes of expression must meet a common test. For Gandhi this test was non-violence.

Gandhi's non-violence begins in the heart and pure manifestation of it is compassion. This is a power, which enables its possessor not only to see but to feel another's plight and to identify himself with it. Gandhi could understand and describe this quality because he was eminently possessed of it. At midnight of August 14, 1947, Jawaharlal Nehru, speaking on the occasion of the transfer of power from the British Empire to the people of India, observed that one was not present, the Father of the Nation who, if he could, would wipe every tear from every eye. This is the power of the heart, which drove Gautama Buddha for more than forty years to walk, to preach and minister to the poor; which caused King Asoka, after the battle of Kalinga, to forswear forever the blood letting-role of conqueror.

Nowhere in our time, perhaps over the past thousand years, have men known one with a greater compassion for his fellowmen than Gandhi. When he could not give them the clothes they needed he reduced his own to the barest minimum. When the removal of untouchable slums was beyond his power, he made his home in one. These untouchables he called Children of God and adopted one of them as his own child. He dedicated his life to the breaking of chains that bound his people to an alien nation. He died a martyr because he dared to fight the cause of a people called enemies by some members of his own religious community. The innocent child and the convict, the harmless beggar at his door and his alien oppressor all alike were the objects of his compassion. Thus he was able to say to others with regard to the masses of the people: "We must first come in living touch with them, working with them and in their midst. We must share their sorrows, understand their difficulties and anticipate their wants. With the pariahs we must be pariahs and see how we feel to clean the closets of the upper classes and have the remains of their tables thrown at us.[3]

The companion of compassion is selflessness, self-renunciation. For to be compassionate one must walk beside the object of his compassion. To renounce a regard for one's body, moreover, is the one way to make others feel safe with oneself. In fact, the capacity to sacrifice is essential to one's own freedom from fear for "He rocks not if he should lose his land, his wealth, his life".[4]

For Gandhi the recurrent theme was "I must reduce myself to zero". Given the human situation he achieved in this the highest measure possible. In England he knew how to play the English gentleman, including the wearing of a gentleman's clothes. All this was changed, however, by his bitter experiences in South Africa and his dogged determination to do something about the evils out of which these experiences arose. He wrote to his son at that time that their lot henceforth should be poverty and that the uses of poverty would be far sweeter than those of riches. At his Tolstoy Farm where he was then engaged, the members ground their own wheat, labored at construction work, and excluded every item of food beyond that necessary to health.

This was the beginning of nearly fifty years of the most rigorous demands upon his frail body. This mode of life entailed the minimum of clothing, food, and every physical comfort. It included, at the age of 61, a walk to the sea of twenty four days to break the law against making salt. Gandhi spent years in prison. At the age of thirty-seven, in marriage he took the vow of sexual abstinence, which he kept to the end of his life. His fasts were numerous. He died a martyr.

Leading India to freedom was a monumental achievement for Gandhi. If, however, freedom had never been attained, leading the people by his own example to sacrifice themselves in the struggle for freedom would also have been an achievement equally great. Thousands upon thousands of them entered the prisons and some died there, including Kasturbai, his wife. They were beaten; they were killed. Following his example, many entered upon the simple life, even the well to do. They spun and wore khadi[5]: they forswore intoxicants; they embraced the lowliest, lived among them and died among them; they reduced themselves to zeros. This was selflessness, self-renunciation. This is what Gandhi called the root of nonviolence.

Gandhi apologized for the use of the word "tolerance" but explained that he could find no other term that conveyed what he felt. No one, certainly, could accuse him of condescension. His spirit was one of deep appreciation for views that differed from his own, especially religious views. All men will never think as one, he said, and truth will always appear in fragments.

For Gandhi all religions are true and all contain some error. All were almost as dear to him as his own Hinduism. His prayer for another person was "NOT" 'God, give him the light that Thou hast given me'. BUT 'Give him all the light and truth he needs for his highest development." This did not mean for him the abandonment of what he believed profoundly in matters religious or cultural. He said: "I do not want my house to be walled in on all sides and my windows to be stuffed. I want the cultures of all lands to be blown about my house as freely as possible, but I refuse to be blown off my feet by any of them. Mine is not a religion of the prison house, it has room for the least among God's creatures, but it is proof against the insolent pride of race, religion or colour."[6]

Here is steadfastness in one's basic beliefs coupled with open-mindedness to change; loyalty to one's faith without blind orthodoxy; freedom from dogmatism without unbelief.

Fearlessness is also a basic principle of non-violence. Gandhi was moulded in the great tradition of *ahimsa* He recoiled at taking life or injuring the living even at the lowest level. One is reminded here of an incident in the life of Dr. Albert Schweitzer. He is reported to have responded as follows when a celebrated American took means to protect the illustrious surgeon against a mosquito bite: "That was my mosquito; and, anyway, it was not necessary to use a battleship to kill him."

Another situation required a different answer from the Mahatma. Gandhi was always surrounded by faithful disciples who expected that his every act would square with his professed convictions. He faced no easy decision, therefore, when a calf in his ashram suffered pitifully from an incurable disease. Despite the horror of his followers, he put a swift end to the calf's existence. When monkeys, held sacred by the faithful, ran amuck in the ashram grounds, destroying precious food, he offended the faithful by having the animals driven away. He had the courage to admit that at this stage of history he saw no answer to the need for killing such insects as flies.

For one who is being beaten by a club, it is difficult for him to understand that he must destroy the system, which spawns club wielding but leave the club wielder untouched. Thus, it required courage for Gandhi to preach that the object of his non-violent movement in India was to destroy the English system of oppression but that not a hair of an Englishman's head should be touched.

Here, however, was man who never wavered once his heart dictated what to him was right. He lived beyond fear. But when men failed to understand or to agree with him, they had the certainty that his act was never born of fear but always of faithfulness to the urgings of an inner voice.

This doctrine of fearlessness held equally in the realm of the physical and the moral. Non-violence requires the act of getting killed without killing, of facing bullets without flinching or lifting a little finger in self- defence. None should seek martyrdom, but none should fear it. One should not seek imprisonment out of bravado, but for the innocent the prison should prove a gateway to liberty and honor.

These, then, are basic qualities of Gandhian non-violence: compassion, selflessness, tolerance, and fearlessness. These are elements upon which he built his version of the great moral concept of *ahimsa.*

The genius of Mr. Gandhi was not simply that he held and preached these views, but that he translated them into a great movement aimed at overcoming social evils in the world. For this aspect of non-violence we use, among other terms, "non-violent resistance". He preferred *satyagraha* (soul or truth force), for his resistance to evil must be consistent with the principles of life, which he held to be basic. *Satyagraha*, on the other hand, has its own laws always consistent; it should be said, with those of non-violence as a way of life.

In urging non-violent resistance, Gandhi very early was confronted with the problem of defining the role of conscience in the presence of the rule of law. We have noted the strength, which he drew from Thoreau's eloquent espousal and practice of civil disobedience. Still Gandhi never discounted the seriousness of his advocacy of lawbreaking and continued throughout his years to justify it. His basic respect for law was expressed in his assurance that if a *satyagrahi* (one who practices *satyagraha*) appears for the moment to disobey a law and constituted authority, he would in the end prove his regard for both of these. The right to civil disobedience, he held, is born of habitual willing obedience to law, as long as it is bearable. When in conscience it becomes unbearable the citizen not only has the right but is under the obligation to disobey it. Blind obedience to law is never binding upon citizens. If their bodies belong to the State, their minds, wills, and souls "must ever remain free like birds of the air..... beyond the reach of the swiftest arrow". One is reminded here of Thoreau's formulation of the principle quoted above[7], distinguishing between bad laws which must be disobeyed and those which may not.

Mr. Gandhi's position on disobedience of the law is illustrated in his statement before a court in India on March 18, 1922. He said: "Non-violence implies voluntary submission to the penalty for non-cooperation with evil. I am here; therefore, to invite and submit cheerfully to the highest penalty that can be inflicted upon me for what in law is a deliberate crime, and what appears to me to be the highest duty of a citizen. The only course open to you, the Judge, is either to resign your post and thus dissociate yourself from evil, if you feel that the law you are called upon to administer is an evil, and that in reality I am innocent; or to inflict on me the severest penalty, if you believe that the system and the law you are assisting to administer are good for the people of this country and that my activity is therefore injurious to the public weal."[8]

The problem of the role of conscience in relation to the rule of law is so fundamental to the non-violent resistance movement and so earnestly debated that a somewhat detailed examination of it here is indicated.

Commenting on the Montgomery, Alabama, U.S.A., bus boycott of 1956, Ralph McGill, editor of *The Atlanta Constitution*, observed that "There will be many future decisions but too few of them will have a King (Dr. Martin Luther King) to provide leadership which stays within the law and thereby manage to become effective". Mr. McGill apparently wished it understood clearly that he was commending action "which stays within the law". Somewhat later in a television debate with Dr. Martin Luther King on the subject "Are Sit-In Strikes Justifiable?" James J. Kilpatrick, editor of *The Richmond News-Leader*, argued categorically that even in such a situation as provoked the sit-in movement, it is right still to abide by the law.

A statement in the American press of a position differing from both of these two is in *The Washington Post* of October 26, 1961. Commenting on the arrest and imprisonment of seventy-five persons in Atlanta involved in a sit-in demonstration it stated: "So the question to be asked is not whether the law makes sense. The law of Georgia will have to give way to what is right." Following the arrest of twenty-one students for refusing to leave a bowling alley in Hyattsville, Maryland, the *Post* made the following editorial comment on October 22: "The managers were within their legal rights, of course. But they will never be able to take much pride in having enforced them."

Supporters of the right of conscience to defy the law will be encouraged by the view of Harris Wofford, Jr., a former member of the faculties of the Howard University Law School and the University of Notre Dame Law School. He writes: "But I am arguing that under our social contract man is to be free, and that a free man should look on each law not as a command but as a question, for implicit in each law is the alternative of obedience or of respectful civil disobedience and full acceptance of the consequences. Once men no longer believe that they as good citizens must obey any law passed by the legislatures, no matter how bad, then they must ask themselves of each law : Is this a law that I should obey ? Is it a just law ? Is it so unjust that it needs to be resisted from the very inception, and cannot wait the slow process of parliamentary reform ? This choice we always have to make. It is the choice which makes us free."[9]

Associate Justice William O. Douglas of the United States Supreme Court reminds us of the choice of Socrates to obey the law protecting Athenian youth against "subversive" doctrine or to drink the hemlock; of Antigone's defiance of Creon's order that her brother Polynices should not be buried; of the Puritans' defiance of English sovereigns; and of Thoreau's celebrated view: "Under a government which imprisons anyone unjustly, the true place for a just man is a prison." Mr. Justice Douglas himself says: "The choice given the individual is not to obey the law or to violate it with impunity, but to obey the law or incur the punishment for disobedience".[10] In this version of the role of conscience in relation to the rule of law the non-violent resister must surely find encouragement.

Success, in *satyagraha* requires, according to Gandhi, two clear convictions, which at initial reading suggest a contradiction. The first is his firm belief in mass action. For years Indian leaders met, made speeches against British rule, and presented resolutions. The turning point came when Gandhi arrived on the scene and galvanized into action the almost forgotten masses. Inspired by him, thousands of women in India collected contraband salt without ill will toward anyone. Thousands of farmers revolted against agrarian evils without hate. Even when their belief in non-violence was without intellectual framework, faith in their leaders was genuine.

There were times when the masses resorted to violence. Gandhi commented that it was manipulated by the intellectuals. He believed that the masses properly trained could exhibit the discipline of the soldier. "My hope lies in the masses", said Gandhi, "as far as the later stages of non-cooperation are concerned."[11]

Having said this Gandhi urged that in *satyagraha* quality mattered rather than numbers. Pointing to Zoroaster, Buddha, Jesus, and Mohammad he argued that the greatest men of the world stood alone always. "Strength of numbers is the delight of the timid", he said. "The valiant of spirit glory in fighting alone".[12] When the struggle became bitter and victory distant, Gandhi declared that his confidence was unshaken in the power even of one *satyagrahi's* ability to bring victory, should he hold out to the end. "Indeed", he said, "one PERFECT civil resister is enough to win the battle of Right against Wrong".[13]

Here we have Gandhi speaking at different times and in each instance emphasizing a different but basic element in a successful non-violent resistance movement.

Whatever ambiguity may appear to exist in Gandhi's idea of the importance of individual and mass contribution to successful non-violent resistance, his position on the indispensable role of integrity is crystal clear. ".......a passive resister", he wrote, "has to be almost, if not entirely, a perfect man"[14]; and, else-where, "a *satyagraha* struggle is impossible without capital in the shape of character."[15]

Among the qualities which Mr. Gandhi regarded as essential to a successful *satyagraha* were common honesty among the participants and a readiness to confess error, since it is better to appear untrue before others than to be untrue to oneself. He enjoined the scrupulous avoidance of exaggeration and of the suppression or modification of the truth even at the price of silence. Secrecy has no place in the *satyagrahi's* code, for his life and plans must be an open book.

Gandhi's code allowed for no compromise on fundamentals. On the other hand, he taught that, while the non-violent resister should be ever ready to press his cause, he must welcome any honourable opportunity for peace. To fail in negotiations one should not prevent him from seizing upon another opportunity, or even making one. He wrote, "It would not do for a *satyagrahi* to argue that the approach must be mutual. That assumes the existence of the spirit of *satyagraha* in the authorities, whereas *satyagraha* is offered in respect of those who make no claim to be *satyagrahis*. Hence the first and the last work of a *satyagrahi* is ever to seek an opportunity for an honourable approach."[16]

The cardinal element in war or other violent methods of inflicting injury or redressing wrongs is the coercive power of the means employed. With non-violence, the purpose is to correct and not to coerce, to awaken in the wrongdoer a sense of justice. Harassment, embarrassment, or injury of any kind is to be adjured, for *satyagraha* is aimed, not at a body or a will to be broken, but at a heart to be moved. The non-violent method, said Gandhi, proceeds on the principle which says, "Love those that despitefully use you."[17] The purpose is not to bring an adversary to his knees, but to lift him up. To employ coercion is to deny not only the cause of non-violence but God Himself.

There are times when reason is not sufficient to arouse a sense of justice and to win one's right. The hearts of men must be moved and for this only self-suffering is sufficient. In September of 1906, upon the occasion of Gandhi's first formal non-violent protest against the discriminations visited upon Indians by the South African Government, he declared: "Nobody has probably drawn up more petitions or espoused more forlorn causes than I have and I have come to the fundamental conclusion that if you want something really important to be done you must not really satisfy the reason, you must move the heart also. The appeal to reason is more to the head but the penetration of the heart comes from suffering. It opens up the inner understanding in man. Suffering is the badge of the human race, not the sword."[18]

This, Mr. Gandhi believed, means no meek submission to the evil-doer, but rather the pitting of one's whole soul against another's will.

With such a spirit one is enabled to defy an unjust empire, to save his own integrity and to lay the ground of that empire's destruction or its regeneration.[19]

As the result of such a spirit the British Empire was confronted for years with a steady stream of men and women going to prison, some dying there; with thousands falling unprotesting beneath the blows of the *lathi*[20] and the hail of bullets. Not only the British, but members of Gandhi's own religious community were faced with the man's entering upon fasts to the death in protest against their acts which to him were morally unbearable. In his death he bore the ultimate testimony to his belief in the efficacy, if indeed there had been the need, of self-suffering.

Gandhi made no pretense to the authorship of a rounded philosophy, not to speak of a rounded theology. Like the Christian theologian, however, he professed a doctrine often basic to which was his belief in the possibility of every man's redemption. "No man", he wrote, "is so bad as to be beyond redemption, no human being so perfect as to warrant his destroying him whom he considers to be wholly evil."[21] He recounts that from early youth he had met human monsters, but that even these he found were not beyond redemption. With such the problem is to know how to touch the right chord. No one in this world is so fallen as to be beyond conversion by love.

It followed naturally, then, that he taught that evil should be the object of resistance and not the evil-doer; that the English system was diabolical but not necessarily the Englishman; that the system must be destroyed at whatever cost, but that the hair of a single Englishman should not be touched.

The philosophy was not without its fruits. One Indian writes of Mahatma Gandhi that "His greatest and noblest achievement lay not in being able to conceive for the Britisher the lesson of Quit India, but in penetrating the soul of Britain and persuading the higher nature of the Britisher to restore to India what had long been hers".[22]

General Jan Christiaan Smuts was responsible for Gandhi's imprisonment at one time during the South African struggle. While in prison, Gandhi made a pair of sandals for the General. At the very least General Smuts was guilty of moral weakness. But Gandhi assumed that he did possess a certain sense of honour. This fact was indeed reflected years later when the General confessed that his was the odium in those earlier years of executing a law which lacked the virtue of strong public support. When in 1942 Gandhi was accused by a British authority of partnership in the sabotage of the allied struggle against Japan, General Smuts answered that this was pure nonsense and that Gandhi was one of the great men of the world.

A secretary to General Smuts, speaking to Gandhi, made the following admission: "I often wish you took to violence like the English strikers, and then we would know at once how to dispose of you. But you will not injure even the enemy. You desire victory by self-suffering alone and never transgress your self imposed limits of courtesy and chivalry. And that is what reduces us to sheer helplessness."[23]

Mahatma Gandhi was confronted with the belief on the part of many—a belief still current—that the end justifies the means. With this philosophy, he took issue in spite of the fact that it had obviously shaped a great part of man's history. For him means and the end are convertible terms, and to take care of the means is to guarantee the ultimate achievement of the end.

Gandhi went even further. He said : "They say 'means are after all means'. I would say 'means are after all everything'. As the means, so the end. There is no wall of separation between means and end. Indeed the Creator has given us control (and that too very limited) over means, none over the end. Realization of the goal is in exact proportion to that of means. This is a proposition that admits of no exception."[24]

The means Gandhi compared to a seed, the end to a tree. The conclusion, of course, is that violent means lead inevitably to a violent end; the obverse has its own reward. He felt, indeed, that it was only through non-violent means that true democracy could result and he cited in this connection both the French and Russian revolutions as proofs. In the same vein, he said to me at the time of the peaceful withdrawal of English soldiers from India in 1947 that Indian might well have staged a violent revolution against the British, killing their officers. In the end, however, this would have proved quite different from the then peaceful transfer of power from Great Britain to India.

In 1947, when rioting between Hindus and Moslems held the city of Calcutta in its grip the Hindus, having come to power became the aggressors. Gandhi expressed great sorrow that after so many years of his leadership his own religious community had not grasped the truth that genuine non-violence is non-violence of the strong and not of the weak, that even when one possesses the power to overcome another violently, if he is truly non-violent, he will not use that power. This marks the difference between non-violence as a technique and non-violence as a creed or moral force. This is the distinction between *satyagraha* and passive resistance as Gandhi saw and appraised it. "Passive resistance", said Gandhi's disciple Mahadev Desai, "acts negatively and suffers reluctantly and infructuously; *satyagraha* acts positively and suffers with cheerfulness because from love, and makes the suffering fruitful."[25]

In relation to non-violence Mahatma Gandhi was not an absolutist. The perfection which Gandhi taught was the perfection of striving and not of attainment, for he believed perfection to be unattainable. He saw perfect non-violence as impossible as long as we are in a physical state, as only a theory like Euclid's point or a straight line. To the very end he was experimenting with truth, and throughout his career he was full of admissions of errors, "Himalayan" errors.

This eloquent and unswearying preacher of non-violence conceded that there were occasions which justified its abandonment. There are times, he said, when the taking of life becomes a duty as when we destroy life to sustain the body or in the interest of health we kill the mosquito or other disease carrier. To dispatch the lunatic who runs amuck killing every one in his path, when there is no possibility of capturing him alive, is to earn the gratitude of the community. When a man or beast helplessly suffers the torture of slow death, when there is no means available to relieve the agony, Gandhi felt the final remedy would be to take the life.

Gandhi approached this difficult problem from a broad philosophical base indicating that the line cannot be drawn the same for all. One needs to remember also that in the effort to discriminate at every step between violence, and non-violence there is no place for shame or cowardice. "The poet has said that the road leading up to God is for the brave, never for the cowardly."

For Gandhi, decisions to participate in war did not come easily. During the First World War, at the time of the Zulu revolt and the Boer War in South Africa, Gandhi, a staunch believer in non-violence, recruited men either to the British army or an ambulance corps. Why? Then he considered himself a citizen of the British Empire, which at that time he believed was not wholly bad. Under these circumstances he felt his duty was to offer his services to the country, then in need. He could not himself, as a believer in non-violence, shoulder a gun, but he advised those who believed in war and were under no such moral restriction that their professed loyalty to the government bound them to support it in its hour of difficulty.

These acts, Gandhi confessed, weighed only in the scales of non-violence, would have been indefensible. But, he said, life is governed by many forces, which permit none to pursue a course as if it were subject to one principle only. To practise so noble a doctrine as non-violence in a world tumultuous, passion-ridden and full of conflicting duties is a task of utmost difficulty. Thus, for him men who professed loyalty to their government and enjoyed its privileges and knew nothing of non-violence were guilty of cowardice in failing to defend their homeland by force of arms.

Gandhi went farther. Though a believer in non-violence, he conceived instances when duty would require him to vote for the military training of those who had no objections to it. Neither a person nor a society can be made non-violent by compulsion. Having said this and professed painful awareness of his failings, he uttered the following testimony of loyalty to his convictions: "But the light within me is steady and clear. There is no escape for any of us save through truth and non-violence. I know that war is wrong, is an unmitigated evil. I know too that it has got to go. I firmly believe that freedom won through bloodshed or fraud is no freedom. Would that all the acts alleged against me were found wholly indefensible rather than that by any act of mine non-violence was held to be compromised or that I was ever thought to be in favour of violence or untruth in any shape or form. Non-violence, not untruth but non-violence. Truth is the law of our being."[26]

Reference is made frequently to Mr. Gandhi's statements on the relationship of cowardice to non-violence, especially by those who believe these expressions justify the use of armed forces under certain conditions. "Non-violence and cowardice go ill together"[27] he said. "I do believe that, where there is only a choice between cowardice and violence, I would advise violence. Thus when my eldest son asked me what he should have done, had he been present when I was almost fatally assaulted in 1908, whether he should have run away and seen me killed or whether he should have used his physical force which he could and wanted to use, to defend me, I told him that it was his duty to defend me even by using violence....I would rather have India resort to arms in order to defend her honour than that she should in a cowardly manner become or remain a helpless witness to her own dishonour."[28]

It is clear that here Gandhi does not make the choice of violence easy except in the case of one for whom cowardice appears to be the only alternative. But the choice is never only between cowardice and violence. Non-violence is also always a live option; but non-violence is for the brave. Once, then—individual or nation—is justified in refusing to fight only if in his inmost convictions he knows that he would have been unafraid otherwise to join battle even unto death. Then let an individual or a nation choose violence as against non-violence and cowardice, if it will, but not under the illusion of moral sanction by the apostle of non-violence.

Gandhi's doctrine of non-violence was subjected to a most searching test in 1947 when Indian troops were sent to Kashmir to repeal tribal invaders from Pakistan and Gandhi approved the sending of troops. How, he was asked, could he advise Churchill, Hitler, Mussolini, and the Japanese to adopt non-violence and condone the use of soldiers by India. His answer lay in a decision reached by him years before, that while a believer in non-violence could not himself resort to violence in defence of anything, he would be justified in presenting no impediments to those whose lives are not governed by non-violence, if justice lies with them. He wrote: "My resistance to war does not carry me to the point of thwarting those who wish to take part in it. I reason with them. I put before them the better way and leave them to make the choice".[29] Moreover, he reasoned that when two parties engage in violence, there can be distinguished a preponderance of justice on one side or the other.

Gandhi believed that whatever the accomplishments of the Indian armed forces in Kashmir, a better way would have been to send unarmed, non-violent men. There, without force of any kind, defending the country against a disciplined army of overwhelming numbers, dying if necessary at their posts, without malice or anger, they would have given an exhibition of heroism unknown in history, and Kashmir would have become a holy land.

Gandhi was confronted with the question of the place of non-violence once India became free. He answered that he would urge upon the new India the adoption of non-violence to the extent possible, but that, in view of the presence of so many "martial races" in India, he anticipated an inclination toward militarism of a modified version. He hoped for a strong party in India to represent the non-violent ideal and thus save from failure the years of efforts to demonstrate the efficacy of non-violence in his country. He declared that under no circumstances, however, could India give non-violent resistance a reasonable chance while maintaining complete military efficiency.

To the question as to whether a modern state based on force could resist either internal or external forces non-violently, his answer was no. A state built on non-violence, he said, could offer non-violent resistance to a world fortified with arms. Such a state was King Asoka's, and the example could be repeated.

Gandhi called himself a practical idealist and perhaps nowhere is the accuracy of this description more evident than in his creation of the "constructive program". He was a social reformer and he saw that preaching, virtue and protesting, even fighting, against evil are not enough. He perceived that a struggle for one's own rights alone will not suffice to reform society. The reformers, both leaders and those in the ranks, have themselves ways to mend towards their fellowmen. Gandhi had the courage, therefore, to say to his fellow Hindus that practitioners of untouchability were undeserving of the freedom they demanded of the British, for he reasoned that *swaraj* was impossible without an indissoluble union between Hindus and Muslims in India.

Gandhi, saw, moreover, that a great civil disobedience struggle for freedom required mass discipline. This, on the other hand, he felt impossible of acquirement except through some constructive cooperative endeavour such as hand spinning and hand weaving to counter the buying of foreign-made cloth. Such a program, requiring great organizing power, brings the masses together and engenders trust between leaders and those whom they lead because of their almost daily touch with each other. Thus, for Gandhi, civil disobedience was only a minor part of *satyagraha*. As a loyal and perceptive follower of Gandhi wrote : "…..to attempt civil disobedience without a constructive program would be like a paralysed hand attempting to lift a spoon."[30]

The constructive program organized by Gandhi was a program of social education aimed to achieve, among other ends, religious unity, the removal of untouchability, the prohibition of strong drinks and drugs, the spread of hand-spun and hand-woven cloth, village sanitation, education through crafts, adult education, the uplift of women, love of the mother tongue, service to the aborigines, the unionisation of labour.

This program mobilized a great army of workers and inspired a dedication which would have to be witnessed to be understood. The high, the low; the poor, the rich; the learned and the illiterate united in labour, self-surrender and abnegation on a level which the forces of an empire could neither ignore nor weaken.

This, then, is the story of Gandhi's concept of non-violent. It begins with a life which includes not only one's acts but as well one's speech and thoughts and embodies the virtues of compassion, selflessness, forbearance, fearlessness. It dictates a way of struggle against the evil forces in society which decries violence in any form and its accompaniment of malice. It requires dedication to the removal of society's ills as far as it lies within one's power so to do. These are the ends to which Gandhi dedicated a lifetime, not in precepts alone, nor simply in leadership of others, but in the endless striving himself to achieve what he urged upon other men. Little wonder then, that Albert Einstein could say that a thousand years from today men will scarcely believe that such a one as this had ever lived.

References:

1. *Gandhi Marg*, July, 1950, p. 247.

2. *Young India*, December 4, 1920.

3. Ibid., September 11, 1924.

4. *Harijan*, September 5, 1936, p. 236, (N.K. Bose, *Selections from Gandhi* (Ahmedabad, 1957) pp. 15 f.).

5. Hand spun and hand woven cloth.

6. Quoted by Indira Gandhi in *Gandhi Marg*, July, 1951, p. 180. Part I, p. 27.

7. Krishnadas, *Seven Months with Mahatma Gandhi* (Ahmedabad, 1951), p. 269.
8. *The Journal of Religious Thought*, Autumn-Winter, 1957-58, p. 31.
9. *The Right of the People* (New York, 1953) p. 169.
10. *Young India*, August 18, 1920, Tagore, p. 370
11. (N.K. Bose, op. cit., p. 228).
12. Ibid., June 17, 1926, p. 217 (Ibid., p. 236).
13. Ibid., November 10, 1921, p. 362 (Ibid., p. 227).
14. *Harijan*, July 21, 1940, p. 214, (Ibid., p. 219).
15. *Satyagraha in South Africa* (Stanford, 1954), p. 218.
16. *Harijan*, June 10, 1939, p. 153 (Gopinath Dhawan, *The Political Philosophy of Mahatma Gandhi* (Ahmedabad, 1951), p. 154.
17. *Harijan*, May 14, 1938, p. 111, (Bose, op.cit., p. 221).
18. *Young India*, November 5, 1931, (Kalidas Nag, *Gandhi and Tolstoy,* Patna, 1950, p. 48).
19. *Young India*, August 11, 1920, Tagore, p. 713, (Bose, op.cit., p. 159).
20. A staff, six to eight feet long, usually made of bamboo and often capped with brass or iron.
21. *Young India*, March 26, 1931, p. 49 (ibid., p. 156).
22. B. Pattabhi Sitaramayya in *Gandhi Marg*, July, 1960, p. 267.
23. M.K. Gandhi, *Satyagraha in South Africa* (Stanford, 1954) p. 325.
24. *Young India*, July 17, 1924, p. 236 (Bose, op.cit., p. 36).
25. *Harijan*, June 25, 1938, p. 164 (Gopinath Dhawan, *The Political Philosophy Mahatma Gandhi,* Ahmedabad, 1951, p. 143.).
26. *Young India*, September 13, 1928, p. 308 (Bose, op.cit., p. 177).
27. *Harijan*, July 15, 1939, p. 201 (ibid., p. 160).
28. Tendulkar, *Mahatma*, II, 5-8 (*All Men are Brothers* – Unesco, p. 104).
29. *Harijan*, August 18, 1940, p. 250 (Pyarelal, *Mahatma Gandhi : The Last Phase*, Ahmedabad, 1958, II, 503).
30. R.R. Diwakar, *Satyagraha : The Power of Truth* (Hinsdale, 1948), p. 42.

31

Violence–Non-violence at Kyoto and Beyond

Homer A. Jack*

Some months before the inauguration of the Gandhi Centenary, the International Seminars Sub-Committee of the Gandhi Centenary Committee sponsored the convening of an International Inter-religious *Symposium on Peace* in New Delhi. This 1968 event was so successful that a larger World Conference on Religion and Peace was held in Kyoto, Japan, in mid-October, 1970—some months after the formal end of the Gandhi Centenary. Although the Kyoto Conference was not sponsored by any Gandhian body, Gandhi and Gandhism were very much on-stage, in the persons of three worldwide practitioners—Dr. Ralph D. Abernathy of the U.S., Archbishop Helder Camara of Brazil, and Thich Thien-Minh of South Vietnam. Also present was a large Indian delegation, partly Gandhian.

The Kyoto Conference frequently discussed the problem of violence of non-violence in social change. This paper deals with how the 212 delegates from the ten major world religions and 39 nations dealt with the problem of violence/non-violence.

Dr. Ralph D. Abernathy, a Protestant and successor to the late Martin Luther King, Jr. as President, of the Southern Christian Leadership Conference, called for "no less than the beginning of a non-violent world revolution...to renounce war, to end poverty, to abolish racism." He asked for "non-violent resistance and struggle following the traditions of a Gandhi in India, a Martin Luther King, J., in America, a Dom Helder Camara in Brazil."

Archbishop Camara, a Roman Catholic, was himself in Kyoto and in his address to the World Conference he said: "without hate, without

---

* Director, Unitarian Universalist Association, U.S.A. .

Published in *Journal of Gandhian Studies*, Vol. 1; October 1973.

incitement to violence, and without fear but with firmness, let us denounce injustice as the great obstacle to peace, injustice (being) the source and cause of all violence."

It was Thich Thien-Minh, a leader of the United Buddhist Church in South Vietnam, who spoke most explicitly about non-violent resistance. He told a plenary of the World Conference: "There are those who assert that non-violent action does not work. I think that this rejection is too facile. In Vietnam, violence has not worked for 25 years. Instead, violence has bred violence. But, the critics will say, non-violence has not worked in Vietnam either. It is true that the non-violent struggle in Vietnam has not been able to bring an end to the war. But that does not mean that non-violence does not work. Permit me to tell you the reasons. Vietnam has become an international conflict in which all the big powers are involved, directly or indirectly. The non-violent struggle, in order to succeed, needs to be carried out on an international scale."

Thich Thien-Minh also said that his associates have been "trying non-violent approaches to end the conflict and external intervention." He added that the "problem of leadership in a non-violent struggle is one of the most important problems....and the leader...must be a man of great compassion, courage and integrity." Thich Thien-Minh affirmed that "the techniques of non-violent action are not non-violent action itself." He asserted that "without the inspiration of love and sacrifice, these techniques (of non-violent action) cannot be successful (and) will lack their deeper strength."

In addition to hearing a number of speeches, the delegates to the Kyoto Conference spent considerable time in three workshops or commissions. These were devoted to the allied topics of disarmament, development and human rights. In all three, the problem of violence/non-violence was discussed and these discussions were reflected in all three final reports.

The Disarmament Commission concluded: "We as religionists should study and teach all forms of non-violence as a measure of bringing about justice. However, the responsibility for violence in extreme cases of injustice rests on oppressive authorities." The Commission said no more, but did attach a footnote to this section of its report asking readers also to read relevant sections of the Development report.

The Development Commission in its report stated: "We strongly support non-violent efforts to replace the unjust structure which marginalize the disinherited. At the same time we warn those who refuse to permit the reform of the unjust structures which support their privilege that their resistance to change will make violence inevitable and that the burden of responsibility will rest with them. We must face the realities, recognizing that development involves a transfer of power from the few to all. This necessarily involves conflict. It must be the task of religion to try to insure that this conflict be creative."

The Human Rights Commission devoted a section of its report to "The Right to Resist Oppression". This stated: "In several regions of the world, the social and economic situation is such that it gives rise to the existence of social classes which are deprived of all possessions and rights. Many people, especially those in the developing countries, feel the need to work towards a profound reorganization of social and economic structures, which they consider to be unjust. Confronted by the obstacles presented by the political order, they are frequently driven to take up positions, which become increasingly more radical. They include a certain number of committed religious leaders who are convinced that by resisting oppression they are bearing witness in their faith. Under the various circumstances, which change according to time and place, their manner of resisting oppression also varies from simple opposition, to disobedience, and even to revolt. We should acknowledge their right to oppose intolerable situations, but strongly recommended the use of non-violent means in the first instance. What is important is that they should act in good faith and from a feeling of love towards their fellowmen. They should respect the rights of those who are not involved in such conflicts. In this respect, it is important that humanitarian laws be reaffirmed and developed to include adequat provisions for the protection of individuals in cases of non-international armed conflicts."

The above quotations are sufficient to indicate that these Commission reports hardly constitute a Gandhian document. This is not even neo-Gandhian doctrine. Too many loopholes are left open for violence albeit for "a good cause." Yet these quotations also show that many world religious leaders, even the activists, still support non-violence. Yet the qualifications reflected at Kyoto are important. The responsibility for violence rests with unjust structure, and their perpetrators (the so-called establishment), and not primarily with those who commit overt violence. The Conference statements also give two additional caveats: Those who commit violence should do so "from a feeling of love towards their fellowmen" and they should "respect the rights of those not involved (directly) in such conflicts."

While the Kyoto Conference did not wholeheartedly endorse non-violence, it has certainly not given a blank cheque to violence as a method of social change. This is indeed the present uneasy stance of many persons in the neo-Gandhian era—religionists and non-religionists alike— even some who have long admired Gandhi. Thus what is needed today is not a new theology (or philosophy or politics) of non-violence, although new formulations are always useful and the old ones should always be brought upto date. What is most necessary are contemporary demonstration that non-violence works and can both topple "unjust structures" and replace them with more just one's.

Why the current vogue of violence not only in totalitarian society but more especially in erstwhile democratic ones today? Just a few years ago, non-violence was "in" in style, from the full wall-posters of Gandhi and King to the more important serious advocacy of the Gandhian rules of social revolution. In a very few years these posters have been replaced by those of Che or Mao. The cult of violence has had widespread currency, even among those of distinctly a non-ideological bent.

Violence does draw attention to recurring if obscured evils. So much injustice is buried under slick public relations in most societies. Injustice seldom makes the headlines. An assassination, a killing, a bombing draws public attention, especially in a television age. Such violence should not be equated with change, but public attention is undeniably a first step towards change.

Violence is also encouraged today in some quarters. It is sometimes covertly welcomed by the establishment (of government or university), for it then makes the subsequent use of counter-violence or repression more respectable.

The frequent strictures against the use of the overt violence obscures the existence of another kind of violence which is widespread and which may be equally evil; covert violence. The strictures of society can kill as well as its guns. When one denounces one kind of violence, the overt in order to perpetuate the other, the covert, and this hypocrisy of the status quo is detected and rightly denounced.

Yet for all the new sympathy for violence, there have been few victories for violence in modern times—only more violence and misery, whether it is violence on the streets of New York or on battlefield outside Saigon.

Violence has rather gained through the defaults of non-violence in our time. It is non-violence that appears to have failed more than having won.

The irony of the assassination of non-violence's two most noted advocates—Gandhi and King—within a single generation has not been lost in the public mind. If even the votaries of a method cannot survive......

Also some of the most publicized projects clearly labelled non-violent in the public press have clearly failed. But not all that carries the mantle of non-violence is in fact the genuine article; on the contrary, much which passes as non-violent even in India today is non-violent in name only perhaps only through default. Often in order to gain respect and thus support, a project which should be relegated to the never-never land; between violence and non-violence is given the non-violent label. When it fails, non-violence appears to have failed.

There have, however, been some current non-violent demonstrations which have been at least moderately successful. The catalogue since the death of Gandhi is not a large one. Yet there are individuals and groups in several parts of the world (Vietnam, India, Italy, U.K., U.S.) who are actively and persistently experimenting with non-violent truth and techniques. These merit the attention and participation of all who demand social change and still have faith in non-violence. The experiments are briefly catalogued in the recent pamphlet "Training for Nonviolent Action", published in London by the Quakers and the War Resister International. And they stand up well against the "achievements" of Fanon Che, and Debray.

Creating a New School of Economic Thought
A New Initiative in the Field of Economics

Paul Ekins*

Overview:

This initiative has two components. The first is to publish a Series of annual books, to be called Living Economics, focusing on an emerging new system of economic ideas. The second is to create a worldwide Living Economy Network of economists and others from the social sciences and related disciplines, to contribute to the creation of the Series and to ensure the maximum dissemination of the ideas it contains, especially through educational and other institutions. This will be a new school of economic thought, in tune with the social and environmental realities of the late twentieth century, come into being and begin to influence the development of the global economy.

The project is based on the hypothesis that such a new school of thought is both an imminent possibility and has become an urgent necessity. Through the work of The Other Economic Summit (TOES), the New Economics Foundation and many other organizations and individuals, its outlines have already become clear and were described in the book based on the first three years of TOES, work *The Living Economy: a New Economics in the Making* (Routledge & Kegan Paul, 1986), edited by Paul Ekins. The essential objectives and concerns of this "Living Economics" may be listed in headline form :

- to develop an economics of fundamental human needs and how they may be satisfied;

---

* Programme Director, Sustainable Economy Unit, London.
Published in *Gandhi Prasang*, Vol. 1 No. 1; October 1998.

- to operationalise an expanded indicator framework for overall human well-being to supplant excessive reliance on figures of GNP and employment;
- to integrate considerations of economy with those of society, ecology and ethics;
- to develop understanding of processes of production - the nature of work, the structures through which it is organised and the technologies it uses;
- to explore issues of operational scale and macro-micro-global relationships, taking into account issues of interdependence organisation and participation as well as of production and its efficiency;
- to develop ways of recognizing the contribution of non-monetary economic activity;
- to address issues of intergenerational equity, particularly by articulating an economics of ecological sustainability;
- to develop an understanding of the appropriate balance to be struck between the four main economic allocative mechanisms - the market, central and local planning and non-monetary production - in order to maximize the overall benefits from each.

This is an agenda, which goes to the heart of the malfunctioning of the current global economy. Many people are working on it and much progress has been made. But the people are isolated and progress is fitful and fragmented. This project will bring people and ideas together and give a coherent thrust to the whole economic approach, from which an influential new school of economic thought can then begin to emerge.

Central Concerns of Living Economics

1. Introduction

Through the work of The Other Economic Summit (TOES), the New Economics Foundation and many other organizations and individuals, it is now possible to perceive the essential features of a political economy, which is here called the Living Economy and was outlined in the book of that name which was based on the first years of TOES' (Ekins 1986).

The Living Economy is radically different from any currently existing economy capitalist or socialist, industrial or non-industrial. Its main features are all recognizably 'economic' in nature, meaning here that they are relevant to decisions about the allocation and distribution of scarce resources between competing uses for the purpose of increasing human well-being. However, conventional economic theory has tended to give these features little if any weight, and economic practice, largely dominated by hostile ideologies and contrary vested interests, has confined them to the margins both of activity and debate. The process of developing a new economics, Living Economics, and a Living Economy thus has three essential and inter-related components :

a) Analysing and describing the basic concerns of Living Economics in a positive (in the economic sense of factual and value-free) way, This amounts to the creation of a new school of economic thought.

b) Developing the normative (i. e. ethical, value-laden) arguments for placing these concerns at the centre of economic debate and formulating the policies to make them operational.

c) Identifying, encouraging and analysing actual economic activities which embody these concerns and thus comprise the Living Economy in practice.

What follows concentrates on the first two of these points.

2. Basic Characteristics

The essential concerns of Living Economics, and thence the basic characteristics of the Living Economy, are:

- An emphasis on human needs and their satisfaction, through a combination of personal responsibility, mutual aid and governmental action. What people actually need and how these needs may be satisfied are important considerations for the allocation of resources for human welfare. The approach so far of Living Economics to this complex subject suggests that a systematic, objective classification of human needs is possible; that the way these needs are satisfied will differ between cultures and over time: and that the decisions about, and the necessary provision for, such satisfaction are best left to the individuals concerned, within the framework of an enabling, liberating social structure, if the satisfaction of needs is to be maximised.

- A holistic approach to human welfare, expressed through an accounting system, which gives value to social and ecological factors as well as to output and employment. Many economists and others have already stressed that wealth and welfare are not mere functions of income and employment. Leisure, working conditions, income distributions, environment, health, safety of the future - all these factors in addition can be and have been modelled economically (see Hueting's contribution to Ekins 1986) to produce a guide to the performance of the economy that dissolves money fetishism and gets to grips with human reality. It is a sign of the immaturity of most present economic assessment that such an expanded framework lies for the most part unused, while governments almost without exception persist with a simple-minded preoccupation with 'growth' and 'jobs'.
- An awareness of the social, ecological and ethical implications of economic activity. The four keywords - economy, ecology, society and ethics - embrace the essential components of human life and interact indivisibly in a single system. Its fragmentation into separate parts diminishes the capacity to understand or to act in a way that benefits the whole. Thus Living Economics is essentially interdisciplinary, and its normative analysis may be expected to stress such concepts as economic and political democracy, social justice, stewardship of the earth's resources and environmental conservation, sustainability, equal opportunity and non-discriminatory access.
- An emphasis on the process of production and exchange, as well as on the ownership of their means and on the product itself. It was one of Schumacher's great insights (Schumacher 1979) that how we work determines to a great extent the sort of humans we become. Yet the boundless possibilities of modern technical change remain crudely fettered to the demand for great labour productivity, ignoring the nature of the economic processes which shape human lives. Concepts in this field which are important to Living Economics are:
  - good work, personally satisfying socially useful and ecologically sound;
  - cooperation, implying democratic participation and control, responsible ownership and non-exploitative social relations;
  - appropriate technology, which develops rather than replaces skills,

makes efficient use of resources, including the avoidance of unemployment and conserves the environment. Good work in cooperative structures with appropriate technologies this is the economic component of human development which along with the provision of goods and services, is the very purpose of production.

- A recognition of the importance of the concept of economic self-reliance as a necessary condition for economic self-determination, without which human groups from villages to nations are dependent, vulnerable and insecure, prone to disruption and exploitation. The concept can be applied to different levels of locality, at each of which self-reliance can be increased in two ways: increased use of local resources to satisfy local needs and a trading strategy that seeks to reduce dependency. Cooperative international economic relationships on the basis of independence and security would then supplant what is for many the anarchic trauma of the international market-place.

- An awareness of the importance of scale, not just with regard to productive efficiency, but also as it affects the ability of people to relate to and participate creatively in the organisational structures involved. Linked to this is a concern with the inter-relationship between various levels of economic analysis, policy-making and activity with a view both to locating decision-making processes at the appropriate level and to ensuring that decisions made at one level do not adversely affect another. The context of these inter-relationships is the emergence of an increasing global dimension to the economy, whether in terms of greater interdependence, the transnationalisation of much economic activity or worldwide communications and ecological impacts. It has long been a tradition in different religions to conceive of humanity as a single family sharing a common home. Such a conception now has physical immediacy and economic analysis must take account of this.

- An understanding that much productive activity essential to human well being, such as reproduction, home-making and child-rearing, is carried out, and is better carried out, in a non-monetary economy. Yet most societies today exclude those engaged in such activity, overwhelmingly, of course, women, from the recognition, status and rewards accorded to productive work. This is not only injustice. It is also economic nonsense, that plays havoc even with the neo-classical allocative mechanisms of incentives and rewards, to pay least well (if at all) those who are the very foundation of the economy and society. It is then, no surprise that there is much social disintegration. The wonder is that there is not more widespread social collapses.

- An emphasis on issues of intergenerational equity, which affect the economic prospects of future generations. This is especially relevant to environmental questions, where the issue is now not so much one of equity as of sustainability for survival. There is no mystery about the steps that need to be taken to improve the present perilous situation. Rich countries, which use some 70% of the world's resources for a quarter of its people, must use fewer of them through a mixture of more efficient use and a redistribution of economic power to poorer countries. Poorer countries must find ways of meeting their people's needs without destroying their resource base. And all countries should work vigorously for stabilisation of the human population with the least possible increase over present numbers. Tragically for today's children and young people (not to mention future generations) the gap between the articulation and imple-mentation of such a programme appears to be politically absolute, presenting the advocates of the Living Economy with their most daunting challenge.

- Balanced use of the four main allocative economic mechanisms: the market, central planning, local planning, and the non-monetary activity of the household and voluntary sector. The costs and benefits of the first two of these are in the main well-documented, although in their promotion they are often distorted by ideology. Local economic planning is an important new emerging dimension, which is being explored and implemented by an increasing number of local government bodies. Broadly, the Living Economy will comprise a competitive, informed market sensitive to the full implications of economic life : a state strong enough to enforce the conditions for such a market and to remedy its inevitable shortcomings in such areas as distribution, concentration of producer power, social costs and the provision of public good : a local planning network able to match local needs and resources with a view to developing the necessary diversity and flexibility for local self-reliance; and a mean such as a basic income for enabling and rewarding productive but unpaid work in the domestic and voluntary sector. Such a framework goes to the heart of present economic problems.

Notes:

This does not mean that the new school of thought will be value-free any more than neoclassical or Marxist economics are value-free. The price choice of basic concerns from the innumerable possible subjects for study is a value judgment in itself. However, once that choice has been made, the analysis should be rigorous and objective, though here again some qualification is necessary. Economic rigour is often taken to mean the application of mathematical and quantitative techniques to economic concepts to arrive at precise conclusions. However, the human economic condition is rarely precise, so that such rigour will often be inappropriate. The school of thought to be developed here will seek to impart an accurate understanding of economic affairs, which will have some elements of mathematical precision but also much qualitative description. It is in the context of striving for accuracy rather than precision that the words rigorous and objective should be here understood.

33

Role of *Shramadana* in Rural Development

A. T. Ariyaratne*

How the Movement Began

The concept and practice of self-help through the sharing of one's mental and physical energy are as old as our civilization itself. At different times in the history of Sri Lanka this was known by different names such as "Samudan", "kaiya", "aththan", "rajakariya" and "athmopakaraya".

The word "Shramadana" was introduced for the first time in this country (Shri Lanka) fourteen years ago by a band of teachers and students of Nalanda Vidyalaya, Colombo. They founded an all-island Movement called the Shramadana Movement for the reconstruction of rural areas, though initially through an Educational Extension Service Programme. Their sustained efforts along with other fraternal groups resulted in the new world famous Sarvodaya Shramadana Movement of Sri Lanka.

Thought and Action

The literal meaning of the word Shramadana is sharing of one's time, thought and energy for the welfare of all. For the founders of this Movement, Shramadana was only a medium of constructive action to bring about a non-violent total revolution in man and society to build up a new social order. Sarvodaya is their ideal society where they expect to see an awakening individual (*Purna Paurushodaya*), an awakening village (*Gramodaya*), an awakening nation (*Deshodaya*), and an awakening world community (*Vishvodaya*). All of these are integrated in a dynamic course of

---

* Hony. Organizing Secretary and Administrative Director, Lanke Jatke Sarvodaya Sammelan and 1969 Ramon Magassy. Awardee for Community Leadership – Sri Lanka.

Published in *Journal of Gandhian Studies*, Vol. 1; January 1974.

non-violent constructive process of social change. For them the Sarvodaya Thought and Shramadana Action are inseparable and must go together.

Liberation of Man and Society

Shramadana action is an excellent instrument for Rural Development provided it is applied in the broader context of the Sarvodaya development ideal. The effectiveness of Shramadana is bound to be lost if this form of action is used only as a money-saving process to realize a physical objective. In the recent past more damage than good has been done in many areas by some people, who knowingly or unknowingly, equated

Shramadana to some form of free-labour movement. They desired to create non-monetized capital to compensate for the serious lack of capital needed for national development. Perhaps they would have served the country better if they concentrated more on an all out effort to prevent waste of capital resources which were already being spent from Government funds; Shramadana to us has had a more profound meaning and significance. To us it is a positive force for the total liberation of man and society from their present social, economic and political deterioration. The bureaucratisation of Shramadana, we maintained, defeated the very object of founding the Shramadana Movement.

Development Without Servitude

Development is primarily an activization of human and material resources of a country for increased production of goods and services which lead to the general progress and welfare of her people. An effective development programme should not of necessity be restricted only to the removal of social injustice already prevailing in that society but should take care not to allow the advent of new forms of oppressive systems be they political, technocratic or bureaucratic in character. In other words economic development programmes should not result in reducing the human being from the status of a 'person' to that of a 'thing', from being a 'subject' to that of being an 'object'.

Shramadana concept was introduced to this country by the Sarvodaya Shramadana workers of Sri Lanka with the above perspective of removing social and economic injustice, ensuring increased economic growth, freeing society from all forms of exploitation of man by man, establishing an equitable distribution system of goods and services, liberating the human being so that he may be able to participate in decision-making as a person and a subject in such a development process in which he is the master and not the slave.

Initiative, Leader, Participation

In shramadana the human being is at the same time the destination, the means and the helmsmen of the development exercise. This is not a vague and theoretical intellectualisation of a distant objective as that which some of those who manage political bureaucratic and technocratic institutions of the country have dubbed as democratic socialism or socialism or socialist democracy, and which they naively expect people to understand and put into concrete form. On the other hand the Sarvodaya concept and Shramadana action are a living philosophy and a concrete practical programme with which the people are already familiar by their cultural conditioning and traditional cooperative way of living.

Then where lies the need for promoting in an organised form the Sarvodaya Shramadana Movement? The answer is that we have to remove the causes that kill the people's leadership and participation in the development of their true constructive vigour flowering forth from the grassroots of their society and spreading through all strata upwards.

A Three-Fold Cause

What now are these causes? I would identify the causes by those, which are thus affected. They are the individual, the group and the community organisation.

Firstly, the prolonged subjugation to colonial domination had resulted in the deterioration of the average individual from his independent stature to that of being a mere dependent, a creature bereft of creature comforts in a highly materialistically motivated society. Secondly, the entire rural infrastructure both in the physical and psychological sense was disintegrated and a replacement of this vital element in village society never took place. Thirdly, the rural population became organisationally the nourishing ground to sustain a centralised form of bureaucratic party political, landed and capitalistic vested interests of those who inhabited the affluent urban areas. Thus the rural areas were sucked out of their vital human leadership, social coherence and freedom to manage their own affairs.

Personality Awakening

The governmental rural development schemes during the last three decades fell far short of their expectation, as they never visualised a bold attempt to remove the aforesaid triple factors from the rural scene. The Sarvodaya Shramadana approach to rural development begins with an apprehension of these fundamental causes and is designed to remove them at their very roots. In this context Shramadana is primarily an attempt to give an opportunity to as many persons as possible both rural and urban to free their personalities from slavish dependence by becoming truly conscious of the causes that have given rise to the problems they are faced with.

Shramadana, while restoring the freedom or action and awakening of personality of the individual should lead him to participate in a Gramodaya or Village Reawakening programme. He becomes a participant in planning and implementing of programmes designed to bring about changes in the educational, health, economic and organisational aspects of the life of his community in an integrated scheme of village (group) development. The personal and the group awakening that takes place through Shramadana and Gramodaya Movement bring about a consciousness in the individual and community about the needs for the removal of unjust social systems that have enslaved the rural peoples for generations. In other words Shramadana and Gramodaya Movement should lead to a revolutionary change in the structural life of the community, which will eventually bring about Purna Swarajya or Total Freedom. A successful rural development programme can only take place under this Total Freedom.

When the Shramadana Movement was launched in Shri Lanka we had illusion about the need for this three-fold approach of Education (through) Shramadana Development (through Gramodaya) and Participation (through Puran Swarajya), if our efforts were to have any true significance in rural and national development. Shramadana always has to be viewed in this revolutionary perspective and I believe the only alternative to violent structural change in this country is this non-violent revolutionary action.

Having mentioned the place of Shramadana practice in the context of a broad social objective I shall next briefly mention some salient operational principles relevant to the role of Shramadana in Rural Development.

Leadership

Motivation and mobilisation of human resources for development need good leadership. The first principle I would stress is effective rural leadership. We have human resources in abundance. But due to the lack of effective leadership at the rural level these resources remain unused, wasted and even become a social burden. The rural areas have had their 'chieftains' but I wouldn't call them leaders. Those who generally went by the name leaders were at most benefactors, heroes or genius as people saw them. They may receive gratitude or admiration from the people but they may not succeed in moving and inspiring the people to a sense of oneness towards the achievement of an objective.

The leaders we need for our village today are those who can help people to learn to perceive social, political and economic contradictions and take action against the oppressive elements that stand in the way to progress. They rise above themselves in a struggle to re-cure the physical and psychological infra-structure of the village by hard labour and sacrifices.

Shramadana Camps

Shramadana Camps provide an excellent opportunity for such true leadership to emerge among rural communities. The provision of opportunities for the emergence of these leaders who truly represent the wishes and aspirations of the people and inconcrete constructive action march with the people towards desired goals. I consider it to be a very positive contribution Shramadana Movement can make towards Rural Development.

Rural Culture

The second principle I would stress is the need to integrate rural culture and the development efforts. Motivation for people to participate in rural development can be brought about by good leaders by inspiring them with relevant cultural values. Mobilisation is brought about by placing before the people realisable objectives that are beneficial to them. This indigenous culture and the science of community development have to be closely combined in Shramadana programme In the Sarvodaya Shramadana Movement *Metta* (loving kindness), *Karunat* (or compassionate action) *Muditha* (or unselfish joy) and *Upekka* (or equanimity) are the four basic values that are used to inspire individuals. Shramadana is an act of *Karuna*. *Dana* (or sharing), *Priya Vachana* (or pleasant speech) *arthacharya* (or constructive action) and *Samanathmatha* (or equality) are the other four traditional values stressed to inspire and motivate the group.

Long Term Planning

The third principle is to utilize Shramadana Camps as the principle instrument for the initiation of a long term development programme. A strict code of self-discipline, a time table which provides for 6 to 8 hours of physical work and 3 to 4 hours of education through dialogue, song and dance, well organised teams and special task groups, preparatory and follow-up programmes, etc. have to be integral parts of any worthwhile Shramadana project. The social and economic surveys of the village as a whole and of every family unit should follow and not precede the Shramadana Camp stage. People should be free to evolve their own development plans based on a simplified understanding of the findings of the surveys.

People's Formations

The fourth principle is the involvement of all people in the village—the young and old, man and women—in organised form in the development exercise with direct benefits accruing to every such formation by their own efforts. An integrated programme to promote educational, health, economic and self-governmental development should be drawn up to enable every man woman and child to participate in building a new life for themselves. In every stage of this exercise they should feel the joy of living and working together.

People are Supreme

I am not going into the logics of Shramadana work as this aspect will be similar to any other serious programme of constructive work involving men, material and knowledge. However, it should be mentioned as a fifth principle that the governmental and other external agencies should smoothly fit into this programme rather than expect the people to fit into a so called village development programme which has been formulated without their participation and imposed on them from above as during colonial times, unless a government has immense capital and human resources and limitless know-how and personnel, has no respect for rural man as a human being and is prepared to negate the elements of much talked theories of democracy and socialism. I believe that, surest way to keep our villages 'undeveloping' is to continue the present exercise of monopolistic planning and implementation from above. Two and a half decades of such planning has proved not only of scant comparative benefit to rural people but also has brought about disastrous social consequences. This haughty thinking at top must be reversed and people must be given total freedom and a chance to think plan and to act. Shramadana Movement has proved that the people are well capable of accepting that responsibility.

Structural Change

The legislators can do better than sermonize on the virtues of Shramadana. They should by law remove the structural injustices that our people are subjected to today such as landlessness, lack of power to participate in decision-making processes that affect their lives and political discrimination in the allocation of governmental resources for development.

Are the Elite Ready?

One final observation. The elite must undergo fundamental change in their attitude to rural development. They should stop playing the dominating Law Giver and Superman role with rural people. On the other hand they should be humble enough to find ways and means of placing their expert knowledge and resources at the disposal of rural people in accordance with latter's needs aspirations and wishes. By personal experience I know that tens of thousands of our rural people have awakened to sacrifice their time, thought and energy through the Shramadana Movement to build up a better Sri Lanka. But how many of our politicians, bureaucrats and the rich are ready to join them in this sacrifice?

34

Non-Violence and The Rule of Law

Horace Alexander*

When we use the expression "non-violence", there is, I think, a tendency to picture in our minds methods of meeting injustice, or of thwarting unjust laws, by methods that involve a breach of the law, but without causing physical harm to the agents of the law. The purpose is to undermine the unjust system, so that it gives way, and reform can be achieved.

But there is another side to the matter, which we, perhaps, too often overlook. When we think of Gandhiji, and the inspiration of his life, we should not forget that he was not primarily a law-breaker. In the situation in which he found himself, through most of his life, he felt driven from time to time to break the laws; whether those imposed on the Indian community in South Africa, or later, those imposed on the Indian people throughout India by the British Government. Yet, even as I write the words "break the laws", I realise that I am overstating the case. He broke some of the laws, some of the time, not all the laws, all the time. And he was always careful to make clear both to his fellow-sufferers from injustice and to the authority he was challenging that he was attacking a specific injustice, even when this act was a symbol of an attack on the whole system of government. The other aspect of his way of life was his deliberate, and even scrupulous, obedience to all the laws he did not feel conscientiously obliged to break. As a good lawyer, he had a healthy respect for law in general, and he would even scrupulously obey prison regulations and other laws, promulgated by those whose moral authority he was disputing, except when he was prepared to suffer to the utmost for disobedience.

One is often tempted to describe Gandhiji as an anarchist; I have myself suggested that he is more nearly an anarchist than a socialist or any

---

* U.S.A. – a close associate of Mahatma Gandhi

Published in *Journal of Gandhian Studies*, Vol. 1; January 1974.

other political category into which we find it convenient to herd our fellowmen. Yet, if an anarchist means one who thinks all law to be evil, then that does not fit Gandhiji at all. He knew that man, the social animal, must accept rules of behaviour if society is to continue to function at all. In an age of fast-moving traffic, there must be a rule of the road, and those who do not obey it must be brought to their sense. So too, there must be sanitary regulations, which all men should be expected to observe; and many other matters need to be regulated for the well-beng of all. Even the ashrams at Sabarmati and at Sevagram had ther rules; and if necessary, steps had to be taken to uphold the rules. Should I say "to enforce the rules"? "Enforce" is a strong word, and does not seem to fit the conception of an ashram. Let us be content to note that every society, including, for nstance, societies for scientific study or for promoting some art, must have certain "sanctions", which are likely to include the right of the majority, or the consensus, to expel an unruly member. In other words, the rule of law is an essential of any human society that is not to degenerate into a mere mob. Gandhiji knew this as well as, or perhaps better than, most of us. His violations of law were especially significant just because he was a believer in the rule of law.

I suggest that this is an important aspect of the struggle against violence in the world today. We see violence on all sides; and the governments of the world build up their mighty military forces, which are inevitably a threat to every other government, especially those of neighbouring States.

There is plenty of room for confusion here. Governments, even the most authori-tarians, are fond of declaring that they must uphold "Law and order" : yet this law and order is often a kind of tyranny, which contain as worse violence to the human spirit than the sporadic violence of those who rise up in anger against it. Thus, those who care deeply for human liberty may find the idea of the "rule of law" unpalatable. They can only conceive of it as a device for supporting tyrannical governments. Or, again, if you are living in the Christian tradition you will recall passages in the New Testament, espe-cially in the writings of the Apostle Paul, where the rule of law seems to be treated as an early stage of development, out of which the Christian has grown into what is called "grace". The law was the schoolmaster; but if we are full-grown, we no longer live under the law. Perhaps this is in part due to the fact that the Apostle was himself living under the rule of the Roman Empire, an alien rule. But essentially, I think we are here concerned with a word that has various shades of meaning. We should live the good life, no doubt, not just to escape the penalties of those who break a law. We live the life of good neighbours, tryng to serve the needs of others, rather than selfishly, because we have been released from the bondage of selfishness and have indeed come into the "glorious freedom of the sons of God". "Love, and do as you like", said St. Augustine; which means, of course, that all your actions will in fact be inspired by love of your fellow-men. You then live, not "under law", but in obedience to the law of love a para-doxical expression, not doubt, but it does not need to be elucidated. The meaning is clear enough.

"Law, not war", was one of the slogans of those who were working for a warless world in the period of the League of Nations. Surely a good slogan. War will not disappear simply through war-resistance, important as the refusal to participate in war and war preparations may be. There must be an adequate substitute for war. And that means a system of world law which all sovereign states will accept and follow. Today, most sovereign States, including, I think, those only recently freed from colonial rule, are inclined to assert their independence in such a way as to allow no place for a superior international law. Too often, loyalty to the United Nations means no more than a readiness to cooperate in common endeavours, but with no readiness to submit to resolu-tions of the U.N. which do not suit immediate convenience. There is little hope for the achievement of "One World" of peace and cooperation until such state sovereignty is curbed, and the rule of law accepted, even when it seems to clash with immediate political interest. The acceptance of obligatory jurisdiction by the World Court of all justiciable disputes would be a great step forward. It is unfortunate that so few States have yet accepted this jurisdiction; and that some who have done so have attached reservations.

The rule of law, when rightly interpreted, means that the weakest member will have his rights upheld by judicial authority against the most powerful. I am not sure where the principle of equality before the law originated. I have heard it said, though I am not sure if it is true, that the main positive contribution that the British made to India was the introduction of this principle; the principle that high-caste Hindu and Harijan, the richest Maharajah and the poorest peasant, were equally protected from illegal actions. It would be idle to pretend that the law in any country is even today truly equal as between the rich and the poor. But the principle of such equality is very widely accepted in the world; and one of the tests of true civilisation is the extent to which the principle is upheld by the courts. The Charter of Fundamental Human Rights, accepted by members of the United Nations, is surely a great step towards a truly non-violent world, even though this too is not fully applied. It is the duty of law-courts, of judges, to uphold it in all countries.

My argument is that one of the main goals of the proponents of non-violence should be the spread through all lands of the principle of equality before the law. This is "the rule of law". It is a noble ideal, and it should remain in the forefront of our minds as we struggle against war and violence and tyranny in their much manifestation.

35

Gandhi's Religious Quest in South Africa

K.L. Seshagiri Rao*

Gandhi's life in South Africa presented to him direct experiences of the bad as well as good aspects of organized religion. He had hardly set foot in South Africa in the spring of 1893 when he became involved in the racial and colour conflict. He tells us about an experience that changed the entire course of his life: he was travelling with a first class ticket and was turned out of his compartment to make room for a white passenger. In the midnight cold of Maritzburg, he was not allowed to enter even a waiting room because of the colour of his skin. Then, the moment of decision came. Should he go back to India or stay in South Africa, and start a long struggle for human justice on the basis of truth and non-violence? He took the decision to stay and fight injustice and not flee. When he was once kicked without the slightest warning by a policeman off a footpath near President Kruger's house, he said to himself: "The insults to which I am subjected are superficial, no more than symptoms of the deep disease of colour prejudice. I should try if possible to root out the disease and endure whatever hardships I would have to suffer in the process."

Gandhi enrolled himself as an advocate of the Supreme Court of Natal. Even in the study and practice of law, he saw the importance of the search for truth. As a lawyer, he was naturally interested in obtaining justice to his clients; but he went a step further. If he found that his client had lied to him, he would discontinue his affiliation with the case. He refused to defend clients he knew to be guilty. The search for truth was his highest goal, and his study of law also influenced him in the same direction.

At Johannesburg, Gandhi built up a flourishing lawyer's practice. He gained increasing influence. His words were heeded by a large section of

---

* Professor of Religious Studies, University of Virginia, U.S.A.

Originally published in *Journal of Gandhian Studies*, Vol. 1; April 1974.

Indians in South Africa. One would perhaps expect him to be satisfied with such a success; but Gandhi was not. He discovered that the life of a successful, moneymaking lawyer was not the best way of furthering the cause of common people. He could not find abiding satisfaction in wealth. There was a deep hunger in him, which could not be satisfied with worldly success.

In his irrepressible search for truth he returned again in South Africa to the study of world religion: Christianity, Islam, Hinduism and Buddhism. He corresponded with religious leaders and sought their advice. Christian influences on him were most powerful during this period. The Sermon on the Mount illumined his spirit and left its imprint on his character and action. Many Christians attempted to convert him. He came across the followers of a wide variety of Christian sects; a Quaker who wanted to save him from ignorance, a Plymouth Brother for whom religion was not necessarily related to morality, a church that would not admit him because he was brown, etc. But Gandhi was looking for the spirit of the Sermon on the Mount in modern Christianity.

John Ruskin's *Unto This Last* (which Gandhi summarised later into Gujarati under the title Sarvodaya) made a decisive impression on him; it was a critical study of modern civilization and a passionate plea for new social values. Mr. Polak had lent him that book to read during one of his journeys from Johannesburg to Durban. "I could not get any sleep that night", wrote Gandhi. "I determined to change my life in accordance with the ideals of that book." The book reflected many ideas that Gandhi was already familiar with, but it brought into focus three points, which he took as being essential to truth. They are:

i) The good of the individual is contained in the good of all;
ii) Everyone has the same right of earning his livelihood from his labour; and a barber's life is as important as a lawyer's;
iii) A life of labour, that is, of the tiller of the soil and the handicraftsman is the life worth living.

He got up at dawn that morning and resolved to give up his career as a successful lawyer in order to become an Indian peasant; to transform from that day his whole mode of existence, his profession and even his personal life.

To realize this new way of life, he established an *ashram*, the Pheonix settlement near Durban; it was a little colony consisting of his Indian and European friends—men, women and children of different races, castes and religions. They all lived and worked happily together in public service. While carrying on his public work, Gandhi was slowly transforming his private life. A passion for simplicity and service took hold of him. He cut down the expenditure of his household—became his own barber and washerman, and taught his children at home without sending them to any school. He volunteered to become a compounder and a nurse in a charitable hospital and gave two hours of his time every morning to this work. It was at this time that he took his vow for *brahmacharya,* celibacy for life, to be able to devote himself solely to the love and service of his fellowmen.

He developed a passion for serving the poor. He wrote: "If I, found myself entirely absorbed in the service of the community, the reason behind it was, my desire for self-realization. I had made the religion of service my own as I felt that God could be realized only through service……I had gone to South Africa for travel, for finding an escape from Kathiawad intrigues and for gaining my livelihood. But I found myself in search of God and striving for self-realization. I began to realize more and more the infinite possibilities of universal 'love'". When the Boer war began in 1899, Gandhi raised an Indian Ambulance Corps and offered its services to the authorities. In 1904 when plague broke out in Johannesburg, he devoted himself to sanitary work and the evacuation and nursing of the victims. In 1906, when there was Zulu rebellion in Natal, he raised from among the Indian community, a Stretcher Bearer Company and offered its services to the government, which accepted its services with Gandhi as Seargent Major.

Possibly one of the most decisive influences which shaped his ideas during this period was that of Tolstoy. Gandhi read *The Kingdom of God is Within You* during his first year in South Africa while he lived in Pretoria. The teaching of the book….that the Sermon on the Mount is a sufficient guide of life, the war, conscription, and oppression are immoral and unjustifiable….was as if written for Gandhi. He was overjoyed to read that 'the power of love is the most potent force on earth.' In Durban, he went to some later works of Tolstoy like the *Gospels in Brief and What To Do*? About their influences, he later told an American correspondent: "Russia gave me in Tolstoy a teacher who furnished a reasoned basis for my non-violence.

Tolstoy blessed my movement in South Africa when it was still in its infancy and of whose wonderful possibilities I had yet to learn. It was he who prophesied in his letter to me that I was leading a movement which was destined to bring a message of hope to the down-trodden people of the earth."

Gandhi soon founded another ashram called Tolstoy Farm devoted to the spiritual training of the members. The training of the spirit conducted there included besides manual labor and public service, the practice of the following virtues among others: (i) *satya*, truthfulness in thought, word and deed; (ii) *ahimsa*, non-injury or freedom from hatred a quality of essential goodwill and compassion even to enemies; (iii) *Brahmacharya*, the control of senses leading to purity of body and mind; (iv) *asteya*, non-stealing or the abstention from mis-appropriation of things that rightfully belong to others; (v) *aparigraha*, non-possession or abstention from the accumulation of wealth that belongs to the whole community; and (vi) *abhaya*, fearlessness of the quality of life that meets the challenging situations of life as they come.

Gandhi shaped a new political weapon for the masses, *satyagraha* —non-violent resistance. He taught the priority of obedience to God over political obedience. He was fascinated by the idea of non-cooperation with an evil system which he obtained from Thoreau's Essay on the Duty of Civil Disobedience. It confirmed his own belief that the individual had a moral right to oppose a law or command that went against divine laws or against the canons of conscience. He condemned all illegitimate social traditions, irrational political privileges and cruel customs. He championed the enormously revolutionary doctrine that the state cannot demand unconditional obedience.

The South African Indians under the leadership of Gandhi used *satyagraha*—non-violent resistance in their fight against the discrimination to which the government had subjected them. Gandhi emphatically advocated freedom and justice for the Indian community; the issue centered on the civil rights of the settlers. Gandhi demanded racial equality and valiantly fought against the dogma of the supremacy of the white man. While he was fighting for the rights of the Indian community, he was opposed to his own community claiming any superiority to the Negro peoples. He attempted to synthesize the political conception of the right and the moral conception of the spiritual personality of man.

He presented a program of four points to the South African government in the interests of political and racial justice. They were: (i) the abolition of the annual tax of three pounds on the Indian settlers; (ii) the civil rights to unrestricted movement in the Union territories; (iii) the legal validation of all non-Christian marriages; and (v) the removal of the anti-Asian bias in the immigration policy of the government. Gandhi was rebuffed and was arrested on orders of General Smuts in 1908. After a protracted struggle, based on the method of non-violent resistance, Gandhi achieved his great victory; and the South African government yielded on all the four points. It was during this eventful period of his life that Gandhi discovered his religion....religion not in the sense of subscription to dogmas or conformity to ritual, but religion in the sense of an abiding faith in the absolute values of truth, love and justice, and a persistent effort to realize them on earth.

36

The Last Hours of Mahatma Gandhi

Stephen Murphy*

PUNCTUALLY at 3.30 am on Friday, January 30, 1948, Mahatma Gandhi awoke to greet the last morning he would ever see.

He was in the tense atmosphere of Delhi. Staying in a ground-floor guest room of Birla House, the mansion of industrialist and benefactor G.D. Birla located in Albuquerque Road, Gandhi had arrived in the strife-torn capital of newly independent India on September 9, 1947 from Calcutta, where he had performed a miracle of peace-making. By January 30, 1947, almost four months had passed since his 78th, and last, birthday. It was 12 days since the successful end of his fast to bring about a reunion of hearts in Delhi. But 10 days before, there had been an aborted attempt on his life during the evening prayer meeting at Birla House. With the situation in Delhi having stabilised, Gandhi was again looking to the future, but his life was in grave danger and he knew it.

The Mahatma's test day would be as methodical and crowded as any other. Upon getting up from his wooden plank, he roused the other members of his party. They included attendants Brij Krishna Chandiwala and Manu and Abha, his grand-nieces. His physician, Dr. Sushila Nayar, who was normally with him, was away in Pakistan. He brushed his teeth with a twig like any ordinary Indian.

At 3.45 am prayers were held on the same cold verandah where the party had slept. With Sushila away, Manu led the Bhagvad Gita recitation. They recited the first and second shlokas. Another female member had failed to rise in time for prayers. This disturbed Gandhi. He mused whether she should leave him, and concluded by saying, "I do not like these signs. I hope God does not keep me here very long to witness these things". When

---

* Secretary-Treasurer, International Gandhian Movement, Hackett, Australia.
Published in *Gandhi Prasang*, Vol. 1 No. 2; January 1999.

Manu asked Gandhi which prayer she should chant for him, Gandhi chose a favourite Gujarati hymn. The song begins, "Whether weary or unweary, O man, do not tarry, stop not, your struggle if single-handed continue, and do not tarry!"

After prayers, leaning on his "walking sticks", Manu and Abha, the old man moved slowly into the inner room where Manu covered his legs with a warm blanket. It was still dark outside as Gandhi began his day's work. He corrected the draft of his proposal for a new Congress constitution written the previous night. This document was to become known as his Last Will and Testament to the nation. At 4.45 he drank a glass of lemon, honey and hot water and an hour later, his daily glass of orange juice. While working, because of weakness caused by the fast, he became tired and allowed himself a sleep.

Waking after only half an hour, Gandhi asked for his correspondence file. The previous day he had written a letter to Kishorlal Mashruwala. One of two matters the letter discussed was a tentative plan for Gandhi to soon leave Delhi and go to Sevagram. The letter had been mislaid, by Manu, and not posted. But it was found and Gandhi gave it to be posted, the last of many thousands. Manu had also wished to convey a message to Mashruwala, who had recently left Gandhi's service. She asked Gandhi whether they were returning to Sevagram on February 2, in which case they would be seeing Mashruwala soon anyway. Gandhi replief, "Who knows about the future? If we come to a decision regarding Sevagram, I shall announce it at the evening prayer meeting. It will then be relayed on the radio at night."

Also a consequence of his fast, Gandhi suffered from a bad cough. To treat it he would take palm-jaggery lozenges with powdered cloves. But by this morning the clove powder had finished. Instead of joining him in his morning walk, a stroll up and down the room, Manu sat down to prepare some more. "I shall join you presently", she said to Gandhi. "Otherwise there will be nothing at hand at night when it is needed". But always focusing on the here-and-now, Gandhi replied, "Who knows what is going to happen before nightfall or even whether I shall be alive. If at night I am still alive you can easily prepare some then." Manu, although well aware of Gandhi's principled stance against modern medicines, could not refrain from offering him penicillin lozenges instead. Unyielding, Gandhi asked her how she could offer him such things when his faith was in Ramanama and prayer.

The Mahatma's first appointment for the day was at 7 am with Rameshwari Nehru who was going to America. Gandhi spoke with her while taking his morning constitutional in the room. He had not yet regained enough strength for his customary long walk in the open air.

Next Gandhi was to have a massage. Passing through his secretary Pyarelal's room, Gandhi handed Pyarelal his draft submission for the new Congress constitution written for the forthcoming Congress Working Committee meeting. Gandhi asked him to go through it carefully. "Fill any gaps that you may find in my thinking", he instructed. "I have prepared it under heavy strain". Brij Krishna gave Gandhi the half-hour massage in a room adjacent to his sitting room. Two electric heaters were needed to warm the chilly air. While laying on the table Gandhi digested the morning newspapers.

After the massage Gandhi asked Pyarelal whether he had finished the revision. Gandhi also requested him to write a note on how, in the light of his work in Noakhali, he believed an impending rice crisis in Madras province could be handled. Manu then gave Gandhi his bath. During this he asked her whether she was doing the hand exercises he had prescribed. Manu told him that she did not like the exercises, then listened to a long but gentle rebuke from her master, who told her of the responsibility he had taken for her health and moral development.

After the bath Manu weighed the little man (who was about five feet and five inches tall). He was 190 — pounds. He had regained two-and-a-half pounds since ending his fast. His strength was returning. Pyarelal thought he looked refreshed after his bath. The strain of the previous night had disappeared. When someone told Gandhi that a woman member of Sevagram Ashram had missed her train that morning because there had been no conveyance for the several mile ride to Wardha station, he asked in all seriousness, "Why did she not talk to the station?" Then Gandhi did his morning Bengali writing exercise. Today he wrote, "Bhairab's home is in Naihati. Shaila is his eldest daughter. Today Shaila gets married to Kailash."

By now it was 9.30 and time for Gandhi's morning meal. The meal included cooked vegetables, 12 ounces of goat's milk, four tomatoes, four oranges, carrot juice and decoction of ginger, sour limes and aloes. While eating Gandhi talked with Pyarelal about the draft Congress constitution, to which Pyarelal had made some alterations. Pyarelal also reported on the outcome of a meeting the previous day with the leader of the extremist Hindu Mahasabha, Dr. Shyama Prasad Mookerjee, of speeches of a particular Hindu Mahasabha worker inciting the assassination of some Congress leaders. Could not Dr. Mookerjee stop these inflammatory speeches? Dr. Mookerjee's reply was halting and unsatisfactory, reported Pyarelal to the Mahatma. Pyarelal observed Gandhi's brow darken as he repeated Dr. Mookerjee's reply. Gandhi and Pyarelal then talked at length about the volatile situation at Noakhali. He told Pyarelal also of his plan to go to Pakistan. He asked Pyarelal to go back to Noakhali, but to wait until he had returned to Sevagram. Pyarelal was surprised at this request, for it was unusual for Gandhi to delay anyone returning to their post. Mid-morning also, an old associate from Gandhi's South African days, Rustom Sorabji, called in with his family.

Next, at about 10.30 Gandhi again slept. The soles of his feet were rubbed with ghee. At midday he awoke and drank a glass of hot water with honey. A little later he walked alone to the bathroom. It as the first time since his fast that he had walked unaided. "Bapuji", Manu called out to him, "how strange you look, walking all alone!" Gandhi laughed and said, "It's nice, isn't it? "Walk alone, Walk alone!". These last words were Tagore's.

Morning had given way to afternoon. At about 12.30 Gandhi talked about the plan of a prominent local doctor to build a nursing home and orphanage. He wanted very much to help. Soon Gandhi was visited by a delegation of Delhi Muslim leaders who were calling daily. Communal tensions and the refugee crisis still darkened the atmosphere in the capital. Gandhi discussed with the leaders his wish to go to Wardha to see about his institutions there and attend a conference on February 2. He would be back in Delhi by the 14th. He sought their permission to leave Delhi. "I do expect to be back here by the 14th. But if Providence has decreed otherwise, that is a different matter, I am not however; sure whether I shall be able to leave here even on the day after tomorrow. It is all in God's hands". The leaders gave their permission for Gandhi to leave Delhi. He would announce his plans at the evening prayer meeting.

On his last day Gandhi also spoke about his late beloved secretary Mahadev Desai. A biography of Mahadev was to be written, but there was disagreement over financial terms. Gandhi expressed his frustration at this. Mahadev's diaries also needed to be edited and compiled. The ideal candidate, Narhari Parikh, was in poor health. The task, Gandhi decided, should fall to Chandrashanker Shukla. Mashruwala had been another candidate.

The Mahatma also met with Sudhir Ghosh, who mentioned an apparent campaign in the British press to highlight a rift that had developed between Prime Minister Jawaharlal Nehru and Deputy Prime Minister Vallabhbhai Patel. Gandhi would raise the matter with Patel who was calling this afternoon, and with Nehru who, with Maulana Azad, was calling at 7 pm this evening.

Gandhi lay down in the afternoon January sunshine and had his abdominal mud pack. To shade his face he donned the peasant's bamboo hat he had brought from Noakhali. Manu and Abha again pressed his feet. A journalist who was there asked Gandhi if information that he was leaving for Sevagram on February 1 was correct. "Who says so?" Gandhi asked. "The papers have it", replied the journalist. "Yes", rejoined Gandhi. "The papers have announced that Gandhi would be going on the 1st. But who that Gandhi is, I do not know."

At about 1.30 p.m. Brij Krishna read out to Gandhi a statement by Master Tara Singh which angrily advised the Mahatma to retire to the Himalayas. A similar attack by a refugee yesterday had shocked him and this also left its mark. Gandhi then took a few ounces of carrot and lemon juice. Some blind and homeless refugees came to meet him. He gave instructions to Brij Krishana about them. Then the Allahabad Riot report was read to him.

Time was ebbing away. It was now mid-afternoon.

The usual daily round of interviews began at about 2.15 p.m. Representatives from all of India and beyond sought an audience. Two Punjabis spoke about the Harijans of their province. Two Sindhis followed. A representative of Ceylon accompanied by his daughter asked Gandhi to give a message for Ceylon's independence day on February 14. The girl obtained Gandhi's autograph, the last he was to give. At about 3 pm a professor who called in told Gandhi that what he was preaching had been advocated in Buddha's time. At about 3.15 a French photographer presented him with a album of his photographs. He met a Punjabi delegation, and a Sikh delegation who asked him to suggest a president for a conference to be held in Delhi on February 15. Gandhi suggested Congress President Rajendra Prasad and added he would give a message himself.

Gandhi finished the last interview by 4 p.m. when the Sardar was due to arrive. Gandhi rose from his sitting place and walked towards the bathroom. He asked Brij Kishore to arrange his railway journey for the very next day, Saturday.

Gandhi was still in the bathroom when Patel and his daughter and secretary Manibehn arrived. Patel and Brij Krishna chatted for a few minutes. When Gandhi emerged, he and Patel immediately fell into conversation. Gandhi told Patel that although earlier he had believed either Patel or Nehru would have to withdraw from Cabinet, he now agreed with Mountbatten, the new Governor-General that both were indispensable. He told Patel that he would make a statement to this effect at the prayer meeting and he would say this to Nehru when he called that evening. He might even postpone his departure for Wardha if he felt there was any trouble between the two.

As Gandhi and Patel were speaking, two Kathiawad leaders came and told Manu they wished to see Gandhi. She enquired of Gandhi whether he would see them. Said Gandhi in Patel's presence, "Tell them that I will, but only after the prayer meeting, and that too if I am still living. We shall then talk things over". Manu conveyed Gandhi's reply to the visitors and invited them to stay for the prayer meeting. Yet again, Gandhi had spoken of his possible imminent demise, and on this occasion in front of the man with prime responsibility for his safety. While Gandhi talked Abha served him his meal. It included goat's milk, vegetable soup, orange and carrot juice. Gandhi then asked for his charkha, which he plied lovingly for the last time.

For Gandhi this fateful Friday had been, more or less, a normal day. But for Nathuram Godse, a 37 year old Hindu extremist, it was a momentous one from the second he awoke that morning in Old Delhi Railway Station's Retiring Room No. 6. For today was the day he was going to kill Mahatma Gandhi.

Early in the morning Godse was joined by fellow conspirators Narayan Apte and Vishnu Karkare. There were actually eight men involved in the plot to kill Gandhi. The three who would carry out their group's second assassination attempt spent the day working out the details of their planned murder and preparing for the awful deed. They would stand at the outer rim of the crowd towards the right as they faced the elevated platform on which Gandhi sat. Godse would shoot at Gandhi with a seven chambered automatic pistol from the distance of about 35 feet. The other two would fend off anyone who tried to interfere. Godse had little experience with guns.

In mid-afternoon they left the railway station and went to Birla Temple. The other two prayed, but Godse did not. At 4.30 Godse, dressed in a newly bought khaki jacket – it would be confrontation of khaki versus khadi – left the temple by tonga for Birla House. Five minutes later, Apte and Karkare took their own tonga.

Before five o'clock Godse reached Birla House, followed by Apte and Karkare. Since the failed assassination attempt on January 20, Gandhi had acceded to the wishes of Patel and Nehru, and permitted about 30 police, uniformed and plainclothes, to be stationed at various points around Birla House and its surrounds. Not to have agreed, Gandhi felt, would have only added to the burdens on the shoulders of the two leaders. But he drew the line at agreeing to the searching of those entering the grounds to attend his prayer meetings. Upon arrival the conspirators observed that the guard had been increased, and, with great relief, that no one was being searched. All three entered the grounds without difficulty. They walked through the front entrance separately, as Gandhi and Patel at the rear of the mansion carried on their conversation.

It was 5 p.m. Afternoon was fading to evening as the winter sun dipped low. Five o'clock was the appointed time for prayers. Gandhi disliked ever being late, especially for prayers. But he was not wearing his familiar ingersoll pocket watch. These days others were his timekeepers. Manu and Abha saw the hour but dared not interrupt such an important conversation. At 5.10 they could wait no longer. Abha showed Gandhi his watch. But he was not distracted. Finally in desperation Manu intervened, and with Gandhi saying, :I must now tear myself away", the talk ended.

Gandhi got up, put on his chappals and stepped through the side door out of the room into the twilight. He wore a shawl for warmth. As usual he lent gently on his two "walking sticks". Manu was on his right and Abha on his left. As usual also Manu carried Gandhi's spittoon, spectacle case and rosary, and her notebook. Brij Krishna was behind them, together with some members of the Birla family and a few others, including the two Kathiawad visitors. Sushila Nayar, who normally walked in front of Gandhi, of course was not there. Nor, momentarily was another attendant Gurbachan Singh, who with one or two other men was usually in front of Gandhi. Also absent from his position at Gandhi's side was A.N. Phatia, the recently introduced plainclothes policeman. He had been assigned elsewhere that day and no replacement had been appointed. The congregation had wondered why the punctual Gandhi was late, but now they could see him coming.

Thus Mahatma Gandhi set out on his final 200 yard journey, his final trek, his final march. He had come from Porbandar, to Rajkot, to the Inner Temple, to Bombay, to Durban, to Pietermaritzburg, to Johannesburg, to Phoenix Settlement to Tolstoy Farm, to Champaran, to Sabarmati, to Yervada, to Dandi, to Kingsley Hall, to St. James Palace, to Sevagram, to the Aga Khan Palace, to Noakhali, to Calcutta, to Delhi.

Today he did not walk as usual through the leafy arbour to the right side of the grounds. Being late he took a short cut directly across the lawn to the steps leading to the terrace where prayers were held.

Despite everything, his mood was light. He joked about the raw carrot Abha had served him that day. "So you are serving me cattle fare!" he exclaimed. Abha replied that Ba, Gandhi's deceased wife, used to call it house fare. Rejoined Gandhi as they hurried along, "Is it not grand of me to relish what no-one else would care for?"

Abha and Manu teased Gandhi for neglecting his watch and his time-keepers both. "It is your fault that I am 10 minutes late", he responded. "It is the duty of nurses to carry on their work even if God himself should be present there. If it is time to give medicine to a patient and you hesitate, the poor patient may die. I hate if if I am late for prayers even by a minute."

With this party had finished the first 170 yards of the journey and had reached the foot of the six curved steps that led onto the prayer ground. Gadhi always insisted on his party stopping all jokes and conversation before they entered the prayer ground. About now Gurbachan Singh caught up the group, but did not move in front of Gandhi.

Around India and the world Gandhi's numberless friends and co- workers old and new, were carrying on in the knowledge that Mahatma Gandhi lived still. Reverend John Haynes Holmes was at his home in New York, Mirabehn was at her ashram in the Himalayas, Mountbatten was at Government House, Nehru was at work in Delhi, Pyarelal was on his way to Birla House, the Life magazine photographer Margaret Bourke-White was just a few streets away. Patel was returning to his bungalow, and American Journalist Vincent Sheean, who also had an appointment with Gandhi that evening was only a few yards away on the Birla House terrace, himself part of the throng.

The hushed crowd was several hundred thick (including possibly about 20 plainclothes policemen). At the top of the steps Gandhi brought his palms together to greet the gathering. As usual, the people parted to make a passage for him to the wooden platform. Critically, today there was no-one in front of Gandhi.

The supreme moment had come. Gandhi trod his final steps to eternity. Through the parting, Godse saw Gandhi coming straight towards him. Godse then made an instant decision to completely change the plan, and to shoot Gandhi there and then from point-blank range. The Mahatma had taken just few paces from the steps. Godse elbowed his way through, parting from the other two, and approached the Mahatma with his palms joined. The tiny black Italian Beretta pistol was concealed between them. He bowed low and said, "Namaste, Gandhiji". Gandhi joined his palms in acknowledgement. Manu thought Godse was going to kiss Gandhi's feet, a practice the Mahatma did not like. She motioned him away. "Brother, Bapu is already late for prayers. Why are you bothering him?" she said.

Gandhi had been expecting another attempt on his life. As this incident occurred, he might have understood.......this was it.

No police intervened. Godse pushed Manu forcefully aside with his hand momentarily exposing the gun in his right. The items in her hands fell to the ground. For a few moments she continued arguing with the unknown assailant. But when the rosary dropped she bent down to pick it up. At this precise moment, a burst of deafening blasts ripped apart the peaceful atmosphere as Godse fired three bullets into Gandhi's abdomen and chest. As the third shot was fired Gandhi was still standing, his palms still joined. He was heard to gasp, "He Ram, He Ram" ("Oh God, Oh God"). Then he slowly sank to the ground, palms joined still, possibly in a final ultimate act of ahimsa. Smoke filled the air. Confusion and panic reigned. The Mahatma was slumped on the ground, his head resting in the laps of both girls. His face turned pale, his white shawl of Australian wool was turning crimson with blood. Within second Mahatma Gandhi was dead. It was 5.17 p.m.

Early that very morning, foreseeing the manner of his death, Gandhi had said to Manu, "If someone fires bullets at me and I die without a groan and with God's name on my lips, then you should tell the world that here was a real Mahatma......."

Gandhi had journeyed through a lifetime from Porbandar to Delhi. He had journeyed from a struggle against disenfranchisement in Natal, to one against British rule of India, to one for peace and justice in free India. He had journeyed from ordinary young man to Mahatma.

He had journeyed "from untruth to truth, from darkness to light, from death to immortality."

His teachings had journeyed from India to the four corners of the world.

Gandhi, the soldier of Truth, lay on the soft, moist earth, his body sacrificed. But Gandhi had never fought with the body but with the spirit, and that remained untouched.

Primary Sources

Brij Krishna Chandiwala, *At the Feet of Bapu*, Navajivan Publishing House, Ahmedabad, 1954.

Larry Collins and Dominique Lapierre, *Freedom at Midnight*, Simmon and Schuster, New York, 1975.

Louis Fischer, *The Life of Mahatma Gandhi*, Granada, London, 1982.

Manubahen Gandhi, *The End of an Epoch*, Navajivan Publishing House, Ahmedabad, 1962. .

K.L. Gauba, *Assassination of Mahatma Gandhi*, Jaico Publishing House, Bombay 1969.

Robert Payne, *The Life and Death of Mahatma Gandhi*, The Bodley Head, London 1969.

Pyarelal, *Mahatma Gandhi : The Last Phase. Vol. II,* Navajivan Publishing House, Ahmedabad, 1958.

D.G. Tendulkar, *Mahatma : Life of Mohandas Karamchand Gandhi*. Vithalbhai K. Jhaveri & DG. Tendulkar, Bombay, 1954.

The Collected Works of Mahatma Gandhi, Vol. XC, Publications Division, New Delhi, 1984.

Author's note: Every effort possible has been made to ensure that the above is a truthful account of Gandhi's last hours. In many instances, in order to give the truest possible picture, actual words and phrases from previously published firsthand accounts have been used. However, there are discrepancies between these accounts, and each account of course is based on the memories of its author.

37

Gandhi for Mere Mortals

Stephen Murphy*

Putting into practice in one's own life the principles for which Gandhi stands is a demanding challenge. Gandhi himself found that it required his complete devotion. Through extraordinary effort and faith in God as deep as an ocean, he was highly successful. In the eyes of his countrymen and women, and others around the world, so successful was he, that he was a 'Mahatma'. As a result of his success, his greatness, it became easy to deify him. This happened easily in India, where processes of deification are part of centuries old religious traditions.

However, deification means the person is to be deeply respected and worshipped but not emulated. With Gandhi in his exalted position with or near the gods, the main focus is on celebrating him and his life rather than on the possibility of emulating his life today. And this when Gandhi said (in 1936): "...I have not the shadow of a doubt that any man or woman can achieve what I have, if he or she would make the same effort and cultivate the same hope and faith.....".

With a new century dawning, and with the Gandhian movement in India having achieved only limited progress since Gandhi's death in 1948, the mission of promoting Gandhian ideals might be advanced considerably if those of us who are Gandhi's 'descendants' but more thought into how living a genuinely Gandhian life can be made more a reachable or attainable goal for the mere mortal. By "Gandhian" is meant not being a devotee of Gandhi, but a devotee of the same ideals of which Gandhi was a devotee.

Many ordinary people undoubtedly would be attracted to the idea of living a life that was guided by the very same principles that guided Mohandas Gandhi. To be able, with honesty and integrity, to call oneself a Gandhian is a special thing in this world. But what does it mean? Immediately when one

---

* Secretary-Treasurer, International Gandhian Movement, Hackett, Australia.
Published in *Gandhi Prasang*, Vol. 1 No. 1; October 1998.

begins to ponder this question the example of Gandhi's own life comes to mind, and with that the negative thought that no one else could attain those heights. This thought process will often lead to a person stopping any attempt before it is started. How can this be overcome?

It would be worthwhile to produce a set of principles, adherence to which would characterise a person as Gandhian. This should be not even difficult. Gandhi did not believe the ideals that guided him were too complex for simple expression. It could simply be a question of stating what the principles and ideals are, and a person committing him or her attaining these not tomorrow, but from tomorrow to work towards their attainment forever more. The mere mortal would find him or herself treading exactly the same path Gandhi trod!

Of course Gandhi progressed far along the path, but the ordinary mortal can attain progress too. The important thing is, the ideals and principles are established and these are the beacons. These are what the ordinary person works towards, and with effort he or she can make gains. If we say that 100 steps is perfection and Gandhi achieved 95 steps, we can aim for 20 or 30 or perhaps more. Even 20 is better than none, or very few. The point is, even one step is better than not trying at all, and simply worshipping Gandhi as a Mahatma beyond the mortal coil.

If we take one example within the Gandhian ambit, that of diet, we can see what a difference such an approach could make it applied on a global scale. The fully Gandhian or non-violent diet is what is known in the West as a vegan diet – the consumption of no animal products whatsoever. The mere mortal may find it too demanding to become a vegan, but he or she may have the capacity to become vegetarian, (consuming dairy products though no meat of any kind). Imagine the revolutionary repercussions that would result if even 50 per cent of the world's population were to become vegetarian!

In all areas of life, so much stands to be gained if individuals can achieve some personal reform. We may not achieve some personal reform. We may not achieve perfect truth or perfect non-violence; our lives may not consist of the purest self-sacrifice, simplicity and service a-al-Gandhi. But if, while acknowle-dging the ideal, significant progress can be made this would be a great gain for humanity. We can still be Gandhians while not being Gandhis!

Here is one possible description of one who could say he or she is Gandhian. They might be called the "Seven Signs of a Seeker".

1. One who believes in God and who daily perceives the living presence of God;
2. One whose life is devoted to the realisation of God through services to His creation;
3. One who, to the greatest extent the individual is capable, is truthful and incorruptible;
4. One who to the greatest the individual is capable, rids him or herself of all violence;
5. One who, to the greatest extent the individual is capable, non-violently resists or non-cooperates with injustices;
6. One whose life, to the greatest extent the individual is capable, displays simplicity, service and sacrifice;
7. One whose life excludes to the maximum extent the individual is capable, the exploitation of the lower species.

Anyone who lived a life according to vows of this kind, I personally would accept as a genuine Gandhian. Let me briefly discuss the rationale and wording of the above points.

The first two, which refer to belief in and service to God, being the bedrock of the Gandhian outlook, are fixed. A person who wishes to regard him or herself as a Gandhian should have such an outlook. Any principle of a sliding scale, which allows for variations in commitment, does not apply here.

However, for the other five such a principles does apply. Of course, this is indicated by inclusion of the phrase "to the maximum extent the person is capable". At one end of the sliding scale is a person whose "maximum extent" is modest, at the other, another Gandhi. These fundamental principles also encompass other less fundamental principles, which may or may not be attempted, depending upon the person. For example, the ideals of simplicity, service and sacrifice can include the practice of *brahmacharya,* bread labour and trusteeship.

The point is, even mere mortals can adopt these principles in their lives. They can be Gandhians. The beacons are the very same ones that guided Gandhi through his life. The only question is to what extent a person can develop the application of the principles in his or her life. As referred to above, if Gandhi took 95 of 100 possible steps mere mortals with effort can still take 20 or 30 or 40 or 50 or more. The ultimate point is, such figures are better than 0. If a significant number of people world-wide were to progress, say, 20 steps, one might contend that the changes that would be brought about in the world be remarkable.

Gandhi did not realistically expect that all would be able to follow in his footsteps. He knew that the effort he had made had been exceptional. But he did believe that everyone could make some effort and achieve some progress along the same path he was treading. He probably believed also that many of us could make more progress if we tried harder.

If in the 21st century we can find a way to make Gandhi more reachable, more attainable to the mere mortal, we as Gandhi's interpreters will have done him and his invaluable legacy a great service. There is no reason why ordinary but sincere and committed people cannot apply the very same principles that Gandhi applied and live their lives in the same spirit. There can be millions of Gandhians. Gandhi is out of reach to no one. As a pre-eminent man of the people, that is the way he wanted it.

38

Implications Of The Limits To Growth Debate – Small Is Beautiful

E.F. Schumacher*

What, it must be asked, is "Growth" in this context? It is impossible to say, because Growth is a purely quantitative concept without any qualitative determination.

As every thing corporal is, as it were, composed of quantity and quality, purely quantitative concepts do not touch reality at any point.

It is not possible to say that Growth is either good or bad, either desirable or undesirable, either possible or impossible. Equally, it is not possible to talk about limits to Growth (except, as concerns the corporal world, in an abstract and ultimate sense, e.g., "infinite growth in a finite framework is impossible") or to talk about the desirability of Non-Growth. Any debate conducted in purely quantitative terms is nothing but a battle of words without meaning.

Of course, it will be said: "When we discuss Growth, Limits to Growth, or Non-Growth, we are merely using a kind of shorthand; we know what we mean in qualitative terms. These are implicit". But even if this were generally true, it would be a highly unsatisfactory state of affairs – to allow the higher factor–quality – to remain implicit, while the lower factor – quantity – is made explicit and, in fact, treated as decisive.

The "Predicament of Mankind" is directly due to the "Reign of Quantity" – materialism, GNP worship, treating money and acquisition as ends in themselves, etc. – in other words, to treating quantity as primary and the qualitative determination implicity as self-understood, i.e., not worth bothering about. A purely quantitative treatment of this predicament is

---

* England

Originally published in *Gandhi Prasang*, Vol 2. No. 1; October 1999.

therefore yet another symptom of the disease and totally incapable of leading to a cure. To substitute the concept of Non-Growth for the concept of Growth is to replace one emptiness with another.

All the same, it can be argued that the Club of Rome study is the kind of symptom which may arouse enough attention so that people become interested in curing the disease which, hitherto, they had studiously interpreted as a condition of excellent health.

It must, however, be quite clearly understood that the attempt to remove symptoms is not equivalent to an attempt to cure the disease; in other words, that the prescriptions given in the Club of Rome study are worthless.

What are these prescriptions? They are marked by total perplexity and helplessness.

p. 173:....we have now arrived at a minimum set of requirements. They are:

1. The capital plant and the population are constant in size. The birth-rate and the capital investment rate equal the depreciation rate.
2. All input and output rates......are kept to a minimum.
3. The levels of capital and population and the ratio of the two are set in accordance with the values of the society.

Now, all this, I suggest, is the most appalling nonsense, to the extent that it has any meaning at all. Why is it nonsense? Because none of the concepts used have any real meaning. They are illegitimate children of a speculative imagination that has lost contact with reality. Capital plant constant in size? A dam built to abolish water erosion in Lesotho may be built only if somebody in England gives up his second car? The farmer in the Transkel may acquire a plough only if your wife goes without a sewing machine? "Of course we don't mean that!" Well, what on earth do we mean? And why don't we say what mean? The world population constant in size? Are there no underpopulated regions in the world – countries like Zambia, where nothing can happen without a greater density of population?

I don't wish to waste your time by dwelling on the truly gigantic nonsensecality of these propositions. They don't point the way to action. They do not identify the disease and therefore cannot point to the possibility of a cure. They are, themselves, a symptom of the disease, because, product of a mindless computer, they are purely quantitative constructs, without any relation to reality.

Let us start from 'first principles'. Man, a child of God, is designed for growth. He is endowed with great gifts which he is called upon to use – see the parable of the talents. Being a composite of body and soul, he is called upon to look after his body, which is the dwelling of his soul and, in fact the temple of God.

This Conference is under the auspices of the World Council of Churches, and we are entitled, therefore, to discuss the fundamental questions of man's existence on Earth – how is man to use the splendid gifts with which he has been endowed? The answer was given – in its most concise form, I believe – by one of Christendom's greatest saints and organizers, as follows:

Man was created to praise, reverence, and severe God our Lord, and by this means to save his soul; and the other things on the face of the earth were created for man's sake, and in order to aid him in the prosecution of the end for which he was created.

Whence it follows, that man ought to make use of them just so far as they help him to attain his end, and that he ought to withdraw himself from them just so far as they hinder him.

As Gandhi said, there is enough for everyman's need but not for everyman's greed.

Now, I know of course, having been around a good while, that there are many who think that saints are there to be admired but on no account to be taken seriously. To me, I must confess, they are the most practical people that have ever been, and as an economist, I cannot help taking them seriously. I believe – not without reason that the statement I have just read – just so far as they help him just so far as they hinder him – is the crux of everything we have come here to discuss. I also believe that Gandhi, another very practical saint, knew what he was talking about.

In other words, it is impossible to talk about "The implications of the Limits to Growth Debate" without considering what man was created for. There is no solution to the problems presented by what the Club of Rome calls the Predicament of Mankind unless we remember what man was created for, because our Earth was also created precisely to serve man just so far as he needs it to do his job, but not just so far as to enable him to worship the false gods of limitless materialism.

During the recent past, it seems to me, the churches had no time for considerations such as these. They wanted to be "with it" and saw their main function in preaching to the working class that they should be good boys and help to produce a bigger cake – then their own slice would be bigger too. I have never been able to see the value of this approach.

However this may be, aimless Growth along the lines of the past is now being called into question. So where do we go from here?

It is perfectly obvious that there is no means whatsoever at our disposal to stop either the Growth of world capital or of world population. What we can do, however, is to fight the growth of what is unsound and promotes the growth of what is sound. The arithmetical balance between the two is of no concern whatever.

To know what is unsound in current patterns of living – growth or no growth – we must divert our attention first of all to the rich countries of which the U.S.A. is the leading example. Here you have a society, containing 5.6% of the world's population, which uses 40% of the world's primary raw materials. A useful table is given on pages 56-60 of The Limits to Growth. Column 10 shows U.S. consumption as % of World Total. The crucial materials are fossil fuels.

Coal 44%

Natural Gas 63%

Petroleum 33% - all non-renewable.

It is obvious that the world cannot afford the U.S.A. Nor can it afford Western Europe or Japan.

In fact, we might come to the conclusion that the earth cannot afford the "Modern World". It requires too much and accomplishes too little. It is too uneconomic. Think of it: one American drawing on resources that would sustain 50 Indians!

The earth cannot afford, say, 15% of its inhabitants – the rich who are using all the marvellous achievements of science and technology – to indulge in a crude, materialist way of life which ravages the earth. The poor don't do much damage; the modest people don't do much damage. Virtually all the damage is done by say, 15%.

It is obvious, therefore, that the Club of Rome exercise, which lumps all people together into a "World population" and also lumps all production and all consumption together, as if everything were much of a muchness, far from clarifying the tense situation, obscures it. The problem passengers on Spaceship earth are the first-class passengers and no one else.

They are now calling a halt to "Growth", and of course, this sounds ominous and hollow in the ears of the other 85% who still travel very uncomfor-tably. (Even the disclaimer, made in the Commentary on p. 191 does not help. Having recommended the cessation of Growth, the commentators "recognize that world equilibrium can become a reality only if the lot of the so-called developing countries is substantially improved", but they fail to tell us how you can fit a quart into a pint pot.)

How can we escape from the perplexity and helplessness which characterize the limits to growth report? First, we need a proper diagno-sis. The modern world has been, and continues to be, shaped by modern technology. Now, from the point of view of survival, modern technology is monstrously inefficient. It lives on capital, not on income, i.e. on non-renewable materials – fossil fuels, on the "tolerance margins of Nature" – hence the ecological crisis, and"also on the "human substance" – hence the universal protest, unrest, violence, resort to crime, drugs, mental breakdowns and so forth.

It appears that our predicaments are not due to our failures but to our successes. Yet it cannot have been wrong to develop Science and to use science to develop technology. Somehow, some where our development of science and technology must have taken a wrong turning. Perhaps I might describe it this way:

If an ancestor of long ago visited us today, what would he be more astonished at-

— The skill of our dentists or the rottenness of our teeth?
— The speed of our transport or the length of time and discomfort incurred in travelling to and from work?
— The progress of medicine or the overcrowding of our hospitals?
— Our ability to land man on the moon or our inability to find work for the workless?

— Our drives for productivity by means of mechanization, rationalization, automation or the staggering inefficiency of the system as a whole?

— The purposefulness of our technological strivings or the aimlessness of our overall policies?

And so forth.

He would certainly feel utterly puzzled and confused. We say we need capital to create jobs, and at the same time use capital primarily to save jobs. We claim that never before in history have so many people been so well educated, but they cannot do anything for themselves, having become utterly dependent on vast and vastly expensive machines and organizations.

We say that earth is overpopulated, but insist on emptying the country side and all crowding together in monster cities many of which have already become quite unmanageable. And so forth.

This sagacious observer, with no axe to grind, might come to the conclusion that all these extraordinary contradictions are due to the fact that we have developed a habit of thinking of goods and profit first and of people – if at all – afterwards. Product comes first, with no holds barred, and then, if it is found to cause human or environmental damage, we try to cope with social and other consequences. But how could one cope with the consequences? The damage has been done! We get someone to pay for it, - if we or he can find the money. The trouble is, however, that money cannot compensate; it cannot undo the damage. Compensation paid to an accident victim does not undo the accident, just as the skill of our dentists cannot compensate us for the rottenness of our teeth. And then, no matter how rich we become, we always find ourselves short of money.

Our observer may come to some further conclusions. He may say: All the remedies you now propose deal only with "consequences" and are not remedies at all.

a) You want to cut out waste; excellent! But the main wastefulness lies in your pattern of production and your pattern of living, not in the often-silly way in which you waste what you have produced.

b) You want to "recycle" materials; but the one material on which every thing depends – energy – cannot be recycled; ever more energy will be required to do the recycling job itself.

c) You want to fight pollution – after it has happened, by using more science and technology to this end. But this is an attempt to get Beelzebub to drive out to the devil.

d) You want to reduce population, but if one person living " American-style" does fifty times as much damage to resources and environment as one person living "Indian-style" how can you ensure that smaller numbers will not do even greater damage by switching from "Indian style" to "American-style"?

Do all these things, he might say, if you can, but do not for a moment believe that they would solve your problems.

Instead of losing patience with this awkward observer, we might ask him for his view of the problem. I do not know what he would reply and shall now give you my own reply for what it is worth.

The trouble arises, of course, - as I have said already – from our basic, metaphysical attitude to life – the Reign of Quantity, Materialism, not knowing where to stop in our pursuit of material satisfaction, disregard of non-material values, and so forth. But I do not propose to remain at this level of argument.

These metaphysical errors have, as it were, incarnated themselves in modern technology which has some very clear and destructive features.

a) It has become too big
b) It has become too complex, and
c) It has become too violent.

These three features, taken together, make it incompatible with:

a) Human nature
b) The rest of living nature, and
c) The resource endowment of the world.

If we want to help ourselves, we must work to use the fullness of our modern knowledge, consciously and with the utmost determination to create – or recreate – a technology, which is:

a) Small, i.e. adapted to the human scale
b) Simple – so that we do not have to become too specialized to be wise and

c) Non-violent, in the sense of working with Nature instead of bludgeoning her all the time.

All material things – including organizations – must have their proper, human, scale, or they become anti-human. This has been known since Genesis. Aristotle knew it and so did Dr. Marx. The best bit in the Club of Rome study is a quotation from Aristotle (p. 156):

To the size of states there is a limit, as there is to other things, plants, animals, implements; for none of those retain their natural power when they are too large or too small; but they either wholly lose their nature or are spoiled.

In protection, small units can find their resources within a short radius and also their markets. There is no need for monster transport.

Small is beautiful: it is also simple and non-violent. Intelligent small-scale technology can use income-energy instead of fossil fuels; it is humanly right because the human mind can encompass it; is socially right because it favours the well-being of small people, not only those already rich and powerful.

There can be no genuine development without small-scale technology, nor can there be a correction of over-development without it.

But size is not all. Keep things simple or, rather, use the fullness of modern knowledge to recapture simplicity. Man's needs are essentially simple, only his extravagances and frivolities are complex. Complexity – any fool can make things complicated; it takes a touch of genius to make them simple.

The complex

— is capital-intensive and expensive
— is produced by gigantism and leads to it
— excludes the majority of people
— demands, as I said before, people too specialized to be wise; and, assuredly, we are now far too clever to be able to survive without wisdom. Wisdom is subtle, but at the same time, simple as a little child.

We now possess such superlative scientific knowledge and technical ability that we can make things simple again.

Thirdly: non-violence. Let us use our great knowledge to find non-violent solutions to our many problems.

Biological processes are non-violent compared with mechanical or chemical processes: e.g. Energy requirements to create artificial polymers in factories, which Nature creates with sunlight

Income energy is non-violent; to use it presupposes smallness.

Organic gardening and farming is non-violent.

Prevention is non-violent compared with cure.

Pollution is the result of violence, almost a measure of it.

The Club of Rome study accepts nuclear energy as a breakthrough extending the 'Limits to Growth' (p. 131): "The technology of controlled nuclear fission has already lifted (?) the impending limit of fossil fuel reserves". The authors give statistics about the expected accumulation of radioactive wastes – but they are evidently so wedded to pure quantity that they cannot appreciate the awesome qualitative impact of what they are talking about.

Indeed, this takes us back to the beginning of talk. The quantitative approach, which almost totally neglects the essence of things and knows nothing but units – whether people, or capital, or hectares – cannot help us to find solutions, because our problems have arisen precisely from this approach.

Such work is already in train. It needs support (e.g. the Intermediate Technology Development Group in the U.K.). Such organizations do not demand sudden, total violent changes. They demand that there should be a gradual change of emphasis.

Here lies the battlefront of the future – between the people of the forward stampede – "a breakthrough a day keeps the crisis at bay" – and the home comers who labour patiently to bring things back to the human scale.

Small is Beautiful.

Simple is Beautiful.

Non-violent is Beautiful.

They labour to make a viable future already visible in the present. The churches, it seems to me, should be on the side of the homecomers.

39

Nonviolence In The 21st Century: Challenges and Choices

Arun Gandhi*

The greatest challenge in promoting non-violence is the English language and its limitations. The next is our perception, rooted for centuries, that violence is the only way we can resolve our problems.

Going back to the first challenge when Mohandas Karamchand Gandhi developed his philosophy of non-violence in South Africa and wanted an appro-priate word to describe it he could not find one "Passive Resistance" and "Civil Disobedience" did not appeal because he said there was nothing passive or disobedient about the movement. He even offered a reward to anyone who could come up with a positive English word to describe what he had in mind but, alas, one could.

At this point Gandhi decided a Sanskrit word may be more appropriate since he was planning to move back to India and lead the Indian struggle for freedom. He found "*Satyagraha*" described his philosophy the best. It is a combination of two Sanskrit words "*Satya*" meaning Truth and "*Agraha*" meaning pursuit of. Thus, "*Satyagraha*" means the "Pursuit of Truth", which is important because it is the opposite of the Western concept of "Possessing the Truth".

Non-violence, therefore, can be described as an honest and diligent pursuit of truth. It could also mean the search for the meaning of life or the purpose of life, questions that have tormented mankind for centuries. The fact that we have not been able to find satisfactory answers to these questions does not mean there is no answer. It only means we have not searched with any degree of honesty. The search has to be both external and

* M.K. Gandhi Institute for Non-Violence, Christian Brother University, 650, East Parkway, South Memphis, TN38104

Published in *Gandhi Prasang,* Vol.2 No.2; January 2000.

internal. We seek to ignore this crucial search because the sacrifices it demands are revolutionary. It means moving away from greed, selfishness, possessiveness and dominance to love, compassion, understanding and respect. It means to be true to our Faith and religion it is not enough that we pray 10 times a day but that we make the scriptures the basis of our existence.

Because of our materialistic and greedy lifestyle we have become very possessive. We seek to possess not only material goods but even our spiritual beliefs and even peace, if we find it. How many times have we heard people say, "I am at peace with myself". Of, when Gurus say to their devotees, "find your peace and hold on to it". Can anyone find peace or spiritual awakening and greedily hold on to it for themselves?

A favourite story that Grandfather liked to tell us was the story of an ancient Indian king who was obsessed with the desire to find the meaning of peace. What is peace and how can we get it and when we find it what should we do with it were some of the issues that bothered him. Intellectuals in his kingdom were invited to answer the King's questions for a handsome reward. Many tried but none could explain how to find peace and what to do with it. At last someone suggested to the King to consult the sage who lived just outside the borders of his kingdom.

"He is an old man and very wise", the King was told. "If anyone can answer your question he can."

The King went to sage and posed the eternal question. Without a word the sage went into the kitchen and brought a grain of wheat to the King.

"In this you will find the answer to your question", the sage said as he placed the gain of wheat in the king's outstretched palm.

Puzzled but unwilling to admit his ignorance, the King clutched the grain of wheat and returned to his palace. He locked the precious grain in a tiny gold box and placed the box in his safe. Each morning, upon waking, the King would open the box and look at the grain to seek an answer but could find nothing.

Weeks later another sage, passing through, stopped to meet the King who eagerly invited him to resolve his dilemma.

The King explained how he had asked the eternal question and this sage gave him a grain of wheat instead. "I have been looking for an answer every morning but I find nothing."

The Sage said: "It is quite simple, your honor. Just as this grain represents nourishment for the body, peace represents nourishment for the soul. Now, if you keep this grain locked up in a gold box it will eventually perish without providing nourishment or multiplying. However, if it is allowed to interact with the elements – light, water, air, soil – it will flourish, multiply and soon you would have a whole field of wheat which will nourish not only you but so many others. This is the meaning of peace. It must nourish your soul and the souls of others, it must multiply by interacting with the elements."

This is the essence of Gandhi's philosophy of "non-violence" or the pursuit of truth. In the life-long pursuit of truth we must always be guided by love, compassion, understanding and respect, allow everything we have to interact positively with the elements and help create a society of peace and harmony. The more possessions we have, the more we have to secure them from those who covet it generating feelings of jealousy and the desire to take by force what the needy cannot get through compassion.

The four essential principles of Gandhi's philosophy are quite simple to understand and implement. At the public level the four principles are: Truth, Ahimsa, Trusteeship and Constructive Action.

While at the personal level the four principles are: Respect, Understanding, Acceptance and Appreciation.

The success in attaining enlightenment or finding the Truth depends on how honest we are and whether we can liberate ourselves from the attachments that tie us down. Gandhi said being liberated politically or socially is not enough. He did not mean that we become careless or adopt a "don't care" attitude towards life and relationship. Freeing yourself of attachments means one must be willing to stand up for truth and justice and not be afraid of the consequences like losing your possessions, your job or even your life. It is only when we reach that level of spiritual power that non-violence will become relevant.

When white racists humiliated Grandfather in South Africa because they did not want a "black" man travelling in a first class compartment of a train he tried to enlist the support of the non-whites in South Africa to stand up for their rights. Instead, he found that fear dominated their response. "What will happen to my family? My job?, My home and possessions?"

The middle-class was content to submit to the white man's injustices rather than stand up to them and risk losing everything. That was when grand-father discovered the corrupting influence of materialism.

This attitude persists everywhere. We still accept injustice because we are afraid of suffering and losing our possessions of our security? True liberation comes when we can liberate ourselves of the FEAR that controls our lives. In the final analysis that is the key. In reality, this is not something impossible that non-violence demands. When we are forced by law to sacrifice our lives to protect our country in war we don't ask who is going to take care of the family or what will happen to my possessions. We just go with the knowledge that we may not come back again. This is a sacrifice that is forced upon an individual by a government. Then, why is it so difficult for the same individual to make the same sacrifice to stand up for justice, ethics and values?

"I am prepared to die but there is no cause for which I am prepared to kill", Gandhi said.

However, to come back to the core principles of non-violence, the meaning of TRUTH is, of course, obvious. We must remember truth has many sides and it is ever changing. What appears true today may not be true tomorrow. Or what appears to be the Truth to us does not necessarily appear to be the Truth to others. We cannot therefore, say that we possess the Truth and so our under-standing of Truth is the right one. We must develop the ability to look at every-thing from different perspectives and have the humility to understand that we could be wrong.

AHIMSA is the Sanskrit word for total non-violence, that is, non-violence in thought, word and deed. Grandfather recognized the limitations of ahimsa. Living the way we do being totally non-violent may not be possible for everyone. It may even not be possible for anyone. Yet, it must be the objective of every individual in the same way as getting an "A+" grade is the objective of every student who goes to school. If any student goes to school with the mindset that he/she will never get an "A+" grade then that student is in big trouble. That person has already discounted himself and will, therefore, only slide down into oblivion.

TRUSTEESHIP is a unique concept that needs to be properly understood. Each individual has the talent or the ability to achieve our goals. We exploit that talent or the ability for personal gains in the belief that we "own" the talent or ability. Gandhi said we don't own the talent but we are appointed "Trustees" by God and so we must use the talent to help others, less fortunate or talented than us. But this "giving" or "sharing" or "helping" must not cripple the receiver.

There is a very thin line that divides "pity" and "compassion" and we often mistake one for the other. Pity is degrading and oppressive while compa-ssion is uplifting for both the giver and the receiver. Pity is when we give a hungry person money to buy food or when we feed the hungry through soup kitchens. When feeding becomes an end in itself then we are causing a problem. Feeding should be a means to constructive action. By feeding the hungry we make them dependent on handouts.

On the other hand compassion requires that we get involved in finding ways in which the unfortunate can be helped to become self-sufficient citizens. The help they receive should be such as to help rebuild their self-confidence and self-respect, which are crushed by poverty and oppression.

CONSTRUCTIVE ACTION is the natural corollary to trusteeship. It means getting involved in finding constructive solutions to problems. We are usually so preoccupied with the Self that we don't have time for anyone or anything. We usually want to hang the responsibility on someone's shoulders, usually the Government's shoulders yet they have severe limitations. Bureaucrats or paid social workers don't always have the compassion needed for this kind of work. In 1970 six young people in Mumbai City in India, each working for a livelihood and committed to raising their children, decided to find a solution to the over-whelming homelessness in the city that is growing rampantly.

Using Gandhi's philosophy of trusteeship and constructive action, this group led by Mahipal Rao Mohite, assembled more than 500 homeless people and challenged them to become a part of the solution by saving a coin everyday to build the necessary capital so that an economic project could be launched. Mohite could have sought donations or applied for grants but that would give the homeless the feeling they could ask for what they need and receive it on a platter.

Mohite said the homeless would have to collectively save a coin every day. Most people would have considered this impossible or even heartless to ask someone to save a coin every day when they did not know where the next meal was going to come from. However, the homeless accepted the challenge and with Mohite's encouragement saved the equivalent of $11,000 in about 19 months.

The money was used to start, in 1971, a small textile factory with second hand power looms in a tin shed in Vita village near Sangli, 200 miles south of Mumbai. Some 70 of the homeless were sent to the village to work in the jointly owned factory under the guidance of Mohite and his friends until the homeless were trained to run the business for themselves. Today all those who contributed to the capital are back in their village living on the earnings of their four textile factories, enjoying a much better life-style and able to send their children to schools and higher education.

The homeless continued saving money and in 1978 opened the Sangli Jilla Kranti Cooperative Bank in Mumbai City. Today the Bank has 7 branch offices and total assets worth $2 million. This is an example of what Gandhi meant by trusteeship and constructive action. Mohite and his friends did not make major sacrifices other than their leisure and vacation time.

The four principles of non-violence to be practiced by individuals begin with RESPECT. We must respect ourselves, respect others and respect our relationship to all of creation. A myth persists, especially in the West, that we are independent individuals with no responsibilities towards others. A cohesive society cannot be built with each individual pulling in different direction. To achieve harmony and cohesiveness we must accept the fact that we are inter-dependent, inter-related and inter-woven working together to build a human society.

It is not enough to respect individual human beings. We must also respect different cultures, different belief systems. Danger lies in our becoming competitive, in believing that ours is the only way and the best way and attempting to impose our way on others. To assume that our way is the best is to say that we "possess" the Truth. When we accept that others could also be right then we join others in an honest search for Truth.

Religion, Grandfather explained, is the beginning of a spiritual journey. When we come to understand Religion properly we reach an understanding of spirituality that is the acceptance and respect for different ways of worship. Salvation is when we reach the mountaintop. When we become one with creation and creation becomes one with us.

UNDERSTANDING is reached when we learn who we are and what is our role in all of creation. In our arrogance we believe that humans are not a part of nature. We are here to conquer nature. In our attempt to conquer nature we are destroying our habitat and cannot expect to survive for very long.

ACCEPTANCE is reached when we accept the differences – physical and philosophical – between human beings. When these differences begin to melt away then we accept each other as human beings and can dispense with the labels that keep people apart.

APPRECIATION of our humanity is achieved at this stage.

The best way, however, to understand Gandhi's philosophy of non-violence is to first understand the extent of violence that we practice, consciously or unconsciously, every day of our lives. Grandfather made me aware of the violence in society, including the violence within myself, by asking me to work on a family tree of violence on the same principles as a genealogical tree.

He said: "Violence has two children – Physical and Passive. Now, everyday before you go to bed I would like you to write under each heading everything that you experienced during the day and the relationship of the violence with each other."

I had to be honest and write about my own acts of violence during the day. This meant that every night I had to analyse my actions and if I found them to be violent then the act had to be put down in its appropriate place. It was an excellent way of introspection and acknowledgement of one's own violence.

We generally deny our violence because we are ignorant about it or because we are conditioned to look at violence only in its physical mani-festation the wars, fighting, killing, beating, rapes etc. where we use physical force. However, we don't consider oppression in all its forms, name-calling, teasing, insulting, disrespectful behaviour etc. as passive forms of violence.

The relationship between passive violence and physical violence is the same as the relationship between gasoline and fire. Acts of passive violence generate anger in the victim and since the victim has not learned how to use anger positively the victim abuses anger and generates physical violence. Thus, it is passive violence that fuels the fire of physical violence, which means if we wish to put out the fire of physical violence we have to cut off the fuel supply.

The choice before humanity, to quote Gandhi's words, is quite simple: "We have to be the change we wish to see". Unless we change individually no one is going to change collectively. For generations we have been waiting for the other person to change first. A change of heart cannot be legislated, it must come out of conviction.

Is non-violence relevant for the 21st century? Non-violence is always relevant because it is the natural response of any civilized human being. Violence is unnatural, a learned behaviour. If violence is human nature then we would not need martial arts institutes and military academies to teach us how to kill. We should be born with the instinct and the ability to kill. The question that we need to ask is, therefore, not whether non-violent is relevant but whether we are willing to move away from greed, selfishness and all the negative attributes that govern our lives to the more positive attributes of love, compassion, understanding and respect. The choice is ours to make.

40

Gandhi and War

George Paxton*

For someone to whom non-violence and truth were guiding stars, Gandhi was surprisingly ambivalent in regard to war during the first 50 years of his life; but his attitude became increasingly anti-war with advancing age.

In contrast to the Western pacifist whose approach tends to emphasise the negative—a rejection of killing in war on ethical ground; Gandhi puts more emphasis on the positive—seeking to replace military violence with active non-violence.

Gandhi's first confrontation with the issue arose in 1899 when tensions between the Boers and the British in South Africa broke into open warfare. At this stage in his life Gandhi still felt that the British Empire was in general a benevolent structure, and although he was more in sympathy with the Boers, the fact that Indians were subjects of the Empire with the possibility of advancement to equality fed him to seek a way of helping the British. Rights demanded had to be accompanied by duties. The aid, which Gandhi decided to offer, was an ambulance team of Indian volunteers. At first the offer was declined but necessity soon resulted in the corps' assignment. The corps was 1100 strong and saw six weeks service on the battlefield removing the wounded to field hospitals.

The second participation in war was similar. A so-called rebellion had broken out among Zulus in 1906. This time Gandhi was given the rank of Sergeant-major and the small (two dozen strong) Indian Ambulance Corps treated mainly Zulus who had been flogged and Zulu 'friendlies' who had been shot by mistake. Gandhi's sympathies were even more with the rebels this time and he was glad that the Corps was nursing them.

---

* Editor, *The Gandhi Way* Quarterly Newsletter, Gandhi Foundation, United Kingdom.

Published in *Gandhi Prasang,* Vol. 2 No.1; October 1999.

In both of the South African episode it was as a non-combatant that Gandhi participated, and in the case of the Zulus it was mainly the 'enemy' who was treated. The case of Gandhi and World War I is different. Leaving South Africa for the last time in the summer of 1914 he called at London where he arrived just two days after the War began. Once more he had the desire to form an ambulance unit. This was done and when casualties started to arrive in Britain they were able to give useful aid. Gandhi however had fallen ill and could not personally participate.

The Great War

Gandhi claimed that arguments similar to those he used in South Africa applied. "I had hoped to improve my status and that of my people through the British Empire.

Whilst in England I was enjoying the protection of the British Fleet, and taking shelter as I did under its armed might, I was directly participating in its potential violence. Therefore, if I desired to retain my connection with the Empire and to live under its banner, one of three courses was open to me: I could declare open resistance to the war and, in accordance with the law of satyagraha, boycott the Empire until it changed its military policy; or I could seek imprison-ment by civil disobedience of such of its law as were fit to be disobeyed; or I could participate in the war on the side of the Empire and thereby acquire the capacity and fitness for resisting the violence of war. I lacked this capacity and fitness, so I thought there was nothing for it but to serve in the war." Not all his friends agreed and Henry Polak had cabled from South Africa to question the consistency with *Ahimsa.* Gandhi admits: "All of us recognised the immorality of war. If I was not prepared to prosecute my assailant, much less should I be willing to participate in a war, especially when I knew nothing of the justice or otherwise of the cause of the combatants......But it is not always given to one be equally clear about one's duty". Once more only non-combatant duties were considered, but Gandhi regarded even that as participation in war.

This was not the end of the matter, however, for, after Gandhi had returned to India and acquainted himself with the country he had been away from for so long, the issue arose again at an advanced stage of the war. At the end of April 1918 Gandhi attended a War conference called by the Viceroy and one outcome was that Gandhi agreed to recruit Indians for the war in Europe. It seems likely that a principal reason was that the Government, so Gandhi imagined, would look favourably on demands for self-government if the Indians supported Britain in its hour of need; a somewhat dubious argument from a moral perspective.

Indians did not see it Gandhi's way, though, and few were willing to cooperate in his recruiting campaign and few recruits came forward. "You are a votary of *Ahimsa,* how can you ask us to take up arms?" "What good has the Government done for India to deserve cooperation"? Not unreasonable questions. The strain of the campaign had its effect on him and he was struck down with illness. Erik Erikson claims that it was a nervous breakdown, although accompanied by physical symptoms.

Gandhi required months to recover his health but by early 1919 the introduction of the oppressive Rowlatt Act brought him back into active politics and within a short time he was the leading figure in the Congress. For almost 20 years interest in international affairs took a subsidiary place to issues of reform in Indian society and to the movement towards independence. Over these years his commitment to non-violence increased.

Fascism and World War II

When Abyssinia was invaded by Fascist Italy in 1935 he did not advise defence under the collective security of the League of Nations. Instead, "If the Abyssinians had adopted the attitude of non-violence of the strong, that is the non-violence which breaks to pieces but never bends, Mussolini would have had no interesting Abyssinia; Thus if they had simply said: 'You are welcome to reduce us to dust and ashes, but you will not find one Abyssinian ready to cooperate with you' what could Mussolini have done? He did not want a desert"

He had a similar message for the Czechs three years later. He considered the Munch agreement between Chamberlain and Daladier and Hitler to be a 'peace without honour', although he realised that it was because the British and French people did not want a repeat of the Great War which had ended only 20 years earlier and they, with the exception of the pacifist minority, did not believe that Gandhi's way was realistic. Nevertheless Gandhi recommended non-violent resistance to the Czechs; "There is no bravery great, and that without bitterness of spirit and in the fullness of faith that the spirit alone lives, nothing else does". He did not believe that even Hitler and Mussolini were beyond redemption. Pragmatically, of course, military resistance in the case of small Czechoslovakia was bound to be ineffective.

To the Jews of Europe he offered the same advice. He considered them to be better equipped than the Indians of South Africa to offer satyagraha: "The Jews are a compact, homogeneous community in Germany. They are far more gifted than the Indians of South Africa. And they have organised world opinion behind them". His Jewish friends, however, for the most part thought the situation of the Jews in Germany to be quite different to that of the South African Indians and considered his advice unwise. Gandhi even wrote to Hitler, though the letter was never delivered due to non-cooperation by the British. It is probable that Gandhi did not expect this advice to be taken, but having been asked to give it, he expressed what he felt in his inner being. "The German persecution of the Jews seems to have no parallel in history. The tyrants of old never went so mad as Hitler seems to have done. If they're ever could be a justifiable war in the name of and for humanity, war against Germany to prevent the wanton persecution of a whole race it would be completely justified. But I do not believe in any war". (*Harijan* 26.11.1938).

When World War II broke out Gandhi became even more isolated as the Congress Working Committee were willing to pledge India's support for the Allies' war effort only if India was promised independence. Gandhi certainly believed the Allied side to be more just and that India should give its support unconditionally — but non-violently. A clear split between Congress and Gandhi came in July 1940 when only Abdul Ghaffar Khan supported him at the Working Committee. After the breakdown of negotiations between the British Government and Congress, Gandhi and Congress came together again.

By early 1942 Japan was becoming a real threat to India. Gandhi's proposed response is spelt out in a letter of Mirabehn (31.5.1942); "Remember that our attitude is that of complete non-cooperation with the Japanese army. Therefore, we may not help them in any way, nor may we profit by any dealings with them.....If, however, the people have not the courage and capacity to evacuate the position invaded by the Japanese, they will do the best they can. One thing they should never do to yield willing submission to the Japanese. That will be a cowardly act, and unworthy of a freedom-loving people. They must not escape from one fire to fall into another and probably more terrible". As relation deteriorated between the Raj and Congress (after the failure of the Cripps mission in April 1942) and the war situation became more acute, Gandhi was prepared, reluctantly, to accede to the 'realist' position of Congress and accept that if India were given independence then its armed forced would defend the country along-side the British Army. It was a tacit recognition that he had failed to win sufficient numbers to the ethics of *Ahimsa*; for most of his colleagues it was a tactic only.

India was spared occupation by the army of an Asian state, and Gandhi spent most of the rest of the war in prison following the launch of the Quit India campaign. The war itself ended with the ultimate manifestation of violence — the atomic bombs dropped on the citizens of Hiroshima and Nagasaki.

Gandhi wrote in *Harijan* 10 February 1946: "There have been cataclysmic changes in the world. Do I still adhere to my faith in truth and non-violence? Has not the atom bomb exploded that faith? Not only has it not done so but it has clearly demonstrated to me that the twins constitute the mightiest force in the world. Before it the atom bomb is of no effect. The two opposing forces are wholly different in kind, the one moral and spiritual, the other physical and material. The one is infinitely superior to the other which by its very nature has an end. The force of the spirit is ever progressive and endless. Its full expression makes it unconquerable in the world". And on 1 July 1946 he wrote: "So far as I can see, the atomic bomb has deadened the finest feeling that has sustained mankind for ages. There used to be the so-called laws of war which made it tolerable. Now we know the naked truth. War knows no law except that of might.....The moral to be legitimately drawn from the supreme tragedy of the bomb is that it will not be destroyed by counterbombs even as violence cannot be by counter-violence. Mankind has to get out of violence only through non-violence. Hatred can be overcome only by love. Counter-hatred only increases the surface as well as the depth of hatred".

Gandhi's Alternative

It is clear that Gandhi's position in regard to war shifted over his lifetime. Although for himself he was committed to non-violence from an early stage in his career, for those who did not share his personal commitment he considered that it was better to take up arms in a good cause than be cowardly or indifferent. It has to be said, though, that a less pure motive operated in the cases of the Boer War and Zulu rebellion and particularly of the First World War since he imagined that support for the ruling power would, probably, bring benefits to the Indians. Up until 1918 support for the military was at least restricted to non-combatant ambulance work. But the recruitment to fighting units in force of the Raj in 1918 surely overstepped the line for a believer in non-violence. Thereafter, his position became much more anti-war until he was advocating non-violence to deal even with Fascism and Nazism.

Gandhi believed that one could substitute non-violent action for violent action. Gene Sharp has identified about 200 different forms of non-violent action. Gandhi's satyagraha, the highest ethical form of such action, uses these diverse forms but places great emphasis on the transforming power of self-suffering. He even believed that Hitler and Stalin might be moved to change through seeing the suffering of dedicated satyagrahis. Whether this ability of undeserved suffering to convert an opponent exists or not, it is clear that non-violent action can be a powerful form of political action, but perhaps more often producing its effects through non-violent coercion. There are many examples of oppressive regimes being brought down by non-violent action, and also attempted coups being thwarted.

Some examples in recent years are the fall of the Marcos regime in the Philippines in 1986; the Shah's rule in Iran in1978; the collapse of totalitarian socialism in eastern Europe beginning in Poland; defeat of the French generals' revolt in Algiers in 1961; the 1991 attempted coup against Gorbachov. Even the most oppressive regime is not immune to the effect of non-cooperation as was demonstrated in Nazi occupied countries such as Norway and Denmark. All of these examples were predominantly pragmatic responses without the principled approach of satyagraha. The latter with its dedicated and trained followers has the potential for even greater effectiveness. This is an important part of the legacy of Gandhi — perhaps even the most important considering the calamitous consequences of war in our age.

Book Review

We Do Not Want Violence; The Buber-Gandhi Controversy:

A Contribution to Practical Philosophy

Christian Bartolf *

In a review on the concise biography on Hermann Kallenbach (the Jewish friend of Mahatma Gandhi in South Africa), I referred to the question that probably more attention should have been given to the discussion in India and elsewhere on the Palestinian problem and Gandhi's reaction to this. I could not foresee that this demand would be so aptly fulfilled. The Buber-Gandhi controversy was a significant and substantial part of the discussion and has now been published based on extensive documentation. The controversy itself has never been thra-shed out and has never become a real and direct exchange of arguments and ideas. The reason for this probably lies in the fact that the two most important reactions by Martin Buber and by Prof. Judah L. Magnes on Gandhi's article "The Jews" in *Harijan* (20.11.1936) on the Arba-Jewish question and the use of *satyagraha*, did most likely never reach Gandhi.

The publication contains documentation and an extensive article by the editor, clarifying the position of Buber and Gandhi. Both Buber and Gandhi belong to the group of thinkers in the twentieth century that declared their philosophy with a concern for practical life. Their ideas touched on many matters of social life. It can only be deplored that a further exchange of arguments and ideas has never taken place.

Gandhi and Buber cherished ideas and principles that showed great affinity and they might have enjoyed discussing these. They would certainly

---

* Gandhi Information Zentrum, Selbst Verlag, 1998, Berlin.
Published in *Gandhi Prasang*, Vol. 1. No.2; January 1999.

have enjoyed discussing their views on society and might have endorsed the idea of a decent society that was recently coined by the Israeli social philosopher Margalit: a society is decent when "its institutions people which are under their authority respect".

The view on a decent society by Gandhi and Buber was best shown in the communities that were established in South Africa and in Palestine. In both cases the influence of Tolstoy was apparent. Gandhi had indirectly come in contact with Tolstoy's thinking by way of his Jewish and Christian friends and later directly through correspondence. The ideas of living in a community and living of the land, as well as the idea of bread labour, are signs of this. Buber was influenced by the founder of the first Kibbutz in Palestine—or as he himself named it, the *Kwuzah* (small community) —Gordon. Gordon was a Russian settler and had established this community under the spell of Tolstoyan thinking. Ideals of manual labour and living from agriculture in close relation to nature and thereby developing the "full potentials of man" were predominant. This met Buber's ideal of the creation of the new man in a free socialist society. The German social anarchist thinker, Gustav Landauer, also shared this idea.

Gandhi had stressed in his article the importance of *satyagraha* in the defence of the Jews against their oppression in German: ".....the Jews in Germany can offer *satyagraha* under infinitively better auspices than the Indians of South Africa. They should seek to convert the Arab heart"......"let them choose the way of non-violence for vindicating their position on earth".

Buber answered Gandhi and clarified his position on non-violence: "You say our non-violence is that of the helpless and the weak". He referred to Gandhi's statement: "I see that our non-violence is skin deep"....."This non-violence seems to be due merely to our helplessness'...'Can true voluntary non-violence come out of this seeming forced non-violence of the weak?" At the time this was written it made a great impression on Buber.

He added: "For I cannot help withstanding evil when I see that it is to destroy the good. I am forced to withstand the evil in the world just as the evil within myself. I can only strive not to have to do so by force. But if there is no other way of preventing the evil destroying the good, I trust I shall use force and give myself up into God's hands". Furtheron Buber refers to the Mahabharata and quotes: ".....there is nothing better for a knight in arms than a just fight" and "there is nothing better for a man than to deal justly, unless it be to love, we should be able even to fight for justice—but to fight lovingly". Buber was certainly influenced by the fateful events in Germany.

Gandhi applied his thinking about *satyagraha* when he wrote: "The satisfaction lies in the effort, not in the attainment. Full effort is full creating. The essence of satyagraha therefore was much more in the process within the satyagraha".

It could again be concluded that in a wider perspective in the present world Gandhi might be right in his thinking about conflict resolution. Yet, many people in the West would opt for a direct solution, very often out of humanitarian reasons and would apply violence as a last resort, forgetting that violence begets violence and does not convert the opponent.

Another divergence of view between Buber and Gandhi was about nationalism. Gandhi's concept of nationalism can be traced back to "*Hind Swaraj*", in which he expressed that Indians have a common identity and that they constitute a "*praja*", a nation, and, what is most important, that Indian nationalism should never legitimate violence as a means of national liberation. Gandhi, as Parel says in his study on "*Hind Swaraj*", believed that his concept of nationalism was neutral as far as religion or sect was concerned. He saw Indians primarily as members of a single nation and only secondary as members of a sect or cast; Indians whose humanity would be strong enough to enable them to tolerate difference within the context of a deeper national reality.

Hind Swaraj's view on the differences and the living together of Hindu and Moslems was strongly influenced by his stay in South Africa and by his co-operation with both groups. He did not go into the relationship between nation and ethnicity; he rejected the adaptation of the modern state as being sufficient for achieving self-government. True self-government requires persons who are able to rule themselves. A modern state without *swaraj* where the British *raj* is replaced by the Indian *raj* will not do. Gandhi wanted to emphasise that both Hindu and Muslim are actually part of the Indian nation. What separated Buber from Gandhi were historical arguments. Gandhi stressed—and this was logical in his thinking about nationalism—the rights of the Arab people in Palestine. In Gandhi's opinion they were a majority having lived in Palestine for centuries, had owned the land (although this might be true for only a small group of landowners) and spoke the same language.

Buber's nationalism on the other hand originated from Zionism, the move-ment that opposed the repressive and humiliating attitudes to the Jewish popu-lation in many European countries. The Zionists wanted to end the "Diaspora", the exile of the Jews, by creating a national home. In their opinion the obvious place for this was Palestine. This implied settlement in Palestine where Arabs already lived and the organisation of a homogenous people already existed. The idea behind this was the historical fact that the Jews had lived there centuries ago and that they should return. Buber shared the idea of returning to Eretz Israel, but differed considerably with other advocates of a return to the former homeland. To Buber it was recognition of being a "nation".

Consequently he resisted a nationalism that stressed the creation of a Jewish state as the main task of the Zionist movement. He analysed nationalism and distinguished between a power oriented nationalism and nationalism that would create an own identity for peoples as well as for individuals. Buber saw real nationalism as a means for a revival of self-consciousness. This was certainly a rejection of the idea of the nation as self-realisation by dominating other people and by a perpetual power drive that prevents fraternal living with other nations.

In rejecting the element of power domination, Buber stressed the opposition of the moral element and the political element. To him it was the existential problem of life and death to draw a line between the legitimate and the illegitimate nationalism. It meant to him a just relationship with the Arab population. Once he said: "We have not lived in Palestine with the Arabas, but have lived next to them"...... "when it does not develop to to-getherness"..... "it will be against each other". Buber's nationalism can best be defined as a cultural, or, as others have defined it, a religious nationalism.

In reflecting upon at least two of the major differences between Buber and Gandhi: non-violence and nationalism, it has become clear that further discussion between the two might have elucidated the problems involved and might have shown solutions that would have been of great value for our present world. In a wider perspective one feels the importance of a profound discussion on violence, force and nationalism. The documentation would probably be complete and therefore of great value for further study. Christain Bartolf's publication in the first place meant for a German audience and this is one of its weaknesses. The main essay by the editor appears in German only. Originally written as a thesis for the Free University of Berlin under the title "On non-violent resistance after Auschwitz", it has been renamed to "The emancipation of the conscious Paria". The latter title is linked to the Gandhian idea of *satyagraha*, being much more than just passive resistance. Much more importance will be placed on the process of conflict rather than on the substance itself. "Satisfaction lies in the effort, not in the statement". As with *swaraj*: "Once you stop regarding yourself as a slave, you cease to be one". It is "a means of providing human dignity". The emancipation of the conscious paria is therefore synonymous with the non-violent rebellion of all oppressed for a life without domination and bondage.

The essay has never got the significance it should have and one wishes for a translation into English, as this could enhance the importance and usefulness of the publication. For those who master both German and English, this publication is a most valuable contribution to a discussion, which would be held in our present situation of a world where violence and ethnic nationalism are rampant.

November 1998, Bergen, The Netherlands — Piet Dijkstra

42

Gandhian Concept of Equitable Equality

Prof. Amalendu Guha*

Introduction: The equitable equality is a new concept in peace studies, which consists of (a) harmony of the heterogeneities, (b) uniformity of diversities, (c) equality with justice and (d) equity of equalities. The goal or end-result of the above is "homonoia" or union of hearts at the behavioural level in society. Gandhi, in his mode of conviction and process life-long action, used justice or equity as value determinant and homonoia as the union of hearts in the human and social behavioural process. Gandhi was not against the Marxist goal of human equalisation creates disorder and discontent at both the social formation and society's functional levels. Gandhi used non-violence as the best and most effective means of changing human mind, effecting revolution in human consc-iousness and uniting the human and social beings under the common platform of human progress and human feeling type of bondage. In his formation of ideology-cum-philosophy and process of action the following elements and actors functio-ned as such:

Violence: as negative to unity as method and means of human and social disorder and destabilisation as method of dominance, suppression and subjugation leading to vertically in human and social relation and as destruction of the human qualities and material values.

Non-Violence: as rational and positive to unity and uniformity as method and means of human and social order and dynamic stabilisation as means of generating human and social sustenance, by gradually destroying the verticality of the human and social relations and as creative and productive for human qualities and socially needed material values.

---

* Chairman, Mahatma M.K. Gandhi Foundation for Non-violent Peace, Oslo, Norway.

Published in *Gandhi Prasang*, Vol. 1 No. 2; January 1999.

Human Marginalisation: as the mechanism of human inequality and human crime.

Homonoia: as the ideology and philosophy of the revolution of human and social conscience and consciousness.

Inequality: as the root of the formation of human and social class or strata relation which generate greed and over-consumption for some at the cost of deprivance and marginalisation of the others.

Equitable Equality: as the stable factor of social order and peace leading to human content.

Search for Truth (*Satyagraha*): as the means for finding the meaning of humanity and human value-oriented life and life's goal.

Search for Human Integrity: as the means and ways of human bondage beyond the religions and fundamentalistic practice of certain religions, classes strata, castes, creeds, origins and artificial human barricades, etc.

Gandhian concept of the positives is not concept of the vertically added multiplied functional points of the qualities; it is the concept of the horizontally-added qualitative social and human values. These positive should not be counted as spiritual. These should be regarded as social and human ethic-based, social norms-based, verified and subjected to tri-dimensions of time, space and circumstances, under the process of continuity. These positives should not be regarded as absolute or static, but as relative, subjected to the transformations and changes as needed and demanded by the above tri-dimensions.

At the same time, the Gandhian concept of the negatives is not the concept of rejection. In logic, two negatives become affirmative. In Gandhian dialectics, the negatives are the roots of, as the failures are regarded as the pillars of success. Negatives are the sources of creativity. Black sharpens and brightens the light. Similarly, the negatives provoke the thoughts for creation in the direction of change towards creative positivity. Gandhi learnt the non-violence from the negatives of violence. However, negatives become the rejections when the same are infiltrated to the human and social life and swallows up the human and social values as well as sicken them. When the negatives contribute to the mal-functioning of the body or organ, it needs dissection. Had the negatives not been present in the social body's functional mechanism, it should not have given birth to the need for discovery of the anti-biotic curative medicines or means.

The sense and essence of the Gandhian Equitable Equality, its theoretical contents and practical contexts are being discussed in this study with a view to establishing a conceptual framework of the same.

Equitable Equality: Premises, Elements and Concept

Gandhi refused to accept the Marxist Moist concept of the floor or scale type of homogenisation. He included the element or space of justice in it and left the case of social and human acceptability to the social and human conscience and consciousness. Equality is the space between the floor and the ceiling and between the margin and justful comfort. The concept of marginality or enforced equality is the concept of reduction, staticity and non-progress. Peace and the process of peace and truth as well as march for truth cannot be marginalized through scale-cuts, because it does not keep pace for dynamicity and dynamic additions. His concept of village or rural socialism contain the labour-input and distribution of output in the following sense:

a) from each according to his wilful capacity, not to the extent of enforced capacity.
b) to each according to his normal and basic needs satisfiable necessities, not to scaled limit.

Can the equities be equals? Equity or Justice, in applicable sense, has to be equal towards and for all. But in the sense of its social and human needs, it is relative depending on the degree, purpose and propensity. The crisis moments and the gravity of crisis determines the extents of relative difference between the a) equity and equality and b) equality and equity.

Since both of these stages and states are possible and realisable only under the conditions and process of sustainable peace in the society and that also under non-violent environment, Gandhi opted for non-violence as the essential condition of social transformation and change, in which, the global marginal or the global periphery could be freed or emancipated. While the above two are the goal motivations of his standpoint he choose non-violence as the means of de-structuralisation of the society and de-marginalisation of the marginal section of the society. This is the human dimension of his concept and conceptual approach. He conceived that:

— A human being or individual cannot be marginalized by birth.

— A human being can be marginalized by denying education and attribution of environment and opportunities for creation and improvement of his physical and intellectual capabilities.

— An individual may be marginalized by being deprived of the means and ways of procuring and satisfying his fundamental basic needs.

— A human being may be marginalized by being denied his right to use his utilities and performing functions.

He conceived that it is the structuralisation which caused the polarisation of wealth, privileges, opportunities and power in the hands of a strate and forced the deprived section towards the social and economic periphery. In today's global structure, a marginal human being has been converted into a factor-input for production, i.e., labour and his social function has been kept out of evaluation. Therefore, Gandhi wanted the evaluation of the social values and potentials of every marginal social being and to integrate his creative values in the socio-economic system, process and functions of each community and society. The survival of the fittest approach, which lacks human dimension and approach, has given birth to social and counterpeace vices like:

War, crime, torture, dominance, dependence, suppression, subjugation, social structuralisation, social and human marginalisation, etc.

If a society cannot use its:

a) Social Resources which is equal to social strength and

b) Social Sources which is equal social potency and potentials.one can find the appearance of Social Destability and Social Destability is a setback stage which hinders the attainment of the society's equitable equality.

The casteless marginalized social community (which numbers around 120 million in today's modern India) is a product of the above negatives. In India, Gandhi termed the rightless casteless people in the plain lands of India as the *Harijans* or the Sons of God and those in the hills and mountains as the *Girijans* or the Sons of the Hills. Gandhi, through revolutionising the human and social consciousness, wanted to effect a GLOBAL SOCIAL ORDER, which has and is to demarginalise this casteless community of India and the apartheid-ridden black people of Africa, where he started the first actions of his non-violent approach and revolution. An equitable-equality can be attained under the conditions of orderly human development and these conditions can be cited as such:

i) Destructuralising the Structural Equality and

ii) Destructuralising the Structural Equity

because both the structured equality and the structured equity are imposed ones and any such imposed social order is social in order of dependency on the the structure.

According to Gandhi, truth which is the condition of human equity is not a professed belief. It is something that has to be lived and that has to be sustained for social and human continuity. As corollary to truth, Gandhi always opted for himself and for others not to have the non-necessities. If charity begins from neighbours and if somebody loves neighbours as himself, he cannot have the superfluities when others lack even the basic necessities of life. And this is the very content and inner essence of both the equal equity and equitable equality and in this very sense these are not contradictory, rather complementary.

Gandhi, besides practising himself, advised others to use "*Samya-Yoga*" or "Practice of Equality" in order to obtain the inner unity of man, whose very essence is based on "Love is One", which is based on unity. And this unity seeks to build an order of equal equity in which all the component humanistic elements will have right place. In the approach of achieving the best essence of the unity and diversity, human welfare can be considered as the most suitable one. Even if such welfare comes from the diversities, the same should not be destroyed.

The practice of equality is opposed to the practice of inequality; however, it is not opposite to the discrimination of the right. The practice of equality provides scope for development to every individual. Because of its very basis of inner unity it seeks for building a balanced order and a balanced order is an equitable and equal order.

As conceptual clarification, Gandhi wrote, "the real implication of equal distribution is that man shall have the wherewithal to supply all his natural wants and no more. For example, if one man has a weak digestion and requires only quarter of a pound of flour for his bread and another needs a pound, both should be in a position to satisfy their wants. This is the concept of equity and ceiling. To bring this ideal into being the entire social order has got to be recon-structed. A society based on non-violence cannot nurture any other ideal". [1] And this is the sense of his equitable equity, which intends to bring contentment to each social member. This concept can be explained as the ceiling concept. For effecting equal distribution in non- violent way Gandhian experiment shows that an individual's want have to be reduced to the minimum. His means of having these bare necessities should be his earnings without dishonesty. There should be a self-restraint on desires, in every sphere of an individual's life, which contains the ecological motivation too, for not over-consuming the natural resources and for stealing the same from the mouth of the forthcoming generation by excessive use.

The rich accumulate the richness and wealth, by exploitation of, as well as, cooperation with the poor. The knowledge is to spread among the poor in order to strengthen them, but by adopting the means of non-violent non-cooperation they can crush the inequalities imposed on them by the rich.

A true human relation in a society ought to be achieved without conflicts and only through harmony and principles of mutual help and love. Such action reveals the very spirit of non-violent democracy. The democratic approach, which is the very basic way realising the equitable equality or equal equity, has to be based on the very essence that it should not be imposed on anybody, either by enforcement or artificially. The spirit and sensitivity of democracy is to come from within. Democracy is a practice and should not be considered as theory. The practice and behaviour of democracy is to begin from and at home which, later on, extends to social level. It is the method of human accommodation in reciprocity. Its success depends on the negation of egoism. Proper functioning of equitable equity or democracy needs the observance of tolerance, patience and preparedness to accept other's views as well as impressing others with own viewpoints. The functional mechanism of democracy demands adjustability.

Two basic premises of the Gandhian Equitable Equality can be as such:

a) Besides the tolerance of various religions and opinion, there should be sincere efforts for realisation of their equality. And under such conditions only the various communities and social groups can live in comity and amity as well as in mutual cooperation and understanding. The essence of such living process and understanding can generate the real Religion of Man and the spirit of Human Co-living.

b) The mankind should feel that "the world is one family" and this should be the goal of humanism. Therefore, peace and love should be the motto of all of our works and thoughts, instead of war.

As methods to materialise these two premises, Gandhi wanted:

i) The means and ends should match completely and both of these should be pure and true to each other, and

ii) Satyagraha or Search for Truth is the only and appropriate way of materialising this unity between the means and the ends and the very essence of Satyagraha contains the qualities of purity, humbleness and non-violence.

The concept of equitable equality or the equal equity needs a culture and its interaction, at the human level for obtaining positive values it is to have two types of approaches, namely, a) sharing with and b) accepting from. The fundamental human behavioural rule confirms that if the approach is positive, the result cannot be in the negative. The functional acceptability and strength of a culture depends on its depth and dynamicity of its character. The human and humanistic contents of a culture of a country or a society is influenced and affected by its geography, climate, important events and societal behaviour in course of the process. Two or several cultures may mix together under the conditions of equitable equality, not on the basis of imposition from any of the partners, and such process can produce many positive and dynamic trends. The means of imposition destroys the very functional method of normal creative acceptability and, also, generates, conflicts and distrusts. The scientific approach to the culture of peace should be the effort to imbibe the social and human values and truth wherever or in which culture the same be found. The culture of peace demands the condition of balanced approach for avoiding negative outcome. In the absence of such an approach, the good can be turned to evil, positive to the negative, amity to enmity, understanding to misunderstanding, trust to distruct and love to hatred.

For the purpose of creating the conditions and spirit of equitable equality, the mankind is to be provided with the essentials of life. When the sufferings, starvation and inequality in a society are not shared by all and some take profit out of these social shortcomings or ills while others bear the burden, then the stage can be called as imbalance. In essence, it becomes a burden on the have-nots and on the principle and practice of equitable equality. Therefore, the abolition of social inequalities should be regarded as an essential condition for realising equalisation with equity. Human beings are primarily the beings of flesh and blood, but this dimension is not the supreme one for and about him. Human beings have minds and passions too. The development of these faculties is necessary not only for the qualitative and creative upliftment of humankind, but also for use as the means of social practice for bringing about a social change in the direction of equity and equality.

There are different social and human groups which cooperate mutually in different social functions. These social groups do have different identities and physionomical structures, habits and traditions, etc. In course of their cooperation they assist each other reciprocally in preserving the conditions for survival and continuity. Force is incompatible to such co-operative social life. But the efforts for establishing uniformity of all social groups and races will be dangerous. Because the differences between and among the social group, races, nations etc. are necessary for preserving the premises and conditions under which further and forthcoming development and promotion are possible. One important factor in the upper trend of human life is his intention and capacity for continuative progressions. In such process, he adopts, from conditions to conditions, climate to climate, mode and habit of life to mode and habit of life, culture-to-culture, thoughts etc. The diversities and distinctiveness among human communities are essential for the purpose of incentive and human spirit. A social group requires from another neighbouring social group or groups something different which it does not possess, something distinctive which draws its attention, something which commands appreciation, etc. These elements enable us to understand the motives and needs for equitable social relation and behaviour. Adjusted accep-tance of these at different social groups and races can be characterised as the equitable equality. What is needed most essentially is the human approach to human problems. Human approaches to problems create scopes for adjustment as regards to the means of attaining the principle goals.

As brain without heart is worse and more dangerous than heart without brain, so is equality without equity. And peace is the essential condition which guarantees equity. Because peace is not a negative state in which conflict is absent. In peace, conflicts are settled by negotiations, mediations, understanding and consensus. In the same way, the social inequality can also be settled by constitutional and democratic ways. The elements and feelings of fear and hatred need be avoided, and, instead, those of equity and quality are to be added. The state should try to create the conditions of the creative norms of equitable equality and implementation of the same during the time of peace. Inequality generates frustration, hatred, suspicion and fear. But the factors of inequalities of every sort needs proper attention for study towards finding out solutions. For removing inequalities and inequities at the human consciousness level, the following negatives ought to be eradicated:

— black and white racial feelings
— religious enmity feelings
— repressive compulsions
— respectlessness and insecurities
— inferiority complex and compensatory cruelties, etc.

Tolstoy's *War and Peace* has been a journey from the destruction of war to the equity and rationality of peace, a journey from the universal violence of war to Gandhian non-violence of peace. A conscientious objector against the compulsory military service of our time, in Europe or elsewhere, is a product of revolution in his conscience between right and wrong, between irrationality and equity and between war and peace. Equity is a force of truth. Destructuralisation of the society is one of the basic premises of creating environment for social equity and non-violent equality. For realisation of a total and equitable equality, one needs the social and economic equality based on equity, too. Otherwise, it will be incomplete and inconsistent to the total sense. Equity and Equality are the two inter-related aspects of human relation. A person should master both the aspects and the same is possible under the following conditions as conceived by both, Confucious and Gandhi:

Confucius:		Gandhi:
(a) Pu-hai (non hurting)	=	(a) Ahimsa (Non-violence)
+		+
(b) Jen (love of friendship)	=	(b) Maitri (Friendship leading to love)

Equity

The conceptual meaning of Jen, as explained by Confucius, under different contexts, contain the following contents [2]:

a) Reply to disciple Fan Chieh:
Jen = Love for all people

b) Reply to disciple Yen Yuah:
Jen = To subdue one's self and return to propriety.

c) Reply to disciple Chung Kung:
Jen = Not to do to others what one would not wish to himself.

d) Reply to disciple Tzu Chang:
Jen = Practising of five things, namely Gravity, Generousity, Sincerity, Earnestness and Kindness.

The essence of the meanings of the aforesaid explanations of Jen, as Confucius gave, under different contexts, is justice or rightfulness. Later on, when Mencius, practised the above doctrine, in political sense, he explained as such:

Jen = Benevolence.

Ye = Righteosness.

to King Hui of the then Liang state in China.

He, further, explained, on several occasions that "Jen (Benevolence) is the tranquil habitation of man and Ye (Righteous) is his straight path [3].

Lao-Tsu, the great social saint of China, perceived that "Tao is eternally inactive, yet it leaves nothing undone.....The simplicity of the nameless Tao brings about an absence of desire. The absence of desire gives tranquillity." [4]. By negation of desire or greed Lao-Tsu intended to mention the righteousness in a man, which symbolises the morality of equity. It means that Lao-Tsu's concept of equity was based, mostly, on non-violent social practice.

Mo-Tsu, another Chinese philosopher, maintained the similar mode of thinking like Gandhi, even during the period 500 BC-400 BC through the following negative arguments, like

"If all look upon others' houses as own house, who will steal ?

If all look upon others' bodies as his own body, who will murder ?

If all look upon others' families as his own family, who will exploit?

......Therefore, when all love each other there will be peace and when all hate each other, there will be chaos and calamity."[5]

Mao Tsu was Buddha's contemporary. As Mao-tsu had been developing the ideology of justful social behaviour, Buddha had been developing his eight noble paths of Nirvana or Human Goal. These very eight means and ways of justful behaviour of a man of equity coincides with the Tri-Ratna or Three jewels of Indian Hindu Jainism indicating the important elements of humanistic justice. To show their complementarities or value-resemblances, their value-elements are being put below:

Jainism	**Buddhism**
Tri-Ratna (3-Jewels)	**Nirvana (8-Noble Paths)**
a) Samyag-Darsana (Just Conviction) with the combination of faith and perception)	a) Samyag-Dristi (Just View)
b) Samyag-jnana (Just Knowledge)	b) Samyag-Samkalpa (Just Thinking)
c) Samyag-Charita (Just Conduct)	c) Samyag-Bac (Just Speaking)
	d) Samyag-Karmanta (Just Conduct)
	e) Samyag-Ajiva (Just Living)
	f) Samyag-Vyayama (Just Effort)
	g) Samyag-Smriti (Just Remembrance)
	h) Samyag-Samadhi (Just Meditation)

These above functions of a person are and have to be performed within the social life and social process. Both Buddha and Mahavira Jaina believed in the process and doctrine of life in Karma or work and Samsara or Social Life. Both of them denied and did not take refuge in the Almighty and Omnipotent God or non-argumentable Absolutism. This metaphysical content is centred around the perception that one's zeal and effort could work out one's own salvation or reaching to the human goal. The principles of righteousness of both the religions had much impact on the Gandhian concept of justice or equitable equality, in which he added two means, namely, Ahimsa or Non-violence and Truth for attaining the same.

Equity is in contrast to wrongdoings and here, Confucius, Jesus Christ, Mohammad and Gandhi conceive and draw the essence as such:

"What you do not want done to yourself, do not do to others" (Confucius as quoted by Tan Yun Shan in Ahimsa in Sino-India Culture, *Harijan* December 29, 1949).

"Whatsoever ye would that man should do to you, do ye even so to them" (Jesus Christ in his *Sermon on the Mount*).

"Followers of the right way follow the correct ways for themselves and for the humankind" (Mohammad in *Sura in the Hordes*).

"If I am a follower of Ahimsa (i.e. Non-violence), I must love my enemy. I must apply the same rules to the wrong doer who is my enemy or stranger to me as I would do to my wrong-doing father or son" (*Speeches and Writings of Mahatma Gandhi*, p. 346).

The ethics of equity become a force when it is practiced at the social level and at this very stage it may attain social equality.

Testing the Validity of the Concept of Equitable Equality:

Gandhi's concept of negation to violent realisation of equality and equity is not one of negation, but of positive nature built up of self-denial and self-assertion. His doctrine and practice as well as political means of non-cooperation is not a negation. Enforced equalisation efforts in the former East European socialism has failed because of the force used above and, at the same time, excluding equity form its concept and action. The Scandinavian social democracy succeeded in obtaining both the equality and equity by balancing the both in its goals and means, alongwith the rights and duties in the direction of satisfying the normal human needs. Under the present context, there does not exist any scope for violent revolution to establish equality in the society, in any part of the world, because such revolution ended with both the human and material destruction in this century and, by excluding equity in its concept and action, it lost the part and particles of human aspects.

The concept of the equitable equality has, so long been a theoretical and intellectual concept as well as a concept for preaching and any concept cannot attain force unless practiced at the mass level. The use of the enforced equality has been proved to be a failure as seen in the collapse of Soviet type of Socialist System and introduction of the liberal socialism by China. At the same time, the equitably equal participation of different social and conflicting groups has produced positive results in problem-solution in the Palestine-Israel relation as well as North Ireland conflict. It has been showing also positive signals towards the resolution of the conflicting situation of Guatemala and unsolved relation between South and North Korea.

By his Non-Cooperation Movement and means Gandhi wanted to mean the non-cooperation with the wrongdoers and its analytical consequence is positive justice or equity. Equity and Equitable equality cannot be achieved by using wrong means and right means only may ensure the achievement of an equitable or just end.

Note and References:

1. Harijan, Vol. XVII, No. 6, Ahmedabad, April 11, 1953.

2. Tan Yun-shan (Professor, Visvabharati University, Santiniketan, West 3. Bengal, India): Ahimsa in Sino-Indian Culture-I, *Harijan*, Vol. XIII, No. 41, Ahmedabad, Gujarat, India, December 11, 1949.

3. As cited by Tan Yun-shan in Sino-Indian Culture-II. *Harijan*, Vol. XIII, No. 41, Ahmedabad, Gujarat, India, December 18, 1949.

4. Idem.

5. Idem, as quoted from "The Works of Mao-Tsu".

43

Non-Violent Philosophy and Culture of Peace: Gandhi's Contribution

Prof. Amalendu Guha*

Introduction

Does the culture of peace means the continuous practice of means and ways for achieving and maintaining peace in conflicting situation? Or, does it mean the effect of the measures used for peace? Again, can the peace diplomacy used in the conflict, conflicting situation or suppressed conflict be considered as the culture of peace? It is inclusive and conclusive of all actions and elements mentioned above. Culture of peace demands that it is to be cultivated and cultured in order to produce positive effects. It is the qualitative output both the quantitative and qualitative inputs.

For creating the basis of the culture of peace at human level, one is to erase the distinction between his self and the other's self, or other selves. Such eradication of the "selves" or "ego-s" promotes the universalisation of outlooks and conduct. Once this is achieved there appears the expectation of the prevalance of human and humanistic peace. Human peace is a culture which is the outcome of the feelings of humanity and humanism. It is like the sparkling rays coming out of diamond, the material form. It is, therefore, the synchronic and synthetised value of the material and immaterial actors and factors of human efforts and function for peace.

Concept and Functional Process of Nonviolence

Nonviolence is the power of the powerless, besides being the force of spirit against the force of violence and arms. Nonviolent protests, again,

---

* Chairman, Mahatma M.K. Gandhi Foundation For Non-violent Peace, Oslo, Norway.

Published in *Gandhi Prasang*, Vol. 3 No. 1; October 2000.

create the conditions for social justice and justful social functioning. Therefore, nonviolence is the positive social functional process for generating a conduct of understandability and peacefulness, at (a) both the individual and social levels and (b) human and universal levels.

By nonviolence is to be meant non-injury, to self, to neighbour, to society, to locality and to the globe. Before thinking of what non-violence is, it is essential to see and feel what it is not. Real nonviolence originates in one's mind and heart and is known by one's own conduct. A non-violent person never forgets that the world is full of love and takes care of not harming any living being or object. He activates and regulates his behaviour or conduct as not to hurt others. He does not intend to frighten others or create an atmosphere of frightfulness, insecurity, instability, terror and tension. Nonviolence is, thus, a clear attitude of both the mind and conduct, without any ambiguity and non-clarity, which does not harm anybody. Nonviolence is a qualitative improvement over the vices and negatives like vengeance, hatred, enmity, disliking, mistrust, misunderstanding, misgiving, etc.

Nonviolence is a power to resistance and it is the greatest and rational force which humankind possesses, because, a human being is not destructive, by nature. There is an argument against the practice of nonviolence, which is often raised, namely, that one does not dare to take up the case of nonviolence to the mighty while cannot be taught to the weak. Nonviolent living may be an example to show its strength to the both.

Nonviolence, as functional process and utility, presumes all-round self-suppression. It is the interest of self-control from ego, malpractices, over-ambitions, hate and hatred. Gandhi conceived the following five axioms for nonviolence:

i) Nonviolence implies as complete self-purification as is humanly possible.

ii) The strength of nonviolence is in exact proportion to the ability, not to the will, of the nonviolent person to inflict violence.

iii) Nonviolence is, without exception, superior to violence, i.e. the power at the disposal of a non-violent person is always greater than he would have if he were violent.

iv) There is no such thing as defeat in nonviolence. The end of violence is surest defeat.

v) The ultimate end of nonviolence is surest victory, if such a term may be used of nonviolence. In reality where there is no sense of defeat, there is no sense of victory. (M.K. Gandhi: *The Greatest Force* Harijan, Vol. III, No. 35, Oct. 12, 1935, p. 276).

The above axioms are based on rationality and logic.

Nonviolence is a matter of experimentation with faith in it. Nonviolent method and means can be regarded as the method and means of constructive revolution. Nonviolent revolution eliminates the obsoletes and evils peacefully by ineffectivising them. Through non-violence every kind of ill may be fought and triumphed through its rationality or judgment force, not through the brutality force. So, this cannot be called as negative function, but a direct and positive fruit-bearing function. Through the power of violence a group of people may get its material goals and subjugate the weaker opponent actor or actors, but the power of nonviolence lies in love, winning through self-restraints and self-sacrifice. These are the potentials and true significance of nonviolence and so nonviolence demands devotion to its causes.

Nonviolence cannot be preached, it is to be practised. Non-violence is invisible and cannot be measured while violence is visible and its effects can be measured. Non-violence, through practice, achieves velocity and its values become strengthened. The functional process of nonviolence has two phases, namely, (a) unconscious phase in the beginning and (b)conscious phase at the end. The consequence of the conscious phase is the visible victory. Therefore, nonviolence is not an emotional philosophy and function, it is a practical and effect-bearing function. Nonviolence is an action of faith within and under the conditions of violence and hostilities. Violence can be administered and executed, but nonviolence can be practised on mass scale and expanded. Therefore, violence and its consequences can be quantified, but non-violence is a quality. Non-violence requires more courage in order to weaken violence.

Non-violence is to be trained. The training of nonviolence and peace suggests the cultivation of certain states of mind like self-respect; respect for and to others and others views, self-cleanliness, and feeling of humanism and brotherhood for and towards others, development of attitude for honouring others, etc. Such activities pave the way for nonviolence self-development. There can be seen, basically, three types of violence, namely:

i) Religious violence under the pretext of divine right to protect and promote religious authority or supremacy.

ii) Individual, group or nationalist-chauvinistic violence under the pretext of the dogma of the survival of the fittest.

iii) Political violence under the pretext of the right of the majority for suppressing and subjugating the minorities whom the majority considers as undesirable.

The knowledge about the above roots of violence is absolutely necessary in order to invent the strategies and tactics of non-violent means and ends.

Non-violence is to be cultivated with fineness in human nature, which is devoid of any anger or malicious wilfulness. A person is to learn how to restrain himself from greed, anger, hate and revenge. Non-violence should be an aspect of inner prompting, instead of outer imposition. Nonviolence is a moral force which can hold the society to constructive unity to produce yields of integrity, which violence cannot. Nonviolence may conceive that if it takes care of the means the ends will strengthen the causes and motivations of the means. Nonviolence being the means, the human realisation as victory becomes the end. Non-violence is, therefore, in essence, an assimilation process of restraintfulness of the malices towards the realisation of violencelessness.

Philosophy of Peace

Philosophy of peace is the outcome of both the inductive and deductive methods, means and procedures used to achieve peace. Peace being the goal or the quality it includes the logical, rational and constructive elements and particles, which are indispensable for achieving peace, peaceful situation and maintenance of the achieved peace. The philosophy of peace starts from the very cardinal questions of "Why peace" and "how peace" and "what are the ethics of peace". Philosophy of peace has, various determinants and dimensions too. It again, has got the behavioural aspect, which may be termed as the conduct of peace.

Philosophy of peace means the sense and essence of the equitable out-come of conflict resolution, in human interest and social interest. It is neither a norm, nor a dictum. Though it is the outcome of both the inductive and deductive procedure and behaviour, yet its very goal is the attainment of just peace. Peace is the result of practice, at the inner and outer levels, at individual and social collectivity levels, at the local and global levels and at the cause and resolution levels. The concept of peace has undergone both the evolutionary and revolutionary processes in different contexts and so its contents have been tested and strengthened in tri-dimensions of time, space and circumstantial condition. Let us present here, in brief, the conceptual evolution of the elements of the concept of peace in different territorial and contextual levels.

a) In Latin, the word "pacis" (or pax) was used to denote the meaning of "to the pacified". It put more attention on the behavioural aspect of the practice of peace, as the means of controlling anger, revenge and violence.

b) In the Indian epics of the Vedas, the word "*om shanti*" (or peace) was used as the expression of both the desire and prayer for peace.

c) Chinese, the word "hoping" expresses the desire for the maintenance of peacefulness or tensionlessness in: social, human and territorial contexts.

d) In Islam, the word "*bismillah*" expresses the desire and practice of peace.

Lao-Tsu, the Chinese philosopher of the 6th Century BC, the founder of Taoism and the author of the Tao-te-ching, meant that "tao" was the "way" of peaceful image-maintenance like the soft behaviour of water or the wind which can win over and erode hard matter and material like stone and iron. Its inward as well as internal meaning is the maintenance of balance and soft or nonviolent attitude towards hardness or hardships, in order to achieve the orderly Tao or way of life, living and continuity. Tao also denotes the absence of desire, because the desire gives birth to greed, conflicts, inequality, injustice etc.

The Confucian doctrine (of the Chinese political and systemic philosopher Confucius, who lived during the period 551-479 BC) of "jen" means the "analect" or empathy which emphasizes that peace originates from social harmony and equilibrium. He further develops the idea that "pu hai" is "non-hurting" and non-hurting is the very basis of nonviolent peace. He explained "jen" in the later periods, as such:

Jen	=	love
	=	own prosperity
	=	abstinence from doing wrong
	=	blessedness
	=	practicing 5 principles of gravity, generosity, sincerity, earnestness and kindness.

These show that Confucius concentrated more on behavioural philosophy, i.e., the philosophy of self control, selflessness, righteousness, etc., which leads an individual or a society to the goal horizontal harmony. Later on, Confucius developed his idea of peace further and he started using "Jen Ye", whose refined meaning is "Benevolence with Righteousness". What Buddha considers as just values for peace Confucius terms it as the righteousness of values.

Mo-tsu, another Chinese philosopher, who lived in the period 468-40 B.C. stated and explained that the "virtue of love is human value". His philosophical expression asserts that "love others and you will be loved one, hate others and you will be hated". The essence of his meaning of peace stems from the very fact of "justful" social/human behaviour.

Buddha, the founder of Buddhist, developed his concept of "nirvana" or peace for escaping the sequence-consequence of human/ social vices in the following ways.

a) samyag Dristi or just view

b) samyag Samkalp or just thinking

c) samyag Bak or just speaking

d) samyag Karmantha or just conduct

e) samyag Vyama or just effort

f) samyag Smriti or just remembrance

g) samyag Samadhi or just meditation

While these can be interpreted and regarded as the just human and social codes of conduct for practice, their combined essence generates the inner and outer peace of and with justice. The meaning of the Buddhist NIRVANA is not escapism from life, but getting rid of the vices or malpractices, which undermines o: hinders the functioning and feelings of justice or justful conduct. Nirvana is the higher stage of proceeding towards perfection by getting rid of the greed. The Buddhist elements/ deeds are the human/social need-based needs, not the greed-based deeds. His "Samyag" or "Justice" means refraining from doing wrongs or injustice. These ethics of human and social behavior intends to mean the modelling of a person in such a way that he should refrain from doing and behaving in excess of what is adjudged as objective and right. Such personal and social behavior of justice, in all the directions of human/ social instincts and desires, educates a man or a society to follow the path of equality type of equity. Buddha did not advise the people to follow the abstinence type of spirituality or ethics. His philosophical concept centred around social and human contexts and, consequently, the contents were social-human. While idealism and metaphysics had been the conceptual basis and determinism of most of the human philosophies of that time, Buddha conceptualised a realistic philosophical way of life in which human life could be guided in such a way as to generate harmony, tranquillity, correctness, objectivity, etc. Its essence and motivation was the attainment of humanistic peace.

Buddha and Confucius based their approaches of righteousness or justice on openness, which we term, now a days, as transparency. Such transparencies approach and attitude help much in resolving the conflicts, contradictions and contrasts, both at the individual and social levels.

The Hindu Jainism of India, famous for its Puritanism, also puts accent on the principles of justice. In its peace philosophy of "Tri-ratna" or Three-Jewels, it proposes the use of

a) Samyag Darshana or just Conviction of Faith and Perception
b) Samyag Janana or just Knowledge and
c) Samyag Charitra or just Conduct

These were the basic criteria of the social philosophy of peace.

Emperor Asoka of India, in the Third Century B.C., who accepted Buddhism and engaged himself in expansion of Buddhism all over Asia, opted for non-violent type of peace and asserted that humanistic love is peace.

Since God, considered as the combined and synthesised essence of all the qualities, nobleness and virtues and, empowerment for leading humankind to the rightful destiny, it was conceptualised in some of the religions that peace is the means and ways of reaching in nearness to the God,

Jesus Christ asserted that peace is the peace of God passed through the tests of understanding.

The Pax Romana concept of peace is the concept of structured peace. It conceptualises that the absence of overt violence is peace. In the Pax Romana type of peace, negative violence can be obtained, but it is obtained through social suppression.

The Greek concept of "*Irene*" means the combination of harmony, justice and peace.

The Arabic "*Salam*" concept and the Hebrew concept of "*Shalom*" mean, the absence of war, with well-being, wholeness and harmony.

The Vedas, written in the Indian Classical language Sanskrit, introduced the peace philosophy with "*Om Shanti*" which means the achievement of peace in both the inward and outward life of the human beings.

The Chinese use "*Ho Ping*" (also mentioned earlier) which means total peace. Ping means the adjustments plus unity of diversities. Therefore, the Chinese concept of peace is inclusive and conclusive of heterogeneous elements or qualities and, in essence, has broader missions and visions. Later on, in the fifties, when the non-aligned countries like India, China, Indonesia, Burma (now Myanmar), Sri Lanka, etc. adopted the non-aligned policy of "Panch Sheel" or five qualitative principles for regional, Asian and World peace, it took into consideration of such broader aspects and prospects. In the mid and late fifties to the 20th century, in Mao's ideology of "Let hundred flowers blossom, let hundred schools of thoughts contend" (though not applied in China) consisted the above peace concept of uniformity through diversities.

The Russian word for peace is "*Mir*", which really means both the peace and the world. It has, thus, an extensive meaning of peace, namely, peace all over the world. Such peace is, therefore, a fundamental whole.

Gandhi, known as the father of the concepts and actions of "*Ahimsa*" or nonviolence and "Satyagraha" or search as well as experiments for truth, opts for selflessness or absence of violence at individual, social and national levels. Gandhi defines this aspect as the condition and means for attaining peace.

The noted peace-researcher of our time John Galtung of Norway, opts for positive peace. The logical assertion of his concept of peace stems from the fact that peace is more than the absence of war and violence. Peace is a condition where overt and structural violence is minimised or eliminated.

The Korean peace scientist Young Seek Choue puts three essential elements for generating peace with justice, namely, (a) "*Jung Ji*" or right under-standing, (b) "*Jung Pan*" or right judgment and (c) "*Jung Haeng*" or right conduct, whose appropriate interaction and inter-adjustment create "consensus synthesis" and the very foundation of global peace and global common human society. These are, however, the cardinal components as well as integral parts of the whole or total peace. Peace has to contain the principle of equity and in order to attain peace with and of equity, as Young Seek Chouse contends, it is to be inclusive and conclusive of (I) justice with truth and (II) justice bound by law.

The Chinese saying of "*Hong-Zhong-Hwa*", which means "the way to right" and "the rule of justice", may contribute to the guaranteeing of peace in the society. For attaining such peace Choue suggests the use of the means like "CHONG-SUNG-HWA" or "TOTALITY OF THE MULTIPLIED HARMONY OR COMBINATION"

CHON or the totality functions as goal or sense.

SUNG or multiplication functions as the means or ways.

HWA or harmony/combination functions as the procedure or strategy-cum-tactics.

Concluding remarks:

Gandhi's concept and philosophy of peace is considered to be secularist and humanist. The sense and essence of his concept of equity denounces wrong doings. Gandhi says, "I must love my enemy, I must apply the same rules to the wrong-doer who is my enemy or stranger to me, as I would do to my wrong-doing father or son." (as quoted in the *Harijan* from Gandhi's speeches and Writings, p. 346).

We find ourselves in a new century and in the new millennium. We are to follow the culture of active peace, not of passive peace. We inherited many wrongs, violence, war-like tensions and incomplete efforts for peace from the 20th century. Through tolerance and non-violent means as well as methods the humankind of this century is to engage itself in the works for peaceful human development.

44

Concept of the Philosophy of Peace

Prof. Amalendu Guha*

Peace has to be a positive peace. The logical assertion of this positive peace concept, as advocated by the contemporary western doyen of peace scientists, John Galtung, stems from the fact that peace is more than the absence of war and violence. Peace is a condition where overt and structural violence can be minimised or eliminated. Peace is, first of all, a need, then a feeling, after that a concept or vision, and finally, an action or mission to achieve the aim or objective. The concepts of and actions for and on peace as well as order have inherited and accepted many elements and principles from various oriental and western schools of thoughts, and these contributed to the formation of the contemporary peace ideology and philosophy as well as the thinking patterns on social peace order. In the formation process of the ongoing concept, the peace philosophers and scientists avoided the negative and obsolete particles, accepted and assimilated the positive and creative elements. Finally, they generated the scientific ideology and philosophy of peace, to be tested in the dynamically stable process of time, space and circumstances in our time as well as in the new millennium. The concepts and ideologies of the following historical personalities, among others, did influence his inter-action and creative process of knowledge accumulation.

Chinese Schools of Thought	Indian Schools of Thoughts	European Schools of Thought	Other Schools of Thought
Taoism	Buddhism Jainism (Hinduism)	Plato	Christianity (Jesus Christ)
Confucianism	Gandhian Non-violence and	Aristotle Leibnitz	Han Culture (Sinocentrism)
I Ching Ideology	Satyagraha (search for Truth)		—
Mo-Tsu Doctrine		Kant Spinoza	—

* Chairman, Mahatma M.K. Gandhi Foundation for Non-violent Peace, Oslo, Norway.

Published in *Gandhi Prasang*, Vol. 5 No. 1; October 2002.

Confucius, the political ideologist of the pre-millennium era, showed the way of Providence and Human Affairs representing internal sacredness of morality and external rule of the home and family affairs, administering a nation and state and establishing peace order in the world. Confucian doctrine also consists of other elements like (a) virtue of righteousness, (b) care for the people, (c) honesty and loyalty for ruling the people based on the Decree of Heaven, (d) humanity and mental training or practice for right behaviour, etc. The oriental peace philosophers embraced the ethical aspects as well as the elements of loyalty, honesty and orderly behaviour from the Confucian doctrine.

Other Confucian teachings and preaching, which moulded the development are as such:

a) Political ethics of virtue and propriety
b) Inner goodness and external righteousness and
c) Studies and ideas related to morality practice

There had been the absence of the elements of human will as well as consciousness because of overemphasis on materialism in, I Ching. Therefore, in order to fulfil the strength of value-combination of philosophy, heart and humanity, there appeared approaches regarding the universe and its functioning, such as: (i) time and (ii) space, both comprising the natural realm, and (iii) living beings and materials, and (iv) environments, comprising the real realm. For the functional approach of the universe, there appeared the necessity of Self-Stabilisation through Self-organisation, which enables Self-Realization. However leaving the function of social inequalities the "Will of Heaven" seems to be the absolute mistake of Confucius. Neo-Confucian principle, as advocated by Chu-his and others in the 11th and 12th centuries, holds that the implied existence of "li" or creative principle and "chi" or passive matter, where "li" generates virtues and "chi" generates vice surrendering to sensual temptation, constitute the two fundamental principles of the universe and mankind. Such ideas, contain that all the matters contain creative potentials and values.

Lao-tsu's Taoism showed, however, the ways of peaceful image or impression building and maintenance, soft and balanced behaviour and attitude of order. This Tao way is the way of life, living and maintaining continuity. The basic ideas of Tao Te Ching or The Canon of Reason and Virtue maintain that all things are mutable and turn into the opposite in the process of mutation and man should adhere to the naturalness of things. The Taoist principle may be accepted in such a way that while preserving his nature intact man should yield the wisdom and knowledge of the truth.

Mao-Tsu's concept of attaining human values through love and justness helped, later on, the formation process of human-centric development philosophy. The Mao-Tsu school of philosophy contends that man's fate and action is not predetermined, and his progress depends on the manner in which he peforms the principles of "Isan al" or universal love. Among his positive principles, the important ones are as such:

a) people should help each other
b) people should follow a useful occupation, and
c) people should reject the use of force and war.

And these principles stay at the very base of the ideology and philosophy as well as social peace. Mo-Tsu also contented that human knowledge is the direct product of his investigation of reality and this is the materialist substance of objective concept of the theory of knowledge in evolution.

But, the evolutionary process plays an important role in the formation of organic social peace order, in the sense that the same moves us from alienation, egoism and isolationalism. It leads the humankind nearer to a social community or collectivity, by embracing the entire people at the local, national, regional and finally, the global level. This vision of an organic world order, as envisaged here, can be obtained by the exercise of the human will of creation and service.

Buddha's abnegation concept of desires, in the sense of greed, and strife of liberation from sufferings, in both the moral perfection and implied sense of social change, impressed most of the social scientists and social reformers in the last two and a half millennia and influenced their formation process of social ideology. Buddha was the first philosopher of the world to preach the principle and practice of equitable equality among the people, which means that all the people are equal and equity is their behavioural basis. Buddha had always been against any type of strata and structural violence. Though his preaching urged for emancipation of man from this earthly sufferings, which is moralistic in essence, yet its objective contents of equality of all men and practice of knowledge, teaching and order are the most ideal humanistic principles. Though he meant these means as "refuge for enlightenment" or "nirvana", their material essence, in the name of perfection, leads a man towards a non-harmful and nonviolent life. The Buddhist Noble Truth asserts that the origin of suffering is desire or greed and getting rid of desire and attachment is the very goal of reaching the state of perfection or Nirvana or Non-Attachment. The means for reaching to this very goal Buddha preached for Right Action including Non-Killing, Practice of Love which does not commit harm, and Right Vocation or Karma (or Work) which does not cause injuries to others.

Jainism is a Hindu version religion, which, in its doctrine, accepted the "Ahimsa" or Nonviolence, as its essence. The pure, enduring and eternal or continuing principle of Jainism (which is the very root of the Gandhian concept of Nonviolence) contends on nonviolence as such:

> One should not kill, mal-use, insult, torment and
> prosecute any kind of living being, any kind of
> creature, any kind of thing having a soul (i.e., life),
> any kind of being.

It can be recognised as the harmony type of outcome from a strong sense of the unity of the universe and mankind. The very humanistic approach of Ahimsa can be found in the writings of an Indian poet Hemchandra, several centuries ago and the following is an excerpt from his writings:

> Nonviolence is like a loving mother of all beings,
>
> Nonviolence is like a stream of juice in the desert of the physical world.
>
> Nonviolence is a course of rain clouds in the suffering fire of forest.

Jesus Christ, who was a non-violent revolutionary, rejected the practice of violence, compromise and escapist aloofness. His proclaimed missions, among others, included the liberation of the oppressed and redistribution of the earth's resources. He also asserted that "Blessed are the peacemakers" and "Love your enemies". Jesus said to his disciples, as such:

> Peace I live with you, may peace I give to you.

This is the very message to the nations of our globe and towards all directions, since:

in Christ there is no East or West,
in Him no South or North.

This concept of Christian Peace had deeper influence in the western part of the world.

Greek philosopher Plato formulated his ethical concept of "dikaiosyne" or justice on the basis of differentiating categories of individual and institution, where justice is considered as virtue that rules, organizes and delimits the action of both the individual and the Polis. In his "Politeia", Plato explains that it is justice that brings the other three virtues: wisdom, courage and temperance. He also contends that the sensible world, which is the product of <<ideas>> and <<matter>>, is an intermediate position. Plato's cosmology is the entity of the world soul.

Another ancient Greek political philosopher Aristotle in his "Nicomachean Ethics" synthesised the following three important principles and their functional utilities:

a) "justitia legalis" for ultimate realization of a good constitution to promote happiness.

b) "justitia commutative" for the community relations of mutual exchange, and

c) "justitia distributive" for assuring proper proportionality in distribution.

These are still considered as the preamble of equity with righteousness in social, moral, political, economic and ecological codes.

Certain aspects of the Kantian Peace Concept ascertains that peace is a category and state of mutual interaction and support and is a combination process of democratic government, economic interdependence, international law and international organizations. This is one of the essences of our millennium's globalisation efforts. Kant also asserts that the perpetual peace is the man's highest goal. Kantian argument that knowledge, independent of experience, and even at all sensuous impressions, is in contradiction to empirical knowledge and, therefore, knowledge is to be based on experiences.

Kantian arguments influenced the cause-effects analysis of peace and cognitive aspects of knowledge. The reasoning behind his assertion are put here from his Critique of Pure Reason:

In respect of time, therefore no knowledge of ours is antecedent to expe-rience but begins within. But thought of all of our knowledge begins with our experience, it by no means follows, that all arises out of experience, for, on the contrary, it is quite a compound of that we receive through impressions, and that the faculty of cognition supplies itself, an addition which we cannot distinguish from the original element given by sense, till long practice has made us attentive to, and skilful in separating it.

This is the subjective-objective basis of the cognitive knowledge formation and its analysis, which impressed, to a great extent, the thinking pattern of certain metaphysicist peace scholars, in course of time. The laws of the (a) Consistency of Substances, (b) of Causality and (c) of Interaction of Substances are the basis of the synthesis of sensuous multiformity in knowledge-formation, Kant, in later stages, affirmed that the world is finite and infinite, all processes are causally conditioned and all processes occur freely. Reason is, by nature, antinomic, Kant's doctrine of the role of antagonisms in the process of social life and the need for permanent peace is objective, the exercised influence on the contemporary peace and social development scientists.

German philosopher Gottfried W. Leibniz, with his theoretical attempt to achieve the synthesis between (a) mechanistic material form and (b) Aristotelian principle of active substantial form, tried to show the genesis of the realities. But his greatest contribution is that the truth of any fact or happening is to be adjudged by (i) the law of identity and (ii) the law of contradiction, without the existence of the in-between middle. It can also be regarded as the Aristotelian version of reasoning.

Dutch philosopher B. Spinoza contended that the possibility of attaining freedom lies in the behaviour based on knowledge and necessity and that the direction of apprehension of the truth, of the intuition of the mind, is the highest type of intellectual knowledge. This explained and supported that the democratic government is the highest form of power and suggested the restriction of all power of the state by freedom. The success of social peace and the democratic peace depend much on the existence of such stage.

There can be observed two faces in the Sino-Centric or Han Culture, which can be traced as such:

a) under the conditions of security and prosperity it inclined towards (i) tolerance, (ii) openheartedness and transparency and (iii) philanthropy, and

b) under the condition of hardness and adversity it inclined towards narrow exclusionism and chauvinism.

The noble part of the Han Culture or Sino-centrism contends that peace and culture are close to each other and that the practice of non-violence should be the main choice for achieving peace and development.

The metaphysical dialectical concept of peace consists of the interaction between the object and the subject in our circular material world. It is almost similar to Plato's perceptive view of "being". Plato elaborated the theory of the existence of immaterial forms of object and he termed them as "forms" or "ideas" and these were his "beings". Plato put "matter" and "space" to counterpose the "ideas" and the interaction between these "beings" and "non-beings" is an inter-mediate position. "Ideas" are eternal or "transcelestiat" which can neither arise, nor vanish, while the sensible objects are transient, relative and depend on time and space. Without going much through this argument one may advocate that the process and action of mutual exchange between the subject and object of the idea and time plus space, enable the change and development in the universe. However, reasoning stands at the very base of Subject-Object interaction for attaining knowledge, which may be characterised as "dialectical linkage". Korean peace scientist Young Seek Choue, in analysis of his "The Meditation of the Heaven" shows the signs of such dialectical linkage as follows:

Object-Subject Interaction	**Reasoning Means**	**Ends-Perception**
There is nothing that has no reason. There is nothing that does not change forever. Everything in this world has beginning and the end.	Logic of Change	Dialectics of Continuity
All the things in this world are mutually inter-related so, nothing exists in isolation.	Logic of interdependence	Dialectics of Centripetally
The theory of total interactions which says that everything interacts.	Logic of interaction.	Dialectics of Interaction.

(Contd.)

(Contd.)

In the interactions, life and death exist. Prosperity and decline exist.	Logic of creation & destruction.	Dialectics of Change
The order is the road for everything.	Logic of bondage	Dialectics of Progress
Harmony is the womb of production..		

Ideological war between and among systems is a cold war and involves many nations taking side with, or divides the people of nations which cause mistrust, suspicion, hatred, revenge, destruction and finally disunity even for noble ideals and missions. Even after the end of the cold was there has not yet appeared the situation of tensionlessness. Again, political, social, economic, cultural, linguistic and religious hegemonism give birth to dominance and enforced dependence relationship. It is against social peace and harmony. Peace diplomacy succeeds sometimes, but not always. The reason is that peace feeling and peace making has not undergone the appropriate processes and levels, which may be traced as such:

a)	Inner-peace or peace in self or heart	= individual or personal dimension
b)	Outer-peace or peace with others	= Social or Territorial Dimension (or Temporal, Spatiao and Circumstantial Dimension).
c)	Personal Peace	At individual level.
d)	Social Peace	At society level.
e)	Local Peace	At the locality level
f)	National Peace	At nationality level.
g)	Regional Peace	At regional level.
h)	Global Peace	At global level
i)	Cross or Vertical Peace	At the majority-minority level
j)	Horizontal Peace	Peace of Consensus for achieving harmony

From confrontation to cooperation, hegemony to harmony, chauvinism to equitable equality, alienation to transparency, are the very basic missions and visions of peace philosophy. Achievement of social peace and realization of the Global Social Peace Order are complementary to each other. While the first one creates the conditions for the second one, the second one can also be the pre-condition for the first one. Therefore, their functional process has to be simultaneous, complementing each other, in course of functions.

As violence may be structured, which is called as structural violence, peace also may be structured and it may be known as structured or structural peace. As centre and sub-centres or dominant nations structure violence on the peripheries or the dependent nations, peace also may be imposed by the centre or the dominant nations on the dependent or helpless peripheries. Such peace is an unjust and non-stable peace. The Oslo peace treaty of Israel-Palestine may be considered as structured peace. We may see its consequence now, which is nothing but a destabilized peace. Social or community peace is its effective alternative. Unless peace is bottom-rooted and flown from the bottom or foundation, one cannot expect any lasting or continuing peace. Both the structured violence and structured peace are subjective in nature. Structured peace can never result or end in positive peace.

Source:

Immanuel Kant, *Critique of Pure Reason*, G. Bell and Sons Ltd., London, p. 15 (as quoted in the *World Encyclopaedia of Peace*, vol. IV, Second Edition, Oceania Publications Inc., New York and Seoul Press, 1999, p.328)

45

From Gautama Buddha and Gandhi to Ikeda: Missions and Visions of Peace and Truth

Amalendu Guha*

Nonviolent Peace has been the mission and vision for humankind, human society and the human abode earth, since Buddha in the pre-millennium era, which got evolved and transcended to Ikeda of our century, getting enriched in concepts and contents in Gandhian era. Nonviolence is *neither a submissive and passive acceptance of violence pressed by the aggressor on non-violent people, nor a coward and subjugated act of the helpless in the society.* Nonviolence is a practical philosophy of human relation that binds the humankind to an understanding of harmless and dominance-dependence-less co-feeling, co-living, co-enduring, co-loving and co-satisfying mode of life.

Gautama Buddha had been one of the world's first practitioner, philosopher and preacher of non-violence, who based his culture and philosophy of non-violence on the premises of the co-existence of (a) human malaise and sufferings and (b) practical means and measures of their ethical cure. Buddha contends that the human life and its sentiments and emotions are, generally, subjected to imperfection and sufferings. The very roots of such sufferings are greed, hatred and ignorance. The biological beings are ignorant of the transitory nature of existence, and as consequence grasp after phenomena or states, believing these to be permanent or eternal. When things change or transform and cease to exist, the human kind suffers more, finding themselves at the state of ignorance or lack of knowledge and grasping. The Buddhist philosophical perception contends that grasping, attachment to self as permanent, surviving in separate entity, etc. give rise to selfishness, obsession state in mind, competition, hostility, attachment to things and

---

* Chairman, Mahatma M.K. Gandhi Foundation for Non-violent Peace, Oslo, Norway.

Published in *Gandhi Prasang*, Vol. 6 No. 2; January 2004.

persons, and finally, to violence. The Buddhist religious culture and principles suggest the practicing of loving kindness, compassion, sympathy, tolerance and even-mindedness in daily life. These are some of the virtues of non-violence. When even-mindedness is developed and promoted, only then mind becomes truly impartial and may get rid of the above vices. Buddhism holds that these should be practiced without any discrimination between self or other, friend or enemy. Buddhist philosophical psychology holds that mind is the source of all wholesome and unwholesome acts, thoughts and actions which are associated and inter-linked. For resolving these problems, Buddha suggests the non-violent percepts of non-killing and non-harming, and, the practice of self-discipline and meditation. Gandhi perceived *Satyagraha,* or the pursuit of truth, which, in sense, means the internal and external search for the true meaning of life and the purpose of life. Such pursuit of truth is based on justice, correctness and dignity, devoid of evils and may be achieved only through non-violence. Non-violent action transforms both the common people and the social ruling top-dogs, in common action or activism, for finding out humanistic solutions to social, economic, political, cultural and ethical problems affecting mankind.

Satyagraha means the *defense of just causes.* Non-violent action does not divide *you and me, me and him or you and him.* It brings all the people into *human whole and onefold.* Non-violence does not recognize enmity and identify with discrimination.

The Buddhist way of life is a life of balance between the society and the ethics, between the earthly life and the nature and between the supportive and cooperative structures. Buddhist peace action is a geo-human action that provides humankind with a working space, within which to stand away from the aggressive culture and to restore balance within imbalances. The culture of non-violence and peace is a *culture of transition from the way of life to the way to life.* The way of life is the ongoing behavioral context; the way to life is and should be the prospected and behavioral context, yet to appear. The humanistic golden rules of human behavior contain the positive essence of balance. When these behavioral rules cross the border of individual dimension and are extended to social and humanistic dimensions, these attain global dimensions. Under such contexts the individual and social conflicts and clashes will disappear from the global arena. As result, there will appear multi-beneficiary new human peace and culture. Peace is obtained by eliminating violence. Buddhism holds that interdependence is the root of all creations and the world floats on this basis. In the network of universal harmony, no entity is irrelevant and threatens the other entity. Buddhism also holds that conflicts can be neutralized and avoided by non-commitment to and exclusion from becoming a partner to conflicts. If any human group or community is kept together with other human groups and communities by force, with the fear of punishment and suppression, such enforced togetherness cannot be regarded as non-violent and ideal. Human beings are bound in togetherness or commonness through socio-moral ethics of horizontal nature, because of the character of mutual and common interdependence. Any other ethics of vertical nature will impede the values and morality of non-violence, as well as, togetherness. A culture of non-violence, in objective or practical sense, creates such a way of life that generates harmony between the human values and ethical moralities.

Gautama Buddha's peace concept is the concept of human emancipation from sorrows, sufferings and attachments. It is, therefore, a spiritual concept of detachment from greed, earthly binding of consumerism and attachment to kith and kin. Gandhi' s concept of peace is based on the combination of idealism and practical actions, as Japanese peace philosopher Daisaku Ikeda perceives. Gandhi's stand on non-violence is the non- violence against wrong, injustice and violence of the authorities or the structure. Daisaku Ikeda observes that "Gandhi demonstrated the unfailing unity with the ordinary people that was indispensable to his original way of thinking".[1] Gandhi succeeded in embodying (i) the non-violent peace idealism with (ii) practical application, in his non-violent resistance movement for attaining the goal or truth he believed in. Gandhi's non-violent revolution and defense is an effective reply to direct violence and structural violence. Gandhi's nonviolence is the effective measure for strengthening the human periphery or the weaker section of the society, as well as weakening the structural center, the stronger section with power. Fighting violence with violence will increase the means, measures and effects of violence manifold, in cumulative way. Had the violent powers re-defined their goals and means, in non- violent ways, they would have attained equity and dignity for their people and the world arena and atmosphere would have been changed. Non-violence is the mission of strengthening the vision of the social and economic peripheries. The strong center penetrates into the mind of the weaker peripheries. The weapon of the weaker peripheries is the non-violent counter-penetration through revolutionizing consciousness, to the structurally violent and dominating societies. Ikeda conceives that liberty, democracy and human rights are the *common human properties,* which may prepare the ground for balance, and such balance, under the condition of non-violence, may generate humanly peace and human prosperity. Violence and Non-Violence constitute the dualism of evils and goods. It can be distinguished the inside evil as primary and the outside evil as secondary, which, in combined form, constitutes the total fault within human beings. Both these evils generate imbalance, which raises the need for *human revolution, the revolution for liquidating both the inner and outer evils.* Historical experience shows us that violence breeds violence. But its contrary, if practiced properly, can prove that non- violence breeds non-violence. The disintegrated Eastern Europe of today, with the exception of the former Yugoslavia and the Cecenian problem in Russia, proves the victory of non-violence, as, the entire South America, proves the validity of the triumph of non-violence, manifested in today's violenceless relation.

Gandhi, like Gautama Buddha, realized that internal revolution and reform in human mind and consciousness is the basis of external revolution and transformation. Inner and outer dialogues constitute the very essence of the Buddhist praxis. Gandhi, like Buddha does not make any distinction between the human + animal and botanical life, or, in other words, between the biological and vegetarian life, or the sentient and non-sentient life. Gandhi rejected, like Shakyamuni, the vertical relation, between and among human beings, expressed and manifested in Indian caste and global class and strata systems, which creates difference and gap in privileges, development of inherent potentials and behavioral aspects. The system of *Kula* or the hereditary occupation structure and *Shila* or the social dignity structure, in the Indian sub-continental structure, hinders the possibility of choosing and developing own aptitude and inherent potentials. Gautama Buddha, Gandhi and Ikeda opt for horizontal socio-human relation and man's need for spiritual and ethical development, which bars the human differentiation, human degradation and de-humanization of humanity. Gautama Buddha and Gandhi wanted a symbiotic union of diverse elements and think-pieces leading to diverse occupations, dignities and vanities. They opted for a casteless and classless society -The Buddhist idea of *sangha* or community life and the Gandhian idea *of village or community* do have much similarity. The basic goal of the both is to provide the need- satisfaction of the people, not the greed enjoyment. Buddha, Gandhi and Ikeda do not want to see want or poverty at the bottom and accumulated wealth and privileges at the top. Gandhi wanted a decentralized and self-reliant village or small-scale socio-economic structure, which might enable production by the masses and mass employment. Gautama Buddha did not engage himself with such problematic.

Gautama Buddha was spiritualist, Gandhi was evolutionary dynamic personality and Ikeda is the combination of the both. He is spiritualist as a convinced and practicing Mahayana Buddhist, witness of the privileges and evils of the high post-war industrialization of Japan and possessor of the expertise knowledge of maldevelopment, comprising of (a) under-development, (b) dependent development and (c) overdevelopment in the underdeveloped peripheries. Ikeda follows the Buddhist idea of the middle way. Buddha followed the middle way, the way between *existence and non-existence, between the material condition and non-material possibilities, between the have and absence, between the having and non-having, etc.* Daisaku Ikeda followed the Buddhist wisdom of the middle way, which is similar to the Gandhian thought and means of gradualist evolution. Capital has not yet been humanized and state welfare system has not yet been effectivized. This is the problem of the 21st century, which neither Buddha, nor Gandhi did experience, which Daisaku Ikeda has undergone through. Ikeda got its spirit and message, Gandhi got the idea and felt the need, but could not put into deeds. The expectation from Daisaku Ikeda is that he can undertake and inspire the fulfilment of the unfinished tasks as envisaged by Buddha, because of circumstantial limitations and Gandhi, because of temporal and spatial limitness. Daisaku Ikeda is the continuation of Buddha's visions and Gandhi's missions.

All these three great preachers for peace – Gautama Buddha, Gandhi and Ikeda opt for horizontal dialogues and approaches for removing wrongdoings, misunderstandings and crisis formation, as well as for reconciliation and self-realization. A life cannot be created and sustained by destroying another life and, similarly, revenge cannot undo injustice. Non-violence develops a culture of peace which (i) develops human instincts of propensity to forgive, (ii) removes the instincts of taking revenge, (iii) develops the rationality of tolerance and (iv) overcomes as well as prevents the evil spirit of direct violence. Buddha and Gandhi, in both the spiritual essence and the sense *of karma* or daily work-performance, suggested the self-practiced means of the reformation of inner life for the entire humankind, Ikeda reconfirms Buddhism's ten states of life as such:

a) hell or the world of sufferings,

b) hunger or the world of the frustrated and unfulfilled desires and greed,

c) animality or the state of non-reasonability,

d) anger or the state of irrationality , and the state of life devoted to conflict and dominance,

e) state of tranquil or calm humanity,

f) heaven or the state of contentment or fulfilled goals,

g) learning or the state of devotion to self-perfection and purification,

h) state of self-realization, discovery of one-self and satisfaction in own world,

i) state of altruistic Bodhisattva, the state of compassion and devotion seeking for enlightenment for self and others, and

j) Buddhatva or the state of enlightenment, in which the individual life and the universal life are merged into the oneness of infinity.

All of these states are the inherent states of the process of life. The first four states are the states of evils, which contain the violent and aggressive instincts. These four states constitute the very foundation of rectifying and proceeding towards the *state of balance.* The next three stages are the stages of such balance. The last two states are the states of (i) self-improvement and realization, (ii) foundation of life subjugating and controlling the evil states of life and {iii) reaching to and finding out the *enlightened meaning and goal of life.* The means of Gandhi' s inner revolution had been non-violent resistance and mobilization of the power and meaningful strength of non-violence for eliminating anger, injustice and inhumanity. Its inherent essence lies in Buddhism and Buddha's preaching. Daisaku Ikeda thinks of materializing the thoughts and ideas of both of Buddha and Gandhi by educating and trails forming the mind of each individual in the spirit of rejecting violence and loving non-violent peace. This has become the very basic ideology of non-violent revolution and activities of the Soka Gakkai International, which Ikeda has been promoting.

Gandhi launched and promoted three important non-violent and human peace ideas, namely,

a) *ahimsa* or non-hatred and non-revengeful non-violence,

b) *satyagraha* or, the quest of and search for truth or justful outcome or result, and

c) non-cooperation or non-violent resistance.

The first one is the ought-to-be goal of human life, the second one is the *meta-idea* for striving, for seeking and for finding out the first one, and the third one is the *practical karma* or function, or duty to perform, for realizing both the above.

Ikeda adds scientific arguments to Buddhist principles discourses, in the sense of strengthening them with modem vitality and viability. He rationally explains the Buddhist middle way of life or the enlightened view of life as such;

Life, as Buddhism conceives is the elusive reality transcending the concepts of existence and non-existence and exhibiting the qualities of the both. It is "the wisdom arising from an enlightened view of life. (that) leads to an ability to reconcile apparently contradictory positions, to transcend the extremes of opposing views, root oneself in the profound reality of life and thus discern a path towards peace".[2] He launches the movement of the dawn *of a global civilization,* comprehensive of:

i) Breaking the cycle of reprisal, in which vengeance invites vengeance,

ii) banishing war which defeats the human spirit,

iii) revitalizing and restoring humanity, in the struggle of which the most creative energy becomes the spiritual struggle,

iv) striving to obtain the spirit of self-mastery,

v) killing the will to kill,

vi) encompassing contradictory entities and finding out consensus,

vii) effecting dialogues between and among civilizations, with a view to live in commonness,

viii) transforming competitions and conflicts to harmony,

ix) lighting the lamp to dispel darkness,

x) building international consensus and cooperation,

xi) supporting peace-building,

xii) alleviating poverty, etc.

At the very core of these functional mechanisms stands a force, which is the source of all human mental activity. Daisaku Ikeda, as true Buddhist perceives that "all the living beings receive their life-force from the fundamental cosmic existence, which supplies the energy for the rhythmic movements of life throughout the cosmos".[3] Ikeda, as Buddhist, recognizes this as a force not outside the cosmos, it is itself the cosmos. Cosmos and life is the infused entity of both the physical law of life and the spiritual law of life. This fusion is regarded as the process of life where life is created and spread out in the infinity or cosmos. Japanese Buddhist philosopher Nichiren (1222-1282) in the *Ongi Kvden (or Orally Transferred Teachings)* taught that -

"Earth is comparable to the physical law of life *(shikiho in Japanese);* cosmic law is comparable to the physical law of life. The two are inseparable". [4] The individual life is a part of the cosmic whole. This is the fundamental relationship between the human beings and cosmos. The physical element forming any living body is composed of the elements in the universe, but every element in the universe reverts to cosmic life. This process is a continuum, and is the cosmic metabolism.

The true entity of life, according to Buddha, consists of three virtues : (i) property of law or *dharmakaya in Sanskrit,* (ii) wisdom or *prajna in Sanskrit* and (iii) emancipation or freedom or *vimukti in Sanskrti.* An *enlightened man* possesses all these three types of virtues. The property of law is the truth or true entity, wisdom is the capability to attain this truth and emancipation or salvation is the state of freedom from the earthly sufferings. In ascending order, the last one is the property of action, the second one is the property of wisdom and the first one is the property of truth. Gandhi's Satyagraha or Search for Truth, contains the following basic values and norms:

a) to be honest and faithful to the cause of resistance and struggle,
b) to be away from the defeatist or doubtful attitude regarding the victory or success of the cause.
c) to stick to the cause of struggle until the final victory, and
d) to remain morally strong even at the time of torture.

Truth, to Gandhi, is a *dialectical unity of goal as well as means of action, because ends emerge from the means and means lead to the goal or end.*[5] Gandhi believed that non-violence brings about (i) radical change inside a man and his consciousness and (ii) accommodative revolutionary transformation within the society. Gandhian dialectics foresaw interaction between (a) the radicality in the change of human mind and consciousness and (b) the sustainability-cum-revolutionary transformation in the social structure and social transformation. Gandhi's concept of the *search for truth* is not a rigid procedure of perfectionism. It follows the middle way, as Daisaku Ikeda does. Because human relations are subjected to constant sensitivity and change and so no society can, absolutely, be perfect. He believed in evolutionary type *of revolution* and continuous dynamicity. His social missions and visions were based on social realities consisting of present needs and future potentialities. Gandhi synthesizes the role of non-violence as such: *nonviolence does not seize, it does not even seek power. Power accrues to it.* To the contrary, violence is bred in inequality. Why and how can non-violence become a social and human power? Non-violence accrues power and strength because:

a) it avoids physical and material destruction

b) it creates the atmosphere of peace for peaceful construction, and

c) it ensures the atmosphere of tensionlessness.

Gandhi's concept of search for truth is the concept of (i) *classless harmony (ii) casteless horizontal equity* and (iii) humanistic efforts for equalizing *the religious values, norms, Interpretation, practices and behaviors.* Gandhian version of the humanistic secularist truth urges (a) the dissolution of hate and hatred, (b) liquidation of the conservatives and static traditions and (c) avoidance of the orthodox fanaticism. Gandhi argued that

"Man and his deeds are two distinct things. Whereas a good deed should call forth approbation and a wicked deed disapprobation, the doer of the deed, whether good or wicked, always deserves respect or pity as the case may be. Hate the sin but not the sinner is a percept which, though easy enough to understand, is rarely practiced, and that is why the poison of hatred spreads in the world".[6]

Different religions and religious beliefs of our time choose different ways and means, in manifestative forms and sense, for reaching to the universal truth But humanistic secularism believes in oneness of mankind and such oneness of mankind is possible only and at the state *of unity of existence survival and continuity.* Gandhi believed that the *crisis of humanity* can be avoided only under the condition of achieving the *spirit-of oneness* in consciousness, which is to undergo the tests of

a) the contradictory aspects of the humanistic and the material dimensions,

b) the cognitive and perceptive aspects of the dimension of knowledge,

c) the humanistic and territorial dimensions,
d) the temporal and spatial dimensions,
e) the temporal and circumstantial dimensions,
f) the circumstantial and spatial dimensions,
g) the attributive and assimilative dimensions,
h) the logical and acceptable value dimensions, etc.

Daisaku Ikeda' s belief rests on the Buddhist percept that there is no beginning and no end. The Buddhist philosophical percept holds that everything appears from the emptiness and disappears to the emptiness. About the evolved process of life the Japanese Buddhist philosopher of the 13th century, Nichiren stated, "life at each moment encompasses both body and spirit and both self and environment of all sentient beings in every condition of life, as well as non-sentient beings -plants, sky, and earth, on down to the most minute particles of dust. Life at each moment permeates the universe and is revealed in all phenomena".[7] Ikeda, in the same perceptual spirit, contends that life- force cannot be considered separately from the life-time and life-space. Life-time and life- space are born because of the fact that life-force is moving pulsating. Simultaneously, life-force is influenced by the lifetime and life-space. Physical life-space and life-time are fused into a *single continuum.* The nearer one approaches to the source of life-force, the larger becomes the space, in which all sentient and insentient lives as well as particles encompass and *become one with the limitless cosmos. At that very point (space) and moment (time) any physical distinctions cease to exist. It can be defined as the cosmic eternity, or cosmic infinity, or cosmic emptiness.* Daisaku Ikeda elaborates the above meta-physical concept further as such: the entire is encompassed in the mind that subsumes every life-point and every life-moment and both of these expand throughout the cosmos and transform into the principles of all elements. This space-time continuum in the cosmic movements is the *cosmic life.* Buddha conceived that *cosmos is the self,* in the sense that *each self in the universe is a part and parcel of the cosmic life, which owes strength to the cosmic life and performs functions in the physical-cum-material 'world. In essence, self of each life is in identity with the cosmic life.* Space and time are the conditions of life activities, to which the creative cosmic energy contributes to the creation of all phenomena. He contends that all the individual selves *are merged together into the cosmic self.* The meaning of cosmic self is that

(a) everything is included in it, (b) everything starts to proceed from it and (c) everything returns to it. Therefore, it is the whole process *of existence with start and end.* The self of the cosmic life is fused with the selves of all the lives. This is the sense and essence of Daisaku Ikeda's philosophical trend, which is in line with the Mahayana Buddhist philosophy, or, better said, *the Buddhayana philosophy, as the father of the Nordic Peace Science, Johan Galtung, coins it on the basis of his talks with a Mongolian Buddhist monk.* Cosmos has infinite energy and its eternal energy is our life-source and resource.

Gandhian concept of survival sustenance, based on the earth's resources to be *enough for everybody' s needs and not enough for everybody's greed,* was influenced by Buddha's eight noble paths of (a) Just View (*Samyag Dristi* in Sanskrit), (b) Just Thinking (*Samyag Samkalpa*), (c) Just Speaking (*Samyag Vac*), (d) Just Conduct (*Samyag Karmantha*), (e) Just Living (*Samyag Ajiva*), (f) Just Effort (*Samyag Vyayama*), (g) Just Remembrance (*Samyag Smriti*) and (h) Just Meditation (*Samyag Samadhi*). These functions being just social functions and their process being the process of equity, the Gandhian percept of need, as replacement to greed, is based on such type of justice of human and social nature.

The Buddhist principle of "just" denotes *equitable equality and excludes any excess or extra.* Gandhi's principle *of just need and non-greed* is also based on the *equality with justice.* Gautama Buddha, Gandhi and Ikeda put emphasis on non-violence, non-exploitation and greed or compassion-free world, which assure human survival. Gandhi developed another concept, namely, *Sarvodaya* or all-round development of each person, or, all-round well being of the entire society, without any discrimination and distinction of class, caste, creed and strata. Its main goal is the demarginalization, besides the equitable equalization of the society.

The essence of the Buddhist concept of peace, based on the principle of "taking care of each other", had much influence on Gandhi's ideology formation. The philosophical essence of Buddhism holds that *human wisdom directs towards Enlightenment (or perfection of thoughts) that leads to Peace of tranquillity and horizontality.* This essence was based on three principles of practical importance, namely, (i) conquering fear, (ii) avoiding greed and lusts and (iii) controlling mind. The Buddhist approach of Enlightenment means self-realization, which depends on the (a) faculty of intuition or *buddhi* and (b) faculty of wisdom, in comparative perspective of good and evil. Both of these give birth to *Human Self.* The sense and essence of the three important Buddhist principles are:

i) Refuge in the Enlightenment *(Buddham saranam gacchami)*

ii) Refuge in the learning and acquisition of knowledge *(Dhammam saranam gacchami)* and

iii) Refuge in the *Order (Sangham saranam gacchami),*

These have been the guiding principles of Gandhi's concept of *Sarvodaya,* as mentioned above, and Ikeda's concept *of New Humanis* or *Renaissance of Humanism.* Buddha and Gandhi had been the social reformers in Indian sub-continental context. Caste system and upper caste dominance, which in modem context may be termed as class system divided by profession, pained Buddha and Gandhi very much. Buddha, in his time, was a protester to the Hindu caste system, in which the *lower and the under caste population was the subjugated and dominated part in the whole social structure.* The under-caste or the non-caste people, whom Gandhi termed as the *Harijan* (or the sons of God*)* and the Girijan (or the sons of the valleys), are the people devoid of human rights, social rights, livelihood rights and right to life. Both of Buddha and Gandhi wanted to create a casteless society, or, in clear term, a *horizontal society of castelessness and classlessness.* The return of the conservative Hinduism and its dominance in the post-Buddhist era and Hindu caste dominance in the pre-and post-independence periods in India made the Buddhist-Gandhian missions and visions a failure, particularly in the very sub-continent.

Maintenance of calmness is regarded as the rational quality for maintaining humanity and promoting humanism. Daisaku Ikeda's New Humanism consists of two aspects: (a) re-humanization from the present state of de-humanization and (b) radicalization and promotion of the newer elements and qualities of humanity and their practical utilization. The way to humanity and humanism consists of the qualitative aspects: balanced and rational consciousness, right judgment, knowledge and wisdom, capacity to distinguish right and wrong as well as proper and improper, intelligence and aptitude to maintain correctness, learning from the humanistic experiences of the past, desire and competence to attain enlightenment or contentment of detachment, etc. The elements of humanism can be characterized as the refined qualities of humanness, which are, really, the tranquil realms. The tranquil state of humanity is attained through proper reasoning, use of right conscience and consciousness, willingness to exercise control over the instinct desires and emotions giving rise to greed and revenge, as well as passion for animosity and evils. The goal of new humanism is the attainment *of human self,* a self of the type of realization of the *Gandhian Sarvodaya,* consisting of greater wisdom and light, insight and judgment, peace and contentment. Human self consists of values and attempts to reach to the goals of the meanings of life, happiness and sense of life's noble mission.

Modem society is a society of desires, in which desires beget more and increased desires. These desires, at individual level, are the desires for wealth, power, controlling and dominating authority, privileges, fame, vanity, dignity, over-consumerism, ego, etc. Ikeda derstands quite well that these are vices or vicious outcome of the modern civilization and culture. This culture is the *culture of desire growth, not of the development of humanism.* Buddha and Gandhi taught *abstinence from desire, though not abstinence from need.* Desire contains greed, lusts and luxuries. Desires consist of material goods, acquisitiveness, vanity, pride, affluence, and above all, ego. New Humanism diverts its direction or goal from *material culture and civilization to the culture and civilization of the basic material and spiritual needs.* Daisaku Ikeda observes that, in modern context spiritual affluence has been traded for material affluence. For this purpose, the use of both the natural and human cream resources are becoming out of balance and control. As long as the people will remain material and ego-cultured, one cannot expect the appearance of new human culture. Human culture is the product of the inner depth of existence for discovering the true nature of humanism. Human beings are born with the potentialities of humanity and such potentialities promote and polish the intelligence and goodness in human beings. Learning and realization are the two basic qualities of the humanism, as Ikeda observes and holds. The basis of the New Humanism will be *the learning and use of the accumulated wisdom from the past and ongoing generations.* The state of learning can be regarded as the step towards enriching the spirit and for enriching the *inner growth and development.*

Daisaku Ikeda holds that the grassroot or the common people should play the leading role and become the deciding factor for changing the world with the creation of new humanism. Ikeda cites the example of Gandhi, as such,

Gandhi's struggle in the name of non-violence was a battle to make the people strong and wise.... Gandhi was a rare leader who chose to live in the midst of the masses, sharing their sorrow and happiness and working to dispel the fear of authority and bred by long years of colonial life". [8]

But the nordic peace philosopher and strategist Johan Galtung holds that

"Grassroot movements alone cannot correct authoritarian elites: no more can democratic elites by themselves prevent the authoritarian grassroot movements from achieving power".[9] He suggests three sets of guideles in this direction, namely,

i) human rights,

ii) lights of Buddhism, and

iii) ecology combining diversity and symbiosis for the enhancementof life.[10]

because these may lead to the formation of international civil society and make the people capable of non-violent intervention. In the society of new humanism and humanity, simply the declaration of human rights cannot be considered as sufficient, there had to be the practical means and measures of achieving the same, particularly, for the grassroot people who are devoid of the same. Again, human rights have to be human needs-based.

Daisaku Ikeda thinks of a new human order, in the era of new humanism and humanity, and the Buddhist principles may become the part of ethos for ordinary human beings in meeting their needs, naturally, not only the spiritual needs. Self-realization of common social usefulness is the humanistic expectation from the new humanism. Ikeda, who is a devoted and true Buddhist, holds that the realization *of self, in complete altruistic sense, is the state of the Bodhisattva Nature, which includes goodness, intelligence, determination, knowledge and happiness, -which deliver happiness and self-perfection.* The state of Bodhisattva is the state of deep thought and insight, besides being the light of wisdom. In *Ikeda's principle of new humanism,* purity constitutes the elements of cleanliness and brilliance of life. It also means that the state of life is devoted to helping others and lights the true wisdom, intelligence and happiness, in the sense of enjoying life and living on an unshakable root of the cosmic life-force. Like Gandhi, Ikeda's philosophy and attitude is more metaphysical than spiritual. In the context of modem-mechanized society, it is essential that man should recover his inherent treasure and potentials of life. An inner human revolution, in appropriate time, makes it felt in the external world and environment, with the function of transformation. Human revolution is based on the dynamics of life, it again creates newer dynamics of life. Power is the potential energy of such dynamics, which can be transmitted towards one's surroundings, because it is the motivating force of a person's life. Power or energy is composed of two types of energy: physical and mental. The visible energy of power is manifested in economic, political or social power. But, mental energy consists of a wide variety of powers like love, affection, willingness to live, capacity to perceive the truth compassion motivated to help others, etc. It is the source and resource of human development.

The following are some of the cardinal principles and aspects, on which Buddha's, Gandhi's and Ikeda's concepts and contents were based and evolved, under, of course, the specific contexts of time, space and circumstances:

Principles & Aspects	**Gautam Buddha**	**Gandhi**	**Ikeda**
Human Emancipation	Nirvan or Enlightenment	Sarvodaya (all-round development	New Humanism through Renaissance
Means	Practice of Bodhsattva or Way to Purification and Detachment	Experiment/Efforts for Self-Realization (Sarvodaya)	Human Revolution
Method	Practice of the three says: (a) Refuge in Learning and acquiring Knowledge followed by (c) Refuge to Order or Life of Non-Attachment	Practice of Non-Violent Participation and Mobilization Continuity based	Practice of Dependent Origination: Human Life on the context of Environment
Nature	Spiritual	Humanist	Meta-ideal
Peace	Spiritual	Self and Social	Inner and Outer
Means	Practice and Meditation	Non-Violent Resistance	Self-Control of inherent nature and removing the casuses of evil and violent effect
Method	Merging Individual Enity with Cosmic	Use of Non-Violent Non-Cooperation	Development of the Consciousness of
Nature	Entity	Strength	Non-violent Struggle
	Inner and Outer peace	Strength of Non-Violent Peace	Individual and Social Peace

Absence of peace generates the need for peace. Peace is the condition in which the individuals are the actors for creation of values for the social community and achieving harmony between themselves as social beings and the environment, the surrounding nature and the circumstances. This can be regarded as the essence of Buddhist concept. Gandhi emphasized on non-violent peace, the peace of potentiality for the weak and structurally violated or the grassroot people. Ikeda considers peace as the condition in which the dignity and human and social rights of all the people are assured guaranteed and respected. He holds that peace culture, with peace education and peace wisdom can become an important and much-needed vehicle for peaceful human development. Buddha, Gandhi and Ikeda are a trialectical unity for promoting non-violent peace and combining the inner and outer peace. Inner peace is the very background of outer peace. Inner peace and outer peace can be explained as self-peace, human peace, social peace, earthly peace and cosmic peace, which are interlinked and interfused from the micro to the mega, or cosmic, or infinity level.

Notes and References:

1. Galtung J. and Ikeda *D. Choose Peace*, Pluto Press, London, 1995, p. 57.
2. Ikeda D. *The Humanism of the Middle Way*. 2002 Peace Proposal,
3. Soka Gakkai International, Tokyo, 2002, p. 21.
4. Ikeda D. *Life. An Enigma, A Precious Jewel*, Kodansha International, Tokyo, 1983, p. 25.
5. Idem, p. 25
6. Guha A. *Gandhi's Non-Violence*, Mahatma M.K. Gandhi Foundation for Non-Violent Peace, Oslo, Norway, 1998, p. 13.
7. Metron Thomas (ed.); *Gandhi on Non-Violence*, London, 1964. As quoted in Ikeda D. *Life. An Enigma, A Precious Jewel*, p. 85-86.
8. Idem, p. 98.
9. Idem, p. 97.
10. Idem, p. 97.

46

Why Gandhi's Principles of Nonviolence are Relevant Today

Michelle Myres*

I am often asked why, at the age of 37, I sold my car, house, and business in San Francisco in order to attend a Master's programme in International Conflict Analysis in Europe. My answer is simply that I could not sit idle as; violence in the form of the threat and use of force escalated around the world. I could not watch both state and non-state actors continue to ignore the United Nations and International Law. As a student at the University of Kent at Canterbury, England, I am now, writing a dissertation on Gandhi's political philosophy of non-violence. When I began research for my dissertation, I was astonished to find that no other student in my programme had written on peace, non-violence, pacifism, or any related subject. This is where e, as a society of nations, have gone wrong. It is imperative that we introduce peace studies in our schools. Children need to learn peaceful alternatives to conflict alongside the histories of war, or history will continue to repeat itself. This is not a time when we can throw up our hands and give in to a coercive and unilateralist actions by dominant hegemonies, nor can we allow our children to grow up with little or no knowledge that there exist viable alternatives to war.

Fortunately, in my teenage years, two events introduced me to peace, non-violence, and Gandhi. They both made indelible impressions on me. First, I spent ninth grade living in an ashram in a community where Hindus, Buddhists and Christians lived, worked, studied and worshipped together in harmony. Prior to this experience, I did not know anything about Hinduism or the way it accepted individuals from every religion. What I remember from growing up in the United States was that each religion preached as if they were the only 'true' religion. Because I had attended many different

* Founding President of the Global Peace Society, U.K.

Published in *Gandhi Prasang*, Vol. 6 No. 1; October 2003.

religious schools, I felt that I could never choose one religion, especially one that excluded all others. When I joined the ashram and learned that Hindus and Buddhist were accepting peoples from all religions, I was happily surprised and knew that I had found something that was more closely aligned with my own beliefs.

Gandhi wrote in 1928, "Let no one even for a moment entertain the fear that a reverent study of other religions is likely to weaken or shake one's faith in one's own. The Hindu system of philosophy regards all religions as containing the elements of truth in them and enjoin an attitude of respect and reverence towards them all...."

The second remarkable event that touched me deeply was the movie, *Gandhi.* I was inspired to learn that this one man was able to achieve such insurmountable goals with his non-violent methods. This was a powerful message that I have carried with me ever since: that conflicts can and should be resolved without war.

Gandhi tied these two issues together and wrote often about religious conflict. If we encourage people to worship together and learn about each other, we will create respect and trust instead of deep divisions of mistrust and animosity. In fact, there is a group called the Inter-ethnic Project Gostivar (IPG) in Macedonia that organises mixed-race activities between Macedonians and Albanians. They found that when these groups lived completely separate lives and never communicated, worshipped, or interacted with each other, conflict erupted much more easily and severely. Now that they have had several years of mixed-race activities, have gotten to know their neighbours, and have developed trust and respect for them, violent conflict has diminished significantly. This shows us that if we treat others with dignity and respect and remove aggression from our lives, we can achieve peace.

As Gandhi explained in July 1926: "If (people) were instinctively violent, the world would end in no time. They remain peaceful.....It is when the mind is unnaturally influenced by wicked men that mankind commits violence."

Violence breeds violence

People often ask, what would Gandhi do in the face of terrorism or with someone like Hitler, Osama bin Laden, or Saddam Hussein? Gandhi wrote the following in March 1937: "(These men) are able to show the immediate effective-ness of violence. But the effects of Buddha's non-violent action persist and are likely to grow with age. And the more it is practised, the more effective and inexhaustible it becomes, and ultimately the whole world stands agape and exclaims: 'A miracle has happened'. All miracles are due to the silent and effective working of invisible force. Non-violence is the most invisible and most effective."

Violence only breeds violence. Unfortunately, many people do not under-stand this way of thinking. They think we can only achieve peace through violent means, i.e., using military force in retaliation and now even as prevention. We need to change people's thinking. For example, far too many people in the US wanted to immediately retaliate after September 11th, but attacking the per-petrators with deadly weapons does not make them stop. They will only attack us again. And then we will attack them again on a more grand scale. Each time the violence gets bigger and more deadly." I am an uncompromising opponent of violent methods even to serve the noblest of cause". Wrote Gandhi.

Gandhi's fundamental philosophy was to make the attacker/ aggressors see the error of his ways. And this he has to realise on his own, you cannot force it upon him. The way to achieve this is to receive his violence without any resistance. If you do this unfailingly, Gandhi felt, he cannot help but learn to respect you and see the error of his ways and reform. He will eventually cease his violent acts. This was Gandhi's method in achieving India's independence from Britain. The British government may not have liked him nor agreed with him, but he did earn their respect and in the end they granted India its inde-pendence."......supposing a people made up their mind that they will never do the tyrant's will, nor retaliate with the tyrant's own methods, the tyrant will not find it worth while to go on with his terrorism." Gandhi wrote in December 1938.

Why is Gandhi still relevant today? His methods are the way to World Peace. There is much that we, as a global society, can learn from this extraordinary man. I hope that by researching and writing my dissertation on his philosophy of non-violence, I can help educate people so that together we can achieve a world at peace, free of weapons of mass destruction, free of hatred, misunderstandings, and religious conflict. We should all begin by encouraging people of different races and religions to participate in activities and worship together, as this will foster understanding, trust, and respect; we should introduce a peace curriculum in schools to show students the alternatives to war; we need to get the word out in order to change the way of thinking that peace=peace and not violence=peace; and lastly, we must convince our leaders and fellow citizens that if we do not react with force and violence, the aggressors of this world will learn the error of their ways and will cease to commit violent acts. If we imple-ment Gandhi's ideas, which will take immense strength, determination, dedication and faith, we will achieve World Peace.

"Unless the world adopts non-violence, (nuclear weapons) will spell certain suicide for mankind."

47

Gandhi's Philosophy and Sufi Doctrine

Mrs. Nageen Sai Zinovieff*

The mysticism of love and self-sacrifice is ancient in both India and Iran and may well have stemmed from the same source in Central Asia, the ancient heartland of both cultures. The teaching of Mahatma Gandhi, India's great spiritual teacher and statesman, which grows out of the Bhakti love-devotional practice of India has much in common with the doctrines of Sufism, which, though in the context of Islam, is in many ways a continuation of the pre-Islamic, is in many ways a continuation of the pre-Islamic gnosis in Iranian Mazdeism. With his own Unitarian and ecumenical view of faith, he had a profound love and respect for the Koran, which he believed was no less divinely inspired than the Bhagavad Gita.

"God has a thousand names", he said, "or rather, He is nameless. We may worship or pray to Him by whichever name that pleases us. Some call Him "Rama", some 'Krishna'; others call Him 'Rahim', and still others call Him 'God'. All worship the same spirit" (*Gandhi*, p. 331).

He stressed one tenet of Hindu philosophy, viz., "God alone is, and nothing else exists, and the same truth you will find emphasized and exemplified in the Kalam (doctrine) of Islạm" (*ibid*, 1931, pp. 427-28).

His basic teaching that God is truth echoes the view of the sufi saints, who actually call God '*Haqq*' (the 'Truth'). Like the Sufis, he taught and practised non-violence, called *ahimsa* in Sanskrit. As with the Sufis, the non-violence is not merely a passive approach to encounters, but it is a dynamic concept, activated by the energy of love.

"Complete non-violence", he said, "is complete absence of ill-will towards all that lives. Non-violence is, therefore, in its active form goodwill towards all life. It is pure love. I read it in the Hindu scriptures, in the Bible, in the Koran" (*ibid.*, p.14).

---

* London, U.K.

Published in *Gandhi Prasang*, Vol. 4 No.1; October 2001.

"In its positive form", he reiterated elsewhere, "Ahimsa means the largest love, the greatest charity, if I'm a follower of Ahimsa, I must love my enemy" (in Nateson 1933, p. 346). To achieve *ahimsa*, Gandhi believed, one must humble oneself as the dust of the earth on which all beings tread and see oneself as on mire than a speck in God's universe, a completely Sufi point of view.

Mohandas Karamchand Gandhi was born in Ahmedabad, Gujarat in 1869 into a family which had been more politically than spiritually oriented, providing statesmen for India over the course of a good four generations. He alludes to the more materialistic tendency of his forebears when in his autobiography he criti-cizes his father for being prey to the temptations of lust, having been married four times.

His spirituality came from his mother, who was a powerful influence on him with her commitment to the devout practice. She went daily to a local ashram to worship and fasted regularly. Given the Hindu tradition of childhood marriage, Gandhi was fortunate that he was all of thirteen before he was forced to wed. In his life story he refers to his marriage with a sign of resignation, commenting, "I would not wish it to anyone".

On his marriage he recalls in *All Men Are Brothers*. "I do not think it meant to me anything more than the prospect of good clothes to wear, drum-beating, marriage processions, rich dinners, and a strange girl to play with" (*Gandhi* 1927, p. 6).

Given his charity of nature, even at that tender age, Gandhi was prepared to love this 'strange girl', who was named Kasturbai, and, indeed, remained lovingly faithful to her for the rest of his life. She bore him several children, the eldest of whom proved a trial for him in time to come.

In his life story he condemns himself for lustfulness at a certain stage, having remorse over a passion, which he had for his wife at the time, a lust, which he felt, was not compatible with God-realization. He spent a lifetime struggling with this sexual passion for his wife and finally succeeded in over-coming it in his early fifties.

"I realized", he recounts, "that the wife is not the husband's bar-slave, but his companion and his helpmeet and an equal partner in all his joys and sorrows".

When he was eighteen, his family sent him to England to study to be a Barrister. His mother was reluctant to lose her son to the corrupt world of

Europe but finally considered on the condition that he abstain from "woman, meat and alcohol".

"There", he writes, "everything was strange—the people, their ways, even their dwellings. I was complete novice in the matter of English etiquette and continually had to be no my guard".

Though he found British society 'strange' and devoted his efforts to oppo-sing British rule in India, he, nevertheless, praised the English as brothers, professing to love them no less than Hindu, Moslem or Parsie.

"I hold myself to be incapable of hating any being on earth. But I can and do hate evil wherever it exists. I hate the system of government that the British people have set up in India. I hate the ruthless exploitation of India even as I hate from the bottom of my heart the hideous system of untouchability for which millions of Hindus have made themselves responsible". (*Gandhi, 1927*).

His first experience of prison life in long struggle to free India of British rule was in 1908. However, much he may have suffered, he says, "I felt then that it was more the fault of the individual British officials than of the British system and that we could convert them by love". (*ibid*).

After receiving his law degree in England and being called to the Bar, he moved to South Africa, where he practised law for several years, used passive resistance in the struggle with the persistent prejudice against the Indian commu-nity there, and won the respect of friend and foe alike.

His protest against oppression was fundamentally non-violent, but it did exclude armed struggle as an alternative to cowardly resignation, despite his lifelong disapproval of the immorality of war. As a result, he urged that Hindus should defend their kith and kin with arms if they were subjected to armed attack.

"Áhimsa in the midst of a world full of strife, turmoil and passions", he writes, "is a task whose difficulty I realize more and more day by day. And yet the conviction, too that without it life not worth living is growing daily deeper". (*ibid* p. 177).

He believed that religion, that is, the realization of moral perfec-tion and virtue and love of God, could not be relevant without service to humanity, which included, for him active participation in the political life of society.

"To see the universal and all-pervading spirit of Truth face to face, one must be able to love the meanest of creation" and see oneself as no more than that. According to Gandhi, one "who aspires after that cannot afford to keep out of any field of life. That is why my devotion to truth has drawn me into the field of politics; and I can say without the slightest hesitation, and yet in all humility, that those who say that religion has nothing to do with politics do not know what religion means" (*Gandhi*, p.66).

This comment could be controversial both from the point of view of political liberalism and from the sufi point of view, until one understands that this is a matter of conscience for Gandhi himself. For the Sufis the word *din*, classically translated 'religion', is rooted in the ancient Persian word *daena*, the word which the Iranian prophet of Mazdaism, Zoroaster, used to mean "truth-guided conscience". The word entered the Semitic languages of the Middle East—first Akkadian, then Hebrew and Aramaic, and finally Arabic—without losing this personal implication.

The word which Gandhi uses is *satyagraha*, 'Truth-force', indicating that whatever actions he takes on the social and/or political stage are driven by a conscience-and consciousness-which is connected to the Truth, or God, and therefore sometimes transcends reason or intellect. In this line, although Sufism in principle opposes political involvement, there are many individual Sufis who have taken action on the official scene out of conscience-motivation such as those Qadiri, Suhrawardi and Naqshandi Sufis in India who felt compelled to advise kings, some of whom were actually their disciples, while the Chishti, masters resolutely opposed this policy, often establishing their capitals as far from the capitals as far from the capital as possible, so that they would remain difficult to contact.

So, if one interprets Gandhi's expression as a call to conscience, as the Catholic liberation theologians of Latin America, such as Archbishop Helder Camara of Recife, Brazil; or Che Guevara's companion Father Camilo Torres of Colombia, or Father Ernesto Cardenal of the Sandinista government in Nicaragua, certainly have done, one can see a valuable dimension to the religious argument.

A time-honored practise has been for people of conscience to participate in the political arena in full vigor at a certain stage in their lives, then to retire in meditation. Hinduism provides for this institutionally with its *grihasta*, or 'house-holder' stage for the person in the prime of life, and its *sunnyasin*, or 'celibate ascetic', stage for the later years.

One must remember that for all Gandhi's involvement in the struggle for the liberation of India and his efforts to bring the faiths together in one common synoptic, Unitarian view, as he was dying from the wound inflicted by a Hindu financial assassin, he appealed for his murdered to be pardoned, so that the retiring, meditative and compassionate *sannyasin* spoke up in the form of the political activist. Thus, when Gandhi calls for the involvement of religion in politics, one must see this in the light of a very particular view of religion, as the motivator of Truth in one's individual conscience, not as a pretext for demagoguery and polemical haranguing.

The question is often stated this way: Is it not better for a devotee to devote the time one spends on spiritual practice in service of others? Gandhi was aware that India's 'speechless millions' could not ponder on God while they were starving.

Gandhi writes, "God Himself seeks for His seat the heart of him who serves his fellowmen" (*Gandhi* 1928). Gandhi believed as do sufi masters, that presence of heart in devotional practice—service being a part of spiritual practice—is vital and that all purification done with remembrance of God is aimed at cleansing the heart.

"My appeal to you", he write, "is to cleanse your hearts and to have charity. Make your hearts as broad as the ocean". (*ibid*).

When he stated that the true service of others is worship, he meant that effective service could be realized only through the self-purification which comes from meditation, so that there is a dynamic interaction between the two states. No service is worthy if the name unless it is guided by the cognition that comes from devotional practice.

Devotional practice cultivates *ahimsa*, the freedom from ill-will towards all living things, fired by self-abnegation and constant striving to be in accord with God's will through the pulse of ceaseless remembrance of God in the heart- what the Hindus call *mantra* and the Sufis call *ahikr*. The *mahabbat* ('living-kindness concept) where one does not simply turn the other cheek when being slapped but actively returns the blow with the warmth of loving-kindness. As for harmlessness itself, the Sufi poet Hafiz says:

How can I offer thanks for this blessing:
That I do not have the power to hurt others?

This consciousness of God comes through the abnegation of self. Returning to Gandhi's metaphor of being humble as the dust, one comes to his statement in a letter to a Western woman whom he had dubbed 'Mira Bahn' (Sister Mira) and who, like so many of his devotees, called him 'Bapu' (an affectionate term for 'father'):

"I feel nearer to God by feeling Him through the earth. In bowing to the earth, I at once realize my indebtedness to Him; and if I am a worthy child of that Mother, I shall at once reduce myself to dust and rejoice in establishing kinship with not only the lowliest of human beings but also with the lowest forms of creation whose fate is reduction to dust, I have to share with them" (*Gandhi* 1927 pp. 147-48).

Gandhi believed that the negation of self through selfless service is vital for one's coming close to God. This is consistent with the Sufi view of God-guided service, focussing the devotee's consciousness a way from self and towards God and what God wills, to the point where the self is annihilated and there is nothing but God's will at work.

Gandhi writes, "Not until we have reduced ourselves to nothingness can we conquer the evil in us. God demands nothing less than complete self-surrender as the price of the only real freedom that is worth having" (*Gandhi* 1928, p.470).

Gandhi believed that the quest and aim of all his writings and activities was self-realization and being united with God.To accomplish this, Gandhi believed that he must serve humanity.

Indeed, he said that all of us are bound to place our resources at the disposal of humanity. And if such is the law, as it evidently is, indulgence ceases to hold a place in life and gives way to renunciation.

When, according to the Sufis, the self has become completely renounced and no longer plays a role in controlling our affairs, then God becomes completely realized in our consciousness. Maghribi (d.ca. 1406), an eminent Sufi master and poet, speaks, as does Gandhi, of the existence of God in every membrane of His creation. According to one of his verses (given in prose paraphrase): "In this lovely melody (creation) behold nothing by the Minstrel, for every sweet strain you hear is played by Him." To see a particle of God in oneself is the quintessence of the Hindu scripture, where God "sees Himself in the hearts of all beings", and the devotee, in turn, "sees all beings in his heart". This is the vision of the yogi of harmony, a vision which is ever one (*Book 6, verse 29*)

Gandhi was a paragon of this teaching, humble on earth, transfigured in the realm of the Divine. "I have no desire for prestige anywhere", he said. "It is the furniture required in the courts of kings. I am a servant of Moslems, Christians, Parsis and Jews, as I am of Hindus" (*Gandhi*, p. 51).

Gandhi was happiest living as the poorest with no personal possessions but as he put it, "six spinning wheels, prison dishes, a can of goat's milk, six homespun lionclothes and towels, and my reputation which cannot be worth" (*Gandhi*, p. 116).

In this society of conspicuous consumption where possessions are accumu-lated for personality, Gandhi writes, "Civilization in the real sense of the term consists not in multiplication but in the deliberate and voluntary reduction of wants".

He stated elsewhere, "I want if I don't give you a shock to realize identity with even the crawling things upon the earth, because we claim descent from the same God, and that being so, all life in whatever form it appears must be essentially one" (*ibid*).

His belief in the sacredness of all life and his modesty about his own saintliness recurs over and over again in his numerous writings, permeating his numerous writings, over again in his numerous writings, permeating his prolific discourse.

"I do believe that it is possible for every human being to become perfect even as God is perfect", he stated. "It is necessary for us all to aspire after per-fection, but when that blessed state is attained, it become indescribable, indefi-nable. And I, therefore, admit, in all humility, that even the Vedas, the Koran and the Bible are imperfect as the word of God and that, imperfect for beings that we are, swayed to and fro by a multitude of passions, it is impossible for us even to understand this word of God in its fullness."

His method of fighting evil with good and fasting often to the point of starvation to death brought about the most massive unarmed uprising in history, as the 'speechless millions' of India rose up in march after march, strike after strike, protest after protest, in opposition to British colonial rule. Yet be blamed his fellow Indians as much as the British for the abuse and exploitation of their country, declaring in a general statement which covered the foibles of all humanity of whatever race, creed or nationality: "The hardest heart and the grossest ignorance must disappear before the rising sun of suffering without anger and without malice".

His asceticism was such that he was the strictest vegetarian until his doctors compelled him to add milk to his diet. He accepted this as a practical measure, since it was seen as necessary for him to maintain a healthy and productive life, for he did not believe in mortification of the flesh as a devotional policy.

"My austerities, fasting and prayer", he said, "are, I know, of no value if I rely on them for reforming myself. But they have an inestimable value if they represent, as I hope they do, the yearnings of a soul striving to lay his weary head in the lap of his Maker". (*ibid.*, p. 87).

In the end although he had been warned of possible assassination attempt in 1947, he went about in the crowds oblivious to the danger. "I know the art of living and dying non-violently", he declared.

Mahatma Gandhi has left a remarkable legacy to the world. Though he claimed no originality in thought and practice, he has left an ineffable impact in his outstanding example for each and every individual.

"There is no such thing as 'Gandhism'," he has written. "I do not want to leave any sect after me. I do not claim to have originated any new principle or doctrine. I have simply tried in my own way to apply the eternal truths to our daily life and problems". (*ibid. p. 62*).

No more fitting words could be found to constitute a leading statement epitomizing the relationship between his political activism and his meditation than these: "Having flung aside the sword, there is nothing except the cup of love which I can offer to those who oppose me" (*Gandhi* [2 April] 1931, p. 54).

References

Gandhi, M.K., 1928, *Young India 24* September 1925, 1 January 1928, 20 December 1928, 2 April 1931, 31 December 1931 – India: Navajivan Publishing House.

Gandhi, M.K. 1927. *Autobiography:My Experiment with Truth*, Penguin.

Gandhi, M.K. *My Religion*, India: Navajivan Publishing House.

Gandhi, M.K. *All Men Are Brothers*, India: Navajivan Publishing House.

Nateson, g.a., 1933: *The Speeches and Writings of Mahatma Gandhi*. Madras.

Nurbakhsh, J., 1996: *Discourses on the Sufi Path*, New York: Khaniqahi-Nimatullahi.

Nurbakhsh, J., 1978: In the avern of Ruin: Seven *Essays* on Sufism, London: Khaniqahi-Nimatullahi.

48

Gandhi and "Imperfect Religions"

Nageen Sai Zinovieff (Mrs.)*

A study of Gandhi's writings may impress many with the idea that he thought man should sacrifice his all on the altar of religion, through service of humanity, disinterested altruism, and love of God, who is Unique yet perceivable even in the spirit of what society may call the lowest of beings.

Yet, in his unassuming and ingenious way, he has often decried the imperfect teachings of the great religions and has emphasised that neither the Bible, the Quran, The Gita, or Avestas are revelation by God directly:

"I exercise my judgment about every scripture, including the Gita I cannot let a scriptural text supersede my reason whilst I believe that the principle books are inspired, they suffer from a process of double distillation. Firstly, they come through a human prophet and then through the commentaries of interpreters. Nothing in them comes from God directly. Mathew may give one version of one text and John may give another. I cannot surrender my reason whilst I subscribe to divine revelation:. (*Truth is God*, p. 87).

The three main religions, which have been purported to convey the word of God, the Bible, Quran, Gita are filled with certain blasphemies in spite of the overall holy messages in them. Moses, in the Old Testament claimed to have spoken with God and like Mohammad said he received direct message from the Lord. In Exodus 31 verse 14. Moses makes the Lord say:

"Observe the Sabbath, because it is holy to you. Anyone who desecrates it must be put to death. Whoever does any work on that day must be cut off from his people". And this is not one off comment in Exodus you find it in Exodus 35 also.

---

* London – U.K.

Published in *Gandhi Prasang*, Vol. 5 No. 1; October 2002.

Moses says God even gives recipes for food: "Do not cook a young goat in its mother's milk" (Exodus 34 verse 26).

It seems in the Old Testament whenever a king wanted to build a temple on the toil and tokens of the people, he would claim it is for God Himself and not for man.

The Lord God says to David:

"Solomon your son is the one who build my house and my courts, for I have chosen him to be my son and I will be his father". (Chronicles 28-29).

Accordingly, David extorts very large sums of gold, talents, bronze, silver and iron from every household to build this temp!e. "The people rejoiced at the willing response of their leaders, for they had given freely and wholeheartedly to the Lord. David the king also rejoiced greatly". (Chronicles 29, verse 9).

Gandhi does not deny the scriptures like some Marxist believing it is the "opium" of the people. He says in Truth is God:

"I am not a literalist. Therefore I try to understand the spirit of the various scriptures of the world. I apply the test of Truth and Ahimsa laid down by these scriptures for interpretation. I reject what is inconsistent with that test and I appropriate all that is consistent with it. (page 88)."

To return to the Old Testament, the whole book of Ecclesiastes is peppered with epicurean philosophy and a nihilism that even Jean Paul Satre could not outdo.

"For a man may do his work with wisdom, knowledge and skill, and then he must leave all he owns to someone who has not worked for it. This too is meaningless and a great misfortune. What does a man get for all the toil and anxious striving with which he labours under the Sun? All his days his work is pain and grief; even at night his mind does not rest. This too is meaningless. A man can do nothing better than to eat and drink and find satisfaction in his work, this too I see from the hand of God." (Verses 21-24 Ecclesiastes 2)

Gandhi who studied the religions of the world with a prayerful heart never fanatically believes in any one prophet.

"I cannot ascribe exclusive divinity to Jesus. He is as divine as Krishna or Rama or Mohammad or Zoroaster. Similarly, I do not regard every word of the Bible as the inspired word of God even as I do not regard every word of the Vedas or the Quran as inspired". (pp. 73-74, *Truth is God*). Gandhi advocates a religion of the service of humanity in the ultimate aim of coming closer to God, for he believed man was created to know his Maker who is LOVE, Light and Truth.

It is true that the media, in particular the Sunday Times often come up with archaeological discoveries, which refute the Bible's claims. But you do not have to have a science in order to see the idiosyncrasies of the Holy Scriptures.

As Gandhi says: "History, imagination and truth have got so inextricably mixed up. It is next to impossible to disentangle them".

There are many inaccuracies in the New Testament which have been passed down from generation for 2000 years. Not the most ludicrous is Jesus teaching "Whoever believes in me has eternal life". Whereas the religious Egyptians three thousand years before Christ saw the after death in astral form, in the form of flying bird, the New Testament seems to think one goes to the spirit world with sinews and flesh!

In Luke 24, Jesus meets his disciples for the first time after being crucified:

"And while they still did not believe it because of joy and amazement, he asked them, Do you have anything to eat". They gave him a piece of broiled fish and he took it and ate it in their presence". (*Luke* 24 verse 41).

Indeed, there is little reason for the followers of one religion to wield the stick of superiority over the other.

Gandhi writes in Harijan (13.3.1937).

"The Allah of Islam is the same as the God of Christians and the Ishwara of Hindus. Even as there are numerous names of God in Hinduism, there are as many names of God in Islam. The names do not indicate individuality but attributes, and little man has tried in his humble way to describe mighty God by giving Him attributes, though He is above all attributes indescribable, inconceivable, immea-surable."

The Quran no less than the Old Testament claims to be directly revealed by God. Yet why should God decree that a thief's hand be cut off, adulterous women stoned to death, Jihad or holy war as an excuse for imperialist designs and machinations and let loose polygamy which is morally reprehensible to all people of moral standing, is anybody's guess. But rather than flagrantly criticise or blindly follow the so-called revealed religions, let us recall Gandhi's advice:

"Tolerance obviously does not disturb the distinction between right and wrong, or good and evil.....in the case of good and evil, we have to cultivate charity for the wicked no less than for the good, the sinner no less than the saint, all the while we cherish inveterate hatred towards wickedness and sin" (*Young India*, 2.10.1930).

Moreover he says:

"The golden rule of conduct, therefore, is mutual toleration, seeing that we will never all think alike and we shall see Truth in fragment and from different angles of vision". (*All Men Are Brothers*, p. 183).

In every scripture there are "misguidance" simply because they are not revealed by God but by the holy souls of the prophets. In the enthusiasm to win faith in God for nations that were heathens a lot of hyperbole has been added and faith has so been sweetened that it is detrimental to one's healthy reason.

Mohammad who prefixed every verse with "it is a book revealed by God" often alludes that God is within the hearing vicinity of every believer. "We created a man and we know what his soul whispereth to him, and We are nearer to him than his jugular vein." (*Surah L Verse* 16).

In Surah verse 51, Mohammad speaking on behalf of God makes another anti-social comment: "O ye who believe take not the Jews and Christians for friends. They are friends one to another. He among you who taketh them for friends is one of them. Lo. God guideth not wrong doing folk."

The Quranic notion of paradise is so human and earthly, promising plenty of food and running streams: "God will say to paradise dwellers: 'Eat and drink to your heart's content.' This is the reward to your labours. They shall recline on couches ranged in rows, to dark eyes houris we shall wed them. It leaves off heterosexuality and goes on to promise boys as fair as virgin pearls". (Surah 52 verse 20).

We still hear suicide bombers in Palestine promised 70 virgins in the hereafter for all eternity. Yet the Quran's is still one of the few holy scriptures that stresses montheism par excellence.

The main and perhaps unforgiving claim of the Gita is that God himself is speaking to us. "He who knows my birth as God and who knows my sacrifice, when he leaves his mortal body, goes no more from death to death, for he in truth comes to me". (*Gita* 4 verse 9).

Mahatma Gandhi believed that those who were near God, referred to themselves as God. Not all of the Gita is filled with profundities. There are verses such as "the evil works or the good works of men are not his work. Wisdom is darkened by unwisdom and this leads them astray". (*Gita* 5 verse 15). Gandhi's own criticism of the Gita which more often inspired him that not, is that "When the Gita was written, although people believed in Ahimsa, wars were not only not taboo but nobody observed the contradiction between them and Ahimsa". (*Truth is God*, p. 96 v. 18).

Need to Revisit Gandhi's Message

Paras Ramoutar*

In the wake of the September 11, 2001 bombings in the New York and Pentagon, Washington D.C., there must be renewed interests in the peace philosophy of Mahatma Gandhi. What would have Gandhi said and done if he was alive today?

"The question is a philosophical, anthropological and psychological one, and perhaps also a religious one. It is, can human nature be changed in such a way that man will forget his being for freedom, for dignity, for integrity, for love—that is to say, can man forget that he is human? Or does human nature has a dynamism which will react to the violation of these basic human needs by attempting to change an inhuman society into a human one?"

Thus writes Eric Fromm in Orwell's *Nineteen Eighty-four*, and when one looks around to see if there was any mortal in this century who was able to meet these requirements, no one can deny that it was Mahatma Gandhi. October 2, 2001 – as the people of Trinidad and Tobago join the world in observing his 312nd birthday with special religious services and wreath laying exercises it is fitting that we reflect on some of his great ideals, thoughts, philosophy, vision and leadership virtues that single him as an extraordinary human personality. For he was a human combination of a saint and a revolutionary; a politician and a social reformer, and economist and a man of religion; an educationist and a Satyagraha; a devotee alike of faith and reason; a Hindu and an inter-religious nationalist and internationalist; a man of action and a dreamer of dreams.

It must be noted that Gandhi's life was engaged in answering and demon-strating through actual experimentation at the grass-roots of society its practical effect. This is a response to Fromm's question.

---

* PRO Mahatma Gandhi Foundation, Trinidad

Published in *Gandhi Prasang*, Vol. 5 No.1; October 2002

Amidst the turmoil and decay on the social, economic and political landscape in his homeland India, and around the globe, Gandhi's message provided fortitude, strength and inspiration to mankind everywhere.

Gandhi pursued and advocated major revolutionary changes in man's way of thinking, in the relationship between man and man, the social set-up and the world economy. He also recognized the ungodly and untruthful and ultimately, unnatural course of life human society had adopted.

His approach was to set out an alternative way of life and, therefore, Satyagraha was the chief weapon for creating the conditions for it. Gandhi's initiatives were to spur an environment rooted in man's essential nature as a human being through means that would not compromise ends but, strengthen them and bring them nearer.

He ignited the philosophy of Satyagraha as a way of life based upon the only Truth – the sound foundation of the essential goodness of man. "non-violence is the law of our species as violence is the law of the brute. The spirit lies dormant in the brute and he knows no law but that of physical might. The dignity of man requires obedience to a higher law – to the strength of the spirit", he writes.

The Father of the Indian Nation believed in God, who is the ultimate Reality of Supreme Power.

'God is Truth", he confides, but later reverses this axioms by saying "Truth is God". His thought on this subject were while God was denied by many: many dare not deny Truth.

Haile Selassie I, writes about Gandhi: "Gandhi's struggle for freedom and justice both in India and Africa has become truth. His philosophy has also been followed throughout the world and has become the corner-stone as well as the deep foundation for the structure of human liberty."

He adds that Gandhi was devoted to the principle that, "man can only exercise perfect love and be completely dispossessed, if he is prepared to embrace death and renounce his body for the sake of human service."

Gandhi believed in God, but for him God was the moral law, the dharma and he considered that all those who believed in the moral law were spiritual even though they were so-called atheists.

We look around and wee an infinite link between India's Gandhi and America's Lincoln. Both men transformed their nations and remain a lasting spirit to shame those who ignored their ideals. They also moved a world and because of them the world remains illuminated by their thoughts and their beings. It is noteworthy to speak of the Gandhian ideal synchronizing with the Periclean Athens. Both Gandhi and Pericles illumine the idea and the era.

Lincoln and Gandhi conceived of their peoples as of the city upon a hill, towards which eyes could turn and wherein could reside a repository of conscience for all mankind. They are symbols for all mankind.

Noted physicist and Nobel Prize Winner, Albert Einstein said of Gandhi when he died; "In our time....., he was the only statesman to stand for a higher human relationship in the political sphere."

At centenary celebrations in 1969 at St. Paul's Cathedral, then Archbishop of Canterbury, Dr. Ramsey was able to recall Gandhi's universalism, noting that Gandhi was inspired by all religions of the world and saw their essential doctrine to be identical, he described Gandhi as God's gift to India and the world – "a gift and a colleague."

Gandhi's vision for peace among mankind can thus be certified: "Peace requires one first to be brave enough to love another, to tolerate another and to trust another. That requires faith in oneself. One has not the strength to be peaceful if he is fighting the internal duel of selfish desires. Good can never result from evil desires or actions, hence the Gita's central teaching of the oneness of the means and ends. The practice of peace is thus a test of the sincerity for diligent work, but must be realized." Former President of South Africa Nelson Mandela, Martin Luther King Jr., late U.S. civil and human rights leader; Vaclav Havel, Lech Walesa and Dalai Lama are men who replenished their service to their communities and the world society through the pursuits of non-violence as reoriented by Gandhi.

Lanza del Vino, French philosopher, writer and artist marched to India searching for the sources for non-violence by discovering Gandhi's way to initiate and develop communities.

He went back to Europe as "Shantidas" (servant of peace) and started to gather friends in the Larzac region in Southern France for an ashram-like "Ark community" as a "Laboratory for Non-Violent Living and Politics."

Political violence is the bane of the world society. In some areas it is more sporadic as opposed to others, but it is fact of life and, daily to continues to escalate. It seems that if present trend continues, political violence will add to the demise of our civilization.

In our country, Trinidad and Tobago, there is a peace at all levels, except for the typical domestic violence and brutal murders. Prime Minister Basdeo Panday's Government continues to place law and order as one of its principal organs of governance, several antiquated pieces of law have been updated as well as new laws are passed in order to meet the changing social, economic and political environment.

We must ask ourselves what do we need to have a world without violence, and therefore, peace, law and order. We need to revisit Gandhi's message for an urgent, pragmatic and paradigm shift.

INDEX